COMMANDING
THE STORM

Major-General Philip Sheridan
with his generals. Left to right:
Wesley Merritt, Philip Sheridan,
George Crook, James William Forsyth,
and George Armstrong Custer.

COMMANDING THE STORM

CIVIL WAR BATTLES IN THE WORDS OF THE GENERALS WHO FOUGHT THEM

JOHN RICHARD STEPHENS

LYONS PRESS
Guilford, Connecticut
An imprint of Globe Pequot Press

To Elaine F. Molina

Text selection and abridgments, copyright © 2012 by John Richard Stephens
First Lyons Paperback Edition, 2014

ISBN 978-0-7627-8790-6

Lyons Press is an imprint of Globe Pequot Press.

Text design and layout: Maggie Peterson
Project editor: Ellen Urban
Maps by Alena Joy Pearce, copyright © 2012 by Morris Publishing, LLC. Based on maps by Hal Jesperson, www.cwmaps.com.

Printed in the United States of America

The Library of Congress has previously catalogued an earlier (hardcover) edition as follows:

Commanding the storm : Civil War battles in the words of the generals who fought them / [selected and abridged by] John Richard Stephens.
    p. cm.
  Includes index.
  ISBN 978-0-7627-8223-9
  1. United States--History--Civil War, 1861-1865--Campaigns--Sources. 2. United States--History--Civil War, 1861-1865--Campaigns--Personal narratives. 3. Command of troops--History--19th century--Sources. 4. Generals--United States--History--19th century--Sources. 5. Generals--Confederate States of America--History--Sources. I. Stephens, John Richard, compiler of edition.
  E470.C6974 2013
  973.7'84--dc23

2012034090

CONTENTS

A NOTE ON THE TEXTS

While there are Civil War battles and officers of greater significance or interest, I have selected what I perceive as the most famous officers and battles since the majority of readers would prefer to know what Custer had to say, as opposed to Major-General Henry Halleck, who played a much greater role in conducting the course of the war from his office in the War Department. Of course, determining what constitutes fame is subjective, so considerable effort went into constructing the list, with consultation of a large variety of sources.

Ranks listed in the heading of each selection represent the highest rank an officer attained, including brevet ranks—some achieved after the war—while ranks listed on battle summary pages, notes, and text are ranks at a specific time, so Lee appears both as colonel and general, depending on the time.

To maintain a degree of impartiality, I have presented the offensive force in each battle first and the defensive force second.

Almost every selection or quotation is abridged for brevity and to remove superfluous material, though I have taken care to maintain context. Occasionally I have integrated material from several sources into a single selection, as indicated in the Sources list. For ease of reading, I have refrained from indicating where edits were made, except where I felt it would be helpful.

I have also corrected typos while generally maintaining the writers' idiosyncratic spelling and punctuation to retain the flavor of the times. As a result, inconsistencies occur between selections, such as General John Bell Hood's spelling of Major-General Rosecrans's name as "Rosecranz."

INTRODUCTION

THE RISING STORM

The storm had been brewing for quite some time—perhaps more than a century. It was about many things, but at the heart of it all lay slavery.

A poll taken on the 150th anniversary of the start of the Civil War showed that most Americans believe that a disagreement over states' rights was the primary cause of the war—this despite the overwhelming opinion of most historians and teachers, who have examined the records and documents that demonstrate clearly that the cause was slavery. The issue of states' rights was a rhetorical smoke screen. As we will see from Secessionist documents, the states' rights they wanted to preserve had to do with owning slaves.

This is all still hotly debated among non-historians, who often ignore facts, with just about everyone confusing the *cause* of the war with the *reasons* for fighting it. Slavery caused the war, but that's not what the fighting ended up being about. Some background material will help clarify the confusion. In order to understand the battles and the men who fought them, we need to know what led them there to kill their friends and relatives.

LEGAL AMERICAN SLAVERY

The first thirty of what later became known as slaves came to the Virginia Colony in 1619. But initially even slaves from Africa were considered indentured servants, released after a specified period of time or on conversion to Christianity. But wealthy whites didn't like losing their best-trained servants, so they turned slavery into an automatic life sentence for both the slaves and their descendants. A 1654 Virginia court decision designated John Casor, an African, as the first official slave in the colonies. Even though he had served well past his period of indentured servitude, the court defined him as his master's property and confirmed the designation as a life sentence.

The trade in Africans, which had gone on since the mid-1500s, escalated in the 1700s. As agriculture grew in the South, plantation owners relied on slaves to plant, tend, and harvest crops. Businesses increasingly used them to generate profits. As larger numbers of slaves were kept together in forced labor camps, the quality of their lives decreased to maximize profits, and increasingly brutal methods kept them in line. As slavery expanded, though, many questioned it—even some slaveholders, such as Thomas Jefferson.

REPUBLICANS VERSUS DEMOCRATS

The Revolutionary War complicated matters. It was a war for autonomy, the Declaration of Independence proclaiming that "all men are created equal." Yet the newly formed United States was one of the largest slaveholding countries in the world. While framing the Constitution, the Founding Fathers compromised on slavery in order to gain the support of Southern states, particularly South Carolina and Georgia, which probably wouldn't have joined the Union otherwise. But the discussion of human rights resulting from the Revolution also led to talk of abolition.

The abolitionist movement grew rapidly in the early 1800s, particularly in the North, lobbying governments and eventually establishing the Underground Railroad to smuggle slaves to freedom. Their extremely vocal and sometimes violent activities sparked equally violent reactions from their opponents, pushing the two factions farther apart. Slavery became a major political issue, and the evolving political parties were forced to take sides, so that by the 1850s there were two main parties—the Republican Party, favoring abolition, and the Democratic Party, favoring slavery.

These two political parties now have essentially inverted what they were then. In general, Republicans were reformers, favoring change, while Democrats favored maintaining the status quo. Then, most Republicans were liberal and lived in cities, while most Democrats were conservative and lived in the country.[1] Up until the war each party had its own liberal and conservative divisions, but when considering the parties of the 1800s, in a general way Abraham Lincoln and the Republicans were more liberal, favored change, and opposed slavery, while Jefferson Davis and the Democrats were more conservative, favored the status quo, and championed slavery. Ultimately slavery defined their parties.

STATES AGAINST STATES

Linking the issue of slavery to individual states ended up dividing the country. Perhaps if the Founding Fathers had established a federal law one way or the other, taking the issue away from the states, the nation could have avoided civil war. But even then the issue was so contentious that the Founding Fathers—who had other matters to handle—for the most part avoided it.

As slavery expanded in the South after the Revolution, Northern states began abolishing it, sometimes converting slaves automatically to indentured servants. By 1810 the Northern states had freed 75 percent of their slaves—which wasn't all that difficult since there weren't many slaves in the North. Only 1 percent of enslaved and free African Americans lived in the North, primarily in cities, while 95 percent lived in the South, with the rest in the territories.

By 1860 the South had nearly four million slaves. A third of all Southern families owned at least one, with half of those owning between one and four. Estimates put 20 to 30 percent of the slaves in the hands of less than 1 percent of the slaveholders, and only nineteen slaveholders owned more than 500 slaves each.

FEAR AND LOATHING

The country divided itself into Northern free states and Southern slave states. The political parties dividing along the same lines, with Republicans in the North and Democrats in the South, made the situation worse. As new states and territories joined the rapidly growing country, Republicans wanted to contain slavery to the South for moral reasons but also to decrease the Democrats' political power. Democrats naturally objected.

The issue became so incendiary that people were being murdered because of their opinions. In the Bleeding Kansas years of 1854–58, Kansas Territory, seeking statehood, tried to establish whether it would be a free or slave state as abolitionists and proslavery forces poured in to battle it out. Both factions fully believed they had God on their side.

---

1 The reversal took place between the two Roosevelts. T. R., one of the last liberal Republicans, curbed the power of corporations, increased the regulation of businesses, promoted environmentalism by creating national parks, and aimed for a Square Deal in which the average citizen got a fair share. After the defeat of liberal Republican President William Howard Taft's reelection bid in 1912 by liberal Democrat Woodrow Wilson, the conservatives in the Republican Party pushed to the fore by 1916. When the Depression hit, conservative Republican Herbert Hoover tried to combat it by launching public works projects and raising taxes on the rich. This was followed by FDR, a liberal Democrat, establishing the New Deal, creating Social Security, and offering government jobs to ease unemployment, while regulating Wall Street and transportation. From then on, the reversal was complete.

Southern Democrats controlled Congress and the White House from 1852 to 1858. The Supreme Court also sided with the South in its infamous 1857 Dred Scott decision, which said that blacks couldn't become American citizens, the Constitution didn't protect them, slaves were strictly property, and Congress and the various territorial governments had no authority to prohibit slavery. The court foolishly thought it was removing the issue of slavery from politics by making it a matter of law. Instead, the decision exploded a bomb among abolitionists and Republicans.

The Dred Scott decision caused a panic in the North, particularly among the political parties. If territories became slave states, slavery would expand and the Democrats could cement total control of the government. It forced many who otherwise were willing to accept slavery, as long it remained in the South, to take sides. Northerners flocked to the newly created Republican Party, formed several years earlier from the antislavery Free-Soil Party. Since the Republican Party had formed around containing slavery, the South became deeply worried. They—particularly Virginians—had to a large extent controlled the federal government since George Washington, but without any new slave states they would lose control of the government forever and the North's power would continue to increase.

When Republicans gained control of the House of Representatives in 1858 and two years later won the presidency and both houses of Congress, Southern politicians suddenly found themselves playing a minor role in government, with the prospect of losing power completely. Nor was their fear baseless. With one party dominating the North and another the South, when one lost, half the country lost. When the majority of voters elected Lincoln, the South could say legitimately that they were subject to a government for which they didn't vote. Lincoln didn't appear on ballots of

ten of the eleven states that seceded. In Virginia, where his name did appear, he received only 1.1 percent of the vote.

Fearing a permanent loss of power, Southern politicians saw an exaggerated future in which the North imposed its will on them and they had no recourse. They believed their rights would be violated —which was already the case to some extent because abolitionists were violating the fugitive slave clause of the Constitution—and that the government would dictate whatever the North wanted, including the abolition of slavery altogether.

By the time Lincoln took the oath of office, Southerners had convinced themselves that much of their fantasy had already happened, seeing Lincoln as a modern-day Julius Caesar, dictatorially leading a tyrannical federal government. They viewed secession as a second war for freedom— except, of course, for the slaves.

Even though most didn't own slaves, Southerners firmly believed abolition would end the "Southern way of life." William Tecumseh Sherman, living in Louisiana before the war, wrote that "all men in Louisiana were dreadfully excited on questions affecting their slaves, who constituted the bulk of their wealth, and without whom they honestly believed that sugar, cotton, and rice, could not possibly be cultivated."

When Southern politicians lost control of the government, they felt they had to form their own government to save themselves. The seven cotton states of the Deep South, which had the greatest number of plantations and slaves, seceded first. Together they formed the Confederate States of America on February 4, 1861, with a government modeled on the one they were leaving.

THE REAL REASONS FOR SECESSION

Many reasons other than slavery are given today as the cause of the war—states' versus federal rights and economic differences between the North and South, among others—and to some extent these played a part. But at the base of it all lay one primary cause: slavery. The South feared losing it, which various declarations of secession clearly spell out. Several discuss slavery at considerable length, with Georgia's the most detailed and reasoned.

Four states—Florida, Louisiana, North Carolina, and Tennessee—gave no reasons for secession. The remaining seven cited the following reasons:

Slavery (four states): This is the only reason Mississippi gave, saying, "Our position is thoroughly identified with the institution of slavery—the greatest material interest of the world. ... A blow at slavery is a blow at commerce and civilization. ... It [abolition] has given indubitable evidence of its design to ruin our agriculture, to prostrate our industrial pursuits, and to destroy our social system. ... For far less cause than this, our fathers separated from the Crown of England."

Georgia, South Carolina, and Texas also mentioned slavery as a reason, and Georgia further specified the exclusion of slavery from new territories, making it illegal for Southerners to take their legal property with them if they traveled or moved to the new territories.

Violations of the Constitution (four states): Alabama, Georgia, South Carolina, and Texas cited violations of the Constitution's fugitive slave clause.

Fear of Lincoln (four states): South Carolina cited the election of Lincoln, "whose opinions and purposes are hostile to slavery," and the fear that under Lincoln's government the "guaranties of the Constitution will then no longer exist; the equal rights of the States will be lost. The slaveholding States will no longer have the power of self-government, or self-protection, and the Federal Government will have become their enemy"—all before Lincoln even became president.

Georgia declared that the avowed purpose of Lincoln and the government dominated by the antislavery Republican Party was "to subvert our society and subject us not only to the loss of our property but the destruction of ourselves, our wives, and our children, and the desolation of our homes, our altars, and our firesides."

Arkansas believed the Republican Party intended to wage war on the seceded states, while Alabama merely cited Lincoln's election.

Abolitionists (three states): Georgia and South Carolina claimed the abolitionists were encouraging their slaves to rise against them, threatening their security and "domestic peace and tranquility." South Carolina also pointed out that the abolitionists were helping slaves run away. Texas was more general, citing the relentless activities of abolitionists.

Federal government (two states): Virginia believed the federal government was perverting its powers in order to injure Virginians and oppress the slave states.

Texas's Declaration of Secession, the most vitriolic, cited the problems in Kansas, claiming that "the disloyalty of the Northern States" and "the imbecility of the Federal Government" allowed "incendiaries and outlaws" to "trample upon the federal laws and to make war upon the lives and property of Southern citizens in that territory." They also cited "an unnatural feeling of hostility to these Southern States and their beneficent and patriarchal system of African slavery, proclaiming the debasing doctrine of equality of all men, irrespective of race or color—a doctrine at war with nature, in opposition to the experience of mankind, and in violation of the plainest revelations of Divine Law."

States' rights (one state): Initially the South used the banner of states' rights as a euphemism for their perceived right to have slaves, but over time they separated and added to it the right to freedom, self-determination, and secession. At the time of secession, Southern documents and speeches clearly reveal a primary concern about the right to own slaves. Only South Carolina mentioned encroachments on states' rights, and the only rights they specifically listed were the "right of property in slaves" and the rather nebulous "right of deciding upon the propriety of our domestic institutions."

Before seceding, the South stood *against* states' rights when it came to restrictions on slavery, such as New York's law that if a slaveholder vacationing in the Empire State brought along a servant, that slave would automatically be free. They also seethed that it was legal in other states for citizens to openly form abolitionist societies and for blacks to vote.

The South wasn't fighting for the right of a state to secede. Every state in the Union had that right—and still does. It was the *method* of secession that Lincoln felt was illegal, and he presented his case in his first inaugural address. The Constitution acted as a contract between the states, and for any state to leave, all parties to the contract had to be in agreement. Obviously the North was not. To join the Union, a territory had to petition Congress and draft a constitution. Both houses of Congress had to approve territorial statehood, and the president signed a bill formally establishing the new state. In theory, the reverse also held true: If a state wanted to secede, the state legislature had to vote as such, and both Congress and the president had to approve. But even Lincoln himself didn't believe the president had authority to force states to remain in the Union. The Southern states, on the other hand, believed in total self-determination, that they could leave the Union only if a majority of their citizens favored it. There was talk in the North of rebellion and treason, but the issue didn't come to a head until after the Battle of Fort Sumter.

Northern businesses (one state): Georgia felt the federal government actively favored Northern businesses.

Tariffs (none): Custom duties comprised 95 percent of the government's revenue in 1860, although by 1863 it only made up 56 percent because the government reintroduced excise taxes and for the first time established income taxes in order to pay for the war debt. Before the Morrill Tariff, America had one of the lowest tariff rates in the world. In 1861 the Morrill Tariff raised the average custom duty from 21 to 36 percent.

Some pro-Confederate people today cite tariffs as a cause of the war, but at the time the cotton states seceded, the government was operating under the 1857 tariff law, which the seceding states helped write. It wasn't until after secession, when those states pulled their members from Congress, that Republicans could pass the Morrill Tariff, which President Buchanan, a Democrat, signed just before Lincoln took office.

Only Georgia and South Carolina cited tariffs in their secession conventions, and even Alexander Stephens, later vice president of the Confederacy, argued that the Morrill Tariff wouldn't affect the South as much as others claimed.

Three weeks before Fort Sumter, Vice President Stephens gave his Cornerstone Speech, in which he outlined the difference between the United States and the Confederate States. "The new [Confederate] constitution has put at rest, forever, all the agitating questions relating to our peculiar institution—African slavery as it exists amongst us—the proper status of the negro in our form of civilization. This was the immediate cause of the late rupture and present revolution. Jefferson in his forecast, had anticipated this, as the 'rock upon which the old Union would split.' He was right. What was conjecture with him, is now a realized fact. Our new government is founded upon exactly the opposite idea; its foundations are laid, its corner-stone rests, upon the great truth that the negro is not equal to the white man; that slavery subordination to the superior race is his natural and normal condition. This, our new government, is the first, in the history of the world, based upon this great physical, philosophical, and moral truth."

His speech demonstrates how deeply slavery had become embedded in the Southern identity.

TRANSITION TO WAR

The Confederacy's attack on Fort Sumter of April 12–13, 1861, gave Lincoln the excuse he needed to call up an army, since the peacetime force was too small to fight a war and a large portion of it, including many of the best officers, had joined the Confederacy. Even though most people knew the war they'd been expecting had begun, only Congress could declare war, so Lincoln issued a proclamation calling for 75,000 volunteers to regain federal property taken by the South. Four wavering states rightly saw the proclamation as Lincoln's call to arms. Arkansas, North Carolina, Tennessee, and most of Virginia used it as their reason for joining the Confederacy. The four border states, Delaware, Kentucky, Maryland, and Missouri, remained with the Union, along with what later became West Virginia.

Kentucky, deeply divided, initially decided on neutrality, but Brigadier-General Leonidas Polk, "the Fighting Bishop," sent the Confederate army to occupy Columbus, prompting the state government to ask the Union army to come to their aid. The majority of Kentucky's elected government was pro-Union, so Southern sympathizers formed a provisional government, creating two Kentucky governments—one with the Union, the other with Confederacy. A similar situation arose in Missouri, where a provisional government formed in opposition to the original elected government.

WHAT THEY WERE FIGHTING FOR

When people argue over what caused the war, they tend to confuse the matter with why they were fighting—two different things. Slavery ultimately caused the war. Without slavery, the war wouldn't have taken place, but that's not what the fight was about. Slavery led to secession, and that split sparked the fighting. For the North the fight was to preserve the Union and suppress an illegal rebellion. For the South it was to uphold the right of self-determination, regardless of what the rest of the country wanted. The South saw the Union army as an invading force against which they had to defend themselves, while the Union saw the Confederacy as a traitorous bunch of rebels trying illegally to seize U.S. soil and establish an illegitimate government.

> I wrote you about my disgust at reading the Reunion speeches: According to [George] Christian the Virginia people were the abolitionists and the Northern people were pro-slavery. The South went to war on account of slavery. South Carolina went to war—as she said in her Secession proclamation—because slavery would not be secure under Lincoln. South Carolina ought to know what was the cause for her seceding. Ask Sam Yost to give Christian a skinning.
>
> I am not ashamed of having fought on the side of slavery—a soldier fights for his country—right or wrong—he is not responsible for the political merits of the course he fights in.
>
> —CONFEDERATE COLONEL JOHN MOSBY, KNOWN AS "THE GRAY GHOST," TO CAPTAIN SAMUEL CHAPMAN

The soldiers themselves gave a wide variety of reasons for fighting. Chief among them was patriotism either for their country or for their state.

Some believed it was the right thing to do—and their duty. Others feared being labeled as cowards if they didn't. (Neighbors sent some men dresses if they refused to join.) Some did it for adventure and excitement or a chance at honor or glory. Some wanted to prove themselves and show their courage. Some wanted to join friends or relatives. A few realized the importance of the events taking place and wanted to take part. Some wanted to defend their homes, while a few wanted the pay or signing bonuses. There were those who saw it as a battle between virtue and vice or good and evil. Some didn't know why they were fighting. For most, it was a combination of these reasons, which changed over time. As the war dragged on, many Union soldiers, sick of it all, wanted to stop the bloodshed by ending slavery altogether. But the Confederates didn't want their world turned upside down. Both sides professed to fight for freedom. Very few risked their lives solely to preserve or to end slavery.

Even Lincoln didn't initially intend to end slavery. Although personally opposed to it, he didn't believe the president had the power to abolish it. The president, through the executive branch, implements and enforces laws. It was up to Congress to create, modify, and abolish them. He also knew the country at large wasn't ready to end slavery.

Lincoln had a higher priority. In a letter to the New York Tribune, he wrote, "My paramount object in this struggle is to save the Union, and is not either to save or to destroy slavery. If I could save the Union without freeing any slave I would do it, and if I could save it by freeing all the slaves I would do it; and if I could save it by freeing some and leaving others alone I would also do that. What I do about slavery, and the colored race, I do because I believe it helps to save the Union; and what I forbear, I forbear because I do not believe it would help to save the Union. I have here stated my purpose according to my view of official duty; and I intend no modification of my oft-expressed personal wish that all men everywhere could be free."

The Emancipation Proclamation was a tool designed to weaken the Confederacy. A prior proclamation, issued in September 1862, freed all slaves in the Confederacy if those states didn't rejoin the Union within three months. But that didn't affect the slave states that remained in the Union. With the Emancipation Proclamation, on January 1, 1863, between 20,000 and 50,000 slaves were freed immediately, with many more to follow as the Union regained control over parts of the South. The Proclamation dramatically shifted the government's perspective on the war from one of preserving the Union to one of establishing freedom for all. Lincoln wanted to sway international opinion in the Union's favor. The Proclamation also allowed freed slaves to join the military and may have hurt the South's economy by encouraging slaves to flee to the North. The Union didn't officially abolish the institution of slavery until after the war, when Congress enacted the Thirteenth Amendment to the Constitution.

Before the war began, no one knew what they were getting into. They hadn't a clue to the unimaginable death, destruction, and devastation they were facing. Each side thought it would end quickly. But both sides were determined and roughly evenly matched, so it turned into a difficult and bloody war that dragged on for four years. Circumstances and events established a situation where war was probably unavoidable—that is, without compromises that neither side was willing to make.

The storm had been brewing since before the birth of the country. When it finally hit, it literally ripped the country apart, and America went to war against itself.

THE WAR BEGINS

Known by the North as
THE WAR FOR THE UNION
THE GREAT REBELLION
THE WAR OF THE REBELLION

Known by the South as
THE WAR OF SECESSION
THE WAR FOR SOUTHERN INDEPENDENCE
THE WAR BETWEEN THE STATES
THE WAR OF NORTHERN AGGRESSION

Known by African Americans as
THE FREEDOM WAR

APRIL 12, 1861

COMMANDERS

Union

Commander in Chief:

President Abraham Lincoln: March 4, 1861–April 15, 1865

Generals in Chief:

Winfield Scott: July 5, 1841–November 1, 1861

George McClellan: November 1, 1861–March 11, 1862

President Abraham Lincoln and Secretary of War Edwin Stanton: March 11–July 23, 1862

Henry Halleck: July 23, 1862–March 9, 1864

Ulysses S. Grant: March 9, 1864–March 4, 1869

Confederate

Commander in Chief:

President Jefferson Davis: February 18, 1861–May 5, 1865

General in Chief:

Robert E. Lee: January 31–April 9, 1865

(Lee commanded the Army of Northern Virginia from June 1, 1862–April 9, 1865)

PARTICIPANTS

20 Northern and Western States and 5 Border States

21,700,000 free population, 400,000 slaves in 1860

The Union Army

Also known as the U.S. Army, the Federal Army, the National Army, and the Northern Army

2,213,363 soldiers, including 7,122 officers, 178,975 enlisted; African Americans

Army of the Cumberland: Tennessee and Georgia

Army of Georgia: the March to the Sea and the Carolinas

Army of the Gulf: the coastal region of the Gulf of Mexico

Army of the James: the Virginia Peninsula

Army of the Mississippi: the Mississippi River

Army of the Ohio: Kentucky, Tennessee, and Georgia

Army of the Potomac: principal army in the eastern theater

Army of the Shenandoah: the Shenandoah Valley

Army of the Tennessee: Kentucky, Tennessee, Mississippi, Georgia, and the Carolinas

Army of Virginia: the Northern Virginia campaign

Navy and Marines

84,000 to 106,000 sailors and marines

725 ships

Militias

Individual states had their own militias, but anyone who wanted to "raise a company" put together informal militias and home guards.

11 Southern States

5,600,000 free population, 3,500,000 slaves in 1860

The Confederate States Army

Also known as the Southern Army

750,000 to 1,100,000 soldiers, plus more than 65,000 slaves and freemen. About 13,000 engaged in combat for the army and state militias.

Army of Mississippi

Army of Missouri

Army of New Mexico

Army of Northern Virginia: the Confederacy's primary force

Army of Tennessee: between the Appalachian Mountains and the Mississippi River

Army of the Trans-Mississippi: states and territories west of the Mississippi

Navy and Marines

About 6,000 sailors and marines

106 ships (including those of individual states and privateers)

THOUGHTS OF WAR FROM WEST POINT

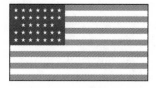

Union

Major-General George Armstrong Custer

George Armstrong Custer infamously lost the Battle of the Little Bighorn in 1876, but he also fought successfully in many battles throughout the Civil War. Born in Ohio, the son of a farmer and blacksmith, he grew up there and in Michigan, graduating from West Point a year early, just after the war began, dead last in the class of 1861. At twenty-three he became the Union army's youngest general, noted for his fearlessness, recklessness, and flamboyance, but also considered an effective cavalry commander.

A cadet at West Point when the war started, George Armstrong Custer graduated and was rushed out to battle. He wrote about his experiences in a series of articles that appeared in The Galaxy magazine right before he was killed attacking a large group of Native American camps in the Battle of the Little Bighorn.

I remember a conversation held at the table at which I sat during the winter of '60–'61. I was seated next to Cadet P. M. B. Young, a gallant young fellow from Georgia, a classmate of mine, then and since the war an intimate and valued friend—a major-general in the Confederate forces during the war and a member of Congress from his native State at a later date. The approaching war was as usual the subject of conversation in which all participated, and in the freest and most friendly manner; the lads from the North discoursing earnestly upon the power and rectitude of the National Government, the impulsive Southron holding up pictures of invaded rights and future independence. Finally, in a half jocular, half earnest manner, Young turned to me and delivered himself as follows:

"Custer, my boy, we're going to have war. It's no use talking: I see it coming. All the Crittenden compromises that can be patched up won't avert it. Now let me prophesy what will happen to you and me. You will go home, and your abolition Governor will probably make you colonel of a cavalry regiment. I will go down to Georgia, and ask Governor Brown to give me a cavalry regiment. And who knows but we may move against each other during the war. You will probably get the advantage of us in the first few engagements, as your side will be rich and powerful, while we will be poor and weak. Your regiment will be armed with the best of weapons, the sharpest of sabres; mine will have only shotguns and scythe blades; but for all that we'll get the best of the fight in the end, because we will fight for a principle, a cause, while you will fight only to perpetuate the abuse of power."

Lightly as we both regarded this boyish prediction, it was destined to be fulfilled in a remarkable degree. Both of us rose to higher commands, and confronted each other on the battlefield.

It is doubtful if the people of the North were ever, or will ever be again, so united in thought and impulse as when the attack on Sumter was flashed upon them. Opponents in politics became friends in patriotism; all differences of opinion vanished or were laid aside, and a single purpose filled and animated the breast of the people as of one man—a purpose unflinching and unrestrained— to rush to the rescue of the Government, to beat down its opposers, come from whence they may. In addition to sharing the common interest and anxiety of the public in the attack upon Sumter, the cadets felt a special concern from the fact that

among the little band of officers shut up in that fortress were two, Lieutenants Snyder and Hall, who had been our comrades as cadets only a few months before.

As already stated, the time of study and instruction at West Point at that period was five years, in the determination and fixing of which no one had exercised greater influence than Jefferson Davis—first as Secretary of War, afterward as United States Senator. There was no single individual in or out of Congress, excepting perhaps the venerable Lieutenant-General [Winfield Scott] at the head of the army, whose opinions on military questions affecting the public service had greater weight than those of Jefferson Davis up to the date of his withdrawal from the Senate in January, 1861. As a Secretary of War he displayed an ability and achieved a reputation which has not since been approached by any of the numerous incumbents of that office, if we except Secretary Stanton.

From New Orleans to Washington, D.C.

Union

General William Tecumseh Sherman

William Tecumseh Sherman took over from Lieutenant-General Grant as commander of the Union forces in the western theater before moving on to the Atlanta campaign, the Savannah campaign—his famous March to the Sea—and the Carolinas campaign.

Born in Ohio, the son of a state supreme court justice, he graduated from West Point in 1840, was assigned to the artillery, and was sent to Florida for the Second Seminole War. Then he went to Georgia, South Carolina, and California. In 1850 he was promoted to captain, and when he married the daughter of the country's first secretary of the interior, President Zachary Taylor attended their wedding. He returned to San Francisco to work as a bank manager, and right before the war took a position as superintendent of the Louisiana State Seminary of Learning and Military Academy near Alexandria, Louisiana. He was the president of a streetcar company in St. Louis, Missouri, when, at age forty-one, he finally decided to return to the army. Lincoln quickly promoted him to brigadier general of volunteers, giving him rank seniority over Brigadier-General Grant.

Before the war, at the Louisiana State Seminary of Learning and Military Academy, which later became Louisiana State University, Sherman was a professor of engineering as well as the superintendent of the Louisiana State Central Arsenal. Although he lived in the South, he remained loyal to the Union.

I think my general opinions were well known and understood, viz., that "secession was treason, was war;" and that in no event could the North and West permit the Mississippi River to pass out of their control.

About this time also, viz., early in December, we received Mr. [President James] Buchanan's annual message to Congress, in which he publicly announced that the General Government had no constitutional power to "coerce a State." The Legislature of Louisiana met on the 10th of December, and passed an act calling a convention of delegates from the people, to meet at Baton Rouge, on the 8th of January, to take into consideration the state of the Union; and, although it was universally admitted that a large majority of the voters of the State were opposed to secession, disunion, and all the steps of the South Carolinians, yet we saw that they were powerless, and that the politicians would sweep them along rapidly to the end, prearranged by their leaders in Washington.

When Louisiana seceded, Sherman tendered his resignation, which was accepted, and he went to New Orleans to finalize matters.

This business occupied two or three days, during which I staid at the St. Louis Hotel. I usually sat at table with Colonel and Mrs. [Braxton] Bragg, and an officer who wore the uniform of the State of Louisiana, and was addressed as captain. Bragg wore a colonel's uniform, and explained to me that he was a colonel in the State service, a colonel of artillery, and that some companies of his regiment garrisoned Forts Jackson and St. Philip, and the arsenal at Baton Rouge.

[G. T.] Beauregard at the time had two sons at the Seminary of Learning. I had given them some of my personal care at the father's request, and, wanting to tell him of their condition and progress, I went to his usual office in the Customhouse Building, and found him in the act of starting for Montgomery, Alabama. Bragg said afterward that Beauregard had been sent for by Jefferson Davis, and that it was rumored that he had been made a brigadier-general, of which fact he seemed jealous, because in the old army Bragg was the senior.

Davis and Stephens had been inaugurated President and Vice-President of the Confederate States of America, February 18, 1860, at Montgomery, and those States only embraced the seven cotton States. I recall a conversation at the tea-table, one evening, at the St. Louis Hotel. When Bragg was speaking of Beauregard's promotion, Mrs. Bragg, turning to me, said, "You know that my husband is not a favorite with the new President." My mind was resting on Mr. Lincoln as the new

President, and I said I did not know that Bragg had ever met Mr. Lincoln, when Mrs. Bragg said, quite pointedly, "I didn't mean your President, but our President." I knew that Bragg hated Davis bitterly, and that he had resigned from the army in 1855, or 1856, because Davis, as Secretary of War, had ordered him, with his battery, from Jefferson Barracks [in St. Louis], Missouri, to Fort Smith or Fort Washita, in the Indian country, as Bragg expressed it, "to chase Indians with six-pounders."

I walked the streets of New Orleans, and found business going along as usual. Ships were strung for miles along the lower levee, and steamboats above, all discharging or receiving cargo. The Pelican flag of Louisiana was flying over the Custom-House, Mint, City Hall, and everywhere. At the levee ships carried every flag on earth except that of the United States, and I was told that during a procession on the 22d of February, celebrating their emancipation from the despotism of the United States Government, only one national flag was shown from a house, and that the house of Cuthbert Bullitt, on Lafayette Square. He was commanded to take it down, but he refused, and defended it with his pistol.

I left New Orleans about the 1st of March, 1861, by rail to Jackson and Clinton, Mississippi, Jackson, Tennessee, and Columbus, Kentucky, where we took a boat to Cairo, and thence, by rail, to Cincinnati and Lancaster. All the way, I heard, in the cars and boats, warm discussions about politics; to the effect that, if Mr. Lincoln should attempt coercion of the seceded States, the other slave or border States would make common cause, when, it was believed, it would be madness to attempt to reduce them to subjection. In the South, the people were earnest, fierce and angry, and were evidently organizing for action; whereas, in Illinois, Indiana, and Ohio, I saw not the least sign of preparation. It

certainly looked to me as though the people of the North would tamely submit to a disruption of the Union, and the orators of the South used, openly and constantly, the expressions that there would be no war, and that a lady's thimble would hold all the blood to be shed. On reaching Lancaster, I found letters from my brother John, inviting me to come to Washington, as he wanted to see me.

Mr. Lincoln had just been installed [on March 4], and the newspapers were filled with rumors of every kind indicative of war; the chief act of interest was that Major Robert Anderson had taken by night into Fort Sumter all the troops garrisoning Charleston Harbor, and that he was determined to defend it against the demands of the State of South Carolina and of the Confederate States. I must have reached Washington about the 10th of March [during inauguration week]. I found my brother there, just appointed Senator, in place of Mr. Chase, who was in the cabinet, and I have no doubt my opinions, thoughts, and feelings, wrought up by the events in Louisiana, seemed to him gloomy and extravagant. About Washington I saw but few signs of preparation, though the Southern Senators and Representatives were daily sounding their threats on the floors of Congress, and were publicly withdrawing to join the Confederate Congress at Montgomery. Even in the War Department and about the public offices there was open, unconcealed talk, amounting to high-treason.

One day, John Sherman took me with him to see Mr. Lincoln. He walked into the room where the secretary to the President now sits, we found the room full of people, and Mr. Lincoln sat at the end of the table, talking with three or four gentlemen, who soon left. John walked up, shook hands, and took a chair near him, holding in his hand some papers referring to minor appointments in the State of Ohio, which formed the subject of conversation.

Mr. Lincoln took the papers, said he would refer them to the proper heads of departments, and would be glad to make the appointments asked for, if not already promised.

John then turned to me, and said, "Mr. President, this is my brother, Colonel Sherman, who is just up from Louisiana, he may give you some information you want."

"Ah!" said Mr. Lincoln, "how are they getting along down there?"

I said, "They think they are getting along swimmingly—they are preparing for war."

"Oh, well!" said he, "I guess we'll manage to keep house."

I was silenced, said no more to him, and we soon left. I was sadly disappointed, and remember that I broke out on John, damning the politicians generally, saying, "You have got things in a hell of a fix, and you may get them out as you best can," adding that the country was sleeping on a volcano that might burst forth at any minute, but that I was going to St. Louis to take care of my family, and would have no more to do with it.

John begged me to be more patient, but I said I would not; that I had no time to wait, that I was off for St. Louis; and off I went.

Virginia Secedes

Confederate

Lieutenant-General Jubal Early

Born into a wealthy Virginia family, Jubal Early graduated from West Point in 1837. As a second lieutenant he was assigned to an artillery regiment and went to Florida to fight the Seminole. After two years he resigned and became a lawyer, returning to the army to fight in the Mexican-American War. He also served for two years in the Virginia House of Delegates.

Early had strongly opposed secession, but when Lincoln called for volunteers to force the South to remain in the Union, he volunteered for the Virginia militia as a brigadier general. He transferred to the Confederate army as a colonel and received command of one of three regiments that he raised. General G. T. Beauregard was impressed with his performance in the First Battle of Manassas (First Bull Run), promoting him to brigadier general. Noted for a short temper and for being highly critical of his subordinates, he fought in just about every major battle in the eastern theater and was wounded in 1862 at Williamsburg, Virginia. His overall performance was mixed, and his inability to inspire his men prompted Lee to relieve him of his duties.

When the question of practical secession from the United States arose, as a citizen of the State of Virginia, and a member of the Convention called by the authority of the Legislature of that State, I opposed secession with all the ability I possessed, with the hope that the horrors of civil war might be averted and that a returning sense of justice on the part of the masses of the Northern States would induce them to respect the rights of the people of the South.

While some Northern politicians and editors were openly and sedulously justifying and encouraging secession, I was laboring honestly and earnestly to preserve the Union.

As a member of the Virginia Convention, I voted against the ordinance of secession on its passage by that body, with the hope that even then, the collision of arms might be avoided and some satisfactory adjustment arrived at. The adoption of that ordinance wrung from me bitter tears of grief; but I at once recognized my duty to abide the decision of my native State, and to defend her soil against invasion. Any scruples which I may have entertained as to the right of secession were soon dispelled by the unconstitutional measures of the authorities at Washington and the frenzied clamor of the people of the North for war upon their former brethren of the South. I recognized the right of resistance and revolution as exercised by our fathers in 1776 and without cavil as to the name by which it was called, I entered the military service of my State, willingly, cheerfully, and zealously.

When the State of Virginia became one of the Confederate States and her troops were turned over to the Confederate Government, I embraced the cause of the whole Confederacy with equal ardor, and continued in the service, with the determination to devote all the energy and talent I possessed to the common defence. I fought through the entire war, without once regretting the course I pursued, with an abiding faith in the justice of our cause.

It was my fortune to participate in most of the great military operations in which the army in Virginia was engaged both before and after General Lee assumed the command. In the last year of this momentous struggle, I commanded, at different times, a division and two corps of General Lee's Army in the campaign from the Rapidan to James River, and subsequently, a separate force which marched into Maryland, threatened Washington City and then went through an eventful campaign in the valley of Virginia.

My operations and my campaign stand on their own merits. And in what I have found it necessary to say in regard to the conduct of my troops, I do not wish to be understood as, in any way, decrying the soldiers who constituted the rank and file of my commands. I believe that the world has never produced a body of men superior, in courage, patriotism, and endurance, to the private soldiers of the Confederate armies. I have repeatedly seen those soldiers submit, with cheerfulness, to privations and hardships which would appear to be almost incredible; and the wild cheers of our brave men, when their thin lines were sent back opposing hosts of Federal troops, staggering, reeling and flying, have often thrilled every fibre in my heart. I have seen, with my own eyes, ragged, barefooted, and hungry Confederate soldiers perform deeds which, if performed in days of yore by mailed warriors in glittering armor, would have inspired the harp of the minstrel and the pen of the poet.

LEE RESIGNS HIS COMMISSION

Confederate

General Robert E. Lee

Raised on a plantation in Alexandria, Virginia, across the Potomac from Washington, D.C., Robert E. Lee graduated from West Point in 1829 and became a second lieutenant in the U.S. Army's Corps of Engineers, spending many years gaining valuable experience positioning troops and artillery. He fought in several battles during the war with Mexico and was slightly wounded in the Battle of Chapultepec. After Mexico, Lee became superintendent of West Point and then second-in-command of the Second U.S. Cavalry in Texas. In 1859, on special assignment, he led a company of Marines to quell John Brown's raid on Harper's Ferry. Lee captured Brown and oversaw his execution.

As the war was about to break out, Colonel Lee was offered top positions in both the Union and Confederate militaries, but he turned both down, not wanting to have to fight against his country or his state—however, that soon changed. When Virginia seceded, he became commander of Virginia's military, soon one of the Confederate army's first five full generals, and personal military advisor to President Jefferson Davis. When General Joseph Johnston sustained severe injuries at the Battle of Seven Pines, Lee took his place as commander of the Confederate Army of the Potomac, which was the Confederacy's primary military force. He changed its name to the Army of Northern Virginia and led it to a number of stunning victories in the face of larger, better-equipped forces.

Robert E. Lee did not condone slavery, but he accepted it. While seeing it as evil, he somehow reasoned that it was God's way of educating Africans, which he explained in a letter written in Texas in December 1856.

There are few, I believe, in this enlightened age who will not acknowledge that slavery as an institution is a moral and political evil. It is idle to expatiate on its disadvantages. I think it is a greater evil to the white than to the colored race. While my feelings are strongly enlisted in behalf of the latter, my sympathies are more deeply engaged for the former. The blacks are immeasurably better off here than in Africa, morally, physically, and socially. The painful discipline they are undergoing is necessary for their further instruction as a race, and will prepare them, I hope, for better things. How long their servitude may be necessary is known and ordered by a merciful Providence.

While we see the course of the final abolition of human slavery is still onward, and give it the aid of our prayers, let us leave the progress as well as the results in the hand of Him who sees the end, who chooses to work by slow influences, and with whom a thousand years are but as a single day.

Is it not strange that the descendants of those Pilgrim Fathers who crossed the Atlantic to preserve their own freedom have always proved the most intolerant of the spiritual liberty of others?

After Texas joined the Confederacy, the general in chief of the United States Army, Brevet[2] Lieutenant-General Winfield Scott, ordered then-colonel Lee to report to the War Department. Leaving behind the regiment he commanded in Fort Mason, Texas, Lee arrived in Arlington, Virginia, on March 1. Forty-eight days later Virginia seceded. The following day Lee met with Scott to discuss his future with the U.S. Army. Two days afterward he submitted his resignation, along with this letter to General Scott:

Arlington, Virginia, April 20, 1861

General:

Since my interview with you on the 18th inst. I have felt that I ought no longer to retain my commission in the Army. I therefore tender my resignation, which I request you will recommend for acceptance. It would have been presented at once but for the struggle it has cost me to separate myself from a service to which I have devoted the best years of my life, and all the ability I possessed.

---

2 A "brevet" or "bvt." rank was a temporary rank awarded for outstanding service. After the war the brevet system was replaced with the awarding of medals.

During the whole of that time—more than a quarter of a century—I have experienced nothing but kindness from my superiors and a most cordial friendship from my comrades. To no one, General, have I been as much indebted as to yourself for uniform kindness and consideration, and it has always been my ardent desire to merit your approbation. I shall carry to the grave the most grateful recollections of your kind consideration, and your name and fame shall always be dear to me.

Save in the defense of my native State, I never desire again to draw my sword.

Be pleased to accept my most earnest wishes for the continuance of your happiness and prosperity, and believe me most truly yours,

R. E. Lee

Military men, when they make speeches, should say but few words, and speak them to the point. I admire, young gentlemen, the spirit you have shown in rushing to the defence of your comrades; but I must commend you particularly for the readiness with which you have listened to the counsel and obeyed the orders of your superior officer. The time may be near at hand when your State will need your services, and if that time does come, then draw your swords and throw away the scabbards.

—Major Thomas "Stonewall" Jackson, as an instructor, to the cadets of the Virginia Military Institute

THE JOURNEY TO RICHMOND

Confederate

Major-General George Pickett

George Pickett was known at West Point as a prankster with little interest in studying, and he graduated last in his class in 1846. He was commissioned as a brevet second lieutenant in an infantry regiment, distinguishing himself during the Battle of Chapultepec. After serving on the Texas frontier, he was sent to Fort Bellingham in Washington Territory, where he was when war broke out. Even though he strongly opposed slavery, he remained loyal to Virginia.

Union major general George McClellan said of him: "There is no doubt that he was the best infantry soldier developed on either side during the Civil War. His friends and admirers are by no means confined to the Southern people or soldiers to whom he gave his heart and best affections and of whom he was so noble a type, but throughout the North and on the Pacific coast, where he long served, his friends and lovers are legion."

When the war started, George Pickett, then a U.S. Army captain, resigned his commission and headed for Richmond by way of New York City. Travel was slow, and the war was under way by the time he finally reached Richmond. There he wrote this letter to LaSalle "Sallie" Corbell, who would eventually become his third wife. She claimed they had first met when she was just nine years old, right after the death of his first wife. He was thirty-six, and she eighteen, when he sent her this letter.

Richmond, September 17, 1861

I had no conception of the intensity of feeling, the bitterness and hatred toward those who were so lately our friends and are now our enemies. I, of course, have always strenuously opposed disunion, not as doubting the right of secession, which was taught in our text-book at West Point, but as gravely questioning its expediency. I believed that the revolutionary spirit which infected both North and South was but a passing phase of fanaticism which would perish under the rebuke of all good citizens, who would surely unite in upholding the Constitution; but when that great assembly, composed of ministers, lawyers, judges, chancellors, states men, mostly white-haired men of thought, met in South Carolina and when their districts were called crept noiselessly to the table in the center of the room and affixed their signatures to the parchment on which the ordinance of secession was inscribed, and when in deathly silence, spite of the gathered multitude, General Jamison arose and without preamble read:

"The ordinance of secession has been signed and ratified; I proclaim the State of South Carolina an independent sovereignty," and lastly, when my old boyhood's friend called for an invasion, it was evident that both the advocates and opponents of secession had read the portents aright.

We did not tarry even for a day in 'Frisco, but under assumed names my friend, Sam Barron [III], and I sailed for New York, where we arrived on the very day that Sam's father, Commodore [Samuel] Barron [II], was brought there a prisoner, which fact was proclaimed aloud by the pilot amid cheers of the passengers and upon our landing heralded by the newsboys with more cheers. [Note: Commodore Barron II was the commander of Virginia and North Carolina's coastal defenses until he was forced to surrender Forts Clark and Hatteras and was taken prisoner on August 29 at the conclusion of the Battle of Hatteras Inlet Batteries.] Poor Sam [the third] had a hard fight to hide his feelings and to avoid arrest. We separated as mere ship acquaintances, and went by different routes to meet again, as arranged, at the house of Doctor Paxton, a Southern sympathizer and our friend.

On the next day we left for Canada by the earliest train. Thence we made our perilous way back south again, barely escaping arrest several times, and finally arrived in dear old Richmond, September 13th, just four days ago. I at once enlisted in the army [as a private] and the following day was commissioned Captain. But so bitter is the feeling here that my being unavoidably delayed so long in avowing my allegiance to my state has been most cruelly and severely criticized by friends, yes, and even relatives, too.

Now, little one, if you had the very faintest idea how happy a certain captain in the C. S. A. (My, but that "C" looks queer!) would be to look into your beautiful, soul-speaking eyes and hear your wonderfully musical voice, I think you would let him know by wire where he could find you. I shall almost listen for the electricity which says, "I am at ——. Come." I know that you will have mercy on your devoted

Soldier[3]

---

3 Pickett didn't actually sign his letters as "Soldier" or "Your Devoted Soldier." Sallie initially published his letters anonymously and used this to hide his identity. She continued using it when the letters were republished under his name. He actually signed his letters, "Ever and forever your own George" or "Ever and 'for ever' your devoted husband George" or a similar variation.

THE BATTLE OF FORT SUMTER

CHARLESTON COUNTY, SOUTH CAROLINA
APRIL 12–13, 1861

COMMANDERS

Confederate
Brig. Gen. G. T. Beauregard

Union
Maj. Robert Anderson

PARTICIPANTS

Approximately 500 (Provisional Forces of the
Confederate States)

85 (First U.S. Artillery)

CASUALTIES

Confederate
4 wounded

Union
2 killed after surrender
9 wounded

VICTORY: CONFEDERACY

OVERVIEW

The Civil War officially began with the Battle of Fort Sumter. After secession South Carolina demanded that Major Anderson evacuate the U.S. Army's facilities in Charleston Harbor. Anderson refused, and during the night of December 26, 1860, he secretly moved his men from Fort Moultrie to the more defensible Fort Sumter. President Buchanan sent supplies to Anderson on January 9, 1861, in an unarmed merchant ship, but Confederate shore batteries opened fire on it, forcing it to depart. While federal property was being seized throughout the Deep South, Anderson resisted.

In March, Brigadier-General G. T. Beauregard became the Confederacy's first general officer, taking charge of Charleston. Beauregard, who had been Anderson's student at West Point, issued his former teacher an ultimatum, to no effect, so at 4:30 a.m. he bombarded the fort from the harbor's artillery batteries. Major Anderson returned fire. But after thirty-four hours—outgunned, low on food and ammunition, and with the quarters destroyed by fire—Anderson finally surrendered. No one had died during the fighting, although a gun exploded during the surrender ceremony's fifty-gun salute, killing two men.

The battle stirred aggression in both the North and South. For the North the fall of Fort Sumter had much the same emotional effect as Pearl Harbor some eighty years later. This finally launched the Union into action. Lincoln issued his call for volunteers to repossess federal property, prompting the wavering states to join the Confederacy.

FORT SUMTER VS. FORT PICKENS

Union

Admiral David Dixon Porter

David Dixon Porter was a son of Commodore David Porter and a brother to the adopted David Farragut. After Admiral Farragut's death he became the second officer in the U.S. Navy to become a full admiral.

Born in Pennsylvania, he hailed from a family of military officers. When his father accepted a position as commander of the Mexican Navy, the ten-year-old Porter, one of his brothers, and a cousin went along. His cousin was killed in battle near Havana, Cuba, while Porter was slightly wounded and captured. He became a midshipman at the belated age of sixteen with the help of his grandfather, a congressman (normally midshipmen started as young boys).

During the Civil War, as part of the West Gulf Blockading Squadron, he took part in the capture of New Orleans and the initial assault on Vicksburg. As commander of the Mississippi River Squadron, he worked closely with Major-Generals Sherman and Grant during the Siege of Vicksburg. Grant said he was "as great an admiral as Lord Nelson."

Mr. Lincoln had been installed in the Presidential office, and the subject of relieving Fort Sumter was under discussion. A small squadron was being fitted out for the supposed purpose of relieving the fort, the final action of which was to be guided by Mr. G. V. Fox, afterward Assistant Secretary of the Navy.

My orders to California were still hanging over me, and I had even engaged my passage in the steamer from New York, and was taking my last meal with my family, when a carriage drove up to the door.

It brought a note from the Secretary of State (Mr. [William] Seward), requesting me to call and see him without delay; so, leaving my dinner unfinished, I jumped into the carriage and drove at once to the Secretary's office.

I found Mr. Seward lying on his back on a sofa, with his knees up, reading a lengthy document.

Without changing his position he said to me, "Can you tell me how we can save Fort Pickens from falling into the hands of the rebels?"[4]

I answered, promptly, "I can, sir."

"Then," said the Secretary, "you are the man I want, if you can do it."

"I can do it," I said, as Mr. Seward rose to his feet.

Those familiar with the history of that period will remember that Lieutenant [Adam] Slemmer was holding Fort Pickens with a small force and had refused the summons of General [Braxton] Bragg to surrender, and all the naval guns and munitions of war that had fallen into the Confederates' hands were being placed in position behind earthworks, preparatory to opening on the Union lines. It was to save Slemmer and the Union works that made Mr. Seward so interested in this affair.

"Now, come," said Mr. Seward, "tell me how you will save that place."

I had talked with Captain (now General) [Montgomery] Meigs a few days before about this matter. Mr. Seward, being anxious to show the Southerners that the Government had a right to hold its own forts, and seeing the likelihood of our losing Fort Sumter, listened very kindly to Captain Meigs's suggestions.

Our plan was to get a good-sized steamer and six or seven companies of soldiers, and to carry the latter, with a number of large guns and a quantity of munitions of war, to Fort Pickens, land them on the outside of the fort under the guns of a ship of war, and the fort would soon be made impregnable—that was all.

I repeated this to Mr. Seward, and said to him, "Give me command of the [steam frigate USS] *Powhatan*, now lying at New York ready for sea,

and I will guarantee that everything shall be done without a mistake."

Mr. Seward invited Captain Meigs—who had come in in the mean time—and myself to accompany him to the President. When we arrived at the White House, Mr. Lincoln—who seemed to be aware of our errand—opened the conversation.

"Tell me," said he, "how we can prevent Fort Pickens from falling into the hands of the rebels, for if Slemmer is not at once relieved there will be no holding it. Pensacola would be a very important place for the Southerners, and if they once get possession of Pickens, and fortify it, we have no navy to take it from them."

"Mr. President," said I, "there is a queer state of things existing in the Navy Department at this time. Mr. [Gideon] Welles is surrounded by officers and clerks, some of whom are disloyal at heart, and if the orders for this expedition should emanate from the Secretary of the Navy, and pass through all the department red tape, the news would be at once flashed over the wires, and Fort Pickens would be lost for ever. But if you will issue all the orders from the Executive Mansion, and let me proceed to New York with them, I will guarantee their prompt execution to the letter."

"But," said the President, "is not this a most irregular mode of proceeding?"

"Certainly," I replied, "but the necessity of the case justifies it."

"You are commander-in-chief of the army and navy," said Mr. Seward to the President, "and this is a case where it is necessary to issue direct orders without passing them through intermediaries."

"But what will Uncle Gideon say?" inquired the President.

"Oh, I will make it all right with Mr. Welles," said the Secretary of State. "This is the only way, sir, the thing can be done." At this very time Mr.

4   Fort Pickens guards the entrance to Pensacola Harbor, near Florida's border with Alabama.

Welles was—or supposed he was—fitting out an expedition for the relief of Fort Sumter. All the orders were issued in the usual way, and, of course, telegraphed to Charleston, as soon as written, by the persons in the department through whose hands they passed.

Mr. Seward was well aware of this, and he wanted to prevent such a thing happening in this instance.

Mr. Welles, no doubt, had the Powhatan on his list of available vessels, and may have relied on her to carry out his plan for the relief of Sumter. Orders had been sent for the several vessels to rendezvous off Charleston on a certain day, but, strange to say, no orders had been issued for the Powhatan to join them.

I observed one thing during this interview, and that was that the best of feeling did not exist between the heads of the State and Navy Departments. Mr. Seward doubtless thought that he had not been as much consulted as he ought to have been in the fitting out of the expedition for the relief of Sumter. He looked upon himself as Prime Minister, and considered that the Secretary of the Navy should defer to him in all matters concerning movements against those in rebellion, in which opinion Mr. Welles did not concur. Mr. Seward was by nature of an arbitrary disposition, and wanted everything done in his own way— not a bad quality on occasions, but apt to create confusion if persevered in in too many cases.

In this instance it was eminently proper that the Secretary of State should take the initiative.

In the course of the conversation Mr. Lincoln remarked: "This looks to me very much like the case of two fellows I once knew: one was a gambler, the other a preacher. They met in a stage, and the gambler induced the preacher to play poker, and the latter won all the gambler's money. 'It's all because we have mistaken our trades,' said

the gambler; 'you ought to have been a gambler and I a preacher, and, by ginger, I intend to turn the tables on you next Sunday and preach in your church,' which he did."

It was finally agreed that my plan should be carried out. I wrote the necessary orders, which were copied by Captain Meigs and signed by the President, who merely said as he did so, "Seward, see that I don't burn my fingers."

Some days later Lincoln told Seward: "Seward, if the Southerners get Sumter we will be even with them by securing Pickens." It is possible Lincoln was awaiting some powerful event to galvanize the public, enabling him to call up soldiers, and expected Fort Sumter would be it. Lincoln had vowed that if there was a war he wouldn't be the one to fire the first shot. Perhaps he knew that for the South to start the war he had to allow them to take Fort Sumter, but he didn't want to sacrifice Fort Pickens. If this was his plan, it worked perfectly. He caught a lot of heat for the loss of Sumter, but in the larger scheme it united the North and enabled him to begin building up the army.

When the Southern states began seceding, Lincoln hadn't yet been inaugurated. Lame-duck president Buchanan took the position that secession was unconstitutional but that the federal government couldn't force those states to stay; it could only use force to protect federal property. That was also the reason Lincoln used for calling up the army. Of course, the Confederacy wasn't about to give up that property without a fight—they certainly didn't want Union forts scattered throughout their fledgling territory—and the North certainly wasn't going to cede control of the Mississippi River, a major transport route and the primary reason President Jefferson had made the Louisiana Purchase.

Porter continued:

As it was, the rebels opened fire on Sumter from their heavy earth-works as soon as the vessels composing Mr. Welles's expedition approached the bar, and they could not have done a particle of good. Had they tried to succor the people in the fort, they would have been sunk in a very few minutes. A more foolish expedition was never dispatched, and Mr. Lincoln remarked, when the news was brought to him, "It's a good rule never to send a mouse to catch a skunk, or a pollywog to tackle a whale."

The attempt to relieve Sumter was a curious muddle, and had, from the first inception of the design, no chance of success. Mr. Seward was evidently opposed to it, feeling sure that it would be a failure, and so he got up the expedition to Pickens, certain that it could not fail to be successful. The Secretary of State wished to show that he was a better sailor than Mr. Welles.

Fort Sumter in the distance, as viewed from Fort Johnson's battery.

Then-lieutenant Porter's expedition succeeded. He drove off Brigadier-General Braxton Bragg's forces with a single warning shot, and Fort Pickens remained under Union control throughout the war—one of the few Southern forts to do so.

LINCOLN'S WAR ROOM

Before the Civil War it took hours or even days for a country's leaders to determine the results of a battle. If the battle took place overseas, it could take weeks for the courier to bring the news in person. Even communicating over short distances proved difficult. Messengers could use smoke signals, like the Native Americans and the Vatican; light beacons, like Paul Revere; or sound, such as firing a cannon.

Shortly before the war began, the telegraph came into popular use, and the war prompted its rapid expansion. By October 1861 the first lines connecting the East and West Coasts went into operation, replacing the Pony Express, which was credited with keeping California and its gold in the Union. Initially the War Department had no telegraph lines, so in order to send a telegram, clerks had to take written messages to the American Telegraph Company office and wait their turn.

It wasn't long before lines ran between the War Department and other significant locations, but not to the White House, which was one reason Lincoln spent so much time next door in the

War Department building. Eventually the telegraph offices ended up on the second floor, next to Secretary of War Edwin Stanton's office. The main telegraph office was actually a large library, with alcoves full of books, and not just military titles and maps. Off to one side lay the cipher room, where outgoing messages were encrypted and incoming messages deciphered. This is where Lincoln seems to have spent most of his time; there and in Stanton's office.

Lincoln often visited the telegraph office several times a day, spending hours there. Sometimes he even spent the night there, using it to dodge the stress of the White House. When a battle was in progress, he practically lived in the telegraph offices and even held cabinet meetings there. In addition to his White House office, it was also here that he was regularly briefed, received updates on plans, formulated strategies, and kept current on the latest military information and intelligence.

Lincoln's office in the White House was also something of a war room, with a conference table in the middle strewn with maps and military books. On one wall hung three giant maps with pencil marks indicating troop movements. Folios of maps leaned against walls and behind the horsehair sofa. In one corner sat a tall clerk's desk with lots of cubbyholes and a row of books on top. He also kept nearby a rolled map that showed in various shades of gray the densities of the slave population in the South, taking it out and referring to it often.

When telegrams came in, they were first deciphered, since most were encrypted using secret codes. Four copies were made—one for the addressee, one for War Department records, one for Secretary of War Stanton, and one for the president.

A. B. Chandler, chief of the War Department's telegraph office, explained how Lincoln read through these dispatches: "President Lincoln's copies were kept in what we called the 'President's drawer' of the 'cipher desk.' He would come in at any time of the night or day, and go at once to this drawer, and take out a file of telegrams, and begin at the top to read them. His position in running over these telegrams was sometimes very curious.

"He had a habit of sitting frequently on the edge of his chair, with his right knee dragged down to the floor. I remember a curious expression of his when he got to the bottom of the new telegrams and began on those that he had read before. It was, 'Well, I guess I have got down to the raisins.'

"The first two or three times he said this he made no explanation, and I did not ask one. But one day, after he had made the remark, he looked up under his eyebrows at me with a funny twinkle in his eyes, and said: 'I used to know a little girl out West who sometimes was inclined to eat too much. One day she ate a good many more raisins than she ought to, and followed them up with a quantity of other goodies. They made her very sick. After a time the raisins began to come.

"She gasped and looked at her mother and said: 'Well, I will be better now I guess, for I have got down to the raisins.'"

As the war progressed and the telegraph system improved, Lincoln could engage in almost real-time communications with his field officers while discussing the situation with military advisors. Thus, the War Department's three telegraph rooms became the president's first situation rooms. The president and his senior generals gained some control over battlefield decisions, but battlefield commanders lost some of their autonomy. Until Lincoln came along and directly involved himself, even the War Department was used to receiving only broad directives and general policies from the White House. Lincoln sent out almost a thousand telegrams during his years as president, but he avoided confrontations and rarely, if ever, gave anyone a direct order. Instead, he tried gently to guide people—especially his commanders—the way he wanted them to go.

By the time Confederate major general Thomas "Stonewall" Jackson launched his Shenandoah Valley campaign, Lincoln had a hand in directing the Union's troop movements against him. Restoring the Union was always Lincoln's top priority, so he immersed himself in learning about the military, strategies, and tactics, while becoming quite knowledgeable on the backgrounds of the officers on both sides. Generally quite modest, he often knew more than even his top generals.

THE BOMBARDMENT OF FORT SUMTER

Confederate

General G. T. Beauregard

Pierre Gustave Toutant Beauregard (he didn't use his first name or first initial) was the Confederacy's leading general at the beginning of the war and later became a primary commander in the western theater.

A Creole born on a sugarcane plantation near New Orleans, he graduated from West Point in 1838, where he specialized in engineering. Serving in the war with Mexico, he was wounded in the shoulder and thigh at Chapultepec, where he worked alongside another engineer, Robert E. Lee. Eventually appointed superintendent of West Point, he served only five days before his orders were revoked after Louisiana's secession. Protesting that he was being forced out because he was a Southerner, he joined the Confederacy and commanded the forces that bombarded Fort Sumter.

Since Union major Robert Anderson, who was in command of Fort Sumter when Beauregard was ordered to pry him loose, had been one of Beauregard's instructors at West Point, Beauregard sent cases of whiskey and brandy, along with boxes of cigars, to Anderson and his officers, but Anderson refused them. Anderson also refused to budge, so Beauregard pulverized the fort with artillery shells for thirty-four hours.

Charleston, S.C., April 27, 1861
Brig. Gen. Cooper, Adjutant-General, C. S. A.
Sir, I have the honor to submit the following detailed report of the bombardment and surrender of Fort Sumter, and the incidents connected therewith:

Having completed my channel-defences and batteries in the harbor, necessary for the reduction

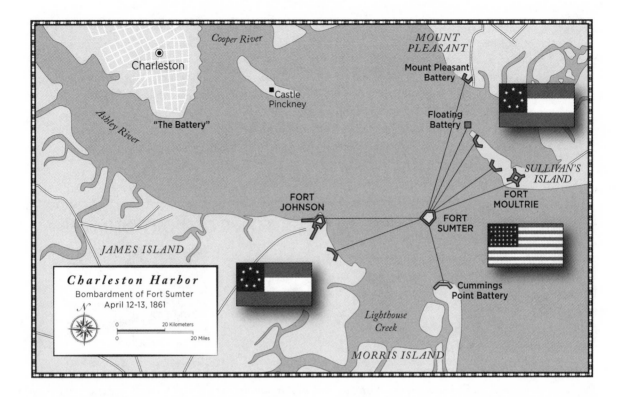

Charleston Harbor
Bombardment of Fort Sumter
April 12-13, 1861

of Fort Sumter, I despatched two of my aids at 2.20 p.m., on Thursday, the 11th of April, with a communication to Major Anderson, in command of the fort, demanding its evacuation. I offered to transport himself and command to any port in the United States he might select; to allow him to move out of the fort with company-arms and property, and all private property, and to salute his flag on lowering it. He refused to accede to this demand. As my aids were about leaving, Major Anderson remarked that if we did not batter him to pieces he would be starved out in a few days, or words to that effect.

As, in consequence of a communication from the President of the United States to the Governor of South Carolina, we were in momentary expectation of an attempt to reinforce Fort Sumter,

or of a descent upon our coast to that end from the United States fleet lying off the entrance of the harbor, it was manifestly an apparent necessity to reduce the fort as speedily as possible, and not to await until the ships and the fort should unite in a combined attack upon us. Accordingly, my aids, carrying out my instructions, promptly refused to accede to the terms proposed by Major Anderson, and notified him, in writing, that our batteries would open upon Fort Sumter in one hour. This notification was given at 3.20 a.m., on Friday the 12th instant [current month]. The signal-shell was fired from Fort Johnson at 4.30 a.m., and, at about 5 o'clock, the fire from our batteries became general. Fort Sumter did not open until 7 o'clock, when it commenced with a vigorous fire upon the Cummings's Point Iron Battery.

> The eyes of the watchers easily detected and followed the burning fuse which marked the course of the shell as it mounted among the stars, and then descended with ever-increasing velocity, until it landed inside the fort and burst. It was a capital shot. Then the batteries opened on all sides, and shot and shell went screaming over Sumter as if an army of devils were swooping around it.
>
> —Union sergeant James Chester

During the day (12th instant) the fire of our batteries was kept up most spiritedly, the guns and mortars being worked in the coolest manner, preserving the prescribed intervals of firing. Towards evening it became evident that our fire was very effective, as the enemy was driven from his barbette guns [on top of the walls], which he had attempted to work in the morning, and his fire was confined to his casemated guns. During the whole of Friday night our mortar batteries continued to throw shells, but, in obedience to orders, at longer intervals. The night was rainy and dark, and as it was confidently expected that the United States fleet would attempt to land troops upon the islands, or throw men into Fort Sumter by means of boats, the greatest vigilance was observed at all our channel batteries, and by our troops on both Morris and Sullivan's islands.

Early on Saturday morning all our batteries reopened on Fort Sumter, which responded vigorously for a while, directing its fire specially against Fort Moultrie. About 8 a.m. smoke was seen issuing from the quarters of Fort Sumter; the fire of our batteries was then increased, for the purpose of bringing the enemy to terms as speedily as possible, inasmuch as his flag was still floating defiantly. Fort Sumter continued to fire from time to time, but at long and irregular intervals, amid the dense smoke. Our brave troops, carried away by their enthusiasm, mounted the different batteries, and, at every discharge from the fort, cheered the garrison for its pluck and gallantry, and hooted at the fleet lying inactive just outside the bar.

About 1.30 p.m., it being reported to me that the Federal flag was down (it was afterwards ascertained that the flagstaff had been shot away), and the conflagration from the large volume of smoke appearing to increase, I sent three of my aids with a message to Major Anderson to the effect that, "seeing his flag no longer flying, his quarters in flames, and supposing him to be in distress, I desired to offer him any assistance he might stand in need of."

Before my aids reached the fort the United States flag was displayed on the parapets, but remained there only a short time when it was hauled down and a white flag substituted in its place. [On] hearing that a white flag was flying over the fort, I sent Major Jones, chief of my staff, and some other aids, with substantially the same proposition I had made to Major Anderson on the 11th instant, excepting the privilege of saluting his flag.

Major Anderson replied that "it would be exceedingly gratifying to him, as well as to his command, to be permitted to salute their flag, having so gallantly defended the fort under such trying circumstances, and hoped that General Beauregard would not refuse it, as such a privilege was not unusual." He furthermore said he "would not urge the point, but would prefer to refer the matter again to me." The point was, therefore, left open until the matter was submitted to me.

I very cheerfully agreed to allow the salute, as an honorable testimony to the gallantry and fortitude with which Major Anderson and his command had defended their post, and I informed Major Anderson of my decision about half-past seven o'clock, through Major Jones, my chief of staff. The arrangements being completed, Major Anderson embarked, with his command, on the transport prepared to convey them to the United States fleet still lying outside of the bar, and our troops immediately garrisoned the fort; before sunset the flag of the Confederate States floated over the ramparts of Sumter.

Charleston, S.C., April 17, 1861
Hon. L. P. Walker, Secretary of War, Montgomery, Ala,

Sir: I have the honor to transmit by Col. E. A. Pryor, one of my aides (who like the others was quite indefatigable and fearless in conveying my orders, in an open boat, from these headquarters to the batteries during the bombardment), a general report of the attack of the 12th instant on Fort Sumter.

Whilst the barracks in Fort Sumter were in a blaze, and the interior of the work appeared untenable from the heat and from the fire of our batteries, whenever the guns of Fort Sumter would fire upon Fort Moultrie the men occupying Cummings Point batteries (Palmetto Guard, Captain Cuthbert) at each shot would cheer Anderson for his gallantry, although themselves still firing upon him, and when on the 15th instant he left the harbor on the steamer *Isabel* the soldiers of the batteries on Cummings Point lined the beach, silent, and with heads uncovered, while Anderson and his command passed before them, and expressions of scorn at the apparent cowardice of the fleet in not even attempting to rescue so gallant an officer and his command were upon the lips of all. With such material for an army, if properly disciplined, I would consider myself almost invincible against any forces not too greatly superior.

The fire of those barracks was only put out on the 15th instant, p.m., after great exertions by the gallant fire companies of this city, who were at their pumps night and day, although aware that close by them was a magazine filled with thirty thousand pounds of powder, with a shot-hole through the wall of its anteroom.

I have the honor to be, very respectfully, your obedient servant,

G. T. Beauregard

THE FIRST BATTLE OF MANASSAS

ALSO KNOWN AS THE FIRST BATTLE OF BULL RUN
PRINCE WILLIAM COUNTY, VIRGINIA
JULY 21, 1861

COMMANDERS

Union
Brig. Gen. Irvin McDowell
Brig. Gen. G. T. Beauregard

Confederate
Brig. Gen. Joseph Johnston

PARTICIPANTS

18,000 engaged
(28,000–35,000 total)

18,000 engaged
(32,000–34,000 total)

CASUALTIES

Union
460 killed
1,124 wounded
1,312 POWs/MIA

Confederate
387 killed
1,582 wounded
13 MIA

VICTORY: CONFEDERACY

OVERVIEW

The capture of Fort Sumter stirred patriotic fervor in the North, and the public and its politicians wanted the U.S. Army to march on Richmond, putting a quick end to the war. With the huge influx of raw recruits, Brigadier-General Irvin McDowell—commander of the Union's Army of Northeastern Virginia, which would have undertaken this invasion—worried more about getting his men into fighting shape. He felt his army wasn't ready, but he was pressured into launching the attack known in the South as the First Battle of Manassas and in the North as the First Battle of Bull Run. It was the first major land battle of the Civil War and at the time the largest battle fought on American soil, though later Civil War battles would dwarf it.

Brigadier-General McDowell planned to attack the Confederate forces under General G. T. Beauregard with two of his columns, while the third circled around the Confederates' right flank, cutting off Beauregard's access to the railroad and attacking him from behind, forcing Beauregard to retreat to the Rappahannock River. The plan almost worked. After an initial Confederate retreat, reinforcements from Brigadier-General Joseph Johnston's Army of the Shenandoah threw the Union forces into disarray, resulting in a humiliating defeat.

Some of Washington's politicians and many of its citizens who had ridden out to watch the battle, armed with picnic baskets, found themselves caught up in the frantic retreat, fleeing for their lives—or so they thought. The Northern public was shocked and outraged, and their patriotic fervor renewed. Realizing that this was not going to be a short war, President Lincoln signed a bill the day after the battle to recruit half a million men for up to three years of service. McDowell was blamed for the defeat, and Major-General George McClellan soon replaced both him and Brevet Lieutenant-General Winfield Scott, the general in chief of all the Union armies.

CUSTER'S FIRST TWO DAYS ON DUTY

Union

Major-General George Armstrong Custer (See biography, page 3.)

After graduating from West Point a year early because of the outbreak of the Civil War, Custer and his classmates were awaiting orders when Custer suddenly found himself under arrest. While he was serving one evening as officer of the guard, a fight broke out between two cadets. Instead of breaking it up, he called out, "Stand back, boys; let's have a fair fight." While his classmates headed to their assignments, Custer was awaiting his court-martial. He pleaded guilty, but several days later, instead of being sentenced, he was released and ordered to report to Washington, D.C. The need for officers outweighed his "crime."

In D.C. the adjutant general, responsible for assignments, offhandedly asked him, "Perhaps you would like to be presented to General Scott, Mr. Custer?"

At the time one of the most important men in the U.S. government, considered one of the country's greatest war heroes, Brevet Lieutenant-General Winfield Scott had commanded forces in the War of 1812, the Mexican-American War, the Black Hawk War, and the Second Seminole War and had run for president in 1852. At the start of the war, Scott was general in chief of the entire U.S. Army, the Union's highest-ranking officer. Custer was stunned.

Following the lead of the officer to whom I had reported, I was conducted to the room in which General Scott received his official visitors. I found him seated at a table over which were spread maps and other documents which plainly showed their military character. In the room, and seated near the table, were several members of Congress, of whom I remember Senator Grimes of Iowa. The topic of conversation was the approaching battle in which General McDowell's forces were about to engage. General Scott seemed to be explaining to the Congressmen the position, as shown by the map, of the contending armies.

The Adjutant-General called General Scott's attention to me by saying, "General, this is Lieutenant Custer of the Second Cavalry; he has just reported from West Point, and I did not know but that you might have some special orders to give him."

Looking at me a moment, the General shook me cordially by the hand, saying, "Well, my young

Brevet Lieutenant-General Winfield Scott

friend, I am glad to welcome you to the service at this critical time. Our country has need of the strong arms of all her loyal sons in this emergency." Then, turning to the Adjutant-General, he inquired to what company I had been assigned.

"To Company G, Second Cavalry, now under Major Innes Palmer, with General McDowell," was the reply. Then, addressing me, the General said, "We have had the assistance of quite a number of you young men from the Academy, drilling volunteers, etc. Now what can I do for you? Would you prefer to be ordered to report to General Mansfield to aid this work, or is your desire for something more active?"

Although overwhelmed by such condescension upon the part of one so far superior in rank to any officer with whom I had been brought in immediate contact, I ventured to stammer out that I earnestly desired to be ordered to at once join my company, then with General McDowell, as I was anxious to see active service.

"A very commendable resolution, young man," was the reply; then, turning to the Adjutant-General, he added, "Make out Lieutenant Custer's orders directing him to proceed to his company at once"; then, as if a different project had presented itself, he inquired of me if I had been able to provide myself with a mount for the field. I replied that I had not, but would set myself about doing so at once.

"I fear you have a difficult task before you, because, if rumor is correct, every serviceable horse in the city has been bought, borrowed, or begged by citizens who have gone or are going as spectators to witness the battle. I only hope Beauregard may capture some of them and teach them a lesson. However what I desire to say to you is, go and provide yourself with a horse if possible, and call here at seven o'clock this evening. I desire to send some dispatches to General McDowell, and you can be the bearer of them. You are not afraid of a night ride, are you?"

Exchanging salutations, I left the presence of the General-in-Chief, delighted at the prospect of being at once thrown into active service, perhaps participating in the great battle which every one there knew was on the eve of occurring; but more than this my pride as a soldier was not a little heightened by the fact that almost upon my first entering the service I was to be the bearer of important official dispatches from the General-in-Chief to the General commanding the principal army in the field.

Custer fortuitously met a former cadet now serving under McDowell who had been sent to Washington to retrieve a horse, which happened to be Custer's favorite horse while he was at West Point. He offered to take Custer to McDowell's command post.

It was between two and three o'clock in the morning when we reached the army near Centreville. The men had already breakfasted, and many of the regiments had been formed in column in the roads ready to resume the march; but owing to delays in starting, most of the men were lying on the ground, endeavoring to catch a few minutes more of sleep; others were sitting or standing in small groups smoking and chatting.

So filled did I find the road with soldiers that it was with difficulty my horse could pick his way among the sleeping bodies without disturbing them. But for my companion I should have had considerable difficulty in finding my way to headquarters; but he seemed familiar with the localities even in the darkness, and soon conducted me to a group of tents near which a large log fire was blazing, throwing a bright light over the entire scene for some distance around. As I approached,

the sound of my horse's hoofs brought an officer from one of the tents nearest to where I halted. Advancing toward me, he inquired who I wished to see. I informed him that I was bearer of dispatches from General Scott to General McDowell.

"I will relieve you of them," was his reply; but seeing me hesitate to deliver them, he added, "I am Major [James] Wadsworth of General McDowell's staff."

While I had hoped from ambitious pride to have an opportunity to deliver the dispatches in person to General McDowell, I could not decline longer, so placed the documents in Major Wadsworth's hands, who took them to a tent a few paces distant, where, through its half-open folds, I saw him hand them to a large, portly officer, whom I at once rightly conceived to be General McDowell. Then, returning to where I still sat on my horse, Major Wadsworth (afterward General Wadsworth) asked of me the latest news in the capital, and when I replied that every person at Washington was looking to the army for news, he added, "Well, I guess they will not have to wait much longer. The entire army is under arms, and moving to attack the enemy to-day."

I was about to witness the first grand struggle in open battle between the Union and secession armies; a struggle in which, fortunately for the nation, the Union forces were to suffer defeat, while the cause for which they fought was to derive from it renewed strength and encouragement.

No battle of the war startled and convulsed the entire country, North and South, as did the first battle of Bull Run, although many succeeding it, both in the East and in the West, were more notable from the fact that greatly superior numbers were engaged, more prominent or experienced chieftains arrayed upon either side, and greater results obtained upon the battlefield. Nor is this difficult to explain. The country, after the

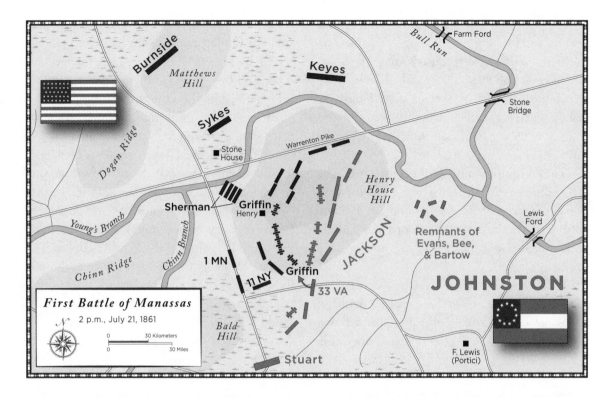

Burnside

Matthews
Hill

Keyes

Bull Run — Farm Ford

Stone
Bridge

Sykes

Dogan Ridge

Warrenton Pike

Stone
House

Griffin
Henry

Sherman

Henry
House
Hill

Lewis
Ford

JACKSON

Young's Branch

Chinn Branch

Remnants of
Evans, Bee,
& Bartow

JOHNSTON

1 MN

Chinn Ridge

11 NY

Griffin

33 VA

First Battle of Manassas

2 p.m., July 21, 1861

N

0   30 Kilometers

0   30 Miles

Bald
Hill

Stuart

F. Lewis
(Portici)

enjoyment of long years of peace and prosperity, was unused to the conditions and chances of war. The people of neither section had fully realized as yet the huge proportions of the struggle into which they had been plunged. This is shown not only by the opinions of the people as shadowed forth in the press, but by the authoritative acts and utterances of the highest officials of the land; for example, the proclamation of President Lincoln as late as April 15, 1861, after Fort Sumter had been fired upon and had been surrendered. In this proclamation, calling for 75,000 troops, or rather in the call sent to the loyal Governors of States, the period of service was limited to three months. To this can be added Mr. Seward's well-known "ninety days" prediction, all tending to incline the people to believe the war was destined to be brief, perhaps to be terminated by a single engagement.

Then again, war was not regarded by the masses as a dreadful alternative, to be avoided to the last, but rather as an enterprise offering some pleasure and some excitement, with perhaps a little danger and suffering. Last of all, the people of the two contending sections had, through the false teachings of their leaders, formed such unjust and incorrect notions in regard to the military prowess and resolution of their opponents, that it required the wager of actual battle to dispel these erroneous ideas.

Beauregard had ordered his forces under arms, and was awaiting his adversary's attack at half-past four o'clock the morning of the 21st.

Reasoning correctly that McDowell was not likely to attack his centre at Blackburn's ford, nor to operate heavily against his right near Union Mills, Beauregard no sooner discovered the movement of Hunter's and Heinzleman's divisions, to pass above and around his left flank at Sudley Springs, than he began moving up his reserves and forming his left wing in readiness to receive the attacking division as soon as the latter should cross Bull Run.

Hunter and Heintzleman were forced to make a much longer detour, in order to reach the designated crossings of Bull Run, than had been anticipated.

The first gun announcing the commencement of the battle was fired from [General Daniel] Tyler's division in front of the Stone bridge. It was not until nearly ten a.m. that the troops of Hunter's division came in contact with the enemy near Sudley Springs.

With the exception of a little tardiness in execution, something to be expected perhaps in raw troops, the plan of battle marked out by General McDowell was carried out with

remarkable precision up till about half-past three p.m. The Confederate left wing had been gradually forced back from Bull Run until the Federals gained entire possession of the Warrenton turnpike leading from the Stone bridge.

It is known now that Beauregard's army had become broken and routed, and that both himself and General Johnston felt called upon to place themselves at the head of their defeated commands, including their last reserves, in their effort to restore confidence and order; General Johnston at one critical moment charging to the front with the colors of the Fourth Alabama. Had the fate of the battle been left to the decision of those who were present and fought up till half-past three in the afternoon, the Union troops would have been entitled to score a victory with scarcely a serious reverse. But at this critical

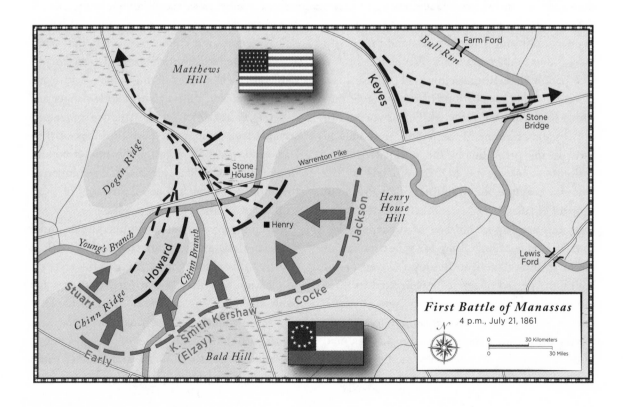

moment, with their enemies in front giving way in disorder and flight, a new and to the Federals an unexpected force appeared suddenly upon the scene. From a piece of timber almost directly in rear of McDowell's right a column of several thousand fresh troops of the enemy burst almost upon the backs of the half victorious Federals.

I was standing with a friend and classmate at that moment on a high ridge near our advancing line. We were congratulating ourselves upon the glorious victory which already seemed to have been won, as the Confederates were everywhere giving way, when our attention was attracted by a long line of troops suddenly appearing behind us upon the edge of the timber already mentioned. It never occurred to either of us that the troops we then saw could be any but some of our reinforcements making their way to the front. Before doubts could arise we saw the Confederate flag floating over a portion of the line just emerging from the timber; the next moment the entire line levelled their muskets and poured a volley into the backs of our advancing regiments on the right.

At the same time a battery which had also arrived unseen opened fire, and with the cry of "We're flanked! We're flanked!" passed from rank to rank, the Union lines, but a moment before so successful and triumphant, threw down their arms, were seized by a panic, and begun a most disordered flight. All this occurred almost in an instant of time. No pen or description can give anything like a correct idea of the rout and demoralization that followed. Officers and men joined in one vast crowd, abandoning, except in isolated instances, all attempts to preserve their organizations.

A moderate force of good cavalry at that moment could have secured to the Confederates nearly every man and gun that crossed Bull Run in the early morning. Fortunately the Confederate army was so badly demoralized by their earlier reverses, that it was in no mood or condition to make pursuit, and reap the full fruits of victory. The troops that had arrived upon the battlefield so unexpectedly to the Federals, and which had wrought such disaster upon the Union arms, were Elzey's brigade of infantry and Beckham's battery of artillery, the whole under command of Brigadier-General E. Kirby Smith, being a detachment belonging to Johnston's army of the Shenandoah, just arrived from the valley. Had this command reached the battlefield a few minutes later, the rout of Beauregard's army would have been assured, as his forces seemed powerless to check the advance of the Union troops.

General McDowell and his staff, as did many of the higher officers, exerted themselves to the utmost to stay the retreating Federals, but all appeals to the courage and patriotism of the latter fell as upon dumb animals. One who has never witnessed the conduct of large numbers of men when seized by a panic such as that was cannot realize how utterly senseless and without apparent reason men will act. And yet the same men may have exhibited great gallantry and intelligence but a moment before.

The value of discipline was clearly shown in this crisis by observing the manner of the few regular troops, as contrasted with the raw and undisciplined three months' men. The regular soldiers never for a moment ceased to look to their officers for orders and instructions, and in retiring from the field, even amid the greatest disorder and confusion of the organizations near them, they preserved their formation, and marched only as they were directed to do.

> Through the abandoned camps of the Federals we found their pots and kettles over the fire, with food cooking; quarters of beef hanging on the trees, and wagons by the roadside loaded, some with bread and general provisions, others with ammunition.
>
> —CONFEDERATE LIEUTENANT GENERAL JAMES LONGSTREET

The long lines of Union soldiery, which a few minutes before had been bravely confronting and driving the enemy, suddenly lost their cohesion and became one immense mass of fleeing, frightened creatures. Artillery horses were cut from their traces, and it was no unusual sight to see three men, perhaps belonging to different regiments, riding the same horse, and making their way to the rear as fast as the dense mass of men moving with them would permit. The direction of the retreat was toward Centreville, by way of the Stone bridge crossing, and other fords above that point. An occasional shot from the enemy's artillery, or the cry that the Black Horse cavalry, so dreaded in the first months of the war in Virginia, were coming, kept the fleeing crowd of soldiers at their best speed. Arms were thrown away as being no longer of service in warding off the enemy. Here and there the State colors of a regiment, or perhaps the national standard, would be seen lying on the ground along the line of retreat, no one venturing to reclaim or preserve them, while more than one full set of band instruments could be observed, dropped under the shade of some tree in rear of the line of battle, and where their late owners had probably been resting from the fatigues of the fight when the panic seized them and forced them to join their comrades in flight. One good steady regiment composed of such sterling material as made up the regiments of either side at the termination of the war, could have checked the pursuit before reaching Bull Run, and could have saved much of the artillery and many of the prisoners that as it was fell into the enemy's hands simply for want of owners. The rout continued until Centreville was reached; then the reserves posted under Mills gave some little confidence to the retreating masses, and after the latter had passed the reserves comparative order began in a slight degree to be restored. General McDowell at first decided to halt and make a stand on the heights near Centreville, but this was soon discovered to be unadvisable, if not impracticable, so large a portion of the army having continued their flight toward Washington. Orders were then given the various commanders to conduct their forces back to their former camps near Arlington opposite Washington, where they arrived the following day.

Custer, assigned to the cavalry under Major Palmer, also described his own experiences of the battle, beginning in the morning.

After arriving at Sudley Springs, the cavalry halted for half an hour or more. We could hear the battle raging a short distance in our front. Soon a staff officer of Gen. McDowell's came galloping down to where the cavalry was waiting, saying that the General desired us to move across the stream and up the ridge beyond, where we were to support a battery. The order was promptly obeyed, and as we ascended the crest I saw Griffin with his battery galloping into position. The enemy had discovered him, and their artillery had opened fire upon him, but the shots were aimed so high the balls passed overhead. Following the battery, we also marched within plain hearing of each shot as it passed over Griffin's men. I remember well the strange hissing and exceedingly vicious sound of the first cannon shot I heard as it whirled through the air. Of course I had often heard the sound made by cannon balls while passing through the air during my artillery practice at West Point, but a man listens with changed interest when the direction of the balls is toward instead of away from him. They seemed to utter a different language when fired in angry battle from that put forth in the tamer practice of drill.

We were formed in column of companies, and were given to understand that upon reaching the crest of the hill we would probably be ordered to charge the enemy. When it is remembered that but three days before I had quitted West Point as a schoolboy, and as yet had never ridden at anything more dangerous or terrible than a three-foot hurdle, or tried my sabre upon anything more animated or combative than a leather-head stuffed with tan bark, it may be imagined that my mind was more or less given to anxious thoughts as we ascended the slope of the hill in front of us.

At the same time I realized that I was in front of a company of old and experienced soldiers, all of whom would have an eye upon their new lieutenant to see how he comported himself when under fire. My pride received an additional incentive from the fact that while I was on duty with troops for the first time in my life, and was the junior officer of all present with the cavalry, there was temporarily assigned to duty with my company another officer of the same rank, who was senior to me by a few days, and who having been appointed from civil life, was totally without military experience except such as he had acquired during the past few days. My brief acquaintance with him showed me that he was disposed to attach no little importance to the fact that I was fresh from West Point and supposed to know all that was valuable or worth knowing in regard to

the art of war. In this common delusion I was not disposed to disturb him. I soon found that he was inclined to defer to me in opinion, and—I recall now, as I have often done when in his company during later years of the war, the difficulty we had in deciding exactly what weapon we would use in the charge to which we believed ourselves advancing. As we rode forward from the foot of the hill, he in front of his platoon and I abreast of him, in front of mine, Walker (afterward Captain) inquired in the most solemn tones, "Custer, what weapon are you going to use in the charge?"

From my earliest notions of the true cavalryman I had always pictured him in the charge bearing aloft his curved sabre, and cleaving the skulls of all with whom he came in contact. We had but two weapons to choose from: each of us carried a sabre and one revolver in our belt. I promptly replied, "The sabre"; and suiting the action to the word, I flashed my bright new blade from its scabbard, and rode forward as if totally unconcerned. Walker, yielding no doubt to what he believed was "the way we do it at West Point," imitated my motion, and forth came his sabre.

I may have seemed to him unconcerned, because I aimed at this, but I was far from enjoying that feeling. As we rode at a deliberate walk up the hill, I began arguing in my own mind as to the comparative merits of the sabre and revolver as a weapon of attack. If I remember correctly, I reasoned pro and con about as follows:

"Now the sabre is a beautiful weapon; it produces an ugly wound; the term sabre charge sounds well; and above all the sabre is sure; it never misses fire. It has this drawback, however: in order to be made effective it is indispensable that you approach very close to your adversary—so close that if you do not unhorse or disable him, he will most likely render that service to you. So much for the sabre. Now as to the revolver, it has this advantage over the sabre: one is not compelled to range himself alongside his adversary before beginning his attack, but may select his own time and distance. To be sure one may miss his aim, but there are six chambers to empty, and if one, two, or three miss, there are still three shots left to fire at close quarters. As this is my first battle, had I not better defer the use of the sabre until after I have acquired a little more experience?"

The result was that I returned my sabre to its scabbard, and without uttering a word drew my revolver and poised it opposite my shoulder. Walker, as if following me in my mental discussion, no sooner observed my change of weapon than he did likewise. With my revolver in my hand I put it upon trial mentally. First, I realized that in the rush and excitement of the charge it would be difficult to take anything like accurate aim. Then, might not every shot be fired, and without result? by which time in all probability we would be in the midst of our enemies, and slashing right and left at each other; in which case a sabre would be of much greater value and service than an empty revolver. This seemed convincing; so much so that my revolver found its way again to its holster, and the sabre was again at my shoulder. Again did Walker, as if in pantomime, follow my example. How often these changes of purpose and weapons might have been made I know not, had the cavalry not reached the crest meanwhile, and after being exposed to a hot artillery fire, and finding that no direct attack upon our battery was meditated by the enemy, returned to a sheltered piece of ground.

A little incident occurred as we were about to move forward to the expected charge, which is perhaps worth recording. Next to the company with which I was serving was one which I noticed as being in most excellent order and equipment. The officer in command of it was of striking appearance, tall, well formed, and handsome, and possessing withal a most soldierly air. I did not then know his name; but being so near to him and to his command, I could not but observe him. When the order came for us to move forward up the hill, and to be prepared to charge the moment the crest was reached, I saw the officer referred to ride gallantly in front of his command, and just as the signal forward was given, I heard him say, "Now, men, do your duty." I was attracted by his soldierly words and bearing; and yet within a few days after the battle he tendered his resignation, and in a short time was serving under the Confederate flag as a general officer. [Note: This was Union cavalry captain Frank Crawford Armstrong, whom the Confederates eventually promoted to brigadier general.]

I little imagined, when making my night ride from Washington to Centreville the night of the 20th, that the following night should find me returning with a defeated and demoralized army.

On the 24th [of May 1862] a very spirited and successful reconnaissance took place near New bridge, which first brought Lieut. (afterwards Gen.) Custer to my notice. His commanding officers commended him highly for his conduct, and I sent for him to thank him. He was then a slim, long-haired boy, carelessly dressed. I thanked him for his gallantry, and asked what I could do for him. He replied very modestly that he had nothing to ask, and evidently did not suppose that he had done anything to deserve extraordinary reward. I then asked if he would like to serve on my personal staff as an aide-de-camp. Upon this he brightened up, and assured me that he would regard such service as the most gratifying he could perform; and I at once gave the necessary orders. He continued on my staff until I was relieved from the command.

In those days Custer was simply a reckless, gallant boy, undeterred by fatigue, unconscious of fear; but his head was always clear in danger, and he always brought me clear and intelligible reports of what he saw when under the heaviest fire. I became much attached to him. In the later days of the war, when he commanded cavalry troops, he displayed a degree of prudence and good sense, in conducting the most dangerous expeditions, that surprised many who thought they knew him well.

—MAJOR-GENERAL GEORGE MCCLELLAN

THE CONFEDERATE BATTLE PLAN

Confederate

General G. T. Beauregard (See biography, page 19.)

Soon after the first conflict between the authorities of the Federal Union and those of the Confederate States had occurred in Charleston Harbor, by the bombardment of Fort Sumter, which, beginning at 4:30 a.m. on the 12th of April, 1861, forced the surrender of that fortress within thirty hours thereafter into my hands, I was called to Richmond, which by that time had become the Confederate seat of government, and directed to "assume command of the Confederate troops on the Alexandria line."

Arriving at Manassas Junction, I took command on the 2d of June, forty-nine days after the evacuation of Fort Sumter by Major Anderson. Although the position at the time was strategically of commanding importance to the Confederates, the mere terrain was not only without natural defensive advantages, but, on the contrary, was absolutely unfavorable. Its strategic value was that, with close proximity to the Federal capital, it held in observation the chief Federal army then being assembled in the quarter of Arlington by General McDowell, under the immediate eye of the commander-in-chief, General Scott, for an offensive movement against Richmond; and while it had a railway approach in its rear for the easy accumulation of reinforcements and all the necessary munitions of war from the southward, at the same time another (the Manassas Gap) railway, diverging laterally to the left from that point, gave rapid communications with the fertile valley of the Shenandoah, then teeming with live-stock and cereal subsistence, as well as with other resources essential to the Confederates. There was this further value in the position to the Confederate army: that during the period of accumulation, seasoning, and training, it might be fed from the fat fields, pastures, and garners of Loudon, Fauquier, and the lower Shenandoah valley counties, which otherwise must have fallen into the hands of the enemy.

Happily, through the foresight of Colonel Thomas Jordan, whom General Lee had placed as the Adjutant-General of the forces there assembled before my arrival, arrangements were made which enabled me to receive regularly, from private persons at the Federal capital, most accurate information, of which politicians high in council, as well as War Department clerks, were the unconscious ducts. Moreover, my enterprising, intelligent pickets [detachment of advance guards] were watchfully kept in the closest possible proximity to General McDowell's headquarters, and, by a stroke of good fortune on the fourth of July, happened upon and captured a sergeant and soldier of the regulars, who were leisurely riding for recreation not far outside their lines. The soldier, an intelligent, educated Scotchman, proved to be a clerk in the Adjutant-General's office of General McDowell, intrusted with the special duty of compiling returns of his army, a work which he confessed, without reluctance, he had just executed, showing the forces under McDowell about the first of July. His statement of the strength and composition of that force tallied so closely with that which had been acquired through my Washington agencies, already mentioned, as well as through the leading newspapers of New York and Washington, Philadelphia and Baltimore, regular files of which were also transmitted to my headquarters from the Federal capital, that I could not doubt them.

In these several ways, therefore, I was almost as well advised of the strength of the hostile army in my front as its commander, who, I may mention, had been a classmate of mine at West Point. Under those circumstances I had become satisfied that a well-equipped, well-constituted Federal army at least fifty thousand strong, of all arms, confronted me at or about Arlington, ready and on the very eve of an offensive operation against me, and to meet which I could muster barely eighteen thousand men with twenty-nine field-guns.

Previously, indeed, or as early as the middle of June, it had become apparent to my mind that through only one course of action could there be a well-grounded hope of ability on the part of the Confederates to encounter successfully the offensive operations for which the Federal authorities were then vigorously preparing in my immediate front; this course was to make the most enterprising, warlike use of the interior lines which we possessed, for the swift concentration at the critical instant of every available Confederate force upon the menaced position, at the risk, if need were, of sacrificing all minor places to the one clearly of major military value, then to meet our adversary so offensively as to overwhelm him, under circumstances that must assure immediate ability to assume the general offensive even upon the territory of the adversary, and thus conquer an early peace by a few well-delivered blows.

This plan was rejected by Mr. Davis and his military advisers (Adjutant-General Cooper and General Lee), who characterized it as "brilliant and comprehensive," but essentially impracticable.

I next acquainted Mr. Davis with the situation, and ventured to suggest that the Army of the Shenandoah, with the brigade at Fredericksburg or Acquia Creek, should be ordered to reënforce me, suggestions that were at once heeded so far that General [Theophilus] Holmes was ordered to carry his command to my aid, and General Johnston was given discretion to do likewise.

I had submitted the proposition to General Johnston, that, having passed the Blue Ridge, he should assemble his forces, press forward by way of Aldie, north-east of Manassas, and fall upon McDowell's right rear; while I, prepared for the operation, at the first sound of the conflict, should strenuously assume the offensive in my front. Our enemy, thus attacked so nearly simultaneously on his right flank, his rear, and his front, naturally would suppose that I had been able to turn his flank while attacking him in front, and, therefore, that I must have an overwhelming superiority of numbers; and his forces, being new troops, most of them under fire for the first time, must have soon fallen into a disastrous panic.

General McDowell, fortunately for my plans, spent the 19th and 20th in reconnaissances; and, meanwhile, General Johnston brought 6,000 men from the Shenandoah valley, with 20 guns, and General Holmes 1,265 rank and file, with six pieces of artillery from Acquia Creek.

The preparation, in front of an ever-threatening enemy, of a wholly volunteer army, composed of men very few of whom had ever belonged to any military organization, had been a work of many cares not incident to the command of a regular army. These were increased by the insufficiency of my staff organization, an inefficient management of the quartermaster's department at Richmond and the preposterous mismanagement of the Commissary-General, who not only failed to furnish rations, but caused the removal of the army commissaries, who, under my orders, procured food from the country in front of us to keep the army from absolute want.

In anticipation of this method of attack, and to prevent accidents, the subordinate commanders had been carefully instructed in the movement by me in conference the night before, as they were all new to the responsibilities of command. They were to establish close communication with each other before making the attack. About half past eight o'clock I set out with General Johnston for a convenient position—a hill in rear of Mitchell's ford—where we waited for the opening of the attack on our right, from which I expected a decisive victory by midday, with the result of cutting off the Federal army from retreat upon Washington.

Meanwhile, about half-past five o'clock [a.m.], the peal of a heavy rifled gun was heard in front of the Stone Bridge, its second shot striking through the tent of my signal officer, Captain E. P. Alexander. At half-past eight o'clock Evans, seeing that the Federal attack did not increase in boldness and vigor, and observing a lengthening line of dust above the trees to the left of the Warrenton turnpike, became satisfied that the attack in his front was but a feint, and that a column of the enemy was moving around through the woods to fall on his flank from the direction of Sudley ford.

The ruins of Judith Henry's house in the middle of the battlefield as they appeared in March 1862. At age eighty-five Mrs. Henry was too infirm to leave her bed and was killed in the battle.

Beauregard's plan of attacking from his right failed because Brigadier-General Richard Ewell didn't receive the order to set his men in motion. Since it was too late to carry out his plan, Beauregard and Johnston decided to use their right to reinforce their left, which was being forced to retreat.

General Johnston and I now set out at full speed for the point of conflict. We arrived there just as [Brig. Gen. Barnard Elliott] Bee's troops, after giving way, were fleeing in disorder behind the height in rear of the Stone Bridge. They had come around between the base of the hill and the Stone Bridge into a shallow ravine which ran up to a point on the crest where [Brig. Gen. Thomas] Jackson had already formed his brigade along the edge of the woods. We found the commanders resolutely stemming the farther flight of the routed forces, but vainly endeavoring to restore order, and our own efforts were as futile. Every segment of line we succeeded in forming was again dissolved while another was being formed; more than two thousand men were shouting each some suggestion to his neighbor, their voices mingling with the noise of the shells hurtling through the trees overhead, and all word of command drowned in the confusion and uproar. It was at this moment that General Bee used the famous expression, "Look at Jackson's brigade! It stands there like a stone wall"—a name that passed from the brigade to its immortal commander.

The disorder seemed irretrievable, but happily the thought came to me that if their colors were planted out to the front the men might rally on them, and I gave the order to carry the standards forward some forty yards, which was promptly executed by the regimental officers, thus drawing the common eye of the troops. They now received easily the orders to advance and form on the line of their colors, which they obeyed with a general movement; and as General Johnston and myself rode forward shortly after with the colors of the Fourth Alabama by our side, the line that had fought all morning, and had fled, routed and disordered, now advanced again into position as steadily as veterans.

> Bee, Bartow, and Evans made valorous efforts, while withdrawing from their struggle on the Matthews plateau. General Thomas J. Jackson also moved to that quarter, and reached the rear crest of the plateau at the Henry House while yet Bee, Bartow, Evans, and Hampton were climbing to the forward crest. Quick to note a proper ground, Jackson deployed on the crest at the height, leaving the open of the plateau in front. He was in time to secure the Imboden battery before it got off the field, and put it into action. Stanard's battery, Pendleton's, and Pelham's, and part of the Washington Artillery were up in time to aid Jackson in his new formation and relieve our discomfited troops rallying on his flank. As they rose on the forward crest, Bee saw, on the farther side, Jackson's line, serene as if in repose, affording a haven so promising of cover that he gave the christening of 'Stonewall' for the immortal Jackson. "There," said he, "is Jackson, standing like a stone wall."
>
> —Confederate lieutenant general
> James Longstreet

As I paused to say a few words to Jackson, while hurrying back to the right, my horse was killed under me by a bursting shell, a fragment of which carried away part of the heel of my boot.

With six thousand five hundred men and thirteen pieces of artillery, I now awaited the onset of the enemy, who were pressing forward twenty thousand strong, with twenty-four pieces of superior artillery and seven companies of regular cavalry. They soon appeared over the farther rim of the plateau, seizing the Robinson house on my right and the Henry house opposite my left center.

I felt that, after the accidents of the morning, much depended on maintaining the steadiness of the troops against the first heavy onslaught, and rode along the lines encouraging the men to unflinching behavior, meeting, as I passed each command, a cheering response.

TURNING THE TIDE

Confederate

Lieutenant-General Thomas "Stonewall" Jackson

During the war the South considered Stonewall Jackson their greatest hero, more famous than General Lee, who rose to prominence later. Descriptions of Jackson's eccentric character have included ambitious, courageous, distrustful, hypochondriacal, fanatical, reticent, secretive, shy, and "strange."

Thomas Jackson grew up in Virginia, becoming a schoolteacher before heading to West Point, where he graduated in 1846 and was assigned to the artillery. During the Mexican-American War he made some bold, perceptive moves that caught the attention of his superiors, but petty disputes caused him to leave the army and become an instructor at the Virginia Military Institute. It was here that he became devoutly Christian, teaching Sunday school classes to black children at his church and continuing to donate to this cause during the war. He owned six slaves and, like many Christian slaveholders, probably believed that God sanctioned slavery. It appears that he treated them humanely.

At the beginning of the war, he became a drill instructor at Harper's Ferry and trained a brigade that, after the First Battle of Manassas, became known as the "Stonewall Brigade." Promoted from colonel to brigadier general just two months into the war, Jackson, a brilliant military tactician, became Lee's left-hand man, next to James Longstreet. Lee knew what to do, and Jackson knew how to do it. An excellent offensive commander, he often took bold chances.

- -

Stonewall Jackson almost never talked of his exploits. He left that to others. People often tried, but he remained silent ... except in private to his wife, as seen in the following excerpts from three of his letters, in which he writes of the incident that gave him his nickname.

Manassas, July 22d

My precious Pet,

Yesterday we fought a great battle and gained a great victory, for which all the glory is due to God alone. Although under a heavy fire for several continuous hours, I received only one wound, the breaking of the longest finger of my left hand; but the doctor says the finger can be saved. It was broken about midway between the hand and knuckle, the ball [actually a piece of shrapnel] passing on the side next the forefinger. Had it struck the centre, I should have lost the finger. My horse was wounded, but not killed. Your coat got an ugly wound near the hip, but my servant, who is very handy, has so far repaired it that it doesn't show very much.

My preservation was entirely due, as was the glorious victory, to our God, to whom be all the honor, praise, and glory. The battle was the hardest that I have ever been in, but not near so hot in its fire. I commanded in the centre more particularly, though one of my regiments extended to the right for some distance. There were other commanders on my right and left. Whilst great credit is due to other parts of our gallant army, God made my brigade more instrumental than any other in repulsing the main attack. This is for your information only—say nothing about it. Let others speak praise, not myself.

While I was dressing General Jackson's hand, at the field-hospital of the brigade at Young's Branch, near the Lewis house, I saw President Davis ride up from the direction of Manassas. He had been told by stragglers that our army had been defeated. He stopped his horse in the middle of the little stream, stood up in his stirrups (the palest, sternest face I ever saw) and cried to the great crowd of soldiers: "I am President Davis; follow me back to the field."

General Jackson did not hear distinctly. I told him who it was and what he said. He stood up and took off his cap and cried: "We have whipped them; they ran like sheep. Give me ten thousand men, and I will take Washington City to-morrow."

—Dr. Hunter McGuire,
Jackson's chief staff medical officer

August 5th

And so you think the papers ought to say more about your husband! My brigade is not a brigade of newspaper correspondents. I know that the First Brigade was the first to meet and pass our retreating forces—to push on with no other aid than the smiles of God; to boldly take its position with the artillery that was under my command—to arrest the victorious foe in his onward progress—to hold him in check until reinforcements arrived—and finally to charge bayonets, and, thus advancing, pierce the enemy's centre. I am well satisfied with what it did, and so are my generals, Johnston and Beauregard. It is not to be expected that I should receive the credit that Generals Beauregard and Johnston would, because I was under them; but I am thankful to my ever-kind Heavenly Father that He makes me content to await His own good time and pleasure for commendation—knowing that all things work together for my good. If my brigade can always play so important and useful a part as it did in the last battle, I trust I shall ever be most grateful. "Truth is mighty and will prevail." When the official reports are published, if not before, I expect to see justice done this noble body of patriots.

August 15th

I am glad that the battle was fought on your birthday, so you can never tell me any more that I forget your birthday. See if I don't always remember it, though I do not my own. If General Lee remains in the Northwest [of Virginia], I would like to go there and give my feeble aid, as an humble instrument in the hand of Providence in retrieving the downtrodden loyalty of that part of my native State. But I desire to be wherever those over me may decide, and I am content here. The success of our cause is the earthly object near my heart; and, if I know myself all I am and have is at the service of my country.

CONFUSION AMONG THE FEDERALS

Union

General William Tecumseh Sherman (See biography, page 4.)
In his official report General Sherman described the nature of the retreat.

Here, about 3.30 p.m. began the scene of confusion and disorder that characterized the remainder of the day. Up to that time all had kept their places, and seemed perfectly cool and used to the shells and shot that fell comparatively harmless all around us; but the short exposure to an intense fire of small-arms at close range had killed many, wounded more, and had produced disorder in all the battalions that had attempted to destroy it. Men fell away talking and in great confusion. Colonel Cameron had been mortally wounded, carried to an ambulance, and reported dying. Many other officers were reported dead or missing, and many of the wounded were making their way, with more or less assistance, to the buildings used as hospitals.

On the ridge to the west we succeeded in partially reforming the regiments, but it was manifest they would not stand, and I directed Colonel Corcoran to move along the ridge to the rear, near the position where we had first formed the brigade. General McDowell was there in person, and used all possible efforts to reassure the men. By the active exertions of Colonel Corcoran we formed an irregular square against the cavalry, which were then seen to issue from the position from which we had been driven, and we began our retreat towards that ford of Bull Run by which we had approached the field of battle. There was no positive order to retreat, although for an hour it had been going on by the operation of the men themselves. I found General McDowell. From him I understood it was his purpose to rally the forces, and make a stand at Centreville. But, about 9 o'clock at night, I received, from General Tyler in person the order to continue the retreat to the Potomac. This retreat was by night, and disorderly in the extreme.

Fort Corcoran, July 22, 1801—10.11

Adjutant-General:

I have this moment ridden in, I hope, the rear men of my brigade, which, in common with our whole Army, has sustained a terrible defeat and has degenerated into an armed mob.

I know not if I command, but at this moment I will act as such, and shall consider as addressed to me the dispatch of the Secretary of this date.

I propose to strengthen the garrisons of Fort Corcoran, Fort Bennett, the redoubt on Arlington road, and the block-houses; and to aid me in stopping the flight, I ask you to order the ferry to transport no one across without my orders or those of some superior.

I am, &c.,

W. T. Sherman

Of course, we took it for granted that the rebels would be on our heels, and we accordingly prepared to defend our posts. By the 25th I had collected all the materials, made my report, and had my brigade about as well governed as any in that army; although most of the ninety-day men, especially the Sixty-ninth [New York], had become extremely tired of the war, and wanted to go home.

Some of them were so mutinous, at one time, that I had Ayres's battery to unlimber, threatening, if they dared to leave camp without orders, I would open fire on them.

Drills and the daily exercises were resumed, and I ordered that at the three principal roll-calls the men should form ranks with belts and muskets, and that they should keep their ranks until I in person had received the reports and had dismissed them.

The Sixty-ninth still occupied Fort Corcoran, and one morning, after reveille, when I had just received the report, had dismissed the regiment, and was leaving, I found myself in a crowd of men crossing the drawbridge on their way to a barn close by, where they had their sinks; among them was an officer, who said: "Colonel, I am going to New York to day. What can I do for you?"

I answered: "How can you go to New York? I do not remember to have signed a leave for you."

He said, "No; he did not want a leave. He had engaged to serve three months, and had already served more than that time. If the Government did not intend to pay him, he could afford to lose the money; that he was a lawyer, and had neglected his business long enough, and was then going home."

I noticed that a good many of the soldiers had paused about us to listen, and knew that, if this officer could defy me, they also would. So I turned on him sharp, and said: "Captain, this question of your term of service has been submitted to the rightful authority, and the decision has been published in orders. You are a soldier, and must submit to orders till you are properly discharged. If you attempt to leave without orders, it will be mutiny, and I will shoot you like a dog! Go back into the fort now, instantly, and don't dare to leave without my consent."

I had on an overcoat, and may have had my hand about the breast, for he looked at me hard, paused a moment, and then turned back into the fort. The men scattered, and I returned to the house where I was quartered, close by.

That same day, which must have been about July 26th, I was near the river-bank, looking at a block-house which had been built for the defense of the aqueduct, when I saw a carriage coming by the road that crossed the Potomac River at Georgetown by a ferry. I thought I recognized in the carriage the person of President Lincoln. I hurried across a bend, so as to stand by the road-side as the carriage passed. I was in uniform, with a sword on, and was recognized by Mr. Lincoln and Mr. Seward, who rode side by side in an open hack. I inquired if they were going to my camps, and Mr. Lincoln said: "Yes; we heard that you had got over the big scare, and we thought we would come over and see the 'boys.'"

I asked if I might give directions to his coachman, he promptly invited me to jump in and to tell the coachman which way to drive. I turned the driver into a side-road which led up a very steep hill, and, seeing a soldier, called to him and sent him up hurriedly to announce to the colonel that the President was coming.

As we slowly ascended the hill, I discovered that Mr. Lincoln was full of feeling, and wanted to encourage our men. I asked him to please discourage all cheering, noise, or any sort of confusion; that we had had enough of it before Bull Run to ruin any set of men, and that what we needed were cool, thoughtful, hard-fighting soldiers—no more hurrahing, no more humbug. He took my remarks in the most perfect good-nature.

Before we had reached the first camp, I heard the drum beating the "assembly," saw the men running for their tents, and in a few minutes the regiment was in line, arms presented, and then brought to an order and "parade rest!"

Mr. Lincoln stood up in the carriage, and made one of the neatest, best, and most feeling addresses I ever listened to, referring to our late

Officers of the Sixty-ninth Regiment, New York State Militia Infantry at Fort Corcoran in 1861, perhaps including the captain whom Sherman confronted.

disaster at Bull Run, the high duties that still devolved on us, and the brighter days yet to come. At one or two points the soldiers began to cheer, but he promptly checked them, saying: "Don't cheer, boys. I confess I rather like it myself, but Colonel Sherman here says it is not military; and I guess we had better defer to his opinion."

In winding up, he explained that, as President, he was commander-in-chief; that he was resolved that the soldiers should have every thing that the law allowed; and he called on one and all to appeal to him personally in case they were wronged. The effect of this speech was excellent.

We passed along in the same manner to all the camps of my brigade; and Mr. Lincoln complimented me highly for the order, cleanliness, and discipline, that he observed. Indeed, he and Mr. Seward both assured me that it was the first bright moment they had experienced since the battle.

At last we reached Fort Corcoran. The carriage could not enter, so I ordered the regiment, without arms, to come outside, and gather about Mr. Lincoln, who would speak to them. He made to them the same feeling address, with more personal allusions, because of their special gallantry in the battle under Corcoran, who was still a prisoner in the hands of the enemy; and he concluded with the same general offer of redress in case of grievance.

In the crowd I saw the officer with whom I had had the passage at reveille that morning. His face was pale, and lips compressed. I foresaw a scene, but sat on the front seat of the carriage as quiet as a lamb. This officer forced his way through the crowd to the carriage, and said: "Mr. President, I have a cause of grievance. This morning I went to speak to Colonel Sherman, and he threatened to shoot me."

Mr. Lincoln, who was still standing, said, "Threatened to shoot you?"

"Yes, sir, he threatened to shoot me."

Mr. Lincoln looked at him, then at me, and stooping his tall, spare form toward the officer, said to him in a loud stage-whisper, easily heard for some yards around: "Well, if I were you, and he threatened to shoot, I would not trust him, for I believe he would do it."

The officer turned about and disappeared, and the men laughed at him. Soon the carriage drove on, and, as we descended the hill, I explained the facts to the President, who answered, "Of course I didn't know any thing about it, but I thought you knew your own business best."

I thanked him for his confidence, and assured him that what he had done would go far to enable me to maintain good discipline, and it did.

By this time the day was well spent. I asked to take my leave, and the President and Mr. Seward drove back to Washington. This spirit of mutiny was common to the whole army, and was not subdued till several regiments or parts of regiments had been ordered to Fort Jefferson, Florida, as punishment.

FRIENDLY FIRE

On chaotic battlefields soldiers often become confused. Unfortunately, it seems inevitable that someone accidently kills one or more of his own men. This was particularly a problem during the Civil War. The most famous incident of this was the death of Stonewall Jackson, accidentally shot by his men while scouting in front of his line, who thought he and his staff were Union cavalry.

Early in the war much of the confusion could have been prevented. The experiences of the Eleventh New York Volunteer Infantry, known as the First Fire Zouaves, at the First Battle of Manassas are an example. The Zouaves, also known as Zoo-Zoos, modeled themselves on Algerian soldiers in the French army. Their distinctive uniforms, often of bright red and dark blue, consisted of baggy trousers tucked into boots, a short open-front jacket buttoned at the collar, a sash, and a large, soft fez with a big tassel or a sort of turban that resembled an upside-down acorn. Their tactics differed as well. They used open-order formations, moving in double time, lying on their backs to load their rifles, and rolling prone or rising on one knee to fire them.

The Union had more than seventy Zouave units, while the Confederates had around twenty-five. The Zouaves considered themselves elite fighting units, and the First Fire Zouaves were particularly tough and fit, all being New York firemen.

The first problem was caused by unusual uniforms. On July 17, as they moved past Fairfax Station, they encountered the Thirty-ninth New York Regiment, known as the Garibaldi Guards. Not recognizing the Garibaldis' Bersaglieri uniforms, the Fire Zouaves shot at them several times before discovering they were fellow New Yorkers.

Uniforms again became a difficulty during the battle when the Fire Zouaves first encountered the Confederate Thirty-third Virginia Infantry, one of Stonewall Jackson's regiments. The New Yorkers' uniforms were gray, while the Virginians were wearing their prewar dark-blue uniforms. They soon sorted it out and went at it.

The Union forces fell back, and passing through some trees, they—alongside the First Minnesota, also dressed in gray—came upon Confederate colonel Jeb Stuart and his Black Horse Cavalry. Some say Stuart thought they were Confederate Zouaves, and by some accounts Stuart's men got within twenty feet of them before spotting their Union flag and opening fire on them.

Later, after re-forming, the Fire Zouaves pursued another group of cavalry up to the Confederate line, where they were almost surrounded. As they were in advance of the Union line, they ended up receiving friendly fire from behind. Then the Thirty-third Virginia in blue charged at the Union artillery, who withheld their fire, thinking the Virginians were Union soldiers, which, in turn, allowed the Virginians to capture the guns.

Nor was it just uniforms that caused trouble at First Manassas. Beauregard realized that from a distance the Union's Stars and Stripes closely resembled the Confederate Stars and Bars, so he ordered a new distinctive battle flag, resulting in the Southern Cross flag, better known now than any of the Confederate national flags.

Fog and artillery smoke also caused difficulties in identifying which side a group of soldiers belonged to, but the darkness of twilight and night really caused problems. Confederate major general Leonidas Polk, "the Fighting Bishop," related an incident to a British observer, Lieutenant-Colonel Arthur Fremantle, that took place in Kentucky on October 8, 1862:

Beauregard's Confederate battle flag

Well, sir, it was at the battle of Perryville, late in the evening—in fact, it was almost dark, Liddell's brigade came into action. Shortly after its arrival I observed a body of men, whom I believed to be Confederates, standing at an angle to this brigade, and firing obliquely at them. I said, 'Dear me, this is very sad, and must be stopped'; so I turned round, but could find none of my young men, who were absent on different messages; so I determined to ride myself and settle the matter. Having cantered up to the colonel of the regiment which was firing, I asked him in angry tones what he meant by shooting his friends, and I desired him to cease doing so at once.

He answered with surprise, "I don't think there can be any mistake about it; I am sure they are the enemy."

"Enemy!" I said; "why, I have just left them myself. Cease firing, sir; what is your name, sir?"

"My name is Colonel ———, of the —th Indiana; and, pray, sir, who are you?"

Then I saw to my great astonishment, that he was a Yankee, and that I was in the rear of a regiment of Yankees. Well, I saw there was no hope but to brazen it out; my dark blouse and the increasing obscurity befriended me, so I approached quite close to him and shook my fist in his face, saying, "I'll soon show you who I am, sir; cease firing, sir, at once."

I then turned my horse and cantered slowly down the line, shouting in an authoritative manner for them to cease firing; at the same time I was conscious of a disagreeable sensation, like screwing up my back, and calculating how many bullets would be between my shoulders every moment. I was afraid to increase my speed until I got to a small copse, when I put the spurs into my horse's flanks and galloped back to my men.

I immediately went up to the nearest colonel, and said to him, "Colonel, I have reconnoitered those fellows pretty closely—and I find there is no mistake who they are; you may get up and go at them." And I assure you, sir, that the slaughter of that Indiana regiment was the greatest I have ever seen in the war.

Polk doesn't mention it, but right before this incident Union colonel Michael Gooding and the Thirtieth Brigade went to assist Major-General Alexander McCook. On riding up to the officer he thought was McCook, he said, "I have come to your assistance with my brigade," and identified himself. The officer turned out to be Polk, who responded, "There is some mistake about this, and you are a prisoner."

Gooding's brigade waited for him to return but attacked without him. On their far left was Lieutenant-Colonel Squire Keith's Twenty-second Indiana Regiment. Keith is the one Polk rode over to, telling him to cease firing. After Polk's close call, his men killed Keith, along with 121 men of the Thirtieth Brigade. A further 314 were wounded, with 35 taken prisoner and 29 missing, for a 35 percent casualty rate. The five brigades in McCook's division suffered even greater casualties, so Polk's deception probably didn't have the effect he thought it did.

ANALYSIS OF THE BATTLE

Confederate

General G. T. Beauregard (See biography, page 19)

Though my adversary's plan of battle was a good one against a passive defensive opponent, such as he may have deemed I must be from the respective numbers and positions of our forces, it would, in my judgment, have been much better if, with more dash, the flank attack had been made by the stone bridge itself and the ford immediately above it.

The commander of the front line on my right, who failed to move because he received no immediate order, was instructed in the plan of attack, and should have gone forward the moment General Jones, upon whose right he was to form, exhibited his own order, which mentioned one as having been already sent to that commander. The Federal commander's flanking movement, being thus uninterrupted by such a counter-movement as I had projected, was further assisted through the imperfection and inefficiency of the staff organization of the army, through which I was left unacquainted with the actual state of affairs on my left. The Federal attack, already thus greatly favored, and encouraged, moreover, by the rout of General Bee's advanced line, failed for two reasons: their forces were not handled with concert of masses (a fault often made later on both sides), and the individual action of the Confederate troops was superior, notwithstanding inferiority in numbers, arms, and equipments, and for a very palpable reason. That one army was fighting for union and the other for disunion is a political expression; the actual fact on the battle-field, in the face of cannon and musket, was that the Federal troops came as invaders, and the Southern troops stood as defenders of their homes.

The military result of the victory was far short of what it should have been. It established as an accomplished fact, on the indispensable basis of military success, the Government of the Confederate States, which before was but a political assertion; but it should have reached much further. The immediate pursuit, but for the false alarm which checked it [where approaching Confederate troops were thought to be a Union attack], would have continued as far as the Potomac, but must have stopped there with no greater result than the capture of more prisoners and material. The true immediate fruits of the victory should have been the dispersion of all the Federal forces south of Baltimore and east of the Alleghanies, the liberation of the State of Maryland, and the capture of Washington, which could have been made only by the upper Potomac.

Confederate

General Joseph Johnston

Joseph Johnston, one of the most senior Confederate generals, fought throughout the war, from First Manassas (First Bull Run) to his surrender following that of General Lee.

Born in Virginia, the son of a judge who had fought in the Revolutionary War, Johnston graduated from West Point in 1829, the same year as Lee. Resigning after eight years, he became a civilian engineer in the Second Seminole War in Florida, but after being involved in more combat than when in the military, he reenlisted. During the Mexican-American War he was wounded several times, prompting Brevet Lieutenant-General Scott to quip, "Johnston is a great soldier, but he had an unfortunate knack of getting himself shot in nearly every engagement."

When the Mexican-American War ended, he became a civilian engineer once again, until he reenlisted for the third time, serving in the Wyoming Territory against the Sioux and during the Bleeding Kansas violence. It was at this time that he became close friends with Captain George McClellan, who would become commander of the Union's primary army. As adversaries, the two would face each other in several battles during the first year of the war.

Shortly before the Civil War began, Johnston became quartermaster general of the U.S. Army and was promoted to brigadier general, becoming the first West Point graduate to achieve the rank of general. When Virginia seceded, he resigned and joined the Virginia militia before transferring to the Confederate Army.

According to Sherman, Johnston was "regarded by many as the most skillful general on the Southern side," and Grant told Sherman at Vicksburg that Johnston "was about the only general on that side whom he feared."

Instead of leaving the command in General Beauregard's hands, I assumed it over both armies immediately after my arrival on the 20th, showing General Beauregard as my warrant the President's telegram defining my position.

As fought, the battle was made by me; Bee's and Jackson's brigades were transferred to the left by me. I decided that the battle was to be there, and directed the measures necessary to maintain

it; a most important one being the assignment of General Beauregard to the immediate command of this left which he held. In like manner the senior officer on the right would have commanded there, if the Federal left had attacked.

If the tactics of the Federals had been equal to their strategy, we should have been beaten. If, instead of being brought into action in detail, their troops had been formed in two lines with a proper reserve, and had assailed Bee and Jackson in that order, the two Southern brigades must have been swept from the field in a few minutes, or enveloped. General McDowell would have made such a formation, probably, had he not greatly under-estimated the strength of his enemy.

All the military conditions, we knew, forbade an attempt on Washington. The Confederate army was more disorganized by victory than that of the United States by defeat. The Southern volunteers believed that the objects of the war had been accomplished by their victory, and that they had achieved all that their country required of them. Many, therefore, in ignorance of their military obligations, left the army—not to return. Some hastened home to exhibit the trophies picked up on the field; others left their regiments without ceremony to attend to wounded friends, frequently accompanying them to hospitals in distant towns. Such were the reports of general and staff officers, and railroad officials. Exaggerated ideas of the victory, prevailing among our troops, cost us more men than the Federal army lost by defeat.

The fortifications upon which skillful engineers, commanding the resources of the United States, had been engaged since April, manned by at least fifty thousand Federal troops, half of whom had not suffered defeat.

The Potomac, a mile wide, bearing United States vessels-of-war, the heavy guns of which commanded the wooden bridges and southern shore [sic].

The Confederate army would have been two days in marching from Bull Run to the Federal intrenchments, with less than two days' rations, or not more. It is asserted that the country, teeming with grain and cattle, could have furnished food and forage in abundance. Those who make the assertion forget that a large Federal army had passed *twice* over the route in question. Many of the Southern people have seen tracts of country along which a Federal army has passed once; they can judge, therefore, of the abundance left where it has passed twice. As we had none of the means of besieging, an immediate assault upon the forts would have been unavoidable; it would have been repelled, inevitably, and our half supply of ammunition exhausted; and the enemy, previously increased to seventy thousand men by the army from Harper's Ferry, and become the victorious party, could and would have resumed their march to Richmond without fear of farther opposition.

And, if we had miraculously been successful in our assault, the Potomac would have protected Washington, and rendered our further progress impossible.

I have never doubted the correctness of my course on that occasion. Had I done so, the results of the invasions made subsequently by disciplined and much more numerous armies, properly equipped and provided, and commanded by the best soldiers who appeared in that war, would have reassured me. The first of these expeditions was after General Lee's victory over Pope, and those of Majors-General Jackson and Ewell over Fremont, Banks, and Shields, in 1862; the second, when the way was supposed to have been opened by the effect of General Lee's victory at Chancellorsville, in 1863.

The armies defeated on those occasions were four times as numerous as that repulsed on the 21st of July, 1861, and their losses much greater in proportion to numbers; yet the spirit of the Northern people was so roused by these invasions of their country, that their armies, previously defeated on our soil, met ours on their own at Sharpsburg and Gettysburg so strong in numbers and in courage as to send back the war into Virginia from each of those battle-fields.

The failure of those invasions, directed by Lee, aided by Longstreet and Jackson, with troops inured to marches and manoeuvres as well as to battle, and attempted under the most favorable circumstances of the war, proves that the Confederacy was too weak for offensive warfare, and is very strong evidence in favor of the course against which Southern writers have declaimed vehemently.

At that time, too, defensive war was regarded by the Southern leaders as our best policy, as, it was apprehended, invasion by us would unite all the people of the North, Democrats and Republicans, in the defense of their country. It is certain that either country could have raised armies stronger, both in numbers and in spirit, for defensive than for offensive war.

MISTAKES AND WHAT COULD HAVE BEEN

Confederate

Lieutenant-General James Longstreet

If Stonewall Jackson was the Confederate army's hammer, Longstreet was its anvil. While Jackson is known for his offensive tactics, Longstreet, another brilliant tactician, is better known for his defense.

Born in South Carolina, he grew up on a cotton plantation. His father called him "Peter" because of his rocklike character, and this became his nickname. Later, his men called him "Old Pete" or variations thereof. At West Point he became friends with a number of fellow young men who would become Union generals, including Grant, Rosecrans, Pope, and Thomas. He served with another West Point friend, George Pickett, in Mexico and was wounded in the thigh at Chapultepec.

Two months into the Civil War, he assumed command of a brigade of three Virginia regiments. Four months later he became commander of a division of the Confederacy's main army. Eight months after that he controlled nearly half of Lee's army, with Stonewall Jackson controlling the other half. When Lee promoted his two division commanders to lieutenant general, he dated Longstreet's promotion one day before Jackson's, making Longstreet the senior officer.

Near the war's end, in a tragic replay of earlier events, Longstreet was shot in the shoulder and throat by friendly fire at a critical moment in the Battle of the Wilderness, and it may have cost the Confederates a victory. Unlike Jackson, Longstreet recovered.

McDowell's first mistake was his display, and march for a grand military picnic. The leading proverb impressed upon the minds of young soldiers of the line by old commanders is, "Never despise your enemy." So important a part of the soldier's creed is it, that it is enjoined upon subalterns pursuing marauding parties of half a dozen of the aborigines. His over-confidence led him to treat with levity the reconnoissance of General Tyler on the 18th, as not called for under his orders, nor necessary to justify his plans, although they involved a delay of three days, and a circuitous march around the Confederate left. Then, he put upon his division commander the odium of error and uncalled-for exposure of the troops. This broke the confidence between them, and worked more or less evil through the ranks in the afterpart of the campaign. Had he recognized the importance of the service, and encouraged the conduct of the division commander, he would have drawn the hearts of his officers and soldiers towards him, and toned up the war spirit and morale of his men. Tyler was right in principle, in the construction of duty, under the orders, and in his more comprehensive view of the military zodiac. In no other way than by testing the strength along the direct route could McDowell justify delay, when time was power, and a long march with raw troops in July weather was pending.

The delay gave Beauregard greater confidence in his preconceived plan, and brought out his order of the 21st for advance towards McDowell's reserve at Centreville, but this miscarried, and turned to advantage for the plans of the latter.

Had a prompt, energetic general been in command when, on the 20th, his order of battle was settled upon, the division under Tyler would have been deployed in front of Stone Bridge, as soon after nightfall as darkness could veil the march, and the divisions under Hunter and Heintzelman following would have been stretched along the lateral road in bivouac, so as to be prepared to cross Sudley's Ford and put in a good day's work on the morrow. Had General Tyler's action of the 18th received proper recognition, he would have been confident instead of doubting in his service. McDowell's army posted as it should have been, a march at daylight would have brought the columns to the Henry House before seven o'clock, dislodged Evans, busied by Tyler's display at the bridge, without a chance to fight, and brought the three divisions, reunited in

gallant style, along the turnpike with little burning of powder. Thus prepared and organized, the compact battle-order of twenty thousand men would have been a fearful array against Beauregard's fragmentary left, and by the events as they passed, would have assured McDowell of victory hours before Kirby Smith and Elzey, of the Army of the Shenandoah, came upon the field.

Beauregard's mistake was in failing to ride promptly after his five-o'clock order, and handling his columns while in action. As events actually occurred, he would have been in overwhelming numbers against McDowell's reserve and supply depot. His adversary so taken by surprise, his raw troops would not have been difficult to conquer.

As the experience of both commanders was limited to staff service, it is not surprising that they failed to appreciate the importance of prompt and vigorous manoeuvre in the hour of battle. Beauregard gave indications of a comprehensive military mind and reserve powers that might, with experience and thorough encouragement from the superior authorities, have developed him into eminence as a field-marshal. His adversary seemed untoward, not adapted to military organization or combinations. Most of his men got back to Washington under the sheltering wings of the small bands of regulars.

The mistake of supposing Kirby Smith's and Elzey's approaching troops to be Union reinforcements for McDowell's right was caused by the resemblance, at a distance, of the original Confederate flag to the colors of Federal regiments. This mishap caused the Confederates to cast about for a new ensign, brought out our battle-flag, led to its adoption by General Beauregard, and afterwards by higher authority as the union shield of the Confederate national flag.

The supplies of subsistence, ammunition, and forage passed as we marched through the enemy's camps towards Centreville seemed ample to carry the Confederate army on to Washington. Had the fight been continued to that point, the troops, in their high hopes, would have marched in terrible effectiveness against the demoralized Federals. Gaining confidence and vigor in their march, they could well have reached the capital with the ranks of McDowell's men. The brigade at Blackburn's Ford (five regiments), those at McLean's and Mitchell's Fords, all quite fresh, could have been reinforced by all the cavalry and most of the artillery, comparatively fresh, and later by the brigades of Holmes, Ewell, and Early. This favorable aspect for fruitful results was all sacrificed through the assumed authority of staff-officers who, upon false reports, gave countermand to the orders of their chiefs.

[After the battle] we were provokingly near Washington, with orders not to attempt to advance even to Alexandria. Well-chosen and fortified positions, with soldiers to man them, soon guarded all approaches to the capital. We had frequent little brushes with parties pushed out to reconnoitre. Nevertheless, we were neither so busy nor so hostile as to prevent the reception of a cordial invitation to a dinner-party on the other side, to be given to me at the headquarters of General Richardson. He was disappointed when I refused to accept this amenity, and advised him to be more careful lest the politicians should have him arrested for giving aid and comfort to the enemy. He was my singularly devoted friend and admirer before the war, and had not ceased to be conscious of old-time ties.

A "GLORIOUS VICTORY"

Confederate

Generals Joseph Johnston and G. T. Beauregard (See biographies, pages 46 and 19.)

Headquarters, Army of the Potomac, Manassas, Va., July 25, 1861

Soldiers of the Confederate States:

One week ago a countless host of men, organized into an army, with all the appointments which modern art and practical skill could devise, invaded the soil of Virginia. Their people sounded their approach with triumphant displays of anticipated victory. Their generals came in almost royal state; their great ministers, senators, and women came to witness the immolation of our army and the subjugation of our people, and to celebrate the result with wild revelry.

It is with the profoundest emotions of gratitude to an overruling God, whose hand is manifest in protecting our homes and our liberties, that we, your generals commanding, are enabled, in the name of our whole country, to thank you for that patriotic courage, that heroic gallantry, that devoted daring, exhibited by you in the actions of the 18th and 21st, by which the hosts of the enemy were scattered and a signal and glorious victory obtained.

Comrades, our brothers who have fallen have earned undying renown upon earth, and their blood, shed in our holy cause, is a precious and acceptable sacrifice to the Father of Truth and of Right. Their graves are beside the tomb of Washington; their spirits have joined with his in eternal communion. We drop one tear on their laurels and move forward to avenge them.

Soldiers, we congratulate you on a glorious, triumphant, and complete victory, and we thank you for doing your whole duty in the service of your country.

J. E. Johnston, General, C. S. Army
G. T. Beauregard, General, C. S. Army

THE BATTLE OF SHILOH

ALSO KNOWN AS THE BATTLE OF PITTSBURG LANDING
HARDIN COUNTY, TENNESSEE
APRIL 6–7, 1862

COMMANDERS

Confederate
Gen. Albert Sidney Johnston†
Gen. G. T. Beauregard

Union
Maj. Gen. Ulysses S. Grant
Maj. Gen. Don Carlos Buell

PARTICIPANTS

44,699 (Army of Mississippi)
17,918 (Army of the Ohio)

48,894 (Army of the Tennessee)

CASUALTIES

Confederate
1,728 killed
8,012 wounded
959 POWs/MIA

Union
1,754 killed
8,408 wounded
2,885 POWs/MIA

VICTORY: UNION

OVERVIEW

Ulysses S. Grant first rose to national prominence following his successful attacks on Fort Henry in Kentucky and on Fort Donelson in Tennessee, the surrenders of which earned him the nickname "Unconditional Surrender Grant." A month later Major-General Halleck ordered him to go down the Tennessee River to Pittsburg Landing, where he would join forces with Major-General Don Carlos Buell to take control of the Memphis & Charleston Railroad, one of the Confederacy's primary supply routes from the west to the East Coast.

Roughly thirty miles downstream from Pittsburg Landing at Corinth, Mississippi, where the railroad crossed the Tennessee River, Confederate general Albert Sidney Johnston had gathered a force of 55,000 soldiers. Johnston knew

Grant was coming with almost 49,000 men and decided to launch a surprise attack on Grant before Buell arrived to strengthen Grant's forces.

Things didn't go as planned, but Johnston and Beauregard did launch a strong attack on Grant's men early in the morning of April 6, 1862, near a small log building called Shiloh Church. The Confederates ferociously forced the Union soldiers back, but the Federals, with a series of short retreats, held off the Confederates until sundown, when hostilities ceased. The Confederates dubbed one of the Union lines, where fighting was particularly fierce, the Hornet's Nest. Johnston, the Confederate commander, was killed early in the battle, and Beauregard took his place. It was a strategic loss; at that time, before Lee's star began to rise, Johnston was considered one of the South's best generals.

Shortly after nightfall Buell arrived with about 18,000 men, providing Grant with the fresh reinforcements, although Buell hesitated to get involved with what he thought was Grant's disaster.

Taken shortly after the war from the roof of a barn, this photograph looks out from the Confederate position over Sarah Bell's peach orchard beyond the fence where some of the heaviest fighting occurred. The Hornet's Nest is in the upper right. General Albert Sidney Johnston died near the edge of this field off the right side of this picture.

The following day Grant pushed the Confederates to retreat back toward Corinth. While Shiloh is considered a Union victory, it was a close call, and both sides took a beating. Bad press and false accusations harmed Grant's reputation in the North, with imputations of drunkenness still persisting today.

A number of generals and religious leaders lobbied Lincoln to replace Grant, but the president put them off, saying, "I can't spare this man—he fights."

Shiloh, a Hebrew word meaning "place of peace," was ironically the bloodiest battle up to this point.

FIGHTING WITH RAW RECRUITS

Union

General Ulysses S. Grant

Born in Ohio, the son of a tanner, Ulysses S. Grant, after graduating from West Point, despite being a natural candidate for the cavalry, was made a regimental quartermaster. In the Mexican-American War he received a couple of brevet promotions for bravery in delivering dispatches. He was stationed at Fort Vancouver in Oregon Territory and Fort Humboldt on the California coast before leaving the military to struggle for seven years to make a living in St. Louis, Missouri, during part of which time he owned a slave.

When Lincoln called for volunteers, Grant helped recruit and train a company in Illinois. He was soon promoted to brigadier general in the U.S. Volunteers. In 1864 Lincoln placed him in charge of all the Union armies, and he became the most successful and highly decorated Union general of the Civil War.

The battle of Shiloh, or Pittsburg Landing, fought on Sunday and Monday, the 6th and 7th of April, 1862, has been perhaps less understood, or, to state the case more accurately, more persistently misunderstood, than any other engagement between National and Confederate troops during the entire rebellion.

Events had occurred before the battle, and others subsequent to it, which determined me to make no report to my then chief, General Halleck, further than was contained in a letter, written immediately after the battle, informing him that an engagement had been fought, and announcing the result. The occurrences alluded to are these: After the capture of Fort Donelson, with over fifteen thousand effective men and all their munitions of war, I believed much more could be accomplished without further sacrifice of life.

Clarksville, a town between Donelson and Nashville, in the State of Tennessee, and on the east bank of the Cumberland, was garrisoned by the enemy. Nashville was also garrisoned, and was probably the best-provisioned depot at the time in the Confederacy. Albert Sidney Johnston occupied

Bowling Green, Ky., with a large force. I believed, and my information justified the belief, that these places would fall into our hands without a battle, if threatened promptly. I determined not to miss this chance. The result proved that my information was correct, and sustained my judgment.

Major-General Henry Halleck

> I met him again when the civil war had broken out—when chaos seemed let loose and the gates of hell wide open in every direction. Then came the news of General Grant's attack on the enemy's camp at Belmont on November 7, 1861, soon followed by the events of Columbus, Paducah, Henry and Donelson—all so simple, so direct, so comprehensible, that their effect on my mind was magical. They raised the dark curtain which before had almost hidden out all hope for the future, and displayed the policy and course of action necessary only to be followed with persistence to achieve ultimate success.
>
> —General William Tecumseh Sherman, whose last year at West Point was Grant's first

What, then, was my surprise, after so much had been accomplished by the troops under my immediate command between the time of leaving Cairo, early in February, and the 4th of March, to receive from my chief a dispatch of the latter date, saying: "You will place Major-General C. F. Smith in command of expedition, and remain yourself at Fort Henry. Why do you not obey my orders to report strength and positions of your command?"

I was left virtually in arrest on board a steamer, without even a guard, for about a week, when I was released and ordered to resume my command.[5]

Again: Shortly after the battle of Shiloh had been fought, General Halleck moved his headquarters to Pittsburg Landing, and assumed command of the troops in the field. Although next to him in rank, and nominally in command of my old district and army, I was ignored as much as if I had been at the most distant point of territory within my jurisdiction; and although I was in command of all the troops engaged at Shiloh, I was

---

5   General Halleck fulminated that Grant wasn't responding to his requests for troop strength reports, so Halleck confined Grant while he investigated. It turned out that a telegraph operator sympathetic to the South wasn't relaying Halleck's telegrams to Grant. The operator soon fled to the South, taking the telegrams with him, and Halleck released Grant. It was many years before Grant discovered that Halleck was responsible for his arrest.

not permitted to see one of the reports of General Buell or his subordinates in that battle, until they were published by the War Department, long after the event. In consequence, I never myself made a full report of this engagement.

When I was restored to my command, on the 13th of March, I found it on the Tennessee River, part at Savanna and part at Pittsburg Landing, nine miles above, and on the opposite or western bank.

The skirmishing in our front had been so continuous from about the 3d of April up to the determined attack, that I remained on the field each night until an hour when I felt there would be no further danger before morning. In fact, on Friday, the 4th, I was very much injured by my horse falling with me and on me while I was trying to get to the front, where firing had been heard. The night was one of impenetrable darkness, with rain pouring down in torrents; nothing was visible to the eye except as revealed by the frequent flashes of lightning. Under these circumstances I had to trust to the horse, without guidance, to keep the road. I had not gone far, however, when I met General W. H. L. Wallace and General (then Colonel) [James] McPherson coming from the direction of the front. They said all was quiet so far as the enemy was concerned. On the way back to the boat my horse's feet slipped from under him, and he fell with my leg under his body. The extreme softness of the ground, from the excessive rains of the few preceding days, no doubt saved me from a severe injury and protracted lameness. As it was, my ankle was very much injured; so much so, that my boot had to be cut off. During the battle, and for two or three days after, I was unable to walk except with crutches.

[On the first day of the battle,] while I was at breakfast heavy firing was heard in the direction of Pittsburg Landing, and I hastened there, sending a hurried note to Buell, informing him of the reason why I could not meet him at Savannah. On the way up the river I directed the dispatch-boat to run in close to Crump's Landing, so that I could communicate with General Lew Wallace. I found him waiting on a boat, apparently expecting to see me, and I directed him to get his troops in line ready to execute any orders he might receive. He replied that his troops were already under arms and prepared to move.

Up to that time I had felt by no means certain that Crump's Landing might not be the point of attack. On reaching the front, however, about 8 a.m., I found that the attack on Shiloh was unmistakable, and that nothing more than a small guard, to protect our transports and stores, was needed at Crump's.

Shiloh was a log meeting-house, some two or three miles from Pittsburg Landing, and on the ridge which divides the waters of Snake and Lick creeks, the former emptying into the Tennessee just north of Pittsburg Landing, and the latter south. Shiloh was the key to our position, and was held by Sherman. His division was at that time wholly raw, no part of it ever having been in an engagement; but I thought this deficiency was more than made up by the superiority of the commander.

The position of our troops made a continuous line from Lick Creek, on the left, to Owl Creek, a branch of Snake Creek, on the right, facing nearly south, and possibly a little west. The water in all these streams was very high at the time, and contributed to protect our flanks. The enemy was compelled, therefore, to attack directly in front. This he did with great vigor, inflicting heavy losses on the Federal side, but suffering much heavier on his own. The Confederate assaults were made with such disregard of losses on their own side, that our line of tents soon fell into their hands. The ground on which the battle was fought was

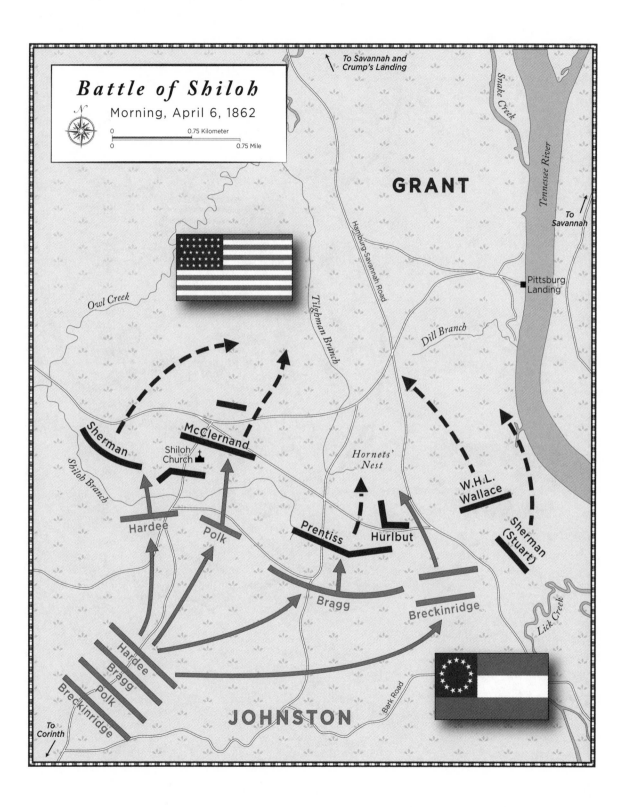

Battle of Shiloh

Morning, April 6, 1862

0 — 0.75 Kilometer
0 — 0.75 Mile

To Savannah and
Crump's Landing

GRANT

Snake Creek

Tennessee River

To
Savannah

Hamburg-Savannah Road

Owl Creek

Tilghman Branch

Pittsburg
Landing

Dill Branch

Sherman

Shiloh Branch

McClernand

Shiloh
Church

Hornets'
Nest

W.H.L.
Wallace

Hardee

Polk

Prentiss

Hurlbut

Sherman
(Stuart)

Bragg

Lick Creek

Breckinridge

Hardee

Bragg

Polk

Breckinridge

Bark Road

To
Corinth

JOHNSTON

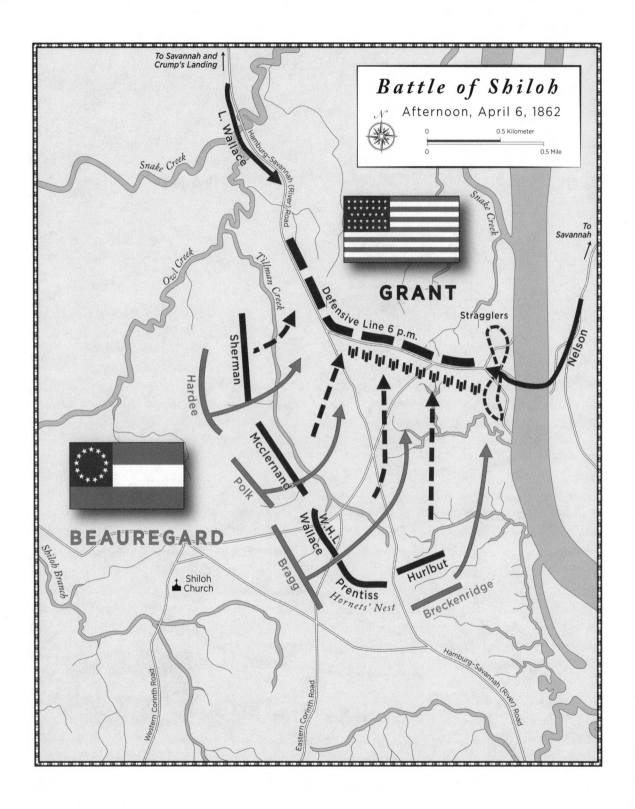

Battle of Shiloh

Afternoon, April 6, 1862

N

0   0.5 Kilometer
0   0.5 Mile

To Savannah and
Crump's Landing

Snake Creek

L. Wallace

Hamburg-Savannah (River) Road

Snake Creek

To Savannah

GRANT

Stragglers

Nelson

Tilman Creek

Defensive Line 6 p.m.

Owl Creek

Sherman

Hardee

McClernand

Polk

W.H.L. Wallace

Bragg

BEAUREGARD

Shiloh Branch

Shiloh Church

Prentiss
Hornets' Nest

Hurlbut

Breckenridge

Western Corinth Road

Eastern Corinth Road

Hamburg–Savannah (River) Road

undulating, heavily timbered, with scattered clearings, the woods giving some protection to the troops on both sides. There was also considerable underbrush.

A number of attempts were made by the enemy to turn our right flank, where Sherman was posted, but every effort was repulsed with heavy loss. But the front attack was kept up so vigorously that, to prevent the success of these attempts to get on our flanks, the Federal troops were compelled several times to take positions to the rear, nearer Pittsburg Landing. When the firing ceased at night, the Federal line was more than a mile in rear of the position it had occupied in the morning.

In one of the backward moves, on the 6th, the division commanded by General [Benjamin] Prentiss did not fall back with the others. This left his flanks exposed, which enabled the enemy to capture him, with about 2,200 of his officers and men.

With this single exception, for a few minutes, after the capture of Prentiss, a continuous and unbroken line was maintained all day from Snake Creek or its tributaries on the right to Lick Creek or the Tennessee on the left, above Pittsburg. There was no hour during the day when there was not heavy firing and generally hard fighting at some point on the line, but seldom at all points at the same time. It was a case of Southern dash against Northern pluck and endurance.

Three of the five divisions engaged the first day at Shiloh were entirely raw, and many of them had only received their arms on the way from their States to the field. Many of them had arrived but a day or two before, and were hardly able to load their muskets according to the manual. Their officers were equally ignorant of their duties. Under these circumstances, it is not astonishing that many of the regiments broke at the first fire. In two cases, as I now remember, the colonels led

their regiments from the field on first hearing the whistle of the enemy's bullets. In these cases the colonels were constitutional cowards, unfit for any military position. But not so the officers and men led out of danger by them. Better troops never went upon a battle-field than many of these officers and men afterward proved themselves to be, who fled, panic-stricken, at the first whistle of bullets and shell at Shiloh.

During the whole of the first day I was continuously engaged in passing from one part of the field to another, giving directions to division commanders. The nature of this battle was such that cavalry could not be used in front; I therefore formed ours into line, in rear, to stop stragglers, of whom there were many. When there would be enough of them to make a show, and after they had recovered from their fright, they would be sent to reinforce some part of the line which needed support, without regard to their companies, regiments, or brigades.

On one occasion during the day, I rode back as far as the river and met General Buell, who had just arrived; I do not remember the hour of the day, but at that time there probably were as many as four or five thousand stragglers lying under cover of the river bluff, panic-stricken, most of whom would have been shot where they lay, without resistance, before they would have taken muskets and marched to the front to protect themselves.

I have no doubt that this sight impressed General Buell with the idea that a line of retreat would be a good thing just then. If he had come in by the front instead of through the stragglers in the rear, he would have thought and felt differently. Could he have come through the Confederate rear, he would have witnessed there a scene similar to that at our own. The distant rear of an army engaged in battle is not the best place from which to judge correctly what is going on in front. In fact, later in the war, while occupying the country between the Tennessee and the Mississippi, I learned that the panic in the Confederate lines had not differed much from that within our own.

So confident was I before firing had ceased on the 6th that the next day would bring victory to our arms if we could only take the initiative, that I visited each division commander in person before any reinforcements had reached the field. I directed them to throw out heavy lines of skirmishers in the morning as soon as they could see, and push them forward until they found the enemy, following with their entire divisions in supporting distance, and to engage the enemy as soon as found. To Sherman I told the story of the assault at Fort Donelson, and said that the same tactics would win at Shiloh. Victory was assured when Wallace arrived with his division of five thousand effective veterans, even if there had been no other support. The enemy received no reinforcements. He had suffered heavy losses in killed, wounded, and straggling, and his commander, General Albert Sidney Johnston, was dead. I was glad, however, to see the reinforcements of Buell and credit them with doing all there was for them to do. My command was thus nearly doubled in numbers and efficiency.

During the night rain fell in torrents, and our troops were exposed to the storm without shelter. I made my headquarters under a tree a few hundred yards back from the river bank. My ankle was so much swollen from the fall of my horse the Friday night preceding, and the bruise was so painful, that I could get no rest. The drenching rain would have precluded the possibility of sleep, without this additional cause. Some time after midnight, growing restive under the storm and the continuous pain, I moved back to the log-house on the bank. This had been taken as a hospital, and all night wounded men were being brought in, their wounds dressed, a leg or an arm amputated, as the case might require, and everything being done to save life or alleviate suffering. The sight was more unendurable than encountering the rebel fire, and I returned to my tree in the rain.

[The next day] in a very short time the battle became general all along the line. This day everything was favorable to the Federal side. We now had become the attacking party. The enemy was driven back all day, as we had been the day before, until finally he beat a precipitate retreat.

About three o'clock, being near that point, and seeing that the enemy was giving way everywhere else, I gathered up a couple of regiments, or parts of regiments, from troops near by, formed them in line of battle and marched them forward, going in front myself to prevent premature or long-range firing. At this point there was a clearing between us and the enemy favorable for charging, although exposed. I knew the enemy were ready to break, and only wanted a little encouragement from us to go quickly and join their friends who had started earlier. After marching to within musket-range, I stopped and let the troops pass. The command, Charge, was given, and was executed with loud cheers, and with a run, when the last of the enemy broke.

During this second day I had been moving from right to left and back, to see for myself the progress made. In the early part of the afternoon, while riding with Colonel McPherson and Major Hawkins, then my chief commissary, we got beyond the left of our troops. We were moving along the northern edge of a clearing, very leisurely, toward the river above the landing. There did not appear to be an enemy to our right, until suddenly a battery with musketry opened upon us from the edge of the woods on the other side of the clearing. The shells and balls whistled about our ears very fast for about a minute. I do not think it took us longer than that to get out of range and out of sight. In the sudden start we made, Major Hawkins lost his hat. He did not stop to pick it up.

When we arrived at a perfectly safe position we halted to take an account of damages. McPherson's horse was panting as if ready to drop. On examination it was found that a ball had struck him forward of the flank just back of the saddle, and had gone entirely through. In a few minutes the poor beast dropped dead; he had given no sign of injury until we came to a stop. A ball had struck the metal scabbard of my sword, just below the hilt, and broken it nearly off; before the battle was over, it had broken off entirely. All were thankful that it was no worse.

After the rain of the night before and the frequent and heavy rains for some days previous, the roads were almost impassable. The enemy, carrying his artillery and supply trains over them in his retreat, made them still worse for troops following. I wanted to pursue, but had not the heart to order the men who had fought desperately for two days, lying in the mud and rain whenever not fighting, and I did not feel disposed to positively order Buell, or any part of his command, to pursue.

Shiloh was the most severe battle fought at the West during the war, and but few in the East equaled it for hard, determined fighting. I saw an open field, in our possession on the second day, over which the Confederates had made repeated charges the day before, so covered with dead that it would have been possible to walk across the clearing, in any direction, stepping on dead bodies, without a foot touching the ground. On our side Federal and Confederate were mingled together in about equal proportions; but on the remainder of the field nearly all were Confederates.

General Albert Sidney Johnston commanded the Confederate forces until disabled by a wound in the afternoon of the first day. His wound, as I understood afterward, was not necessarily fatal, or even dangerous. But he was a man who would not abandon what he deemed an important trust in the face of danger, and consequently continued in the saddle, commanding, until so exhausted by the loss of blood that he had to be taken from his horse, and soon after died.

General Beauregard was next in rank to Johnston, and succeeded to the command, which he retained to the close of the battle and during the subsequent retreat on Corinth, as well as in the siege of that place. His tactics have been severely criticised by Confederate writers, but I do not believe his fallen chief could have done any better under the circumstances. The fact that when he was shot Johnston was leading a brigade to induce it to make a charge which had been repeatedly ordered, is evidence that there was neither the universal demoralization on our side nor the unbounded confidence on theirs which has been claimed.

Up to the battle of Shiloh, I, as well as thousands of other citizens, believed that the rebellion against the Government would collapse suddenly and soon if a decisive victory could be gained over any of its armies. Donelson and Henry were such victories. But when armies were collected which not only attempted to hold a line from Memphis to Chattanooga, and Knoxville, and on to the Atlantic, but assumed the offensive, and made such a gallant effort to regain what had been lost, then, indeed, I gave up all idea of saving the Union except by complete conquest.

Shiloh was one of the most important battles in the war. It was there that our Western soldiers first met the enemy in a pitched battle. From that day they never feared to fight the enemy, and never went into action without feeling sure they would win. Shiloh broke the prestige of the Southern Confederacy so far as our Western army was concerned. I have every reason to be fully satisfied with the battle of Shiloh. In its results it was one of our greatest victories.

What won the battle of Shiloh was the courage and endurance of our own soldiers. It was the staying power and pluck of the North as against the short-lived power of the South; and whenever these qualities came into collision the North always won. I used to find that the first day, or the first period of a battle, was most successful to the South; but if we held on to the second or third day, we were sure to beat them, and we always did.

> The class next after us [1843] was destined to furnish the man who was to eclipse all, to rise to the rank of general, an office made by Congress to honor his services; who became President of the United States, and for a second term; who received the salutations of all the powers of the world in his travels as a private citizen around the earth; of noble, generous heart, a lovable character, a valued friend, Ulysses S. Grant. I had the pleasure to ride with him on our first visit to Mr. Frederick Dent's home, a few miles from the garrison, where we first met Miss Julia Dent, the charming woman who, five years later, became Mrs. Grant.
>
> —Confederate lieutenant general James Longstreet, who attended West Point with Grant

MILITARY INTELLIGENCE

Military intel often determines who wins and who loses. In order to make proper decisions, commanders need accurate information. When marching to battle, sometimes they have no idea where the enemy lies or the size of its forces. A perennial fear is to suddenly receive enfilading fire (i.e., from the side) or to be attacked from behind. Knowing the lay of the land and which roads are passable is necessary for properly moving and positioning troops, and knowing the capability and range of the enemy's weapons also forms a major part of military intel.

At this time generals used their cavalry as one of the primary methods of gathering information. Cavalry moved rapidly and probed the enemy's strengths and weaknesses. Scouts provided another source of information, although some generals considered them less reliable since they tended to be rough-and-tumble daredevils. Spies could obtain even better information, operating behind enemy lines, but they always attracted suspicion or doubt. Spies and scouts often blended together, with scouts sometimes operating as spies and reconnaissance bleeding into espionage.

The Confederacy established the Secret Service Bureau as its intelligence-gathering service; it was a clandestine unit within the Signal Corps, in turn part of the War Department in Richmond. The bureau established secret offices in Toronto and Montreal, Canada, for running spies and sabotage operations.

Much of the South's intel came straight from regular news reports in Northern newspapers. Early in 1863 Sherman had a journalist arrested and tried as a spy for publishing details about the army, but he couldn't prove the Confederates received that particular newspaper. He wrote to his brother: "These newspaper correspondents hanging on about the skirts of our army reveal all plans, and are worth a hundred thousand men to the enemy."

The Union, on the other hand, never really had a central service. Each general handled this on his own. Major-General George McClellan hired Allan Pinkerton, while Scott had Lafayette Baker. Even President Lincoln hired William Lloyd, who reported only to him. Pinkerton called his semiofficial organization the Union Intelligence Service. Baker sometimes called his the National Detective Police. When Major-General Ambrose Burnside replaced McClellan, Pinkerton resigned, taking his organization with him.

When Major-General Joseph Hooker took over the Army of the Potomac, he had Colonel George Sharpe, his deputy provost marshal, set up an intelligence organization that Sharpe called the Bureau of Military Information. With about seventy agents, the bureau produced thorough reports containing information from cavalry, infantry, spies, deserters, refugees, POWs, Southern newspapers, Union pickets in touch with Confederate pickets, observation balloons, and documents found on battlefield corpses. Runaway slaves, called contrabands, also proved a valuable source of information since they were eager to help and many had been doing the manual labor at Confederate camps or had built their fortifications. Some even had served the officers and overheard their conversations. By the Siege of Petersburg, Sharpe, by then a brigadier general, could provide Grant with just about any information requested.

Gathering intel was the primary goal, but it was also important to mislead the enemy, concealing one's own intentions and capabilities. When counterintelligence ferreted out enemy spies, they could send false reports through the enemy's spy channels. Planting disinformation in newspapers offered another method to fool the opposition.

Confederate major general John Magruder was well-known for deceiving Union major general George McClellan. As McClellan was preparing for the Battle of Yorktown, Magruder had small groups of soldiers march around in circles in the gaps between trees so they looked like long lines of troops, convincing McClellan that he had a large force. McClellan decided not to risk an attack, so he entrenched and the battle turned into a siege. Magruder's 12,000 men (35,000 with later reinforcements) stopped McClellan from marching into Richmond.

General Joseph Johnston used Quaker guns, an excellent example of Confederate

A Union soldier pretends to light a Confederate Quaker gun at Centreville, Virginia, in March 1862.

deception, around Centreville, Virginia. Quakers being pacifists, of course, Quaker guns were simply logs carved and painted black to resemble cannons, tricking the Federals into thinking the Confederates had more artillery than they actually did. The Confederates employed fake guns at the Sieges of Corinth and Petersburg as well.

Before the Battle of Chickamauga, Confederate general Braxton Bragg sent false deserters into Union lines, where, when interrogated, they gave deceptive information that helped convince Union major general William Rosecrans that Bragg's demoralized army was fleeing—when instead they were preparing to attack. The ruse worked, and Bragg routed Rosecrans.

THE EXTREME FURY OF BATTLE

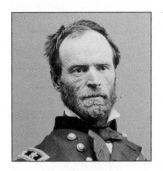

Union

General William Tecumseh Sherman (See biography, page 4.)

On Sunday morning, the 6th, early, there was a good deal of picket-firing, and I got breakfast, rode out along my lines, and, about four hundred yards to the front of Appier's regiment, received from some bushes in a ravine to the left front a volley which killed my orderly, Holliday. About the same time I saw the rebel lines of battle in front coming down on us as far as the eye could reach. All my troops were in line of battle, ready, and the ground was favorable to us. I gave the necessary orders to the battery and cautioned the men to reserve their fire till the rebels had crossed the ravine of Owl Creek. In a few minutes the battle of "Shiloh" began with extreme fury, and lasted two days.

The battle began by the enemy opening a battery in the woods to our front and throwing shells into our camp. Our infantry and artillery opened along the whole line and the battle became general. I saw at once that the enemy designed to pass my left flank and fall upon Generals [John] McClernand and Prentiss, whose line of camps was almost parallel with the Tennessee River and about 2 miles back from it. Very soon the sound of musketry and artillery announced that General Prentiss was engaged, and about 9 a.m. I judged that he was falling back. About this time Appier's regiment broke in disorder, soon followed by fugitives from Mungen's regiment, and the enemy pressed forward on Waterhouse's battery, thereby exposed.

Although our left was thus turned and the enemy was pressing on the whole line, I deemed

Shiloh so important that I remained by it, and renewed my orders to Colonels McDowell and Buckland to hold their ground, and we did hold those positions till about 10 o'clock a.m., when the enemy got his artillery to the rear of our left flank, and some change became absolutely necessary.

While we were so hardly pressed two Iowa regiments approached from the rear, but could not be brought up to the severe fire that was raging in our front, and General Grant, who visited us on that ground, will remember our situation about 3 p.m.; but about 4 p.m. it was evident that Hurlbut's line had been driven back to the river, and knowing that General Wallace was coming from Crump's Landing with re-enforcements. General McClernand and I, on consultation, selected a new line of defense, with its right covering the bridge by which General Wallace had to approach. We fell back as well as we could, gathering, in addition to our own, such scattered forces as we could find, and formed a new line.

General McClernand's division made a line charge on the enemy, and drove him back into the ravines to our front and right. I had a clear field about 200 yards wide in my immediate front, and contented myself with keeping the enemy's infantry at that distance during the rest of the day. In this position we rested for the night.

General Grant and Buell visited me in our bivouac that evening, and from them I learned the situation of affairs on the other parts of the field. General Wallace arrived from Crump's Landing shortly after dark, and formed his line to my right and rear. It rained hard during the night, but our men were in good spirits and lay on their arms, being satisfied with such bread and meat as could be gathered from the neighboring camps, and determined to redeem on Monday the losses of Sunday.

> On the 6th Sherman was shot twice, once in the hand, once in the shoulder, the ball cutting his coat and making a slight wound, and a third ball passed through his hat. In addition to this he had several horses shot during the day.
>
> —Major-General Ulysses S. Grant of General Sherman, who didn't mention this in his official report or his memoirs

At daylight on Monday I received General Grant's orders to advance and recapture our original camps. Under cover of their fire we advanced till we reached the point where the Corinth road crosses the line of McClernand's camps, and here I saw for the first time the well-ordered and compact columns of General Buell's Kentucky forces, whose soldierly movements at once gave confidence to our newer and less-disciplined forces. Here I saw Willich's regiment advance upon a point of water-oaks and thicket, behind which I knew the enemy was in great strength, and enter it in beautiful style. Then arose the severest musketry fire I ever heard, which lasted some twenty minutes, when this splendid regiment had to fall back.

The enemy had one battery close by Shiloh and another near the Hamburg road, both pouring grape and canister upon any column of troops that advanced toward the green point of water-oaks. Rousseau's brigade moved in splendid order steadily to the front, sweeping everything before it, and at 4 p.m. we stood upon the ground of our original front line and the enemy was in full retreat. I directed my several brigades to resume at once their original camps. Several times during the battle cartridges gave out, but General

Grant had thoughtfully kept a supply coming from the rear. When I appealed to regiments to stand fast, although out of cartridges, I did so because to retire a regiment for any cause has a bad effect on others. I commend the Fortieth Illinois and Thirteenth Missouri for thus holding their ground under a heavy fire, although their cartridge boxes were empty.

My division was made up of regiments perfectly new, nearly all having received their muskets for the first time at Paducah. When individual fears seized them the first impulse was to get away. To expect of them the coolness and steadiness of older troops would be wrong. My Third Brigade did break much too soon, and I am not yet advised where they were during Sunday afternoon and Monday morning.

Probably no single battle of the war gave rise to such wild and damaging reports. It was publicly asserted at the North that our army was taken completely by surprise; that the rebels caught us in our tents; bayoneted the men in their beds; that General Grant was drunk; that Buell's opportune arrival saved the Army of the Tennessee from utter annihilation, etc. These reports were in a measure sustained by the published opinions of Generals Buell, Nelson, and others, who had reached the steamboat-landing from the east, just before nightfall of the 6th, when there was a large crowd of frightened, stampeded men, who clamored and declared that our army was all destroyed and beaten.

[After the first day of battle, Grant] again came to me just before dark, and ordered me to be ready to assume the offensive in the morning, saying that, as he had observed at Fort Donelson at the crisis of the battle, both sides seemed defeated, and whoever assumed the offensive was sure to win. About half an hour afterward General Buell himself rode up to where I was. Buell said he had come up from the landing, and had not seen our men, of whose existence in fact he seemed to doubt. I insisted that I had five thousand good men still left in line, and thought that McClernand had as many more, and that with what was left of Hurlbut's, W. H. L. Wallace's, and Prentiss's divisions, we ought to have eighteen thousand men fit for battle. I reckoned that ten thousand of our men were dead, wounded, or prisoners, and that the enemy's loss could not be much less.

Buell said that Kelson's, McCook's, and Crittenden's divisions of his army, containing eighteen thousand men, had arrived and could cross over in the night, and be ready for the next day's battle. I argued that with these reinforcements we could sweep the field. Buell seemed to mistrust us, and repeatedly said that he did not like the looks of things, especially about the boat-landing, and I really feared he would not cross over his army that night, lest he should become involved in our general disaster.

Buell did cross over that night, and the next day we assumed the offensive and swept the field, thus gaining the battle decisively. Nevertheless, the controversy was started and kept up, mostly to the personal prejudice of General Grant, who as usual maintained an imperturbable silence.

Striking a Sudden Blow

Confederate

General G. T. Beauregard (See biography, page 19.)

On the 2d, having ascertained conclusively, from the movements of the enemy on the Tennessee River and from reliable sources of information, that his aim would be to cut off my communications in West Tennessee with the Eastern and Southern States, by operating from the Tennessee River, between Crump's Landing and East-port, as a base, I determined to foil his designs by concentrating all my available forces at and around Corinth.

It was then determined to assume the offensive, and strike a sudden blow at the enemy, in position under General Grant on the west bank of the Tennessee, at Pittsburg, and in the direction of Savannah, before he was re-enforced by the army under General Buell, then known to be advancing for that purpose by rapid marches from Nashville via Columbia. About the same time General Johnston was advised that such an operation conformed to the expectations of the President.

By a rapid and vigorous attack on General Grant, it was expected he would be beaten back into his transports and the river, or captured, in time to enable us to profit by the victory, and remove to the rear all the stores and munitions that would fall into our hands in such an event before the arrival of General Buell's army on the scene. It was never contemplated, however, to retain the position thus gained and abandon Corinth, the strategic point of the campaign.

The formation of our lines of battle was not completed until late on the afternoon of the 5th. It had actually taken us upwards of two days to go over a distance of less than eighteen miles. As soon as it became certain that no engagement on our part could begin that evening, General Johnston invited his Corps Commanders, and the Commander of the Reserves, as well as myself, to an informal conference, near his head-quarters, which were, at that moment, less than two miles from the enemy's line of encampments. There it was ascertained that most of our men were already without rations; and that the transportation wagons, with the extra rations and extra ammunition, were still far in the rear, with no certainty of their soon coming up with the troops.

When I understood the true condition of affairs, which, it will be admitted, was far from promising, I told General Johnston and the other officers present, that, anxious as I was to carry out the aggressive movement, I was not certain but that the delays

General Albert Sidney Johnston in 1860, just before he switched from the U.S. Army to the Confederate Army.

we had met with on our march, and the lack of food threatening the army, and, added to these, the boisterous and regretful conduct of some of our cavalry the day before, had not already frustrated the object we had in view upon marching our forces from Corinth, namely, to reach our present position, take the enemy by surprise, and especially and above all, give him battle before General Buell's junction with General Grant. That none could be more sorely disappointed than I was, at seeing the great purpose we were about to execute probably lost to us through accident and mismanagement. I no longer favored an attack, but now preferred inviting one from the enemy, and thus change our offensive movement into a reconnoissance in force; the result of which might bring him nearer to our base and, therefore, farther from his own, and give us, eventually, the chance of retrieving the present lost opportunity. My remarks were listened to with much attention both by the Corps Commanders and by General Johnston. He admitted the correctness of my views, but said that he still hoped the enemy would be unprepared to meet our onset, and that we could accomplish our end before the arrival of General Buell's army. That our troops were in line of battle at last, and it were better to make the venture.

It was clear that I only proposed this alternative because I deemed my first plan unsafe at this particular juncture, too much time having been lost by us to justify a fair hope of success.

It is singular that notwithstanding the evidence furnished by all Confederate and many Federal authorities, some northern writers and northern generals persevere in the idle assertion—idle because it has been proven groundless—that the Federal forces were not taken by surprise

at Shiloh on the 6th of April, 1862. I, myself, for reasons already referred to in this paper, had deemed a surprise improbable; but that it was effected is, nevertheless, a fact.

On the 5th General Sherman sent this telegram to General Grant at Savannah: "I do not apprehend anything like an attack upon our position." General Grant on the same day telegraphs General Halleck as follows: "I have scarcely the faintest idea of an attack (general) being made upon us, but will be prepared should such a thing take place." And on the same evening (April 5th) General Grant, being then at Savannah, and addressing Colonel Ammen, who commanded a brigade of Nelson's Division, Buell's Army, said: "There will be no fight at Pittsburg Landing; we will have to go to Corinth, where the rebels are fortified. If they come to attack us, we can whip them, as I have more than twice as many troops as I had at Fort Donelson."

On the evening of the 5th of April, our army, amounting to some forty thousand men, was within a mile and a half of the Federal encampments. We had formed our lines of battle in the woods fronting these encampments. We had remained there a whole night, using but few precautionary measures to conceal our presence. We had moved on the next morning within easy sight of the enemy, without encountering any obstacle worthy of notice. When the first encampments were taken, many Federal officers and soldiers were yet lying in bed. Bread was being baked and was taken hot from the ovens by our men. Sutlers' stores were left wide open. Whole companies ran from their quarters, without having time to take their muskets or rifles with them. Our first columns of attack entered the first Federal lines as freely and as unimpeded as if by invitation.

> We did not know that we had been surprised
> and slaughtered in our beds. We believed
> we had heroically defended our position
> till reinforcements, near and long expected,
> did arrive, until the newspapers came from
> the North full and complete. Our families
> mourned us as dead, with the blush of shame
> that we had set down like a parcel of cowards,
> to be knocked over with clubs.
>
> These accounts were written by cowards,
> and fugitives who fled from the field and did
> not stop till they reached Paducah, Cairo, and
> Cincinnati. Their accounts were verified by
> men who never commanded even a brigade,
> and who reached the battle-field from the rear,
> always presenting a sickening sight, and sent
> forth their reports damaging to the brave and
> gallant men of the Army of the Tennessee,
> who did fight hard and successfully on the 6th
> of April, 1862.
>
> —GENERAL SHERMAN IN A PRIVATE LETTER, LATER
> PUBLISHED, ON THE CLAIMS THAT SOME OF HIS MEN
> WERE BAYONETTED IN THEIR SLEEP

At dawn of day I had ridden to General Johnston's head-quarters, to advise with him about our respective action in the impending battle. It was agreed between us that he would lead the attack on our right, and that I would supervise the movements of the field and direct the reserves. When the firing became heavier he mounted his horse and rode forward. I took the position which General Johnston should have occupied himself, near the center and in rear of our line; and, from the spot I sent instructions and orders to various portions of the field, as, in my opinion, the exigencies required.

At 5.30 a.m. our lines and columns were in motion, all animated, evidently, by a promising spirit. The front line was engaged at once, but advanced steadily. Like an Alpine avalanche our troops moved forward, despite the determined resistance of the enemy, until after 6 p.m., when we were in possession of all his encampments between Owl and Lick Creeks but one; nearly all of his field artillery; about 30 flags, colors, and standards; over 3,000 prisoners, including a division commander (General Prentiss), and several brigade commanders; thousands of small-arms; an immense supply of subsistence, forage, and munitions of war, and a large amount of means of transportation, all the substantial fruits of a complete victory, such, indeed, as rarely have followed the most successful battles; for never was an army so well provided as that of our enemy.

The remnant of his army had been driven in utter disorder to the immediate vicinity of Pittsburg, under the shelter of the heavy guns of his iron-clad gunboats, and we remained undisputed masters of his well-selected, admirably-provided cantonments, after over twelve hours of obstinate conflict with his forces, who had been beaten from them and the contiguous covert, but only by a sustained onset of all the men we could bring into action.

General Johnston had been, for nearly three-quarters of an hour, in rear of General [John] Breckinridge's division, which was, at that time, the advanced right of the main Confederate line. The firing was unusually heavy in that quarter; and General Johnston was astonished at the resolute resistance encountered there. After causing General Breckinridge to appeal to the soldiers, and after doing so himself, he ordered a charge, which he led, in person, with his well-known valor, and during which he was wounded in the leg, without at first realizing the extent of his injury. The Federal line thus charged had slowly and reluctantly given way, retiring to the next ridge beyond; but the temporary advantage we had gained was dearly bought by the death of the General-in-Chief, a gallant soldier and noble citizen, whose life, had it been spared, would have been of inestimable value to his country. General Johnston died in the arms of Governor Harris, of Tennessee, one of his volunteer aides, at about 2.30 o'clock p.m.

General Johnston was not wounded while leading a charge, as has been so frequently asserted, but while several hundred yards in the rear of Statham's brigade after it had made a successful advance, and during the absence of Governor Harris of his staff, whom he had dispatched to Colonel Statham, some two hundred yards distant, with orders to charge and take a Federal battery on his left.

It is but true to state here, that never from the opening of the battle up to the hour of his death, had General Johnston occupied on the field the position which was properly his own, as Commander-in-Chief of our forces. From the place he had himself selected on our line, and where he remained to the last, he was but acting the part of a Corps or Division Commander, and as such, uselessly exposing his person. From where he was, he could not—nor in fact did he ever attempt to—direct the general movements of our forces. That most important trust devolved upon me, the second in command, and I performed it throughout the whole day, before, as well as after, the death of General Johnston.

Messengers were hurriedly sent by me to the Corps Commanders, to inform them of what had occurred, and to urge upon them the necessity of concealing the fact from the troops; and, feeling all the more the weighty responsibility resting upon me, I gave orders that the attack be continued and pushed forward with the utmost vigor.

It was after 6 p.m. when the enemy's last position was carried, and his forces finally broke and sought refuge behind a commanding eminence covering the Pittsburg Landing, not more than half a mile distant, and under the guns of the gunboats, which opened on our eager columns a fierce and annoying fire with shot and shell of the heaviest description.

Darkness was close at hand; officers and men were exhausted by a combat of over twelve hours without food, and jaded by the march of the preceding day through mud and water. It was, therefore, impossible to collect the rich and opportune spoils of war scattered broadcast on the field left in our possession, and impracticable to make any effective dispositions for their removal to the rear.

I accordingly established my headquarters at the church of Shiloh, in the enemy's encampments, with Major-General Bragg, and directed our troops to sleep on their arms in such positions in advance and rear as corps commanders should determine, hoping, from news received by a special dispatch, that delays had been encountered by General Buell in his march from Columbia, and that his main force, therefore, could not reach the field of battle in time to save General Grant's shattered fugitive forces from capture or destruction on the following day.

The continuous fighting, marching, counter-marching and manoeuvring of the troops all day long—and that mostly without food—finally produced the most telling effect upon them. Almost every position of the enemy was carried. His lines of encampments were taken. The Tennessee River was in sight, on several points of our line. We had captured small arms, guns, flags, and upwards of three thousand prisoners; but the victory, none the less, was not wholly ours. Straggling among the men, which had begun before noon, had now assumed fearful proportions. And worse even than straggling, was the fact that the men in front, who had never been out of action, were absolutely outdone by the need of food and by fatigue.

During the night the rain fell in torrents, adding to the discomforts and harassed condition of the men. The enemy, moreover, had broken their rest by a discharge at measured intervals of heavy shells thrown from the gunboats; therefore on the following morning the troops under my command were not in condition to cope with an equal force of fresh troops, armed and equipped like our adversary.

About 6 o'clock on the morning of April 7, however, a hot fire of musketry and artillery, opened from the enemy's quarter on our advanced line, assured me of the junction of his forces, and soon the battle raged with a fury which satisfied me I was attacked by a largely superior force. But hour by hour, thus opposed to an enemy constantly re-enforced, our ranks were perceptibly thinned under the unceasing, withering fire of the enemy, and by 12 m. eighteen hours of hard fighting had sensibly exhausted a large number.

My last reserves had necessarily been disposed of, and the enemy was evidently receiving fresh re-enforcements after each repulse; accordingly about 1 p.m. I determined to withdraw from so unequal a conflict, securing such of the results of the victory of the day before as was then practicable. The line of troops established to cover this movement had been disposed on a favorable ridge commanding the ground of Shiloh Church. From this position our artillery played upon the woods beyond for a while, but upon no visible enemy and without reply.

> In this result we have a valuable lesson, by which we should profit—never on a battle-field to lose a moment's time, but leaving the killed, wounded, and spoils to those whose special business it is to care for them, to press on with every available man, giving a panic-stricken and retreating foe no time to rally, and reaping all the benefits of a success never complete until every enemy is killed, wounded, or captured.
> —Confederate general Braxton Bragg's official report

No one on the hard-fought field of Shiloh had the hope of victory more at heart than I had. The entire conception of the campaign had been mine; and I had directed the general movements of the troops throughout the day. But human endurance has its limits; and to quote the language of General Bragg, not as found in his report, written more than three months after the battle of Shiloh, but as used by him while leaving the front on the 6th of April with his exhausted men: They had done all that they would do and had better be withdrawn.

"Our Condition Is Horrible"

Confederate

General Braxton Bragg

One of the primary commanders in the western theater, Braxton Bragg later became a military advisor to Confederate president Jefferson Davis. An 1837 graduate of West Point, he went as a second lieutenant in the artillery to the Second Seminole War, in Florida, though he didn't have a combat role. In 1843 he was stationed at Fort Moultrie, across Charleston Harbor from Fort Sumter, where he became friends with William Tecumseh Sherman, George Thomas, and John Reynolds, all later Union major generals. He won national acclaim for his use of artillery at the Battle of Buena Vista in the war with Mexico, fighting under Major-General Zachary Taylor, whom he helped to win the presidency. There he also fought alongside his friend Sherman and Colonel Jefferson Davis.

After Mexico, Bragg left the military and bought a sugar plantation with more than a hundred slaves. He opposed secession, but when it occurred he was a colonel in the Louisiana militia. After a series of rapid promotions, at the age of forty-four he became a major general and one of the top commanders in the Confederate army. After the Battle of Shiloh, he became one of the Confederacy's seven full generals.

> Three Miles on Road from Mickey's to Corinth,
> April 8, 1862, 7.30 a.m.

My Dear General [Beauregard]:

Our condition is horrible. Troops utterly disorganized and demoralized. Road almost impassable. No provisions and no forage; consequently everything is feeble. Straggling parties may get in to-night. Those in rear will suffer much. The rear guard, Breckinridge commanding, is left at Mickey's in charge of wounded, &c. The enemy, up to daylight, had not pursued. Have ordered Breckinridge to hold on till pressed by the enemy, but he will suffer for want of food. Can any fresh troops, with five days' rations, be sent to his relief?

It is most lamentable to see the state of affairs, but I am powerless and almost exhausted.

Our artillery is being left all along the road by its officers; indeed I find but few officers with their men.

Relief of some kind is necessary, but how it is to reach us I can hardly suggest, as no human power or animal power could carry empty wagons over this road with such teams as we have.

Yours, most truly,

Braxton Bragg

"RECRUITS WANTED"

Confederate

Lieutenant-General Nathan Bedford Forrest

Nathan Bedford Forrest became one of the most controversial of the war's generals. Born in Tennessee to a poor blacksmith, he was the eldest of twelve. After moving to Mississippi, his father died and he began supporting his family when he was seventeen. Never attending school, he was entirely self-taught and had a talent for business. He traded in livestock before moving to Memphis to trade in horses, slaves, and real estate, with some gambling on the side. He soon became one of the richest men in the South, owning two cotton plantations and more than 3,000 acres, farmed by more than a hundred slaves. Slave dealers were tolerated but socially avoided in the South—this was overlooked in Forrest's case probably because of his riches.

When the war started, he immediately joined as a private. Quickly realizing how badly equipped the Confederate forces were, he used his own money to recruit and equip a mounted battalion, known as Forrest's Tennessee Cavalry Battalion, and he was promoted to lieutenant colonel. He formed an elite group within his command of forty to ninety of his best men, his escort company, which included eight of his slaves.

He had minimal military training but a talent for tactics, along with enthusiasm and determination, which led to a promotion to brigadier general and fifteen months into the war, the command of a cavalry brigade, which he used like mechanized infantry. He and his men moved around quickly on horses, from which they dismounted and fought on the ground, enabling lightning strikes against the enemy more in line with guerrilla warfare.

The Fort Pillow Massacre and his postwar position as the Ku Klux Klan's first grand wizard have marred his military reputation. Some say he left the Klan because of its violence, and near the end of his life he did give a speech espousing racial reconciliation and equality.

CITY DIRECTORY. 251

FORREST & MAPLES,

SLAVE DEALERS,

87 Adams Street,
Between Second and Third,

MEMPHIS, TENNESSEE,

Have constantly on hand the best selected assortment of

FIELD HANDS, HOUSE SERVANTS & MECHANICS,

at their Negro Mart, to be found in the city. They are daily receiving from Virginia, Kentucky and Missouri, fresh supplies of likely Young Negroes.

Negroes Sold on Commission, and the highest market price always paid for good stock. Their Jail is capable of containing Three Hundred, and for comfort, neatness and safety, is the best arranged of any in the Union. Persons wishing to purchase, are invited to examine their stock before purchasing elsewhere.

They have on hand at present, Fifty likely young Negroes, comprising Field hands, Mechanics, House and Body Servants, &c.

Forrest's slave advertisement in Memphis City Directory.

Then-colonel Forrest first distinguished himself at the Battle of Fort Donelson in February 1862 when, after chafing over the proposal to surrender, he sneaked himself and 700 cavalrymen from the fort during the siege. At Shiloh two months later, the terrain largely obviated the use of cavalry, so he provided rear guard for the Confederate retreat.

On April 8 a reconnaissance group of Sherman's soldiers came upon one of the Confederate camps protected by Forrest and about 350 men six miles to the southwest of Pittsburg Landing. Forrest spotted Sherman's men and led a cavalry charge across a field toward them, breaking through Sherman's line and causing some of Sherman's men to throw down their weapons and flee. Forrest outdistanced the rest of his men and ended up alone among the enemy. During the hand-to-hand combat, a Union soldier shoved his musket into Forrest's side and fired a shot through Forrest's left hip, the bullet lodging against his spine. Sherman rallied his men and launched a countercharge, forcing Forrest's men back. The Confederates captured about a hundred Union soldiers, but Sherman captured the camp. Some claim Colonel Forrest was the last man wounded in the Battle of Shiloh.

The bullet was removed a week later, and upon recovering from his wound, he set about forming a new cavalry brigade by running this advertisement in the Memphis Appeal from May 18 to 29:

200 Recruits Wanted!

I will receive Two Hundred stout, able-bodied men if they will present themselves at my headquarters by the 1st of June, with good horse and gun. I wish none but those who desire to be actively engaged. My headquarters, for the present, is at Corinth, Mississippi. Come on boys, if you want a heap of fun, and kill some Yankees. N. B. Forrest, Col. Commanding Forrest's Regiment.

On July 13 he raided Murfreesboro, Tennessee, capturing the Union garrison and its supplies. Eight days later he was promoted to brigadier general. In December, against Forrest's wishes, General Bragg reassigned his cavalry to another commander, and Forrest had to raise a new brigade of 2,000 men, many without weapons. Bragg then ordered Forrest, once again against his wishes, to conduct a raid through Tennessee with his raw recruits. Successful, Forrest returned with a larger force than he set out with, while leading Union forces on a wild-goose chase. He disrupted Union operations enough that Grant had to delay his Vicksburg campaign.

THE BATTLE OF ANTIETAM

ALSO KNOWN AS THE BATTLE OF SHARPSBURG
WASHINGTON COUNTY, MARYLAND
SEPTEMBER 17, 1862

COMMANDERS

Union
Maj. Gen. George McClellan

Confederate
Gen. Robert E. Lee

PARTICIPANTS

75,500 (Army of the Potomac)

35,255 (Army of Northern Virginia)

CASUALTIES

Union
2,108 killed
9,540 wounded
753 POWs/MIA

Confederate
1,546 killed
7,752 wounded
1,018 POWs/MIA

VICTORY: UNION (STRATEGICALLY, BUT TACTICALLY INCONCLUSIVE)

OVERVIEW

While Grant was capturing Fort Donelson and fighting at Shiloh, Major-General George McClellan was working his way up the Virginia Peninsula toward Richmond. But McClellan's continuous delays, overly cautious method of fighting, and constant demands for more troops, while greatly overinflating the numbers of the opposing forces, galled President Lincoln. Eventually McClellan claimed he was facing 200,000 Confederates around Richmond, when there actually were only 85,000.

His force was usually larger than the Confederacy's, but he always thought himself outnumbered.

The problem was that McClellan was popular with the soldiers. Lincoln had removed him as general in chief just before the Peninsula campaign, leaving open whether he would be restored once the campaign terminated. When it went badly, Lincoln gave the position to Major-General Henry Halleck.

Halleck ordered McClellan to abandon his failed campaign and bring his army back to Washington, but McClellan continued to stall, hoping to find an opening to capture Richmond and redeem himself, while blaming his "enemies" in Washington—mainly Lincoln, Halleck, and Secretary of War Edwin Stanton—not only for his failures but also of plotting against him and trying to make him fail. Lincoln only wanted him to fight.

On July 11, 1862, a couple of weeks prior to Halleck's appointment, McClellan wrote his wife that people were urging him "to march on Washington & assume the Govt!" A week later, anticipating Halleck's appointment, he wrote her: "I owe no gratitude to any but my own soldiers here; none to the government or to the country. I have done my best for the country; I expect nothing in return; they are my debtors, not I theirs."

Halleck continued to order McClellan to return his army to Washington and to send reinforcements to Major-General John Pope's Army of Virginia, but McClellan stalled again, apparently with devious intent. He wrote his wife: "I have a strong idea that Pope will be thrashed during the coming week—& very badly whipped he will be & ought to be—such a villain as he is ought to bring defeat upon any cause that employs him."

When Halleck telegraphed with news that Pope and Burnside had run into trouble, McClellan wrote his wife: "I believe I have triumphed!!" After more than three long weeks of deferral, he finally began moving his men—after the Second Battle of Manassas was well under way. Only two of the four corps arrived in time to take part in the end of the battle. McClellan's delay contributed to the Union's defeat.

When McClellan returned to Washington, Lincoln, against all advice, placed him in charge of its defenses, knowing him to be an excellent organizer. Explaining this unpopular reappointment, Lincoln told his private secretary, John Hay: "He has acted badly in this matter, but we must use what

tools we have. There is no man in the Army who can man these fortifications and lick these troops of ours into shape half as well as he. Unquestionably he has acted badly toward Pope. He wanted him to fail. That is unpardonable. But he is too useful just now to sacrifice." On another occasion Lincoln said, "If he can't fight himself, he excels in making others fight."

On the Confederate side, after General Joseph Johnston was wounded at the Battle of Seven Pines, Lee took command of the Confederate Army of the Potomac, which then combined with the Army of the Shenandoah under a new name, the Army of Northern Virginia. Lee secured a series of victories, including forcing Major-General Pope and the Union's Army of Virginia to retreat from the Second Battle of Manassas. This time he chased the Federals all the way behind the barricades of Washington, D.C. Pope was relieved of command and sent west to fight Native Americans, and his army was absorbed into the Union's Army of the Potomac.

Emboldened by success, Lee launched a campaign into Maryland to draw the wounded Union army out, away from its entrenched defenses and its base of supplies. After crossing the Potomac and reaching the town of Frederick, Lee sent Stonewall Jackson southwest to take Harper's Ferry and Longstreet northwest to Hagerstown.

When Lee's army marched into Maryland, the Union army went out to fight without a commander. Before one could be appointed, McClellan rushed out to take command, hoping a decisive victory would redeem him and teach those in Washington a lesson. Once in control, McClellan cautiously moved the army through Maryland. Some of his men fought against Longstreet's soldiers at Crampton's Gap, Turner's Gap, and Fox's Gap on September 14 in the Battle of South Mountain, while Stonewall Jackson's soldiers captured Harper's Ferry on the fifteenth. Lee quickly tried to gather his forces at Sharpsburg to make a stand. Because McClellan moved so slowly, Lee was just able to do this.

Antietam (sometimes called the Battle of Sharpsburg) remains the single bloodiest day in American military history. Bloodier battles took place—Spotsylvania Court House, the Wilderness, and Gettysburg—but these were spread out over two or more days.

After the battle Lee headed back across the Potomac, while McClellan refused to pursue him against entreaties from the War Department and President Lincoln. This despite the fact that one-third of his men, held in reserve, hadn't fought in the battle.

McClellan was removed from command and told to await further orders, which never came. Referring to McClellan and Antietam, the U.S. Congress's Committee on the Conduct of the War concluded, "The same mind that controlled the movements upon the [Virginia] Peninsula controlled those in Maryland, and the same general features characterize the one campaign that characterized the other. In each may be seen the same unreadiness to move promptly and act vigorously; the same desire for more troops before advancing; and the same references to the great superiority of numbers on the part of the enemy."

Two years later McClellan ran for president as a Democrat against Lincoln and lost.

THE INVASION OF MARYLAND

Confederate

Lieutenant-General James Longstreet (See biography, page 48.)

When the Second Bull Run campaign closed we had the most brilliant prospects the Confederates ever had. We then possessed an army which, had it been kept together, the Federals would never have dared attack. With such a splendid victory behind us, and such bright prospects ahead, the question arose as to whether or not we should go into Maryland. General Lee, on account of our short supplies, hesitated a little, but I reminded him of my experience in Mexico, where sometimes we were obliged to live two or three days on green corn. I told him we could not starve at that season

of the year so long as the fields were loaded with "roasting ears." Finally he determined to go on, and accordingly crossed the river and went to Frederick City.

On the 6th of September some of our cavalry, moving toward Harper's Ferry, became engaged with some of the Federal artillery near there. General Lee proposed that I organize a force, and go and surround the garrison and capture it. I objected and urged that our troops were worn with marching, were on short rations, and it would be a bad idea to divide our forces while we were in the enemy's country, where he could get information, in six or eight hours, of any movement we might make.

The surrender of the Ferry and the twelve thousand Federal troops there was a matter of only a short time. If the Confederates had been able to stop with that, they might have been well contented with their month's campaign. They had had a series of successes and no defeats; but the division of the army to make this attack on Harper's Ferry was a fatal error, as the subsequent events showed.

While a part of the army [under Stonewall Jackson] had gone toward Harper's Ferry, I had moved up to Hagerstown. In the meantime Pope had been relieved and McClellan was in command of the army, and with ninety thousand refreshed troops was marching out to avenge Second Manassas. The situation was a very serious one for us. McClellan was close upon us. As we moved out of Frederick he came on and occupied that place, and there he came across a lost copy of the order assigning position to the several commands in the Harper's Ferry move.

This lost order has been the subject of much severe comment by Virginians who have written of the war. It was addressed to D. H. Hill, and they charged that its loss was due to him, and that the failure of the campaign was the result of the lost order. As General Hill has proven that he never received the order at his headquarters it must have been lost by some one else.

Ordinarily upon getting possession of such an order the adversary would take it as a decoy, but it seems that General McClellan gave it his confidence, and made his dispositions accordingly. He planned his attack upon D. H. Hill under the impression that I was there with twelve brigades, nine of which were really at Hagerstown, and

R. H. Anderson's division was on Maryland Heights with General [Lafayette] McLaws. Had he exercised due diligence in seeking information from his own resources he would have known better the situation at South Mountain and could have enveloped General D. H. Hill's division on the afternoon of the 13th, or early on the morning of the 14th, and then turned upon McLaws at Maryland Heights, before I could have reached either point.

As it was, McClellan, after finding the order, moved with more confidence on toward South Mountain, where D. H. Hill was stationed as a Confederate rear guard with five thousand men under his command.

As I have stated, my command was at Hagerstown, thirteen miles further on. General Lee was with me, and on the night of the 13th we received information that McClellan was at the foot of South Mountain with his great army. General Lee ordered me to march back to the mountain early the next morning. I suggested that instead of meeting McClellan there, we withdraw Hill and unite my forces and Hill's at Sharpsburg, at the same time explaining that Sharpsburg was a strong defensive position from which we could strike the flank or rear of any force that might be sent to the relief of Harper's Ferry. I endeavored to show him that by making a forced march to Hill my troops would be in an exhausted condition and could not make a proper battle. The general listened patiently enough, but did not change his plans, and directed that I should go back the next day and make a stand at the mountain.

We marched as hurriedly as we could over a hot and dusty road, and reached the mountain about three o'clock in the afternoon, with the troops much scattered and worn. In riding up the mountain to join General Hill I discovered that everything was in such disjointed condition it would be impossible for my troops and Hill's to hold the mountain against such forces as McClellan had there. We got as many troops up as we could, and by putting in detachments here and there managed to hold McClellan in check until night, when Lee ordered the withdrawal to Keedysville, and on the march changed the order, making Sharpsburg the point of assembly.

That night [September 15] we heard of the fall of Harper's Ferry, and Jackson was ordered to Sharpsburg as rapidly as he could come. Right then, we should have retired from Sharpsburg and gone to the Virginia side of the Potomac. The moral effect of our move into Maryland had been lost by our discomfiture at South Mountain, and it was then evident we could not hope to concentrate

in time to do more than make a respectable retreat, whereas by retiring before the battle, we could have claimed a very successful campaign.

On the afternoon of the 15th, the blue uniforms of the Federals appeared among the trees that crowned the heights on the eastern bank of the Antietam. The number increased and larger and larger grew the field of blue until it seemed to stretch as far as the eye could see, and from the tops of the mountains down to the edges of the stream gathered the great army of McClellan, ninety thousand strong. It was an awe-inspiring spectacle as this grand force settled down in sight of the Confederates, then shattered by battles and scattered by long and tiresome marches. On the 16th Jackson came and took position with part of his command on my left.

RUSHING TO DEFEND THE NORTH

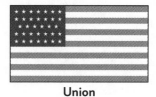

Union

Major-General George McClellan

Major-General George McClellan took over as commanding general of the U.S. Army from Brevet Lieutenant-General Winfield Scott until Lincoln removed him from that position four months later. He also established the Army of the Potomac—the Union's main force—and commanded it during the Peninsula campaign and against General Lee's Maryland campaign.

McClellan's grandfather had been a general in the Revolutionary War. At thirteen McClellan began studying law at the University of Pennsylvania, but after two years he decided to join the military. With the help of President John Tyler, he got into West Point a year ahead of the minimum age of sixteen. He graduated just in time to serve in the Mexican-American War alongside Lee and Beauregard.

In the 1850s he surveyed in Mexico and Washington Territory, and because he spoke French, he was selected to be an official observer of the Crimean War in 1855–56. Based on saddles he saw there, he designed the McClellan saddle, which became standard issue for the U.S. cavalry. He also wrote a manual on cavalry tactics and translated one from the French on bayonet tactics. In 1857 he left the military to become chief engineer and vice president of the Illinois Central Railroad and then president of the Ohio and Mississippi Railroad.

While he didn't believe the government should get involved in the issue of slavery, he strongly opposed secession, so he took command of the Ohio militia. When he reentered the U.S. Army as a major general, he outranked everyone except the general in chief, Winfield Scott. He soon formed the Army of the Potomac and became its first commander. By November 1861 Scott had retired, and McClellan took over as leader of the Union armies.

McClellan worked hard to build the U.S. Army into a disciplined, confident, professional force. He was extremely popular but also too cautious, continually overestimating the number of Confederates he was facing. Unwilling to take risks, he hesitated putting his men in danger. His men appreciated this, but Lincoln didn't. When McClellan did attack, he was slow to use reinforcements and quick to retreat, turning potential victories into draws. Lincoln replaced him with Major-General Ambrose Burnside.

In spite of his shortcomings, General Lee had considerable respect for McClellan. Lee's grand-nephew once said: "I asked him [Lee] which of the Federal generals he considered the greatest, and he answered most emphatically 'McClellan by all odds.'"

The Army of the Potomac was thoroughly exhausted and depleted by its desperate fighting and severe marches in the unhealthy regions of the Chickahominy and afterwards, during the second Bull Run campaign; its trains, administration services and supplies were disorganized or lacking in consequence of the rapidity and manner of its removal from the Peninsula, as well as from the nature of its operations during the second Bull Run campaign. In the departure from the Peninsula, trains, supplies, cavalry, and artillery were often necessarily left at Fort Monroe and Yorktown for lack of vessels, as the important point was to move the infantry divisions as rapidly as possible to the support of General Pope. The divisions of the Army of Virginia were also exhausted and weakened, and their trains and supplies disorganized and deficient by the movements in which they had been engaged.

Had General Lee remained in front of Washington it would have been the part of wisdom to hold our own army quiet until its pressing wants were fully supplied, its organization restored and its ranks filled with recruits in brief, prepared for a campaign. But as the enemy maintained the offensive and crossed the Upper Potomac to threaten or invade Pennsylvania, it became necessary to meet him at any cost notwithstanding the condition of the troops; to put a stop to the invasion, save Baltimore and Washington, and throw him back across the Potomac. Nothing but sheer necessity justified the advance of the Army of the Potomac to South Mountain and Antietam in its then condition.

Partly in order to move men freely and rapidly, partly in consequence of the lack of accurate information as to the exact position and intention of Lee's army, the troops advanced by three main roads. We were then in condition to act according to the development of the enemy's plans and to concentrate rapidly in any position. If Lee threatened our left flank by moving down the river road or by crossing the Potomac at any of the forks from Coon's Ferry upward, there were enough troops on the river road to hold him in check until the rest of the army could move over to support them; if Lee took up a position behind the Seneca near Frederick the whole army could be rapidly concentrated in that direction to attack him in force; if he moved upon Baltimore the entire army could rapidly be thrown in his rear and his retreat cut off; if he moved by Gettysburg or Chambersburg upon York or Carlisle we were equally in position to throw ourselves in his rear.

The first thing was to gain accurate information as to Lee's movements, and meanwhile to push the work of supply and reorganization as rapidly as possible.

General Lee and I knew each other well in the days before the war. We had served together in Mexico and commanded against each other in the Peninsula. I had the highest respect for his ability as a commander, and knew that he was not a general to be trifled with or carelessly afforded an opportunity of striking a fatal blow. Each of us naturally regarded his own army as the better, but each entertained the highest respect for the endurance, courage, and fighting qualities of the opposing army; and this feeling extended to the officers and men. It was perfectly natural under these circumstances that both of us should exercise a certain amount of caution; I in my endeavors to ascertain Lee's strength, position, and intentions before I struck the final blow; he to abstain from any extended movements of invasion, and to hold his army well in hand until he could be satisfied as to the condition of the Army of the Potomac after its second Bull Run campaign, and as to the intentions of its commander.

McClellan was writing this account of the Battle of Antietam when he died in 1885. His unfinished manuscript ended above. Fortunately, we have his earlier writings on the subject.

[On September 15] I went rapidly to the front by the main road, being received by the troops, as I passed them, with the wildest enthusiasm. Near Keedysville I met Sumner, who told me that the enemy were in position in strong force, and took me to a height in front of Keedysville whence a view of the position could be obtained. He [the enemy] occupied a strong position on the heights, on the west side of Antietam creek, displaying a large force of infantry and cavalry, with numerous batteries of artillery. After a rapid examination of the position I found that it was too late to attack that day.

The corps were not all in their positions until the next morning after sunrise. On all favorable points the enemy's artillery was posted, and their reserves, hidden from view by the hills on which their line of battle was formed, could manoeuvre unobserved by our army, and from the shortness of their line could rapidly reinforce any point threatened by our attack. Their position, stretching across the angle formed by the Potomac and Antietam, their flanks and rear protected by these streams, was one of the strongest to be found in this region of country, which is well adapted to defensive warfare.

It was afternoon before I could move the troops to their positions for attack, being compelled to spend the morning in reconnoitring the new position taken up by the enemy, examining the ground, finding fords, clearing the approaches, and hurrying up the ammunition and supply-trains.

At daylight on the 17th the action was commenced by the skirmishers of the Pennsylvania reserves. The whole of Gen. Hooker's corps was soon engaged.

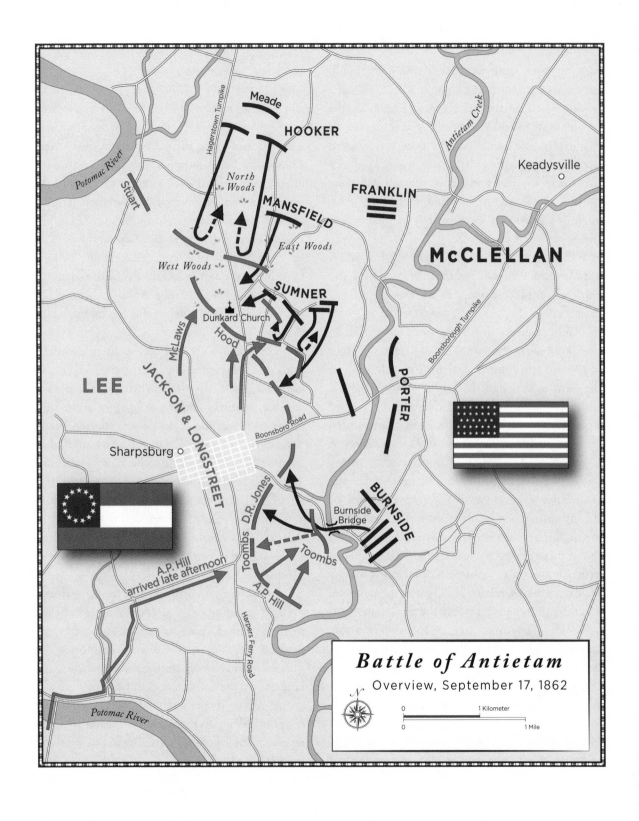

Meade

HOOKER

Hagerstown Turnpike

North
Woods

MANSFIELD

East Woods

FRANKLIN

Keadysville

McCLELLAN

West Woods

SUMNER

Dunkard Church

Hood

McLaws

LEE

JACKSON & LONGSTREET

Boonsboro Road

PORTER

Boonsborough Turnpike

Sharpsburg

D.R. Jones

Burnside
Bridge

BURNSIDE

A.P. Hill
arrived late afternoon

Toombs

Toombs

A.P. Hill

Harpers Ferry Road

Potomac River

Stuart

Potomac River

Antietam Creek

Battle of Antietam

Overview, September 17, 1862

N

0   1 Kilometer

0   1 Mile

AERIAL RECONNAISSANCE

Union War Balloons, September 1861–August 1863

Usually cavalry or scouts conducted reconnaissance during the Civil War, but it was hard to determine what the other side was doing. Then, in September 1861, the Union introduced a new form of technology: observation balloons.

The first military use of balloons occurred in France in 1794, but although the U.S. military discussed using balloons over the next half century, it didn't get around to using them until the Civil War in the battles of Yorktown, Seven Pines (Fair Oaks), the Seven Days Battles, Antietam, Fredericksburg, Vicksburg, and smaller battles in between.

Thaddeus Lowe, who had flown balloons for several years as a showman, put on a demonstration for President Lincoln and received an Army contract to establish and direct the Union's primary balloon program. Unofficially known as the Balloon Corps, Lowe's small group of civilian aeronauts had six hydrogen balloons, each with two gas-generating wagons. The three larger balloons could carry two men and a telegraph key set to a height of 5,000 feet—the end of their tethers. The smaller one-man balloons stopped at 1,000 feet.

Observation balloons were cumbersome, unruly, and dangerous. Amazingly, none of them ever caught fire, as hydrogen is highly flammable. From 1,000 feet the observer would discern the enemy's numbers, position, armaments, and whatever else he could spot. With a telescope on a clear day, an aeronaut had a radius of vision of thirty miles.

The Confederates understandably didn't like being observed from above and generally shot at the balloons, though rarely hitting them. Just in case, aeronauts eventually lined their baskets with lead. The balloons generally were safe from gun and artillery fire above 300 feet. The balloons forced the Confederates to hide or disguise their movements, camouflage their large artillery, and black out their camps at night. They even offered a $750 reward for Thaddeus Lowe since he headed the corps and did most of the flying. Newspapers called him "the most shot-at man of the Civil War." Not officially in the military, he probably would have been hanged as a spy if caught.

Often commanders didn't know what to do with the balloons. Shells fired at balloons came close to hitting Union soldiers on the ground, so they didn't like the artillery attention they attracted. Some felt the program was ineffective and more suited to the circus. German emigrant and aeronaut John Steiner suffered considerable hostility and derision from Brigadier-General John Pope's staff when he was sent to Cairo, Illinois. He complained to Lowe: "I can not git eny ascistence here. Thay say thay know nothing about my balloon business. Thay even laugh ad me. […] Give me a paper from Headvuarters to show theas blockheads hoo I am." Again, a couple of weeks later: "All the officers hear are as dum as a set of asses."

On the other hand, balloon-sourced intelligence pleased many generals, and it definitely influenced some battles. A number of generals even went up in the balloons: George McClellan, Daniel Sickles, George Stoneman, Irvin McDowell, Benjamin Butler, and particularly Fitz John Porter, who went up more than a hundred times. Custer was also one of the first aeronauts.

The Union used observation balloons until August 1863, when bureaucratic wrangling and the shortsightedness of officials finally deflated the program. In all, Union war balloons made more than 3,000 ascents.

The Confederate Air Corps, April 13, 1862–1863

The first known Confederate balloon was used at Yorktown on April 13, 1862. A hot-air balloon made of cotton fabric with a wooden frame, it used a stove burning pine knots soaked in turpentine for lift. Their second balloon was used from June 27 to July 4, 1862, during the Seven Days Battles. This one, called the *Gazelle*, consisted of bolts of silk, giving it a patchwork appearance and earning it the nickname of "silk-dress balloon." They filled it at Richmond's gasworks and hauled it by railroad or boat to wherever they wanted to launch it. When it was captured, they made another petticoat balloon with a "bright flowered pattern, squared off by multi-colored plaids and iridescent blues," which they used in and around Charleston, South Carolina, until it broke loose from its mooring and was lost.

"The Hardest Fought Battle"

Confederate

General John Bell Hood

John Bell Hood was born in Kentucky. His cousin was G. W. Smith, who became a Confederate major general. Future Union generals James McPherson and John Schofield were his classmates at West Point, and George Thomas his artillery instructor. He later fought all of them. West Point's superintendent, Colonel Robert E. Lee, became his commander.

As a brevet second lieutenant, he served in the California infantry, then in Texas in the U.S. Cavalry. He was twenty-nine when Beauregard bombarded Fort Sumter, and since his home state of Kentucky was neutral, he resigned from the U.S. Army to join the Texas cavalry and was soon promoted to colonel of the Fourth Texas Infantry. When it became part of the Confederate Army of the Potomac in 1862, he rose to brigadier general and his unit became known as Hood's Texas Brigade. He was the youngest Confederate to achieve the rank of full general.

[At the opening of battle, early in the morning:] Not far distant in our front were drawn up, in close array, heavy columns of Federal infantry; not less than two corps were in sight to oppose my small command, numbering, approximately, two thousand effectives. Notwithstanding the overwhelming odds of over ten to one against us, we drove the enemy from the wood and corn field back upon his reserves, and forced him to abandon his guns on our left.

This most deadly combat raged till our last round of ammunition was expended. The First Texas Regiment had lost, in the corn field, fully two-thirds of its number; and whole ranks of brave men, whose deeds were unrecorded save in the hearts of loved ones at home, were mowed down in heaps to the right and left. Never before was I so continuously troubled with fear that my horse would further injure some wounded fellow soldier, lying helpless upon the ground.

Our right flank, during this short, but seemingly long, space of time, was toward the main line of the Federals, and, after several ineffectual efforts to procure reinforcements and our last shot had been fired, I ordered my troops back to Dunkard Church.

Upon the arrival of McLaws's Division, we marched to the rear, renewed our supply of ammunition, and returned to our position in the wood, near the church, which ground we held till a late hour in the afternoon, when we moved somewhat further to the right and bivouacked for the night. With the close of this bloody day ceased the hardest fought battle of the war.

FIGHTING AT THE DUNKARD CHURCH

Confederate

Lieutenant-General Jubal Early (See biography, page 7.)

The facts were, as I subsequently ascertained from the brigade commanders, that, at light, after skirmishing along the front of Lawton's and Trimble's brigades in a piece of woods occupied by him, the enemy had opened a very heavy enfilading fire [fire from the side down a line of troops] from the batteries on the opposite side of the Antietam, and then advanced very heavy columns of infantry against them, at the same time pouring a destructive fire of canister and shells into their ranks from the front. Lawton's brigade had sustained a loss of very nearly one-half, Hays of more than one-half, and Trimble's of more than a third. General Hood then came to their relief and the shattered remnants of these

brigades, their ammunition being exhausted, retired to the rear.

Jackson's division in the meantime had been very heavily engaged, and had shared a like fate, all of it that was left being what I found Grigsby and Stafford rallying, after General Jones had retired from the field stunned by the concussion of a shell bursting near him, and General Starke, who had succeeded him, had been killed.

After having discovered that there was nothing of the division left on the field for me to command except my own brigade, and seeing that, what I supposed were Hood's troops, were very hard pressed, and would probably have to retire before overpowering numbers, I sent Major J. P.

Wilson to look after the brigades which had gone to the rear, and I rode to find General Jackson to inform him of the condition of things in front.

I found the General on a hill in rear of the Dunkard Church, where some batteries were posted, and when I informed him of the condition of things, he directed me to return to my brigade and resist the enemy until he could send me some reinforcements, which he promised to do as soon as he could obtain them.

After my return, the enemy continued to press up towards the woods in which I was, in very heavy force, and I sent Major Hale, my Assistant Adjutant General, to let General Jackson know that the danger was imminent, and he returned with the information that the promised reinforcements would be sent immediately. Just as Major Hale returned, a battery opened on the Hagerstown pike where the field, or plateau, and woods joined. This was in rear of my right flank and not more than two hundred yards from it. I had been anxiously looking to my front and left flank, not dreaming that there was any immediate danger to my right, as I had seen our troops on the eastern side of the pike, at an advanced position, engaged with the enemy, and I took it for granted that this was one of our batteries which had opened on the enemy, but it was one of the enemy's batteries. Major Hale examined it himself and immediately informed me of the fact, but I doubted it until I rode to the edge of the woods and saw for myself that it was really one of the enemy's batteries, firing along the pike in the direction of the Dunkard Church.

While I was looking at it for a minute to satisfy myself, I saw a heavy column of infantry move up by its side. The fact was that Hood, after resisting with great obstinacy immensely superior numbers, had fallen back to the vicinity of the Dunkard Church, and the enemy had advanced to this position. My position now was very critical, as there was nothing between Hood and myself, thus leaving an interval of from a quarter to a half mile between my command and the rest of the army. Fortunately, however, my troops were concealed from this body of the enemy, or their destruction would have been inevitable, as it was nearly between them and the rest of the army, and the body, moving up on the left in my front, had now got into the woods. Hoping the promised reinforcements would arrive in time, I quietly threw back my right flank under cover of the woods to prevent being taken in the rear.

The situation was most critical and the necessity most pressing, as it was apparent that if the enemy got possession of this woods, possession of the hills in their rear would immediately follow, and then, across to our rear on the road leading back to the Potomac, would have been easy. In fact the possession of these hills would have enabled him to take our whole line in reverse, and a disastrous defeat must have followed.

I determined to hold on to the last moment. I saw the column on my right and rear suddenly move into the woods in the direction of the rear of the church. I could not now remain still, and I at once put my brigade in motion by the right flank on a line parallel to that of the enemy's movements, skirmishing with the enemy coming up on the left. The limestone ledges enabled my troops to keep out of view of the enemy moving in the woods on my right, and they moved rapidly so as to get up with them. I now saw two or three brigades moving in line to our assistance, at the further end of the woods, and my brigade was faced to the front as soon as the whole of it had passed from behind the ledge, and opened fire on the enemy, who commenced retiring towards the pike in great confusion, after delivering one or two volleys.

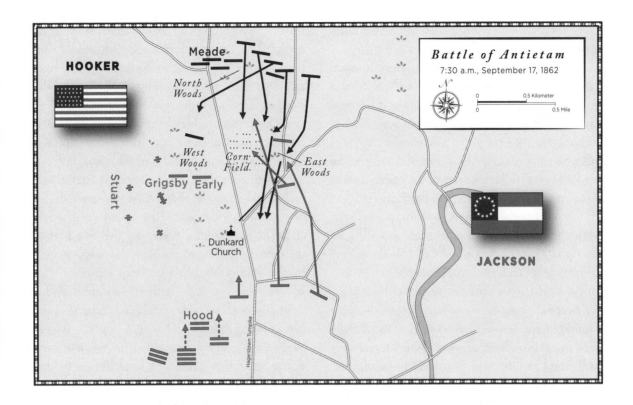

I then saw other troops of the enemy moving rapidly across the plateau from the pike to the column. Just as I was reforming my line, Semmes brigade, and two regiments of Barksdale's brigade, of McLaws' division, and Anderson's brigade of D. R. Jones division came up, advanced and swept the enemy from the woods into the fields, and the enemy retreated in great disorder to another body of woods beyond that from which he had been thus driven. As soon as his infantry had retired the enemy opened a tremendous fire with canister and shell upon the woods occupied by us, which was continued for some time.

During his advance, the enemy's columns had received a galling fire from the guns under General Stuart on a hill in the rear of our left which contributed very materially to the repulse, and

General Stuart pursued the retreating force on its flank for some distance, with his pieces of artillery and the remnant of the 13th Virginia Regiment.

We remained in position during the rest of the day, as did the troops on my left, and those immediately on my right. The enemy made no further attack on us on this part of the line. There were, however, some attempts against our line further to the right, and late in the afternoon a fierce attack was made on our extreme right by Burnside's corps, which drove some of our troops from the bridge across the Antietam on that flank, and was forcing back our right, when some of A. P. Hill's brigades, which were just arriving from Harper's Ferry, went to the assistance of the troops engaged on that flank, and the enemy was driven back in considerable confusion.

This affair, which terminated just before dark, closed the fighting on the 17th.

The enemy in my immediate front showed a great anxiety to get possession of his dead and wounded on that part of the ground, and several flags of truce approached us, but, I believe, without authority from the proper source. However, a sort of informal truce prevailed for a time, and some of the dead and very badly wounded of the enemy and of that part of our army which had been engaged first on the morning of the 17th, were exchanged even while the skirmishers were firing at each other on the right. This was finally stopped and the enemy informed that no flag of truce could be recognized unless it came from the headquarters of his army.

Since crossing the Rappahannock we had been without regular supplies of food, and had literally been living from hand to mouth. Our troops were badly shod and many of them became barefooted, and they were but indifferently clothed and without protection against the weather. Many of them had become exhausted from the fatigues of the campaign, and the long and rapid marches which they had made while living on short rations and a weakening diet and many were foot-sore from want of shoes; so that the straggling from these causes, independent of that incident to all armies, had been frightful before we crossed the Potomac, and had continued up to the time of the battle.

The truth is that the substantial victory was with us, and if our army had been in reach of reinforcements, it would have been a decisive one; but we were more than 200 miles from the point from which supplies of ammunition were to be obtained, and any reinforcements which could have been spared to us were much further off, while large reinforcements were marching to McClellan's aid. We had, therefore, to recross the Potomac.

The question had been mooted as to the propriety of the campaign into Maryland, and in regard thereto I will say: General Lee, on assuming command of the army at Richmond, had found that city, the seat of the Confederate Government, beleaguered by a vast army, while all Northern Virginia, including the best part of the beautiful valley of the Shenandoah, was held by the enemy. With a herculean effort, he had broken through the cordon surrounding his army, and with inferior numbers fallen upon the beleaguering enemy, and sent it cowering to the banks of the lower James. He had then moved north, and, after a series of hard fought battles, had hurled the shattered remains of the army that had been marauding through Northern Virginia, with all the reinforcements sent from the lately besieging army, into the fortifications around Washington. With the diminished columns of the army with which he accomplished all this, he had crossed the Potomac, captured an important stronghold defended by a strong force, securing a large amount of artillery, small arms, and stores of all kinds, and had fought a great battle with the newly reorganized and heavily reinforced and recruited army of the enemy, which later was so badly crippled that it was not able to resume the offensive for near two months.

HOLDING THE LINE WITH TWO CANNONS

Confederate

Lieutenant-General James Longstreet (See biography, page 48.)

The battle ebbed and flowed with terrific slaughter on both sides. The Federals fought with wonderful bravery and the Confederates clung to their ground with heroic courage as hour after hour they were mown down like grass. The fresh troops of McClellan literally tore into shreds the already ragged army of Lee, but the Confederates never gave back.

I remember at one time they were surging up against us with fearful numbers. I was occupying the left over by Hood, whose ammunition gave out. He retired to get a fresh supply. Soon after, the Federals moved up against us in great masses.

We were under the crest of a hill occupying a position that ought to have been held by from four to six brigades. The only troops there were Cooke's regiment of North Carolina infantry without a cartridge. As I rode along the line with my staff I saw two pieces of the Washington artillery, but there were not enough men to man them. The gunners had been either killed or wounded.

This was a fearful situation for the Confederate center. I put my staff-officers to the guns while I held their horses. It was easy to see that if the Federals broke through our line there, the Confederate army would be cut in two and probably destroyed, for we were already badly whipped and were only holding our ground by sheer force of desperation. Cooke sent me word that his ammunition was out.

I replied that he must hold his position as long as he had a man left. He responded that he would show his colors as long as there was a man alive to hold them up. We loaded up our little guns with canister and sent a rattle of hail into the Federals as they came up over the crest of the hill.

There was more business to the square inch in that little battery than in any I ever saw, and it shot harder and faster and with a sort of human energy as it seemed to realize that it was to hold the thousands of Federals at bay or the battle was lost. So warm was the reception we gave them that they dodged back behind the crest of the hill. We sought to make them believe we had many batteries before them instead of only two little guns.

As the Federals would come up they would see the colors of the North Carolina regiment waving placidly and then would receive a shower of canister. We made it lively while it lasted. In the meantime General Chilton, General Lee's chief of staff, made his way to me and asked, "Where are the troops you are holding your line with?"

I pointed to my two pieces and to Cooke's regiment and replied, "There they are; but that regiment hasn't a cartridge."

Chilton's eyes popped as though they would come out of his head, he struck spurs to his horse and away he went to General Lee. I suppose he made some remarkable report.

Meantime General Lee was over toward our right, where Burnside was trying to cross to make an attack there. [Brigadier General Robert] Toombs, who had been assigned as guard at that point, did handsome service. His troops were footsore and worn from marching, and he had only twelve hundred men to meet Burnside, who had ten thousand. The little band fought bravely, but the Federals were pressing them slowly back. The delay that Toombs caused saved that part of the battle, however, for at the last moment A. P. Hill came in to reënforce him and D. H. Hill discovered a good place for a battery and opened with it. Thus the Confederates were enabled to drive the Federals back, and when night settled down the army of Lee was still in possession of the field. But it was dearly bought, for thousands of brave soldiers were dead on the field and many gallant commands were torn as a forest in a cyclone.

It was heartrending to see how Lee's army had been slashed by the day's fighting. Nearly one-fourth of the troops who went into the battle were killed or wounded that day. We were so badly crushed that at the close of the day ten thousand fresh troops could have come in and taken Lee's army and everything it had. But McClellan did not know it, and even feared when Burnside was pressed back that Sharpsburg was a Confederate victory, and that he would have to retire.

As it was, when night settled down both armies were content to stay where they were.

During the progress of the battle of Sharpsburg General Lee and I were riding along my line and D. H. Hill's, when we received a report of movements of the enemy and started up the ridge to make a reconnoissance. General Lee and I dismounted, but Hill declined to do so. I said to him, "If you insist on riding up there and drawing

Gunsmoke from the Battle of Antietam can be seen to the right, while horses and their artillery caissons are in the field to the left.

the fire, give us a little interval so that we may not be in the line of the fire when they open upon you."

General Lee and I stood on the top of the crest with our glasses, looking at the movements of the Federals on the rear left. After a moment I turned my glass to the right and the Federal left. As I did so I noticed a puff of white smoke from the mouth of a cannon.

"There is a shot for you," I said to General Hill.

The gunner was a mile away, and the cannon-shot came whisking through the air for three or four seconds and took off the front legs of the horse that Hill sat on and let the animal down on his pegs. The horse's head was so low and his croup so high that Hill was in a most ludicrous position. With one foot in the stirrup he made several efforts

to get the other leg over the croup, but failed. Finally we prevailed on him to try the other end of the horse and he got down. He had a third horse shot under him before the close of the battle.

That was the second best shot I ever saw. The best was at Yorktown. There a Federal officer came out in front of our line, and sitting down to his little platting table began to make a map. One of our officers carefully sighted a gun, touched it off, and dropped a shell into the hands of the man at the little table.

The great mistake of the campaign was the division of Lee's army. If General Lee had kept his forces together he could not have suffered defeat. The next year, when on our way to Gettysburg, there was the same situation of affairs at Harper's Ferry, but we let it alone.

General Robert E. Lee (See biography, page 9.)

STRAGGLERS

Confederate

In a letter to President Davis dated September 21, 1862, Lee discussed one of the major problems he faced.

The army is resting to-day on the Opequon, below Martinsburg [in what would become West Virginia]. Its present efficiency is greatly paralyzed by the loss to its ranks of the numerous stragglers. I have taken every means in my power from the beginning to correct this evil, which has increased instead of diminished. A great

many men belonging to the army never entered Maryland at all; many returned after getting there, while others who crossed the river kept aloof. The stream has not lessened since crossing the Potomac, though the cavalry has been constantly employed in endeavoring to arrest it. It occasions me the greatest concern in the future operations of the army. Some immediate legislation, in my opinion, is required, and the most summary punishment should be authorized. It ought to be construed into desertion in face of the enemy, and thus brought under the Rules and Articles of War.

> Thus it very often happens in war that there are on each side, two armies in the field, one of the fighting men with the colors, the other of stragglers and marauders in the rear; the relative strength of these two armies depends upon the state of discipline and the peculiar circumstances of the time.
>
> —Union major general George McClellan

To give you an idea of its extent in some brigades, I will mention that, on the morning after the battle of the 17th, General Evans reported to me on the field, where he was holding the front position, that he had but 120 of his brigade present, and that the next brigade to his, that of General Garnett, consisted of but 100 men. General Pendleton reported that the brigades of Generals Lawton and Armistead, left to guard the ford at Shepherdstown, together contained but 600 men. This is a woeful condition of affairs, and I am pained to state it, but you ought not to be ignorant of the fact, in order, if possible, that you may apply the proper remedy.

It is true that the army has had hard work to perform, long and laborious marches, and large odds to encounter in every conflict, but not greater than were endured by our revolutionary fathers, or than what any army must encounter to be victorious. There are brilliant examples of endurance and valor on the part of those who have had to bear the brunt in the battle and the labor in the field in consequence of this desertion of their comrades.

Battlefield Promotion

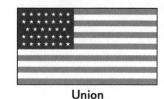

Union

Major-General George Meade

Major-General George Meade is best known for defeating Lee at the Battle of Gettysburg just three days after assuming command of the Army of the Potomac, a position he held until the end of the war.

Meade's father was a naval agent and consul to Spain until shortly after Meade's birth in Cádiz. Meade fought in the Second Seminole War in Florida until illness forced him to be reassigned. For a short time he became a civilian engineer, surveying future railway lines. In 1842 he reenlisted as a second lieutenant in the Corps of Topographical Engineers. He fought in the Mexican-American War, receiving a promotion to brevet first lieutenant. Returning to the United States, he built lighthouses.

When the Civil War started, he received an appointment as brigadier general of the Pennsylvania Volunteers, his brigade becoming part of McClellan's Army of the Potomac for the Peninsula campaign.

He was badly wounded in one of the Seven Days Battles but recovered and returned to his command. He replaced Major-General Joseph Hooker as commander of the Army of the Potomac right before Gettysburg.

According to General Grant, "He was brave and conscientious, and commanded the respect of all who knew him. He was unfortunately of a temper that would get beyond his control, at times, and make him speak to officers of high rank in the most offensive manner. No one saw this fault more plainly than he himself, and no one regretted it more." His short temper earned him the nickname "Old Snapping Turtle."

Brigadier-General George Meade wrote the following letters to his wife:

September 18, 1862

Yesterday and the day before my division commenced the battle, and was in the thickest of it. I was hit by a spent grape-shot, giving me a severe contusion on the right thigh, but not breaking the skin. When General Hooker was wounded, General McClellan placed me in command of the army corps, over General Ricketts's head, who ranked me. This selection is a great compliment, and answers all my wishes in regard to my desire to have my services appreciated. I cannot ask for more, and am truly grateful for the merciful manner I have been protected, and for the good fortune that has attended me. I go into the action to-day as the commander of an army corps. If I survive, my two stars are secure, and if I fall, you will have my reputation to live on.

September 20, 1862

The battle of the day previous had been a very severe one, and our army was a good deal broken and somewhat demoralized—so much so that it was deemed hazardous to risk an offensive movement on our part until the reinforcements arriving from Washington should reach the scene

of action. Yesterday morning, at early dawn, we moved forward, when lo! the bird had flown, and we soon ascertained from prisoners, taken straggling on the field, and from the evidences the field itself bore, that we had hit them much harder than they had us, and that in reality our battle was a victory.

At South Mountain, on the 14th, I was on the extreme right flank, had the conduct of the whole operations, and never saw General Hooker, commanding the corps, after getting his instructions, till the whole affair was over. I must, however, do Hooker the justice to say that he promptly gave me credit for what I did, and have reason to believe it was his urgent appeal to McClellan, that I was the right man to take his place when he was wounded, which secured my being assigned to the command of the corps.

October 5, 1862

Since writing to you the President of the United States has visited our camp and reviewed our corps. I had the distinguished honor of accompanying him to the battle-field, where General McClellan pointed out to him the various phases of the day, saying here it was that Meade did this and there Meade did that; which all was very gratifying to me. He seemed very much interested in all the movements of Hooker's corps.

I prepared a statement, showing that Hooker's corps on paper was thirty-one thousand five hundred strong; that of this number there were present for duty only twelve thousand, and of these, a numerical list, made on the day of the battle, after we came out of action, showed only seven thousand. It would take too much time to explain this apparent paradox. Suffice it to say, it results from a serious evil, due to the character and constitution of our volunteer force, and from the absence of that control over the men, which is the consequence of the inefficiency of the officers commanding them—I mean regimental and company officers.

Three days after the battle this corps numbered twelve thousand officers and men, though on the evening of the battle we could only muster seven thousand. Now, the difference of five thousand constituted the cowards, skulkers, men who leave the ground with the wounded and do not return for days, the stragglers on the march, and all such characters, which are to be found in every army, but never in so great a ratio as in this volunteer force of ours. I believe all that saves us is the fact that they are no better off on the other side.

"A GREAT BATTLE HAS BEEN FOUGHT"

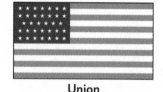

Union

Major-General Joseph Hooker

After the Union's defeat at the first Battle of Fredericksburg, Major-General Joseph Hooker replaced Major-General Ambrose Burnside as commander of the Army and Department of the Potomac, launching the Chancellorsville campaign. He held this position for five months until Meade replaced him after petty bickering with U.S. Army headquarters.

Hooker's grandfather had been a captain in the Revolutionary War. Assigned to the artillery, Hooker fought in the Second Seminole War and received several promotions during the Mexican-American War. He left the military after testifying against Major-General Winfield Scott in the insubordination court-martial of Major-General Gideon Pillow. As a civilian, Hooker became a farmer and developer in Sonoma, California, where he gained a reputation for drinking and gambling. After trying to reenter the military and being ignored, he became a colonel in the California militia.

Borrowing money to travel back to the East Coast, he eventually talked Lincoln into giving him a command. As a brigadier general of volunteers, he was assigned to the defenses of Washington, D.C., and became part of the Army of the Potomac during the Peninsula campaign. He took over from Burnside as commander of the Army and Department of the Potomac.

He was popular with his men, but senior officers alongside and above him didn't trust him. Some hated him. Grant, after complimenting Hooker on one maneuver, wrote, "I nevertheless regarded him as a dangerous man. He was not subordinate to his superiors. He was ambitious to the extent of caring nothing for the rights of others."

Centreville, Md., Wednesday, September 17

A great battle has been fought and we are victorious. I had the honor to open it yesterday afternoon, and it continued until ten o'clock this morning, when I was wounded, and compelled to quit the field.

The battle was fought with great violence on both sides. The carnage has been awful. I only regret that I was not permitted to take part in the operations until they were concluded, for I had counted on either capturing their army or driving them into the Potomac.

My wound has been painful, but it is not one that will be likely to lay me up. I was shot through the foot.

"A MASTERPIECE OF ART"

Union

Major-General George McClellan (See biography, page 79.)

After a night of anxious deliberation and a full and careful survey of the situation and condition of our army, the strength and position of the enemy, I concluded that the success of an attack on the 18th was not certain. I am aware of the fact that, under ordinary circumstances, a general is expected to risk a battle if he has a reasonable prospect of success; but at this critical juncture I should have had a narrow view of the condition of the country had I been willing to hazard another battle with less than an absolute assurance of success. At that moment—Virginia lost, Washington menaced, Maryland invaded—the national cause could afford no risks of defeat. One battle lost, and almost all would have been lost. Lee's army might then have marched as it pleased on Washington, Baltimore, Philadelphia, or New York.

In the last battles the enemy was undoubtedly greatly superior to us in number, and it was only by very hard fighting that we gained the advantage we did. As it was, the result was at one period very doubtful, and we had all we could do to win the day. If the enemy receives considerable reinforcements and we none, it is possible that I may have too much on my hands in the next battle.

McClellan wrote privately to his wife:

[September 18, 1862, near Sharpsburg]
We fought yesterday a terrible battle against the entire rebel army. The battle continued fourteen hours and was terrific; the fighting on both sides was superb. The general result was in our favor; that is to say, we gained a great deal of ground and held it. It was a success, but whether a decided victory depends upon what occurs to-day. I hope that God has given us a great success. It is all in His hands, and there I am content to leave it. The spectacle yesterday was the grandest I could conceive of; nothing could be more sublime. Those in whose judgment I rely tell me that I fought the battle splendidly and that it was a masterpiece of art.

[First letter, September 20, 1862, near Sharpsburg]
Our victory was complete, and the disorganized rebel army has rapidly returned to Virginia, its dreams of "invading Pennsylvania" dissipated for ever. I feel some little pride in having, with a beaten and demoralized army, defeated Lee so utterly and saved the North so completely. Well, one of these days history will, I trust, do me justice in deciding that it was not my fault that the campaign of the Peninsula was not successful.

Lincoln joked that the ailment McClellan suffered from was "the Slows." A number of days after the battle, Lee's exhausted and starved army sat just ten miles west of McClellan. For more than a month, Lincoln and the War Department urged McClellan to pursue Lee, but he refused, defying orders and using all sorts of excuses. Exasperated, Lincoln sent him a telegram on October 25: "I have just read your despatch about sore tongue and fatigued horses. Will you pardon me for asking what the horses of your army have done since the battle of Antietam that fatigues anything?"

McClellan's cavalry had in fact been chasing Jeb Stuart's cavalry as it circled all the way around the Army of the Potomac, just as Stuart did in Virginia during McClellan's Peninsula campaign.

I knew McClellan, and had great confidence in him. I have, for that matter, never lost my respect for McClellan's character, nor my confidence in his loyalty and ability. I have never studied his campaigns enough to make up my mind as to his military skill, but all my impressions are in his favor. But the test which was applied to him would be terrible to any man, being made a major-general at the beginning of the war. It has always seemed to me that the critics of McClellan do not consider this vast and cruel responsibility—the war, a new thing to all of us, the army new, everything to do from the outset, with a restless people and Congress. McClellan was a young man when this devolved upon him, and if he did not succeed, it was because the conditions of success were so trying.

If McClellan had gone into the war as Sherman, Thomas, or Meade had fought his way along and up, I have no reason to suppose that he would not have won as high a distinction as any of us. McClellan's main blunder was in allowing himself political sympathies, and in permitting himself to become the critic of the President, and in time his rival.

—General Ulysses S. Grant,
writing long after the war had ended

WHAT MIGHT HAVE BEEN

Confederate

Lieutenant-General James Longstreet (See biography, page 48.)

In the confusion about Washington, incident to the Bull Run campaign, General McClellan was ordered to receive the retreating columns and post them to defend and hold their fortified lines. He had not emerged from the clouds that hung about his untoward campaign in Virginia, but, familiar with the provisions that had been made for defence, he was most available for the service.

He had hardly posted the troops and arranged the garrison when he found that the Confederates, instead of moving against his fortifications, had turned the head of their columns north, and were marching to invade Union territory. He was quick to discover his opportunity, and, after posting guards for the works about the capital, assumed command of the army and took the field, lest another commander should be assigned. His clouded fame and assumption of authority committed him to early aggressive work. He had nothing to lose, but the world to gain, and that upon the field of battle.

All that the Confederates had to do was to hold the army in hand and draw the enemy to a field wide enough for manoeuvre; then call him to his battle. It is possible that ragged affairs about the mountain passes might have given him safe retreat to his capital, leaving the army of the South afield, a free lance. It had been arranged that the Southern President should join the troops, and from the head of his victorious army call for recognition.

It is about time the North understood the truth that the entire South, man, woman, and child, is against us, armed and determined. It will call for a million men for several years to put them down. They are more confident than ever; none seem to doubt their independence, but some hope to conquer the Northwest. My opinion is, there never can be peace and we must fight it out. I guess you now see how, from the very first, I argued that you all underestimated the task. None of you would admit for a moment that after a year's fighting the enemy would still threaten Washington, Cincinnati, and St. Louis.

You doubtless, like most Americans, attribute our want of success to bad generals. I do not. With us you insist the boys, the soldiers, govern. They must have this or that, or will cry down their leaders in the newspapers, so no general can achieve much. They fight or run as they please, and of course it is the general's fault. Until this is cured, you must not look for success.

—MAJOR-GENERAL SHERMAN TO HIS BROTHER,
SEPTEMBER 22, 1862

The full significance of Sharpsburg to the Federal authorities lay in the fact that they needed a victory on which to issue the Emancipation Proclamation, which President Lincoln had prepared two months before and had held in abeyance under advice of members of his Cabinet until the Union arms should win a success. Although this battle was by no means so complete a victory as the President wished, and he was sorely vexed with General McClellan for not pushing it to completion, it was made the most of as a victory, and his Emancipation Proclamation was issued on the 22d of September, five days after the battle. This was one of the decisive political events of the war, and at once put the great struggle outwardly and openly upon the basis where it had before only rested by tacit and covert understanding.

If the Southern army had been carefully held in hand, refreshed by easy marches and comfortable supplies, the proclamation could not have found its place in history. On the other hand, the Southern President would have been in Maryland at the head of his army with his manifesto for peace and independence.

The Emancipation Proclamation represented an important step in ending slavery but also had significance in another way. After the South seceded, Britain and France debated whether to recognize the Confederacy. In November 1861 a U.S. warship stopped a British ship and removed two Confederate diplomats. The Trent Affair, as it was known, brought Britain and the Union dangerously close to war. Meanwhile, Russia, which had lost the Crimean War to France and Britain, made it clear that it would side with the Union and even sent its fleets on a goodwill tour of America's Pacific and Atlantic coasts with secret orders to prevent Britain and France from sending convoys of troops and supplies to the Confederacy. Preparing for war, Britain shipped 11,000 troops to Canada with orders to capture New York City if war broke out. The Civil War was verging on world war.

Lincoln released the diplomats, but the issue of international recognition of the Confederacy remained. The Emancipation Proclamation brought slavery back to the forefront of the conflict with the South. Britain had abolished slavery about twenty years earlier and strongly opposed it. Lincoln's proclamation made it more difficult for it to side with the Confederacy, further averting world war.

President Lincoln on the battlefield at Antietam, Maryland, in October 1862. Major-General George McClellan is second from the left, and Brigadier-General George Armstrong Custer is on the right.

THE BATTLE OF FREDERICKSBURG

SPOTSYLVANIA COUNTY AND FREDERICKSBURG, VIRGINIA
DECEMBER 11–15, 1862

COMMANDERS

Union
Maj. Gen. Ambrose Burnside

Confederate
Gen. Robert E. Lee

PARTICIPANTS

About 114,000 (Army of the Potomac)

About 72,500 (Army of Northern Virginia)

CASUALTIES

Union
1,284 killed
9,600 wounded
1,769 POWs/MIA

Confederate
608 killed
4,116 wounded
653 POWs/MIA

VICTORY: CONFEDERACY

OVERVIEW

After Burnside reluctantly took over from McClellan, Lincoln and the general public placed considerable pressure on him to accomplish something big. They wanted a major victory, a major blow to the Confederacy. Unfortunately, winter was rapidly approaching, and it would be difficult to do much until spring. This pressure led to the famous Battle of Fredericksburg in December 1862. Instead of a great victory, it became one of the most lopsided Union defeats of the war, where the number of Union dead was twice that of the Confederate dead, with similar figures for the wounded and casualties in general.

Burnside and the Army of the Potomac were supposed to zip around Lee's army and attack Richmond. To do this, Burnside had to cross the Rappahannock River at the chosen spot of Fredericksburg. Then they would march sixty miles dead south to their destination. Burnside rapidly brought his army to the river, but red tape delayed the delivery of his pontoon bridges. By the time he could move his army across, the Confederates had manned the hills behind Fredericksburg and were blocking his way.

Burnside had to do something. After all the planning and expense, and burdened with the weight of everyone's expectations, he couldn't just walk away. Lee's army was there, and he felt he had no choice but to attack. His army outnumbered Lee's by about 40,000 men. He had better equipment and supplies. His artillery was along the ridge to the north of the river, giving his forces coverage of the river basin they had to cross. His artillery had greater range than Lee's, and the ridge lay higher than the hills that Lee's men were on, but Lee's artillery lay just out of the reach of the Union artillery. Burnside's men had to march across open ground to attack.

Burnside launched a two-pronged attack. To the southeast, against Stonewall Jackson's corps, Meade's division charged into A. P. Hill's men and broke through their line. Unprepared for this, the Union army failed to give Meade the support he needed. Meanwhile, Early's men came to Hill's assistance, pushing Meade back and patching the Confederate line. Brigadier-General John Gibbon's division then moved in to attack, and after both sides ran out of ammunition, the battle devolved into hand-to-hand fighting with bayonets and rifle butts.

General Lee and his top officers were observing the battle from Telegraph Hill—also called Lee's Hill—in the center of the Confederate line. The Union army didn't attack it because of its rugged sides and its position slightly back from the other hills. They would have been fired down upon on three sides.

Burnside launched the other prong of his attack against the northeast end of the Confederate line, not realizing that Longstreet's men were entrenched behind a stone wall at the base of Marye's Heights. Longstreet had 3,000 men behind the stone wall and another 3,000 on top of Marye's Heights about fifty feet above the plain. Six waves of Union soldiers charged this position, only to be mowed down or forced to retreat. Burnside originally assigned one division to the attack, but three more went in after it. All the soldiers fell or fled before reaching the wall. Brigadier-General Winfield Scott Hancock's Irish Brigade went in with 1,200 men. Only 250 survived.

By midafternoon both prongs of the attack had failed. Instead of altering his line of attack, Burnside ordered his officers to repeat the attacks. Major-General William Franklin ignored the order, so no further attacks took place in the southeast. To the northwest Hooker personally made a reconnaissance of the line and returned to Burnside, advising against the attack. Burnside insisted that Hooker proceed, so he reluctantly complied. In all, fourteen waves of Union soldiers fell in charges on Marye's Heights.

The dead and wounded covered the ground, sometimes three bodies deep. Some soldiers stood the frozen bodies up to shield themselves from the heavy fire. Many of the wounded remained on the battlefield for forty-eight hours before they were retrieved.

Extremely upset at the terrible number of casualties, Burnside insisted on renewing the attacks the following morning, even saying that he'd lead one of the attacks against Marye's Heights himself, but his officers talked him out of it. He eventually brought his army back across the river and left. About 50,000 Union soldiers fought in this battle against about 20,000 Confederates. Casualties were fairly even in the fight against Stonewall Jackson's men, but at Marye's Heights the Union suffered an exceedingly high rate of casualties. Longstreet reported 241 dead, with 1,894 total casualties, while the divisions of Major-Generals Hooker and Edwin Sumner had 875 killed and a total of 8,799 casualties.

Burnside tried to launch another campaign on January 20, 1863, in which he once again attempted to sneak around Lee's army. Weather was mild the day he began, but it rained heavily that night, and soon mud mired his army. While his men struggled for two days to move, Lee took position on the other side of the river. Burnside finally gave up and returned to camp. This incident became known as the Mud March. A few days later Lincoln removed Burnside from command, replacing him with Major-General Hooker.

PREPARATION FOR BATTLE

Confederate

Lieutenant-General James Longstreet (See biography, page 48.)

In the early fall of 1862, a distance of not more than thirty miles lay between the Army of the Potomac and the Army of Northern Virginia. A state of uncertainty had existed for several weeks succeeding the battle of Sharpsburg, but the movements that resulted in the battle of Fredericksburg began to take shape when on the 5th of November the order was issued removing General McClellan from command of the Federal forces. The order assigning General Burnside to command was received at General Lee's headquarters, then at Culpeper Court House, about twenty-four hours after it reached Warrenton, though not through official courtesy. General Lee, on receiving the news, said he regretted to part with McClellan, "for," he added, "we always understood each other so well. I fear they may continue to make these changes till they find some one whom I don't understand." The Federal army was encamped around Warrenton,

Virginia, and was soon divided into three grand divisions, whose commanders were Generals Sumner, Hooker, and Franklin.

Lee's army was on the opposite side of the Rappahannock River, divided into two corps, the First commanded by myself and the Second commanded by General T. J. (Stonewall) Jackson. At that time the Confederate army extended from Culpeper Court House (where the First corps was stationed) on its right across the Blue Ridge down the Valley of Virginia to Winchester. There Jackson was encamped with the Second Corps, except one division which was stationed at Chester Gap on the Blue Ridge Mountains.

About the 18th or 19th of November, we received information through our scouts that Sumner, with his grand division of more than thirty thousand men, was moving toward Fredericksburg. Evidently he intended to surprise us and cross the Rappahannock before we could offer resistance. On receipt of the information, two of my divisions were ordered down to meet him. We made a forced march and arrived on the hills around Fredericksburg about 3 o'clock on the afternoon of the 21st. Sumner had already arrived, and his army was encamped on Stafford Heights, overlooking the town from the Federal side.

About the 26th or 27th it became evident that Fredericksburg would be the scene of a battle, and we advised the people who were still in the town to prepare to leave, as they would soon be in danger if they remained. The evacuation of the place by the distressed women and helpless men was a painful sight. Many were almost destitute and had nowhere to go, but, yielding to the cruel necessities of war, they collected their portable effects and turned their backs on the town. Many were forced to seek shelter in the woods and brave the icy November nights to escape the approaching assault from the Federal army.

Very soon after I reached Fredericksburg the remainder of my corps arrived from Culpeper Court House, and as soon as it was known that all the Army of the Potomac was in motion for the prospective scene of battle, Jackson was drawn down from the Blue Ridge. In a very short time the army of Northern Virginia was face to face with the Army of the Potomac.

When Jackson arrived he objected to the position, not that he feared the result of the battle, but because he thought that behind the North Anna was a point from which the most fruitful results would follow. He held that we would win a victory of Fredericksburg, but it would be a fruitless one to us, whereas at North Anna, when he drove the Federals back, we could give pursuit to advantage, which we could not do at Fredericksburg. General Lee did not entertain the proposition, however, and we continued our preparations to meet the enemy at the latter place.

PLANNING THE ATTACK

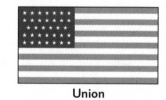

Union

Major-General Joseph Hooker (See biography, page 94.)

On December 20 Hooker testified before a congressional investigating committee looking into how the war was being conducted.

About this time a council of war was held to determine in what manner we should attack the enemy after crossing the river. It was determined,

as I supposed—for I left the council with that impression—that we should attack them without any separation or division of the army, attacking the enemy on their right, below here. That was what I advocated, the keeping the army together, and turning the enemy's right. I did not approve the attempt to pierce so strong a line at two points, when one would be as much as we would be likely to succeed in.

A prisoner, a German, had been taken and brought into this very room (General Sumner's headquarters). This prisoner said he had no objection to communicating everything that he knew in regard to the rebel forces, provided the rebel authorities were not informed of it. He had been impressed into their service, and wanted to quit it. His appearance and his story were such as to carry conviction to the minds of every one who heard him. He told us precisely of the arrangements for defence they had made on the right, but in regard to the left he knew less. He said that it was impossible for us to carry this position. He informed us of the batteries they had, the positions they had taken, and the defences they had thrown up, and said that the rebels regarded it as an impossibility for them to be driven from it. But General Burnside said that his favorite place of attack was on the telegraph road. The army was accordingly divided to make two attacks.

THE UNION ARMY ENTERS THE TOWN

Confederate

General Robert E. Lee (See biography, page 9.)

A letter from Lee to his daughter Mary:

Camp Near Fredericksburg, November 24, 1862
My Dear Daughter:

General Burnside's whole army is apparently opposite Fredericksburg, and stretches from the Rappahannock to the Potomac. What his intentions are he has not yet disclosed. I am sorry he is in position to oppress our friends and citizens of the Northern Neck. He threatens to bombard Fredericksburg, and the noble spirit displayed by its citizens, particularly the women and children, has elicited my highest admiration. They have been abandoning their homes, night and day, during all this inclement weather, cheerfully and uncomplainingly, with only such assistance as our wagons and ambulances could afford, women, girls, children, trudging through the mud and bivouacking in the open fields.

Believe me always your affectionate father,
R. E. Lee

This next excerpt comes from Lee's final official report on the battle.

On the 21st, it became apparent that General Burnside was concentrating his whole army on the north side of the Rappahannock.

On the same day, General Sumner summoned the corporate authorities of Fredericksburg to surrender the place by 5 p.m., and threatened, in case of refusal, to bombard the city at 9 o'clock next morning. The weather had been tempestuous for two days, and a storm was raging at the time of the summons. It was impossible to prevent the execution of the threat to shell the city, as it was completely exposed to the batteries on the Stafford hills, which were beyond our reach. The city authorities were informed that, while our forces would not use the place for military purposes, its occupation by the enemy would be resisted, and directions were given for the removal of the women and children as rapidly as possible. The threatened bombardment did not take place, but, in view of the imminence of a collision between the two armies, the inhabitants were advised to leave the city, and almost the entire population, without a murmur, abandoned their homes. History presents no instance of a people exhibiting a purer and more unselfish patriotism or a higher spirit of fortitude and courage than was evinced by the citizens of Fredericksburg. They cheerfully incurred great hardships and privations, and surrendered their homes and property to destruction rather than yield them into the hands of the enemies of their country.

While the threatened bombardment on November 22 didn't take place, Union artillery did bombard the city on December 11 in preparation for crossing the river. They were trying to stop Confederate snipers from picking off their men, so they aimed at the buildings on the northeastern side of town along the river, about three blocks deep. The Confederates also bombarded Fredericksburg as Union troops emerged from the town during both this battle and five months later at the Second Battle of Fredericksburg. Damage from the Confederate bombardment occurred two blocks deep on the town's southwestern side.

Later in the day of the river crossing, Lee wrote in a letter to his wife:

The enemy, after bombarding the town of Fredericksburg, setting fire to many houses and knocking down nearly all those along the river, crossed over a large force about dark, and now

Fredericksburg, Virginia

occupies the town. We hold the hills commanding it, and hope we shall be able to damage him yet. His position and heavy guns command the town entirely.

Several days later he wrote to the Confederate secretary of war:

Sir: On the night of the 10th instant, the enemy commenced to throw three bridges over the Rappahannock—two at Fredericksburg, and the third about 1¼ miles below, near the mouth of the Deep Run. The plain on which Fredericksburg stands is so completely commanded by the hills of Stafford, in possession of the enemy, that no effectual opposition could be offered to the construction of the bridges or the passage of the river, without exposing our troops to the destructive fire of his numerous batteries. Positions were, therefore, selected to oppose his advance after crossing. The narrowness of the Rappahannock, its winding course and deep bed, afforded opportunity for the construction of bridges at points beyond the reach of our artillery, and the banks had to be watched by skirmishers. The latter, sheltering themselves behind the houses, drove back the working parties of the enemy at the bridges opposite the city, but at the lowest point of crossing, where no shelter could be had, our

The lower pontoon bridges about a mile south of Fredericksburg. The hills in the distance are where Stonewall Jackson's men were. This picture was taken on June 7, 1863, after the bridges were rebuilt in the same place where Burnside had them in the Battle of Fredericksburg. The pontoon bridges were built here the previous month for the Battle of Chancellorsville and once again in May 1865 when the Union army returned to Washington, D.C., for the Grand Review celebrating the end of the war.

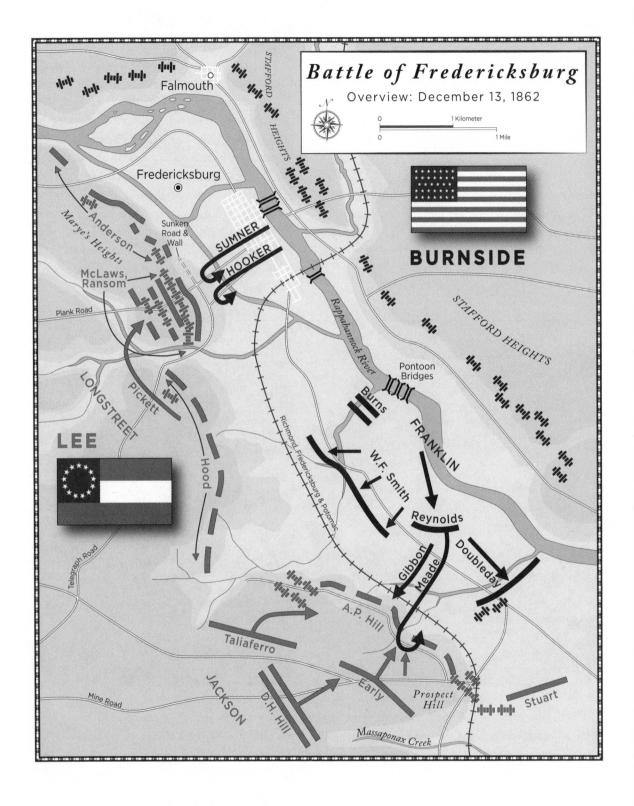

Battle of Fredericksburg

Overview: December 13, 1862

0 — 1 Kilometer
0 — 1 Mile

BURNSIDE

LEE

Falmouth

STAFFORD HEIGHTS

Fredericksburg

Anderson

Marye's Heights

Sunken Road & Wall

McLaws, Ransom

SUMNER

HOOKER

Plank Road

LONGSTREET

Pickett

Hood

Rappahannock River

STAFFORD HEIGHTS

Pontoon Bridges

Burns

FRANKLIN

W.F. Smith

Richmond, Fredericksburg & Potomac

Reynolds

Gibbon

Meade

Doubleday

Telegraph Road

A.P. Hill

Taliaferro

JACKSON

D.H. Hill

Early

Prospect Hill

Stuart

Mine Road

Massaponax Creek

sharpshooters were themselves driven off, and the completion of the bridge was effected about noon on the 11th.

In the afternoon of that day the enemy's batteries opened upon the city, and by dark had so demolished the houses on the river bank as to deprive our skirmishers of shelter—and, under cover of his guns, he effected a lodgment in the town.

The troops which had so gallantly held their position in the city, under the severe cannonade, during the day, resisting the advance of the enemy at every step, were withdrawn during the night, as were also those who, with equal tenacity, had maintained their post at the lowest bridge. Under cover of darkness and of a dense fog, on the 12th, a large force passed the river and took position on the right bank, protected by their heavy guns on the left.

The morning of the 13th, his arrangements for attack being completed, about 9 o'clock (the movement veiled by a fog) he advanced boldly in large force against our right wing. General Jackson's corps occupied the right of our line, which rested on the railroad; Gen. Longstreet's the left, extending along the heights to the Rappahannock above Fredericksburg. Gen. Stuart, with two brigades of cavalry, was posted in the extensive plain on our extreme right.

As soon as the advance of the enemy was discovered through the fog, Gen. Stuart, with his accustomed promptness, moved up a section of his horse-artillery, which opened with effect upon his flank, and drew upon the gallant Pelham a heavy fire, which he sustained unflinchingly for about two hours.

I have the honor to be, very respectfully, your obedient servant,

R. E. Lee, General

SHARPSHOOTERS

Sharpshooters played an important role in the Civil War. At the Battle of Fredericksburg, Confederate snipers in the town and along the waterfront seriously delayed Union forces from crossing the Rappahannock River, giving Lee time to entrench and prepare for the battle. During the Sieges of Vicksburg and Petersburg, they forced the soldiers to hide in trenches to keep from being picked off.

In September 1861 the engineer, inventor, and self-made millionaire Colonel Hiram Berdan formed the First and Second U.S. Volunteer Sharpshooter Regiments, gathering together the Union's most accurate shooters. To qualify, applicants had to shoot all ten bullets through a ten-inch target at 200 yards and again, off hand, at 100 yards. They were armed mainly with breech-loading Sharps rifles, particularly good for long-distance shooting. Some had tube sights—brass tubes longer than the barrel with crosshairs but no lenses. Wearing green uniforms, brigades were usually detached for special assignments. Their duties involved skirmishing and scouting more often than actual sniping.

While Berdan's Sharpshooters operated in the eastern theater, Birge's Western Sharpshooters were formed for the western theater, and later renamed the Fourteenth Missouri Volunteers and then the Sixty-sixth Illinois Veteran Volunteer Infantry Regiment. In order to qualify, a candidate had to put three bullets within a three-inch pattern from 200 yards. These men were initially armed with half-stock plains rifles, although many used their own rifles. In the fall of 1863, some men began spending their own money to buy sixteen-shot Henry repeating rifles, which cost forty-two dollars (three months' pay for a private). Firing quickly at shorter ranges was more useful than long-range accuracy as they took on a new role as shock troops leading assaults. The Western Sharpshooters fought in sixteen major battles and more than fifty actions, including counterguerrilla operations in northern Missouri and northern Mississippi.

Considered elite, sharpshooters often received more difficult assignments. One company of the First Regiment Michigan Volunteer Sharpshooters was made up entirely of Native Americans, mainly from the Odawa, Ojibwa, and Potawatomi nations, who had particularly adept sharpshooting skills.

The Confederates also had their sharpshooters—such as the First and Second Battalions Georgia Sharpshooters and the Ninth Battalion Missouri Sharpshooters—but they also used them more widely as semipermanent detached units assigned to regiments. These Confederates had muzzle-loading British Whitworth rifles and Enfield rifled muskets. A few were equipped with long-tube telescopic sights. Even though they had less than 4x magnification, they could kill at a range of up to 1,200 yards.

Like Union sharpshooters, they also functioned as skirmishers and scouts, in addition to serving as advance, flank, and rear guards. In trench warfare the sharpshooters pushed their trenches and rifle pits as close to Union lines as they could. Sometimes they manned their pits during the day and were relieved by pickets at night. Other times they remained at their post for several days before being relieved for a day. After the Battle of Gettysburg, the five sharpshooter battalions were brought together—about 1,000 men—to cover the Confederate retreat. Lee then ordered that every one of his infantry brigades have its own sharpshooter battalion, which they did beginning in 1864.

In one of the most noted sniper shots of the war, a Confederate sharpshooter killed Major-General John Sedgwick—the highest-ranking Union officer killed in the war—at the beginning of the Battle of Spotsylvania Court House. He was hit from about 1,000 yards away while directing artillery placements.

Brevet Major-General Martin McMahon, who was with Sedgwick at the time, described what happened.

I gave the necessary order to move the troops to the right, and as they rose to execute the movement the enemy opened a sprinkling fire, partly from sharp-shooters. As the bullets whistled by, some of the men dodged.

The general said laughingly, "What! what! men, dodging this way for single bullets! What will you do when they open fire along the whole line? I am ashamed of you. They couldn't hit an elephant at this distance."

A few seconds after, a man who had been separated from his regiment passed directly in front of the general, and at the same moment a sharp-shooter's bullet passed with a long shrill whistle very close, and the soldier, who was then just in front of the general, dodged to the ground. The general touched him gently with his foot, and said, "Why, my man, I am ashamed of you, dodging that way," and repeated the remark, "They couldn't hit an elephant at this distance."

The man rose and saluted and said good-naturedly, "General, I dodged a shell once, and if I hadn't, it would have taken my head off. I believe in dodging."

The general laughed and replied, "All right, my man; go to your place."

For a third time the same shrill whistle, closing with a dull, heavy stroke, interrupted our talk; when, as I was about to resume, the general's face turned slowly to me, the blood spurting from his left cheek under the eye in a steady stream. He fell in my direction; I was so close to him that my effort to support him failed, and I fell with him.

DISCUSSIONS WITH LEE AND STONEWALL JACKSON

Confederate

General John Bell Hood (See biography, page 84.)

On the 11th of December, 1862, General Burnside having completed all necessary preparation, began to lay pontoons above and below the railroad bridge which had been destroyed. That entire day and night he consumed in crossing his forces to the southern bank of the river, under cover of, at least, one hundred pieces of artillery. During the 12th he formed his line below and above Deep Run, whilst upon the range of hills overlooking the valley, Lee's forces lay in readiness to receive the attack. General Jackson had, meantime, moved up to form a line on our right, and that day, if I remember correctly, as we were riding together in direction of General Lee's headquarters, the conversation turned upon the future, and he asked me if I expected to live to see the end of the war. I replied that I did not know, but was inclined to think I would survive; at the same time, I considered it most likely I would be badly shattered before the termination of the struggle. I naturally addressed him the same question, and, without hesitation, he answered that he did not expect to live through to the close of the contest. Moreover, that he could not say that he desired to do so. With this sad turn in the conversation, the subject dropped.

It was now past nine o'clock, and the sun, mounting up the eastern sky with almost a summer power, was rapidly exhaling the mist. As the white folds dissolved and rolled away, disclosing the whole plain to view, such a spectacle met the eyes of the generals as the pomps of earth can seldom rival.

Marshaled upon the vast arena between them stood the hundred and twenty-five thousand foes, with countless batteries of field-guns blackening the ground. Long triple lines of infantry crossed the field from right to left, and hid their western extreme in the streets of the little city; while down the valleys, descending from the Stafford Heights to the bridges, were pouring in vast avalanches of men, the huge reserves. For once, war unmasked its terrible proportions to the view with a distinctness hitherto unknown in the forest-clad landscapes of America; and the plain of Fredericksburg presented a panorama that was dreadful in its grandeur.

Lee stood upon his chosen hill of observation, inspiring every spectator by his calm heroism, with his two great lieutenants beside him, and reviewed every quarter of the field with his glass. It was then that Longstreet, to whose sturdy breast the approach of battle seemed to bring gayety, said to Jackson: "General do not all these multitudes frighten you?"

He replied: "We shall see very soon whether I shall not frighten them."

—Rev. Dr. Robert Dabney, Stonewall Jackson's chief of staff and biographer, describing the armies on the morning of the battle

My division was again the centre of the Confederate Army, as it rested in line of battle opposite Deep Run, full of spirit and impatient for action. The following morning, after the fog had disappeared, and at about 10 o'clock, the heavy lines of the enemy advanced upon our right and against Jackson's forces, but were driven back beneath the fire of our guns posted on that part of the line. Again, at about 1 p.m., the attack was renewed, and the Federals penetrated into a gap left in Jackson's front line. They were, however, speedily repulsed by his brigades held in reserve. My troops repelled with ease the feeble attack made on their immediate front, whilst Longstreet's remaining forces on the left drove the enemy back repeatedly with great slaughter near Marye's Hill.

I was directed in this battle, as at Second Manassas, to obey the orders either of Generals Lee, Jackson, or Longstreet. About sunset, after the musketry fire had nigh ceased, I received instructions through an officer of Jackson's staff to join in a movement on my right as soon as A. P. Hill's division advanced. The order was accompanied with a message from General Jackson that he intended to drive the enemy into the river. I responded that I was in readiness to act, but, for some reason unknown to me, these orders were countermanded.

About 10 o'clock that night I rode back to my encampment to procure a cup of coffee, and, General Lee's quarters being within a few hundred yards, I walked up the ridge and presented myself at his tent. He immediately asked me what I thought of the attack by the enemy during the day. I expressed my opinion that Burnside was whipped; that no good general would ever make an assault similar to that upon my right and left, without intending it as his main effort, and that the heavy roll of musketry I had heard clearly convinced me that the hardest part of the battle had been fought. He then remarked that he did not think Burnside had made his principal attempt, but would attack again the next day, and that we would drive him back and follow him up to the river. After conversing a few moments longer, during which time he was in the highest spirits, I returned to my line, where I continued the remainder of the night.

The morning of the 14th both Armies still lay face to face, no aggressive movement having been initiated by either side, when about noon Generals Lee and Jackson rode by my position, and invited me to accompany them on a reconnaissance towards our right. We soon reached an eminence, not far distant from Hamilton's Crossing on the railroad, and upon which some of our batteries were posted. From this point we had a magnificent view of the Federal lines on their left, some seven in number, and each, seemingly, a mile in length.

General Jackson here turned to me, and asked my estimate of the strength of the enemy then in sight and in our immediate front. I answered fifty thousand, and he remarked that he had estimated their numbers at fifty-five thousand.

Strange to say, amid this immense assemblage of Federal troops not a standard was to be seen; the colors were all lowered, which circumstance induced me to abide by the opinion I had expressed to General Lee the night previous. The two Armies stood still during this entire day, and the following morning we awoke to find the enemy on the north side of the Rappahannock.

"I Should Have Been the Great Hero"

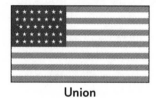

Union

Major-General George Meade (See biography, page 92.)

Brigadier-General Meade led the only Union attack that was partially successful. After the attack he raged that his colleagues didn't give him the support that he needed. In particular, he fired a long string of profanities directly at Brigadier-General David Birney.

Camp opposite Fredericksburg, Va., December 16, 1862
To Mrs. George G. Meade:

On the 12th we crossed [the river]. Sumner at the town, Franklin below, and Hooker remaining in reserve. On the 13th it was determined to make an attack from both positions, and the honor of leading this attack was assigned to my division. I cannot give you all the details of the fight, but will simply say my men went in beautifully, carried everything before them, and drove the enemy for nearly half a mile, but finding themselves unsupported on either right or left, and encountering an overwhelming force of the enemy, they were checked and finally driven back.

As an evidence of the work they had to do, it is only necessary to state that out of four thousand five hundred men taken into action, we know the names of eighteen hundred killed and wounded. There are besides some four hundred missing, many of whom are wounded. All the men agree it was the warmest work the Reserves had ever encountered.

I cannot enumerate all the casualties, but among them was poor [First Lieutenant Arthur] Dehon [General Meade's aide-de-camp], who fell pierced through the heart and expired almost immediately. Yesterday, under a flag, we found his body, and Coxe has taken it this morning to Washington. I had become very much attached to Dehon for his many excellent qualities, and it does seem as if the good luck that attends me is to be made up in the misfortunes of my staff. I was myself unhurt, although a ball passed through my hat so close, that if it had come from the front instead of the side, I would have been a "goner." The day after the battle, one of their sharpshooters took deliberate aim at me, his ball passing through the neck of my horse.

The fact being, as I advised you, they had prepared themselves, in a series of heights covered with woods, where they had constructed redoubts and connected them with rifle pits, so that it was pretty much one fortification. On the town side, the works were so near that our people could make no progress out of the town, they coming immediately under the fire of the works. The 14th and 15th were spent in reconnaissances and deliberations, the result of which was, that last night we had the humiliation to be compelled to return this side of the river; in other words, acknowledge the superior strength of the enemy and proclaim, what we all knew before, that we never should have crossed, with the force we have, without some diversion being made on the James River in our favor.

What will be done next I cannot tell. Burnside, I presume, is a dead cock in the pit, and your friend Joe Hooker (fighting Joe) is the next on the list, except that it is said fighting Joe recommended the withdrawal of the army.

Meade was promoted to major general a few days later.

★ ★ ★

Camp opposite Fredericksburg, December 20, 1862
To Mrs. George G. Meade:

My last letter was dated the 17th instant. Since that day I have been quite busy moving camp, and to-day have been occupied in writing my official report of the recent battle. I am quite anxious to know what you think and hear of my doings. For my part, the more I think of that battle, the more annoyed I am that such a great chance should have failed me. The slightest straw almost would have kept the tide in our favor. We had driven them for some distance. Lee in his report acknowledges that two brigades of A. P. Hill's division gave way before our attack.[6] All we had to do was to have held our own, to have organized on the hill we had gained, and prepared for their assault till our reinforcements could get up. Instead of that, owing to the death of General [C. Feger] Jackson and the wounding of Colonel Sinclair, two brigades were without commanders. It being in the woods, and no one being able to see what was going on around, our men pushed too far, and got right on a large body of the enemy [under Brigadier-General Early], drawn up in line ready to receive them. Of course they immediately poured in a deadly fire, which staggered my disorganized line, and finally

6 They must have captured someone familiar with Lee's dispatches, or perhaps the report was published in one of the Southern newspapers.

drove it back, with the loss of all it had gained. Had it been otherwise—that is to say, had we held the position gained till our reinforcements came up—I should have been the great hero of the fight, as every other attack had not only failed, but without even the success we could boast of. Well, I suppose it is all for the best, and cannot be helped; but it made me feel worse at the time than if we had been repulsed from the first.

THE ATTACK HAD TO BE ABANDONED

Confederate

Lieutenant-General Thomas "Stonewall" Jackson (See biography, page 37.)

In his official report on the battle of December 13, Jackson wrote:

About 1 o'clock, the main attack was made by heavy and rapid discharges of artillery. Under the protection of this warm and well-directed fire, his infantry in heavy force advanced, seeking the partial protection of a piece of wood extending beyond the railroad. The batteries on the right played on their ranks with destructive effect. The advancing force was visibly staggered by our rapid and well-directed artillery, but, soon recovering from the shock, the Federal troops, consisting of the main body of Franklin's grand division, supported by a portion of Hooker's grand division, continued to press forward. Advancing within point-blank range of our infantry, and thus exposed, to the murderous fire of musketry and artillery, the struggle became fierce and sanguinary.

Repulsed on the right, left, and center, the enemy soon after reformed his lines, and gave some indications of a purpose to renew the attack. I waited some time to receive it; but he making no forward movement, I determined, if prudent, to do so myself. The artillery of the enemy was so judiciously posted as to make an advance of our troops across the plain very hazardous; yet it was so promising of good results, if successfully executed, as to induce me to make preparations for the attempt. In order to guard against disaster, the infantry was to be preceded by artillery, and the movement postponed until late in the evening, so that, if compelled to retire, it would be under the cover of night. Owing to unexpected delays, the movement could not be gotten ready until late in the evening. The first gun had hardly moved forward from the wood 100 yards when the enemy's artillery reopened, and so completely swept our front as to satisfy me that the proposed movement should be abandoned.

The next day (14th), the enemy continued in our front all day, apparently awaiting an attack from us.

On the 15th, the enemy still remained in our front, and in the evening of that day sent in a flag of truce requesting a cessation of hostilities between his left and our right wings, for the purpose of removing his wounded from the field, which, under previous instructions from the commanding general, was granted.

Our troops patiently remained in position on that, as they had done the previous day, eagerly awaiting another attack from the enemy, and such was the desire to occupy the front line, when such an attack should be made, that the division of Maj. Gen. D. H. Hill sent in a written request to be permitted to remain in the front line until next day. But our brave troops were disappointed in the expectation of another attack, for while they patiently waited during the night of the 15th in the hope of another encounter on the following day, and of visiting upon the invaders of their sacred homes and firesides a just retribution for the outrages of this most unprovoked and unchristian war, the enemy hurriedly and silently during that night made good his retreat by recrossing the river.

I trust that the victory of Fredericksburg, with which God has blessed our cause, will continue to be gratefully remembered.

I am, general, your obedient servant,

T. J. Jackson, Lieutenant-General

DEFENDING MARYE'S HEIGHTS

Confederate

Lieutenant-General James Longstreet (See biography, page 48.)

While Meade attacked Jackson's men on the southeast portion of the battlefield, Sumner and Hooker were attacking Longstreet's men below Marye's Heights at the northwestern end of the battlefield. This was the other prong of the Union's two-pronged attack.

Before daylight on the morning of the eventful 13th, I rode to the right of my line held by Hood's division. General Hood was at his post in plain hearing of the Federals south of Deep Run, who were marching their troops into position for the attack. The morning was cold and misty, and everything was obscured from view, but so distinctly did the mist bear to us the sounds of the moving Federals that Hood thought the advance was against him. He was relieved, however, when I assured him that the enemy, to reach him, would have to put himself in a pocket and be subjected to attack from Jackson on one side, Pickett and McLaws on the other, and Hood's own men in front. The position of Franklin's men on the 12th with the configuration of the ground had left no doubt in my mind as to Franklin's intentions. I explained all this to Hood, assuring him that the attack would be on Jackson. At the same time I ordered Hood, in case Jackson's line was broken, to wheel around to his right and strike in on the attacking bodies, telling him that Pickett, with his division, would be ordered to join in the flank movement. These orders were given to both division generals, and at the same time they were advised that I would be attacked near my left center, and that I must be at that point to meet my part of the battle. They were also advised that my position was so well defended I could have no other need of their troops. I then returned to Lee's Hill, reaching there soon after sunrise.

Thus we stood at the eve of the great battle. Along the Stafford Heights a hundred and forty-seven guns were turned on us, and on the level plain below, in the town, and hidden on the opposite bank ready to cross, nearly a hundred thousand men were assembled, eager to begin the combat. Secure in our hills, we grimly awaited the onslaught. The valley, the mountaintops, everything was enveloped in the thickest fog, and the preparation for the fight was made as if under cover of night. The mist brought to us the sounds of the preparation for battle, but we were blind to the movements of the Federals. Suddenly, at ten o'clock, as if the elements were taking a hand in the drama about to be enacted, the warmth of the sun brushed the mist away and revealed the mighty panorama in the valley below.

Franklin's forty thousand men, reenforced by two divisions of Hooker's grand division, were in front of Jackson's thirty thousand. The flags of the Federals fluttered gayly, the polished arms shone brightly in the sunlight, and the beautiful uniforms of the buoyant troops gave to the scene the air of a holiday occasion rather than the spectacle of a great army about to be thrown into the tumult of battle. From my place on Lee's Hill I could see almost every soldier Franklin had, and a splendid array it was. But off in the distance

was Jackson's ragged infantry, and beyond was Stuart's battered cavalry, with their soiled hats and yellow butternut suits, a striking contrast to the handsomely equipped troops of the Federals.

In front of Marye's Hill is a plateau, and immediately at the base of the hill there is a sunken road known as the Telegraph road. On the side of the road next to the town was a stone wall, shoulder high, against which the earth was banked, forming an almost unapproachable defense. It was impossible for the troops occupying it to expose more than a small portion of their bodies. Behind this stone wall I had placed about twenty-five hundred men. It must now be understood that the Federals, to reach what appeared to be my weakest point, would have to pass directly over this wall held by [Brigadier General Thomas] Cobb's infantry.

An idea of how well Marye's Hill was protected may be obtained from the following incident. General E. P. Alexander, my engineer and superintendent of artillery, had been placing the guns, and in going over the field with him before the battle, I noticed an idle cannon. I suggested that he place it so as to aid in covering the plain in front of Marye's Hill. He answered, "General, we cover that ground now so well that we will comb it as if with a fine-tooth comb. A chicken could not live on that field when we open on it."

About 11 a.m. I sent orders for the batteries to play upon the streets and bridges beyond the city, by way of diversion in favor of our right. The batteries had hardly opened when the enemy's infantry began to move out toward my line. Our pickets in front of the Marye house were soon driven in, and the enemy began to deploy his forces in front of that point. Our artillery, being in position, opened fire as soon as the masses became dense enough to warrant it. This fire was very destructive and demoralizing in its effects, and frequently made gaps in the enemy's ranks that could be seen at the distance of a mile. The enemy continued his advance and made his attack at the Marye Hill in handsome style.

The Federal troops filed out of the city like bees out of a hive, coming in double-quick march and filling the edge of the field in front of Cobb. This was just where we had expected attack and I was prepared to meet it. As the troops massed before us, they were much annoyed by the fire of our batteries. The field was literally packed with Federals from the vast number of troops that had been massed in the town. From the moment of their appearance began the most fearful carnage. With our artillery from the front, right, and left tearing through their ranks, the Federals pressed forward with almost invincible determination, maintaining their steady step and closing up their broken ranks. Thus resolutely they marched upon the stone fence behind where quietly awaited the Confederate brigade of General Cobb.

As the Federals came within reach of this brigade, a storm of lead was poured into their advancing ranks and they were swept from the field like chaff before the wind. A cloud of smoke shut out the scene for a moment, and, rising, revealed the shattered fragments recoiling from their gallant but hopeless charge.

The artillery still plowed through the ranks of the retreating Federals and sought the places of concealment into which the troops had plunged. A vast number went pell-mell into an old railroad cut, to escape fire from the right and front. A battery on Lee's Hill saw this and turned its fire into the entire length of the cut, and the shells began to pour down upon the Federals with the most frightful destruction. They found their position of refuge more uncomfortable than the field of the assault.

Thus the right grand division of the Army of the Potomac found itself repulsed and shattered on its first attempt to drive us from Marye's Hill. Hardly was this attack off the field before we saw the determined Federals again filing out of Fredericksburg and preparing for another charge. The Confederates under Cobb reserved their fire and quietly awaited the approach of the enemy. The Federals came nearer than before, but were forced to retire before the well-directed guns of Cobb's brigade and the fire of the artillery on the heights. By that time the field in front of Cobb was thickly strewn with the dead and dying Federals, but again they formed with desperate courage and renewed the attack and were again driven off.

The ranks [behind the stone wall] were four or five deep, the rear files loading and passing their guns to the front ranks, so that the volleys by brigade were almost incessant pourings of solid sheets of lead.

ASSAULTING MARYE'S HEIGHTS

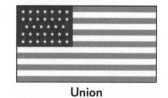

Union

Major-General Winfield Scott Hancock

Winfield Scott Hancock gained his reputation as a war hero primarily at Gettysburg, where he was wounded facing Pickett's Charge. Born as a twin in Pennsylvania, he was named after Brevet Lieutenant-General Winfield Scott.

The son of a staunch Democratic schoolteacher, lawyer, and local politician, he graduated from West Point in 1844 and served in the infantry under Scott in Mexico, where he was wounded in the knee during the Battle of Churubusco. Later stationed in Kansas during the Bleeding Kansas violence and in Utah Territory during the Utah War against the Mormons, he became friends in southern California with Albert Sidney Johnston and Lewis Armistead, the latter of whom he faced at Gettysburg.

Soon after the war began, Grant said of him: "Hancock stands the most conspicuous figure of all the general officers who did not exercise a separate command. He commanded a corps longer than any other one, and his name was never mentioned as having committed in battle a blunder for which he was responsible."

At 1 p.m. the first wave attacked the stone wall and failed. Hancock's men, led by Colonel Samuel Zook, made the second assault.

The troops then advanced, each brigade in succession, under a most murderous fire of artillery and musketry, the artillery fire reaching the troops in a destructive manner in the town, even before they had commenced the movement. The distance to overcome by the way the troops were obliged to march before reaching the enemy's works was probably 1,700 yards. It took an unusually long time to advance that distance, as the planking of one of the bridges was found to be partly taken up, requiring the men to cross on the stringers.

Colonel Zook's brigade was the first in order. As soon as it had formed a line, it advanced to the attack with spirit, passing the point at which the preceding troops had arrived, and being joined as it passed by the brave regiments of Kimball's brigade and some other regiments of French's division. It failed, however, to take the stone wall, behind which the enemy was posted, although our dead were left within 25 paces of it. These troops still held their line of battle in front of the enemy and within close musketry range.

The Irish Brigade next advanced to the assault. The same gallantry was displayed, but with the same results. Caldwell's brigade was next ordered into action, and, although it behaved with the utmost valor, failed to carry the enemy's position. All the troops then formed one line of battle, extending from a point a little distance to the right of Hanover street, in a line nearly parallel to the enemy, with the left thrown back, the extreme left extending about the front of two regiments to the left of the railroad culvert. This line was held during the entire day and until it was relieved, some of the regiments not coming off the field until 10 o'clock the following morning. This line was held for hours after the troops had exhausted their ammunition, and after the ammunition of the killed and wounded within reach had been expended.

Shortly after the last of my brigades came into action, it appeared as if the front crest of the enemy's hill might have been taken had there been other troops at hand, for the enemy were at that time running from their rifle-pits and works on

The Union view of Marye's Heights from the direction the attacks were made. Many of the soldiers marched down Hanover Street on the right heading to the stone wall at the foot of the hill. The area in front of Marye's Heights became known as the Bloody Plain. This photograph was taken in 1864.

the crest directly in front of our right. But by the time Howard's troops were ready to attack, the enemy had repaired this, and making a strong attack at the same time toward our left, it became necessary that a portion of that division should be detached toward that flank.

YET ANOTHER FUTILE ASSAULT

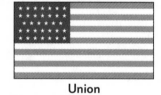

Union

Major-General Joseph Hooker (See biography, page 94.)

Hooker continued in his testimony before the congressional investigating committee:

About 2 o'clock on that day I received an order from General Burnside to cross over my other two divisions and attack the enemy on the telegraph road—the same position we had been butting against all day long. As soon as I received the order my divisions commenced crossing.

I rode forward to see what I could learn from the officers who had been engaged in the attack— General French, General Wilcox, General Couch, and General Hancock. Their opinion, with one exception, was that the attack should not be made on that point. After conferring with them, I went to examine the position to ascertain whether or not it could be turned. Discovering no weak point, and seeing that many of the troops that had been already engaged in the attack were considerably demoralized, and fearing that should the enemy make an advance, even of but a small column, nothing but disaster would follow, I sent my aide-de-camp to General Burnside to say that I advised him not to attack at that place. He returned, saying that the attack must be made. I had the matter so much at heart that I put spurs to my horse and rode over here myself, and tried to dissuade General Burnside from making the attack. He insisted on its being made.

I then returned and brought up every available battery in the city, with a view to break away their barriers by the use of artillery. I proceeded against the barriers as I would against a fortification, and endeavored to breach a hole sufficiently large for a "forlorn hope" to enter. Before that the attack along the line, it seemed to me, had been too general—not sufficiently concentrated. I had two batteries posted on the left of the road, within four hundred yards of the position upon which the attack was to be made, and I had other parts of batteries posted on the right of the road at the distance of five hundred or six hundred yards. I had all these batteries playing with great vigor until sunset upon that point, but with no apparent effect upon the rebels or upon their works.

During the last part of the cannonading I had given directions to General Humphrey's division to form, under the shelter which a small hill afforded in column for assault. When the fire of the artillery ceased I gave directions for the enemy's works to be assaulted. General Humphrey's men took off their knapsacks, overcoats, and haversacks. They were directed to make the assault with empty muskets, for there was no time there to load and fire. When the word was given the men moved forward with great impetuosity. They ran and hurrahed, and I was encouraged by the great good feeling that pervaded them. The head of General Humphrey's column advanced to within, perhaps, fifteen or twenty yards of the stone wall, which was the advanced position which the rebels held, and

then they were thrown back as quickly as they had advanced. Probably the whole of the advance and the retiring did not occupy fifteen minutes. They left behind, as was reported to me, 1,760 of their number, out of about 4,000.

Another council of war was held. The opinion of most of the council was, that the place could not be taken at all. My own opinion was that, if there was any chance to take the place, it was by forming a heavy column of attack at night, when the enemy could not see to use their artillery.

Mr. Chandler: What was there to prevent flanking them on our right, beyond their batteries?

Answer: Water—a lake and a mill-race, which was reported to me to be impassable.

Chairman: If they [the pontoons] had been here [on time], what would have been the result?

Answer: When Sumner's advance column reached here there were only some 500 of the rebels in Fredericksburg. I do not know why they did not take possession of Fredericksburg. But the feeling seemed to be that they could take possession of Fredericksburg at any time; only a few days before, Lieutenant Dahlgren, of the cavalry, with fifty-five men, crossed the river and took possession of the town.

When I was at Hartwood I heard that there was going to be a delay of three or four days in getting the pontoons here, and that was one reason why I asked permission of General Burnside to cross at the ford there, and come down on the other side of the river. When we got here we should have been in condition to march right forward without stopping a day anywhere. But the same mistake was made here that has been made all along through this war. I think it would here been better to have held the line where we were, by retaining a sufficient force there to threaten the enemy and keep them up to their works at Culpeper and Gordonsville. But instead of that we withdrew every man, and even burned the bridges, thus exposing our plan to the enemy the very moment we did so. If General Summer's corps had come down here and left me up there threatening to advance on that line, or led them to believe that we were going to advance on both lines, it would have been better. But the enemy saw at once what we were at, and came right down here, and they nearer here then we were; and this country is such that wherever you give them two or three weeks to fortify, 100,000 men can make any place impregnable to any other 100,000 men.

Further Attacks on Marye's Heights

Confederate

Lieutenant-General James Longstreet (See biography, page 48.)

At each attack the slaughter was so great that by the time the third attack was repulsed, the ground was so thickly strewn with dead that the bodies seriously impeded the approach of the Federals. I think the fourth time the Federals came, a gallant fellow reached within one hundred feet of Cobb's position and then fell. Close behind him came some few scattering ones, but they were either killed or fled from certain death.

A fifth time the Federals formed and charged and were repulsed. A sixth time they charged and were driven back, when night came to end the dreadful carnage, and the Federals withdrew, leaving the battle-field literally heaped with the bodies of their dead. Before the well-directed fire of Cobb's brigade, the Federals had fallen like the steady dripping of rain from the eaves of a house. Our musketry alone had killed and wounded at least five thousand; and these, with the slaughter by the artillery, left over seven thousand killed and wounded before the foot of Marye's Hill. The dead were piled sometimes three deep, and when morning broke, the spectacle that we saw upon the battle-field was one of the most distressing I ever witnessed. The charges had been desperate and bloody, but utterly hopeless. I thought, as I saw the Federals come again and again to their death, that they deserved success if courage and daring could entitle soldiers to victory.

A series of braver, more desperate charges than those hurled against the troops in the sunken road was never known, and the piles and cross-piles of dead marked a field such as I never saw before or since.

The stone wall was not thought before the battle a very important element. We assumed that the formidable advance would be made against the troops of McLaw's division at Lee's Hill, to turn the position at the sunken road, dislodge my force stationed there, then to occupy the sunken road, and afterwards ascend to the plateau upon which the Marye mansion stands; that this would bring their forces under cross and direct fire of all of our batteries short- and long-range guns in such concentration as to beat them back in bad disorder.

Preparations were made to meet the grand attack of the enemy, confidently expected on Monday morning. As the attack was not made, this artillery and General Ransom's sharpshooters opened upon the enemy and drove him back to cover in the city.

During the night the enemy recrossed the river. His retreat was not discovered until he had crossed the river and cut his bridges at this end. Our sharpshooters were moved forward and our old positions resumed. Four hundred prisoners, 5,500 stand of small-arms, and 250,000 rounds of small-arm ammunition were taken.

TRYING TO DETERMINE THE UNION'S INTENTIONS

Confederate

General Robert E. Lee (See biography, page 9.)

Near Fredericksburg, Va., December 16, 1862
Hon. James A. Seddon, Secretary of War, Richmond, Va.

Sir: I have the honor to report that the army of General Burnside recrossed the Rappahannock last night, leaving a number of his dead and some of his wounded on this side. Our skirmishers again occupy Fredericksburg and the south bank of the river. Large camps and wagon trains are visible on the hills of Stafford, and his heavy guns occupy their former position on that bank. There is nothing to indicate his future purpose. I have sent one brigade of cavalry down the Rappahannock, and have put Jackson's corps in motion in the same direction. I think it probable an attempt will be made to cross at Port Royal. Another brigade of cavalry has been sent up

the Rappahannock, with orders, if opportunity offers, to cross and penetrate the enemy's rear and endeavor to ascertain his intention.

I learn from prisoners that the three grand divisions of General Burnside's army, viz, Hooker's, Sumner's, and Franklin's, crossed this side, and were engaged in the battle of the 13th. They also state that the corps of Generals Heintzelman and Sigel reached Fredericksburg Sunday evening. Should the enemy cross at Port Royal in force before I can get this army in position to meet him, I think it more advantageous to retire to the Annas and give battle than on the banks of the Rappahannock. My design was to have done so in the first instance. My purpose was changed not from any advantage in this position, but from an unwillingness to open more of our country to depredation than possible, and also with a view of collecting such forage and provisions as could be obtained in the Rappahannock Valley.

The loss of the enemy in the battle of the 13th seems to have been heavy, though I have no means of computing it accurately. An intelligent prisoner says he heard it stated in the army to have amounted to 19,000, though a citizen of Fredericksburg who remained in the city computes it at 10,000. I think the latter number nearer the truth than the former.

I have learned that on the side of the enemy Generals Bayard and Jackson were killed, and Generals Hooker and Gibbon wounded; the former said to be severely so.

I am, most respectfully, your obedient servant,
R. E. Lee, General

EXPLAINING THE DEFEAT

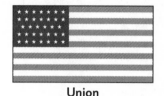

Union

Major-General Ambrose Burnside

History remembers Major-General Ambrose Burnside for his sideburns—the word deriving from his name—and for being a poor military tactician. Unable to see better alternatives, he relied on standard frontal assaults that proved deadly to many of his men.

Burnside's father owned slaves in South Carolina but freed them and moved to Indiana, where Burnside was born. He worked as a tailor before entering West Point, where he graduated in 1847. He arrived in Mexico just after the war ended. In the early 1850s he left the military to design and develop his breech-loading Burnside carbine, the third-most-common carbine in the Civil War.

When the war broke out, he was a brigadier general of the Rhode Island militia, having remained in the militia since his time in the army. Offered command of the Army of the Potomac after the failed Peninsula campaign, he refused out of loyalty to McClellan and because of his own inexperience. He declined again after Second Manassas (Second Bull Run). When Lincoln removed McClellan after Antietam, telling Burnside that if he didn't accept, the job would go to Hooker—whom Burnside wanted court-martialed for insubordination—Burnside finally agreed to take the position. He commanded the Army of the Potomac for two and a half months during the Fredericksburg campaign, until his defeat, when Hooker replaced him.

"General Burnside was an officer who was generally liked and respected," wrote Grant. "He was not, however, fitted to command an army. No one knew this better than himself."

Headquarters Army of the Potomac, December 17, 1862
Maj. Gen. H. W. Halleck, General-in-Chief, Washington, D.C.

I have the honor to offer the following reasons for moving the Army of the Potomac across the Rappahannock sooner than was anticipated by the

President, Secretary, or yourself, and for crossing at a point different from the one indicated to you at our last meeting at the President's:

During my preparations for crossing at the place I had at first selected, I discovered that the enemy had thrown a large portion of his force down the river and elsewhere, thus weakening his defenses in front; and I also thought I discovered that he did not anticipate the crossing of our whole force at Fredericksburg; and I hoped, by rapidly throwing the whole command over at that place, to separate, by a vigorous attack, the forces of the enemy on the river below from the forces behind and on the crests in the rear of the town, in which case we should fight him with great advantages in our favor. To do this we had to gain a height on the extreme right of the crest, which height commanded a new road, lately built by the enemy for purposes of more rapid communication along his lines; which point gained, his positions along the crest would have been scarcely tenable, and he could have been driven from them easily by an attack on his front, in connection with a movement in rear of the crest.

How near we came to accomplishing our object future reports will show. But for the fog and unexpected and unavoidable delay in building the bridges, which gave the enemy twenty-four hours more to concentrate his forces in his strong positions, we would almost certainly have succeeded; in which case the battle would have been, in my opinion, far more decisive than if we had crossed at the places first selected. As it was, we came very near success. Failing in accomplishing the main object, we remained in order of battle two days—long enough to decide that the enemy would not come out of his strongholds and fight us with his infantry. After which we recrossed to this side of the river unmolested, and without the loss of men or property.

As the day broke, our long lines of troops were seen marching to their different positions as if going on parade; not the least demoralization or disorganization existed.

To the brave officers and soldiers who accomplished the feat of this recrossing in the face of the enemy I owe everything. For the failure in the attack I am responsible, as the extreme gallantry, courage, and endurance shown by them was never excelled, and would have carried the points, had it been possible.

To the families and friends of the dead I can only offer my heartfelt sympathy, but for the wounded I can offer my earnest prayers for their comfort and final recovery.

The fact that I decided to move from Warrenton onto this line rather against the opinion of the President, Secretary, and yourself, and that you have left the whole management in my hands, without giving me orders, makes me the more responsible.

I will add here that the movement was made earlier than you expected, and after the President, Secretary, and yourself requested me not to be in haste, for the reason that we were supplied much sooner by the different staff departments than was anticipated when I last saw you.

Our killed amounted to 1,152; our wounded, about 9,000; our prisoners, about 700, which have been paroled and exchanged for about the same number taken by us. [These numbers were later revised to 1,284 killed, 9,600 wounded, and 1,769 captured or missing.] The wounded were all removed to this side of the river before the evacuation, and are being well cared for, and the dead were all buried under a flag of truce. The surgeon reports a much larger proportion than usual of slight wounds, 1,630 only being treated in hospitals.

I am glad to represent the army at the present time in good condition.

Thanking the Government for that entire support and confidence which I have always received from them, I remain, general, very respectfully, your obedient servant,

A. E. Burnside, Major-General,
Commanding Army of the Potomac

On December 19, while in Washington, D.C., Burnside explained his plan in his testimony to the investigating committee.

The plan I had in contemplation was, if the stores and those bridges had come here as I had expected, to throw Sumner's whole corps across the Rappahannock, fill the wagons with as many small stores as we could, and having beef-cattle along for meats, then to make a rapid movement down in the direction of Richmond, and try to meet the enemy and fight a battle before Jackson could make a junction there. We knew that Jackson was in the valley, and felt that there was force enough on the Upper Rappahannock to take care of him. We felt certain that as soon as the enemy knew of our coming down here the force under Jackson would be recalled, and we wanted to meet this force and beat it before Jackson could make a junction with them, or before Jackson could come down on our flank and perhaps cripple us, I had recommended that more supplies should be sent to the mouth of the Rappahannock, with a view to establishing a depot at Port Royal after we had advanced to Fredericksburg.

After it was ascertained that there must be a delay, and that the enemy had concentrated in such force as to make it very difficult to cross except by a number of bridges, we commenced bringing up from Aquia creek all the pontoons we could. After enough of them had been brought up to build the bridges, I called several councils of war to decide about crossing the Rappahannock. It was first decided to cross down at Skinker's Neck, about

twelve miles below here. But our demonstration in that direction concentrated the enemy at that place, and I finally gave up the idea of crossing there. I still continued operations at Skinker's Neck by way of demonstration, simply for the purpose of drawing down there as large a force of the enemy as possible. I then decided to cross here, because, in the first place, I felt satisfied that they did not expect us to cross here, but down below; in the next place, I felt satisfied that, this was the place to fight the most decisive battle, because if we could divide their forces by piercing their lines at one or two points, separating their left from their right, then a vigorous attack with the whole army would succeed in breaking their army in pieces.

The enemy had cut a road along in the rear of the line of heights where we made our attack, by means of which they connected the two wings of their army, and avoided a long detour around through a bad country. I obtained from a colored man from the other side of the town information in regard to this new road, which proved to be correct. I wanted to obtain possession of that new road, and that was my reasons for making an attack on the extreme left. I did not intend to make the attack on the right until that position had been taken, which I supposed would stagger the enemy, cutting their line in two; and then I proposed to make a direct attack on their front, and drive them out of their works.

I succeeded in building six bridges, and taking the whole army across. The two attacks were made, and we were repulsed; still holding a portion of the ground we had fought upon, but not our extreme advance.

Contrary to his generals' opinions, Burnside still believed that by throwing waves of men at the stone wall in quick succession he could have overwhelmed the Confederates entrenched there.

WHAT BURNSIDE SHOULD HAVE DONE

Confederate

Lieutenant-General James Longstreet (See biography, page 48.)

I have been asked if Burnside could have been victorious at Fredericksburg. Such a thing was hardly possible. Perhaps no general could have accomplished more than Burnside did, and it was possible for him to have suffered greater loss. The battle of Fredericksburg was a great and unprofitable sacrifice of human life made, through the pressure from the rear, against a general who should have known better and who doubtless acted against his judgment. If I had been in General Burnside's place, I would have asked the President to allow me to resign rather than execute his order to force the passage of the river and march the army against Lee in his stronghold.

Viewing the battle after the lapse of more than twenty years, I may say, however, that Burnside's move might have been made stronger by throwing two of his grand divisions across at the mouth of Deep Run, where Franklin crossed with his grand division and six brigades of Hooker's. Had he thus placed Hooker and Sumner, his sturdiest fighters, and made resolute assault with them in his attack on our right, he would in all probability have given us trouble. The partial success he had at that point might have been pushed vigorously by such a force and might have thrown our right entirely from position, in which event the result would have depended on the skillful handling of the forces. Franklin's grand division could have

made sufficient sacrifice at Marye's Hill and come as near success as did Sumner's and two-thirds of Hooker's, combined. I think, however, that the success would have been on our side, and it might have been followed by greater disaster on the side of the Federals; still they would have had the chance of a possible success in their favor, while in the battle as fought it can hardly be claimed that there was a chance.

Burnside made a mistake from the first. He should have gone from Warrenton to Chester Gap. He might then have held Jackson and fought me, or have held me and fought Jackson, thus taking us in detail. The doubt about the matter was whether or not he could have caught me in that trap before we could concentrate. At any rate, that was the only move on the board that could have benefited him at the time he was assigned to the command of the Army of the Potomac. By interposing between the corps of Lee's army, he would have secured strong ground and advantage of position. With skill equal to the occasion, he should have had success. This was the move about which we felt serious apprehension, and were occupying our minds with plans to meet it, when the move towards Fredericksburg was reported.

General McClellan, in an account recently published, speaks of this move as that upon which he was studying when the order for Burnside's assignment to command reached him. When Burnside determined to move by Fredericksburg, he should have moved rapidly and occupied the city at once, but this would only have forced us back to the plan preferred by General Jackson.

VICTORY

Confederate

General Robert E. Lee (See biography, page 9.)

Hdqrs. Army of Northern Virginia, December 31, 1862
 General Orders, No. 138

I. The general commanding takes this occasion to express to the officers and soldiers of the army his high appreciation of the fortitude, valor, and devotion displayed by them, which, under the blessing of Almighty God, has added the victory of Fredericksburg to the long list of their triumphs.

An arduous march, performed with celerity, under many disadvantages, exhibited the discipline and spirit of the troops and their eagerness to confront the foe.

The immense army of the enemy completed its preparation for the attack without interruption, and gave battle in its own time, and on ground of its own selection. It was encountered by less than 20,000 of this brave army, and its columns crushed and broken, hurled back at every point with such fearful slaughter that escape from entire destruction became the boast of those who had advanced in full confidence of victory. That this great result was achieved with a loss small in point of numbers, only augments the admiration with which the commanding general regards the prowess of the troops, and increases his gratitude to Him who has given us the victory.

The war is not yet ended. The enemy is still numerous and strong, and the country demands of the army a renewal of its heroic efforts in her behalf. Nobly has it responded to her call in the past, and she will never appeal in vain to its courage and patriotism.

THE BATTLE OF CHANCELLORSVILLE

SPOTSYLVANIA COUNTY, VIRGINIA
APRIL 30–MAY 6, 1863

COMMANDERS

Union
Maj. Gen. Joseph Hooker

Confederate
Gen. Robert E. Lee

PARTICIPANTS

133,868 (Army of the Potomac)

60,892 (Army of Northern Virginia)

CASUALTIES

Union
1,606 killed
9,672 wounded
5,919 MIA

Confederate
1,665 killed
9,081 wounded
2,018 MIA

VICTORY: CONFEDERACY

OVERVIEW

The Battle of Chancellorsville—called Lee's "perfect battle"—came as a tremendous blow to the Confederacy. It was during this battle that Stonewall Jackson was accidentally killed by his own men during a skirmish as he approached their line from the direction of the Union fire. Near the end of Lee's life, he said, "If I had had Stonewall Jackson at Gettysburg, we should have won a great victory. And I feel confident that a complete success there would have resulted in the establishment of our independence."

At Chancellorsville, Lee was facing an army more than twice as large, yet he made the bold move of splitting his army in two, while a third part—Longstreet and about 20 percent of Lee's army—was away and unable to take part in the battle. Leaving Major-General Early and another 20 percent to face Union major general John Sedgwick in the Second Battle of Fredericksburg, the remaining 60 percent went to attack the Union's main force. As if that wasn't daring enough, after Jeb Stuart's cavalry found Hooker's weak spot, Lee left just 13,000 men to face Hooker's main force head-on, while Stonewall Jackson took 28,000 around to flank Hooker in a surprise attack on the Union's right. Lee's brashness in the face of Hooker's reticence made Fighting Joe Hooker look more like George "McDawdle" McClellan.

Hooker's plan was good—hitting Lee with a two-pronged attack on his front and rear, while sending cavalry to cut off Lee's communications and harass Richmond—but when it came to its execution, Hooker proved too slow and indecisive. He sent in troops and then pulled them back, sometimes even when they were successful. In the end, he felt he didn't have the space to maneuver in the Wilderness, so he ended his Chancellorsville campaign by retreating to safety. Overlooking all this, Lincoln allowed Hooker to continue as commander of the Army of the Potomac.

In spite of the loss of Stonewall Jackson, this Confederate victory no doubt increased Lee's confidence and his faith that God was giving them victories. This line of thought, combined with the loss of Jackson, contributed to his defeat at Gettysburg.

THE PERFECT BATTLE

Confederate

General Robert E. Lee (See biography, page 9.)

Headquarters Army of Northern Virginia,
September 21, 1863
General S. Cooper, Adjt. and Insp. Gen. C. S. Army, Richmond, Va.

After the battle of Fredericksburg, the army remained encamped on the south side of the Rappahannock until the latter part of April. The Federal Army occupied the north side of the river opposite Fredericksburg, extending to the Potomac. General Longstreet, with two divisions of his corps, was detached for service south of James River in February, and did not rejoin the army until after the battle of Chancellorsville.

On April 14, intelligence was received that the enemy's cavalry was concentrating on the Upper Rappahannock. Their efforts to establish themselves on the south side of the river were successfully resisted by Fitzhugh Lee's brigade and two regiments of W. H. F. Lee's, the whole under the immediate command of General Stuart.

About the 21st, small bodies of infantry appeared at Kelly's Ford and the Rappahannock Bridge, and almost at the same time a demonstration was made opposite Port Royal, where a party of infantry crossed the river about the 23d. These movements were evidently intended to conceal the designs of the enemy, but, taken in connection with the reports of scouts, indicated that the Federal Army, now commanded by Major-General Hooker, was about to resume active operations.

At 5.30 a.m. on April 28, the enemy crossed the Rappahannock in boats near Fredericksburg, and, driving off the pickets on the river, proceeded to lay down a pontoon bridge a short distance below the mouth of Deep Run. Later in the forenoon another bridge was constructed about a mile below the first. A considerable force crossed on these bridges during the day, and was massed out of view under the high banks of the river.

As in the first battle of Fredericksburg, it was thought best to select positions with a view to resist the advance of the enemy, rather than incur the heavy loss that would attend any attempt to prevent his crossing. Our dispositions were accordingly made as on the former occasion.

No demonstration was made opposite any other part of our lines at Fredericksburg, and the strength of the force that had crossed and its apparent indisposition to attack indicated that the principal effort of the enemy would be made in some other quarter. This impression was confirmed by intelligence received from General Stuart that a large body of infantry and artillery was passing up the river. The routes they were pursuing after crossing the Rapidan converge near Chancellorsville, whence several roads lead to the rear of our position at Fredericksburg.

On the night of the 29th, General Anderson was directed to proceed toward Chancellorsville. Learning that the enemy were approaching in strong force, General Anderson retired early on the morning of the 30th to the intersection of the Mine and Plank roads, near Tabernacle Church, and began to intrench himself.

In the meantime General Stuart had been directed to endeavor to impede the progress of the column marching by way of Germanna Ford. By this means the march of this column was delayed until 12 m., when, learning that the one from Ely's Ford had already reached Chancellorsville,

General Stuart marched by Todd's Tavern toward Spotsylvania Court-House, to put himself in communication with the main body of the army.

The enemy in our front near Fredericksburg continued inactive, and it was now apparent that the main attack would be made upon our flank and rear. It was, therefore, determined to leave sufficient troops to hold our lines, and with the main body of the army to give battle to the approaching column.

The enemy was soon encountered on both roads, and heavy skirmishing with infantry and artillery ensued, our troops pressing steadily forward. His whole line thereupon retreated rapidly, vigorously pursued by our troops until they arrived within about 1 mile of Chancellorsville. Here the enemy had assumed a position of great natural strength, surrounded on all sides by a dense forest filled with a tangled undergrowth, in the midst of which breastworks of logs had been constructed, with trees felled in front, so as to form an almost impenetrable abatis.[7] His artillery swept the few narrow roads by which his position could be approached from the front, and commanded the adjacent woods.

Darkness was approaching before the strength and extent of his line could be ascertained, and as the nature of the country rendered it hazardous to attack by night, our troops were halted and formed in line of battle in front of Chancellorsville, at right angles to the Plank road, extending on the right to the Mine road and to the left in the direction of the Catharine Furnace.

It was evident that a direct attack upon the enemy would be attended with great difficulty and loss, in view of the strength of his position and his superiority of numbers. It was, therefore, resolved

---

7   An *abatis* (pronounced ab-uh-TEE) is a barrier in front of fortifications usually consisting of felled trees with sharpened branches pointing toward the opposing line.

to endeavor to turn his right flank and gain his rear, leaving a force in front to hold him in check and conceal the movement. The execution of this plan was intrusted to Lieutenant-General Jackson with his three divisions.

Early on the morning of the 2d, General Jackson marched by the Furnace and Brock roads, his movement being effectually covered by Fitzhugh Lee's cavalry, under General Stuart in person. After a long and fatiguing march, General Jackson's leading division, under General [Robert] Rodes, reached the old turnpike, about 3 miles in rear of Chancellorsville, at 4 p.m. As the different divisions arrived, they were formed at right angles to the road—Rodes in front, Trimble's division, under Brigadier-General [Raleigh] Colston, in the second, and A. P. Hill's in the third line.

At 6 p.m. the advance was ordered. The enemy were taken by surprise, and fled after a brief resistance. General Rodes' men pushed forward with great vigor and enthusiasm, followed closely by the second and third lines. Position after position was carried, the guns captured, and every effort of the enemy to rally defeated by the impetuous rush of our troops. In the ardor of pursuit through the thick and tangled woods, the first and second lines at last became mingled, and moved on together as one.

The enemy made a stand at a line of breastworks across the road, at the house of Melzie Chancellor, but the troops of Rodes and Colston dashed over the intrenchments together, and the flight and pursuit were resumed, and continued until our advance was arrested by the abatis in front of the line of works near the central position at Chancellorsville.

It was now dark, and General Jackson ordered the third line, under General Hill, to advance to the front, and relieve the troops of Rodes and

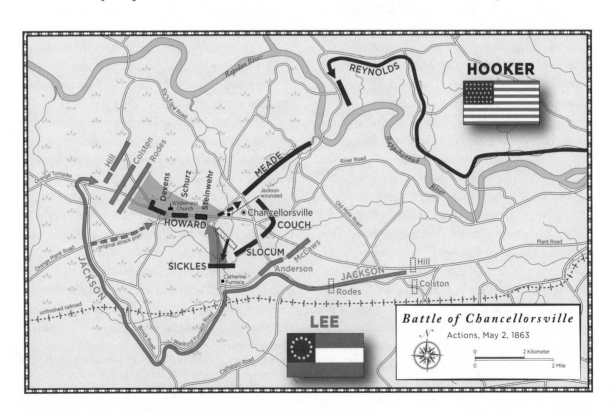

Colston, who were completely blended and in such disorder, from their rapid advance through intricate woods and over broken ground, that it was necessary to reform them. As Hill's men moved forward, General Jackson, with his staff and escort, returning from the extreme front, met his skirmishers advancing, and in the obscurity of the night were mistaken for the enemy and fired upon. Captain Boswell, chief engineer of the corps, and several others were killed and a number wounded. General Jackson himself received a severe injury, and was borne from the field.

The command devolved upon Major-General Hill, whose division was advanced to the line of intrenchments which had been reached by Rodes and Colston. A furious fire of artillery was opened upon them by the enemy, under cover of which his infantry advanced to the attack. They were handsomely repulsed by the Fifty-fifth Virginia Regiment, under Colonel Mallory, who was killed while bravely leading his men. General Hill was soon afterward disabled, and Major-General [Jeb] Stuart, who had been directed by General Jackson to seize the road to Ely's Ford, in rear of the enemy, was sent for to take command. The darkness of the night and the difficulty of moving through the woods and undergrowth rendered it advisable to defer further operations until morning, and the troops rested on their arms in line of battle.

As soon as the sound of cannon gave notice of Jackson's attack on the enemy's right, our troops in front of Chancellorsville were ordered to press him strongly on the left, to prevent re-enforcements being sent to the point assailed. They were directed not to attack in force unless a favorable opportunity should present itself, and, while continuing to cover the roads leading from their respective positions toward Chancellorsville, to incline to the left so as to connect with Jackson's right as he closed in upon the center.

The breastworks at which the attack was suspended the preceding evening were carried by assault under a terrible fire of musketry and artillery. The enemy was driven from all his fortified positions, with heavy loss in killed, wounded, and prisoners, and retreated toward the Rappahannock. By 10 a.m. we were in full possession of the field.

The troops, having become somewhat scattered by the difficulties of the ground and the ardor of the contest, were immediately reformed preparatory to renewing the attack. The enemy had withdrawn to a strong position nearer to the Rappahannock, which he had previously fortified. His superiority of numbers, the unfavorable nature of the ground, which was densely wooded, and the condition of our troops after the arduous and sanguinary conflict in which they had been engaged, rendered great caution necessary.

Before dawn on the morning of the 3d, General [William] Barksdale reported to General Early that the enemy had occupied Fredericksburg in large force and laid down a bridge at the town. Very soon the enemy advanced in large force against Marye's and the hills to the right and left of it. Two assaults were gallantly repulsed by Barksdale's men and the artillery. After the second, a flag of truce was sent from the town to obtain permission to provide for the wounded.

Three heavy lines advanced immediately upon the return of the flag and renewed the attack. They were bravely repulsed on the right and left, but the small force at the foot of Marye's Hill, overpowered by more than ten times their numbers, was captured after a heroic resistance, and the hill carried. The success of the enemy enabled him to threaten our communications by moving down the Telegraph road, or to come upon our rear at Chancellorsville by the Plank road.

The Battle of Chancellorsville

The enemy began to advance up the Plank road, his progress being gallantly disputed by the brigade of General [Cadmus] Wilcox. General Wilcox fell back slowly until he reached Salem Church, on the Plank road, about 5 miles from Fredericksburg. Information of the state of affairs in our rear having reached Chancellorsville, General McLaws was ordered to re-enforce General Wilcox.

The assault was met with the utmost firmness, and after a fierce struggle the first line was repulsed with great slaughter. The second then came forward, but immediately broke under the close and deadly fire which it encountered, and the whole mass fled in confusion to the rear. They were pursued by the brigades of Wilcox and Semmes, which advanced nearly a mile, when they were halted to reform in the presence of the enemy's reserve, which now appeared in large force. It being quite dark, General Wilcox deemed it imprudent to push the attack with his small numbers, and retired to his original position, the enemy making no attempt to follow.

In the meantime the enemy had so strengthened his position near Chancellorsville that it was deemed inexpedient to assail it with less than our whole force, which could not be concentrated until we were relieved from the danger that menaced our rear. It was accordingly resolved still further to re-enforce the troops in front of General Sedgwick, in order, if possible, to drive him across the Rappahannock.

Looking southeast from a Federal artillery position on Stafford Heights on May 2, 1863, gunsmoke from the battle can be seen in the distance above the sitting man. The smoke closer and to the right is from cooking fires in the Union camp. The lower pontoon bridges are hidden from view right below the camp.

The attack did not begin until 6 p.m., when Anderson and Early moved forward and drove General Sedgwick's troops rapidly before them across the Plank road in the direction of the Rappahannock. The speedy approach of darkness prevented General McLaws from perceiving the success of the attack until the enemy began to recross the river. His right brigades advanced through the woods in the direction of the firing, but the retreat was so rapid that they could only join in the pursuit. A dense fog settled over the field, increasing the obscurity, and rendering great caution necessary to avoid collision between our own troops.

The next morning it was found that General Sedgwick had made good his escape and removed his bridges. Fredericksburg was also evacuated, and our rear no longer threatened. Preparations were made to assail the enemy's works [at Chancellorsville] at daylight on the 6th, but, on

advancing our skirmishers, it was found that under cover of the storm and darkness of the night he had retreated over the river.

The movement by which the enemy's position was turned and the fortune of the day decided was conducted by the lamented Lieutenant-General Jackson. I do not propose here to speak of the character of this illustrious man, since removed from the scene of his eminent usefulness by the hand of an inscrutable but all-wise Providence. I nevertheless desire to pay the tribute of my admiration to the matchless energy and skill that marked this last act of his life, forming, as it did, a worthy conclusion of that long series of splendid achievements which won for him the lasting love and gratitude of his country.

Respectfully submitted.

R. E. Lee, General

STONEWALL JACKSON IS SHOT

Confederate

Lieutenant-General Jubal Early (See biography, page 7.)

About the close of the winter or beginning of the spring of 1863, two of Longstreet's divisions, one-fourth of our army, were sent to the South side of James River; and, during their absence, Hooker, who had succeeded Burnside in the command, commenced the movement which resulted in the battle of Chancellorsville, in the first days of May. Throwing a portion of his troops across the

river just below Fredericksburg, on the 29th of April, and making an ostentatious demonstration with three corps on the North bank, he proceeded to cross four others above our left flank to Chancellorsville. Having accomplished this, Hooker issued a gasconading order to his troops, in which he claimed to have General Lee's army in his power, and declared his purpose of crushing it.

Leaving my division, one brigade of another, and a portion of the reserve artillery, in all less than nine thousand men, to confront the three corps opposite and near Fredericksburg, General Lee moved with five divisions of infantry and a portion of the artillery to meet Hooker, the cavalry being employed to watch the flanks. As soon as General Lee reached Hooker's front, he determined to take the offensive, and, by one of his bold strategic movements, he sent Jackson around Hooker's right flank, and that boastful commander, who was successively reinforced by two of the corps left opposite Fredericksburg, was so vigorously assailed, that he was put on the defensive, and soon compelled to provide for the safety of his own defeated army.

It is a little remarkable that Hooker did not claim, on this occasion, that we had the odds against him; but when he went back, under compulsion, he issued an order, in which he stated, that his army had retired for reasons best known to itself, that it was the custodian of its own honor and advanced when it pleased, fought when it pleased, and retired when it pleased.

As glorious as was this victory, it, nevertheless, shed a gloom over the whole army and country, for in it had fallen the great Lieutenant to whom General Lee had always entrusted the execution of his most daring plans, and who had proved himself so worthy of the confidence reposed in him.

West of the Wilderness Church [about two miles west of Chancellorsville] General Jackson had crossed the Plank road to the old Stone turnpike and moved along the latter, with his lines across it at right angles, until he struck the enemy, and until the two roads united.

[Stopping to rearrange the columns,] General Jackson was slowly riding to the front, while making every effort to hurry forward the troops, when he was fired upon by a portion of his own men on the right (south) of the road and obliquely from the rear, and that then the horses of his party that were not shot down wheeled to the left, and he galloped into the woods on the left to escape the fire, when he was fired upon by another body of troops on the north side of the road.

> I always respected Jackson personally, and esteemed his sincere and manly character. He impressed me always as a man of the Cromwell stamp, a Puritan—much more of the New Englander than the Virginian. If any man believed in the rebellion he did. And his nature was such that whatever he believed in became a deep religious duty, a duty he would discharge at any cost. It is a mistake to suppose that I ever had any feeling for Stonewall Jackson but respect. Personally we were always good friends; his character had rare points of merit, and although he made the mistake of fighting against his country, if ever a man did so conscientiously he was the man.
>
> —GENERAL ULYSSES S. GRANT

This firing, lamentable as were its consequences, was in both instances the result of accident, or rather of that confusion inevitable in all attempts to operate with troops in the dark while they are under excitement. The writer of this has perhaps been under fire as often as any man of his day, and the result of his experience and observation has been to convince him that the dangers attending offensive movements of troops in the night, especially in the forepart of the night, when the opposite side is on the alert, from mistakes or collision on the part of those taking the offensive, are not counterbalanced by any advantages likely to result; and to sustain him in this opinion he can confidently appeal to the judgment of those who have had any experience. In operating in a thickly-wooded country the dangers are increased very greatly.

The firing from the right (the first in point of time) was undoubtedly the cause of the other, for when General Jackson's party came crashing through the brushwood in the dark towards the infantry in line of battle expecting soon to encounter the enemy, a fire upon it was inevitable.

In the current accounts of the affair it is generally represented that a number of officers were shot at the same time the General was shot, in such a manner as to produce the impression that they were with him; but the fact is, that the only officer with General Jackson at the time was Captain Wilbourn, the rest of the party being composed of couriers and signal-men.

Facing south, this is approximately the spot where Lieutenant-General Stonewall Jackson was shot and he rode off into the trees trying to escape.

General Jackson thought, while awaiting General Hill's movements, he would ride to the front as far as the skirmish line or pickets, and ascertain what could be seen or heard of the enemy and his movements, supposing there was certainly a line of skirmishers in front, as his orders were always very imperative to keep a skirmish line in front of the line of battle. When we had ridden only a few rods, to our great surprise our little party was fired upon by about a battalion, or perhaps less, of our troops, a little to our right and to the right of the pike the balls passing diagonally across the pike, and being apparently aimed at us. Many of the escort and their horses were shot down.

At this firing our horses wheeled suddenly to the left, and General Jackson (at whose side I kept), followed by the few who were not dismounted by this first fire, galloped into the woods to get out of range of the bullets, and approached our line a little obliquely; but we had not gone over twenty paces from the edge of the pike, in the thicket, ere the brigade just to the left of the pike (to our right as we approached from the direction of the enemy), drawn up within thirty yards of us, fired a volley also, kneeling on the right knee (as shown by the flash of their muskets) as though prepared to guard against cavalry. By this fire General Jackson was wounded. These troops evidently mistook us for a party of the enemy's cavalry.

—Capt. R. E. Wilbourn, chief signal officer for
Jackson's corps, in an 1873 letter to
General Early

The firing, however, as usual in case of false alarms, passed along the line, and some officers with the party of General Hill in the road were shot; Captain Boswell and Lieutenant Morrison were with this party, or were going forward to join General Jackson. General Hill and some others were subsequently struck by the enemy's fire.

General Jackson did not get out of hearing of his own men, nor out of sight of General Hill's party, and was riding slowly to the front when first fired on. When wounded he had not gone obliquely towards his line more than twenty paces before he was fired on by the troops, not more than thirty yards distant. Therefore, while he was being carried off by Wilbourn and Wynn, he was not more than fifty yards from the troops that had wounded him.

To complete the narrative of the circumstances attending the wounding of General Jackson until he was placed in the ambulance to be carried to the hospital, it is only necessary to state that when Captain Wilbourn left him to obtain some whiskey, after the first fall of the litter, Captain Leigh and the General's two aids, Lieutenants Smith and Morrison, remained with him and faithfully administered to him. The party had to lie down in the road for a time to escape the enemy's fire, and when it ceased along the road, the General was assisted for a short distance to move on foot, but was again placed upon a litter, from which he had a second very painful fall, caused by one of the litter-bearers entangling his foot in a vine as the litter was borne through the brushwood on the side of the road. He was placed a third time upon the litter and carried to the rear, until he met the ambulance Dr. McGuire had provided for him; and in this he was carried to the hospital, along with his Chief of Artillery, Colonel Crutchfield, who had been painfully wounded during the engagement.

SURGERY AND MEDICINE

The Civil War helped bring the medical profession out of its dark ages. Prior to the war, many physicians still believed in the ancient idea of four bodily humors: blood, associated with the liver; yellow bile, with the spleen; black bile, with the gall bladder; and phlegm, with the lungs and brain. They thought ailments resulted from humors falling out of balance, so treatments generally involved bloodletting, emetics, and purges. It was probably bloodletting that killed the ailing George Washington, from whom physicians drained 35 percent of his blood.

Prior to the Civil War, only a handful of larger cities, such as New York and New Orleans, had hospitals, these mainly for the poor. Everyone else was treated at home. When the war began, the Union had only 87 men in its medical corps; four years later 11,000 medical officers were serving or had served in the corps. The U.S. Army Medical, Ambulance, and Nurse Corps was formed, introducing an ambulance service that didn't previously exist. By the end of the war, they had treated more than ten million injuries and ailments.

There were more than sixty medical schools in the country providing a year of lectures, followed by apprenticeships. Some students traveled to Europe for more advanced training. Doctors didn't yet know about bacteria. Frenchman Louis Pasteur was discovering them at the time—developing his germ theory and pasteurization—but doctors were learning the importance of sanitation only slowly.

Sanitary practices in army camps were very lax. Many soldiers had been cared for by women all their lives. Some didn't know how to cook, so they ate their food raw until they learned. Others didn't bother with bathing or washing their clothes. Vermin, particularly lice and fleas, quickly infested even those who did wash. Each company was supposed to dig a trench eight feet deep and two feet wide nearby where they could deposit all their excrement and garbage. Each night they were to cover the trench's contents with half a foot of dirt. Some didn't like digging these sinks, while others didn't want to use them.

The Sanitary Commission's report to the Secretary of War in December 1861 found that of 200 regimental camps, 24 percent were "decidedly bad, filthy and dangerous," while an additional 26 percent were "negligent and slovenly." The report said the dangers included "drains wanting or clogged up, and retentive of stagnant water; the camp streets and spaces between the tents littered with refuse food and other rubbish, sometimes in an offensive state of decomposition; slops deposited in pits within the camp limits, or thrown out broadcast; heaps of manure and offal close to the camp, and the privies neglected."

This led to infestations of flies, which spread bacteria and viruses among the men and onto their food. With the physical exertion, exposure, and poor diet weakening their immune systems, along with the crowding and unsanitary conditions, diseases spread like fire.

Approximately two-thirds of the deaths among soldiers of both sides came from disease. Only about one-third derived from battle wounds or accidents. Typhoid fever caused about a quarter of noncombat fatalities. Mosquitoes spread malaria, infecting a million Union soldiers; fortunately, treatment with quinine reduced these fatalities. Of every 1,000 Union soldiers, more than 995 contracted chronic dysentery at some point. Among all the diseases prevalent during the war, dysentery was the deadliest.

The Confederates had it roughly the same. They had about 4,000 doctors, and medicines were always running low or out, but they improvised with native plants and herbal remedies, which worked out very well.

When a soldier was wounded on the battlefield, his first stop was the field dressing station just out of range of gunfire. Here an assistant surgeon administered an opium pill for pain or rubbed morphine powder into the wound and gave the patient whiskey or brandy for shock. He cleaned the wound, packed it with lint—essentially the unraveled threads of cloth—and bandaged it, applying a splint if needed. Later in the war, morphine was injected by syringe.

If further treatment was required, the patient walked or was carried to a field hospital, generally a tent or barn well away from the battlefield. Here doctors triaged soldiers into the slightly wounded, mortally wounded, and those headed for surgery. Head, neck, chest, and abdominal wounds were usually considered fatal, so arm and leg wounds went first into surgery. Despite common misconceptions, more than 90 percent of operations took place under anesthesia—even in the South—usually under chloroform, ether, or morphine.

Among Union soldiers 71 percent of gunshot wounds affected the arms and legs, perhaps from fighting behind cover. Minié balls tended to inflict extensive wounds largely because of their power and weight, so amputations were the usual treatment. When they struck the abdomen, they usually perforated the colon, causing peritonitis, which was fatal. Round shot, because of its slower speed, tended to push the intestines out of the way without puncturing them, so these wounds were more survivable. The reverse was true for chest wounds. The velocity of Minié balls enabled them to pass right through, while round shot lacerated large areas of lung tissue. Surprisingly, those treated for saber and bayonet wounds usually survived.

But none of the physicians knew that bacteria or viruses existed; therefore, they didn't sterilize anything. They shoved dirty fingers into wounds to remove bullets, shrapnel, and bone fragments. There was little water for washing anything, so they reused bloody bone saws and instruments from one operation to the next. If they dropped a sponge or instrument on the ground, they might rinse or brush it off before employing it. They reused bandages, didn't change them often, and kept them wet, which helped bacteria grow. Most doctors knew that cleanliness helped—but didn't realize how vitally important it was.

As a result, just about every wound developed infection. It was so common that the doctors thought pus was a sign of healing. Instead, it was destroying tissue and releasing deadly toxins into the bloodstream. Sometimes gangrene followed. Still, almost 75 percent of amputees survived.

Both soldiers and the press referred to military physicians as butchers, but some estimate that without them twice as many men would have died in the war.

THE PROBLEM WITH CHANCELLORSVILLE

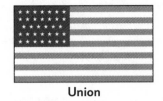

Union

Major-General Joseph Hooker (See biography, page 94.)

Hooker testified before the Committee on the Conduct of the War:

When I returned from Chancellorsville, I felt that I had fought no battle; in fact, I had more men than I could use, and I fought no general battle for the reason that I could not get my men in position to do so; probably not more than three or three and a half corps on the right were engaged in that fight. When I marched out on the morning of the 1st of May, I could get but few troops into position; the column had to march through narrow roads, and could not be thrown forward fast enough to prevent their being overwhelmed by the enemy in his advance. On assuming my position, Lee advanced on me in that manner, and was soon repulsed, the column thrown back in confusion into the open ground. It could not live there. The roads through the forest were not unlike bridges to pass. A mile or more in advance of the position I had would have placed me beyond the forest, where, with my superior forces, the enemy would in all probability have been beaten.

I may say here the battle of Chancellorsville has been associated with the battle of Fredericksburg, and has been called a disaster. My whole loss in the battle of Chancellorsville was a little over 17,000. I may say that the enemy's surgeons admitted to the surgeons I left on the field at Chancellorsville that their loss was not less than 18,000 men in that battle.[8]

I said that Chancellorsville had been called a disaster. I lost, under those operations, one piece artillery, I think five or six wagons, and one ambulance. Of course, many of the 11th corps lost their arms and knapsacks. In my opinion there is nothing to regret in regard to Chancellorsville except the failure to accomplish all I moved to accomplish. The troops lost no honor, except in one corps, and we lost no more men than the enemy; but expectation was high, the army in splendid condition, and great results were expected from it. It was at a time, too, when the nation required a victory.

Mr. Loan: What corps had you in the action of the 3d of May?

Answer: The 12th and part of the 2d, the 3d and a small part of the 5th. The 11th corps I put on the left, where it was not exposed. The 11th and 1st corps were not engaged at all; as was also the case with perhaps two-thirds of the 5th corps.

---

8   Final figures put Union loses at 17,197, with Confederate losses of 12,764, including those killed, wounded, missing, and captured.

Mr. Loan: Why were not those corps brought into action?

Answer: They could not be put into position. When the corps commanders assembled on the night of the 4th and 5th, I submitted to them the mode of attack I should have to adopt in case of an advance; that it could only be with slender columns, if an advance was made at all. On the roads that we would have to make use of for that purpose the enemy was particularly strong, and was behind his defences throughout the line. Early in the campaign I had come to the conclusion that, with the arms now in use, it would be impossible to carry works by an assault in front, provided they were properly constructed, and properly manned. I was of that impression at the battle of Fredericksburg, and requested General Burnside not to insist upon an attack being made under those circumstances; I said to him that I would advise him not to attack there; he said it was necessary, and of course I made it, and it was made with great vigor.

"I Am Sorry for Hooker"

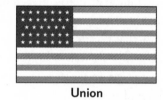

Union

Major-General George Meade (See biography, page 92.)

In letters to his wife, Meade wrote:

Camp near Falmouth, Va., April 26, 1863

Hooker seems very confident of success, but lets no one into his secrets. I heard him say that not a human being knew his plans either in the army or at Washington. For my part I am willing to be in ignorance, for it prevents all criticism and faultfinding in advance. All I ask and pray for is to be told explicitly and clearly what I am expected to do, and then I shall try, to the best of my ability, to accomplish the task set before me.

Camp near Falmouth, Va., May 7, 1863

I reached here last evening, fatigued and exhausted with a ten days' campaign, pained and humiliated at its unsatisfactory result, but grateful to our heavenly Father that, in His infinite goodness, He permitted me to escape all the dangers I had to pass through.

The papers will give you all the details of the movement, so that I shall confine myself to a general account of my own doings. General Hooker's plan was well conceived and its early part well executed. It was briefly thus: A portion of the army were to make a forced march, cross the Rappahannock so high up as to preclude opposition, cross the Rapidan at the lower fords, drive away the defenders of the works placed at the crossings of the Rappahannock nearest to Fredericksburg, and when one of these was opened, the rest of the army was to join the advanced corps, be concentrated, and push the enemy away from Fredericksburg.

On the 30th we advanced and concentrated at Chancellorsville, a small place on the plank road from Fredericksburg to Gordonsville, and distant some ten miles from Fredericksburg. On the 1st inst. two more corps were brought over to Chancellorsville, and the Fifth and Twelfth corps advanced from Chancellorsville towards Fredericksburg; but just as we reached the enemy we were recalled. On our retiring the enemy attacked [Major-General George] Sykes's division of my corps and we had a smart fight till dark.

The next day, May 2d, the enemy attacked in force, and after a day's hard fighting, owing to the bad behavior of a portion of our troops, the Eleventh Corps, we had to fall back and draw in our lines.

I ought to have mentioned that, simultaneously with our crossing the Rappahannock above, Sedgwick and [Major-General John] Reynolds crossed below Fredericksburg, and after occupying the attention of the enemy, so soon as we were established at Chancellorsville, they were withdrawn, and Reynolds joined us on the 30th. When the force of the enemy was perceived, Sedgwick was ordered to recross at Fredericksburg and attack in their rear, which he did, on the 2d inst.

On the 3d we had a very heavy fight, in which we held our own, but did not advance, awaiting Sedgwick's operations. On the 4th remained quiet, and in the evening learned that Sedgwick was held in check by superior forces, and his position critical. The enemy not attacking us on the 5th, as we hoped, and finding him too strong to attack without danger of sacrificing the army in case of defeat, Hooker determined to withdraw to this side of the river, which we did without pursuit, on the night of the 5th.

Camp near Falmouth, Va., May 8, 1863

Just after closing my letter yesterday I was summoned to headquarters, where I found the President and General Halleck. The former said he had come down to enquire for himself as to the condition of affairs and desired to see corps commanders. He and Halleck spent a couple of hours, took lunch, and talked of all sorts of things, but nothing was said of our recent operations, or any reference made to the future, nor was any corps commander called on for an opinion. The President remarked that the result was in his judgment most unfortunate; that he did not blame any one—he believed every one had done all in his power; and that the disaster was one that could not be helped. Nevertheless he thought its effect, both at home and abroad, would be more serious and injurious than any previous act of the war. In this I agree with him; and when it comes to be known that it might and should have been avoided, I think the country will hold some one responsible.

My conscience and record are fortunately clear. I opposed the withdrawal with all my influence, and I tried all I could, on Sunday morning, to be permitted to take my corps into action, and to have a general battle with the whole army engaged, but I was overruled and censured for sending in a brigade of Humphreys's, which I did in spite of orders to the contrary.

General Hooker has disappointed all his friends by failing to show his fighting qualities at the pinch. He was more cautious and took to digging quicker even than McClellan, thus proving that a man may talk very big when he has no responsibility, but that it is quite a different thing, acting when you are responsible and talking when others are. Who would have believed a few days ago that Hooker would withdraw his army in opposition to the opinion of a majority of his corps commanders? Yet such is absolutely and actually the case.

My corps did not have much of a chance. On Friday, Sykes's division had a very handsome little affair, in which his command behaved very well and gained decided advantages, driving the enemy before them; but Sykes was recalled just as his advance was successful.

The heavy fighting, however, of Saturday and Sunday was done by [Generals Henry] Slocum, [Darius] Couch and [Daniel] Sickles, particularly the latter, whose losses are greater than any other corps, unless it be Sedgwick's, which suffered very severely in his attempt to attack the enemy from Fredericksburg.

I have been a good deal flattered by the expression of opinion on the part of many officers, that they thought and wished I should be placed in command, and poor Hooker himself, after he had determined to withdraw, said to me, in the most desponding manner, that he was ready to turn over to me the Army of the Potomac; that he had enough of it, and almost wished he had never been born.

Since seeing the President, however, he seems in better spirits, and I suppose, unless some strong pressure is brought to bear from external sources, he will not be disturbed. Hooker has one great advantage over his predecessors in not having any intriguer among his subordinate generals, who are working like beavers to get him out and themselves in.

Camp near Falmouth, May 10, 1863

There is a great deal of talking in the camp, and I see the press is beginning to attack Hooker. I think these last operations have shaken the confidence of the army in Hooker's judgment, particularly among the superior officers. I have been much gratified at the frequent expression of opinion that I ought to be placed in command. Three of my seniors [Couch, Slocum, and Sedgwick] have sent me word that they were willing to serve under me. Couch, I hear, told the President he would not serve any longer under Hooker, and recommended my assignment to the command.

I mention all this confidentially. I do not attach any importance to it, and do not believe there is the slightest probability of my being placed in command. I think I know myself, and am sincere when I say I do not desire the command; hence I can quietly attend to my duties, uninfluenced by what is going on around me, at the same time expressing, as I feel, great gratification that the army and my senior generals should think so well of my services and capacity as to be willing to serve under me. Having no political influence, being no intriguer, and indeed unambitious of the distinction, it is hardly probable I shall be called on to accept or decline.

I see the papers attribute Hooker's withdrawal to the weak councils of his corps commanders. This is a base calumny. Four out of six of his corps commanders were positive and emphatic in their opposition to the withdrawal, and he did it contrary to their advice. Hooker, however, I should judge, feels very secure, and does not seem concerned. I have no idea what his next move will be. For my part it would seem that all projects based on pursuing this line of operations having been tried and failed, we should try some other route. Yet the Administration is so wedded to this line that it will be difficult to get authority to change.

Camp near Falmouth, Va., May 12, 1863

I did not suppose you would credit the canard in the papers about our crossing and Lee's retreating. This story, however, with minute details, I see is published in *Forney's Press*, an Administration organ, that must have known and did know better. It has been circulated for some purpose, and is doubtless considered a great piece of strategy. There is no doubt Hooker assured the President that he would soon cross again and repair all disaster, but I fear he finds the execution of this promise more difficult than the making. The enemy have all returned to their old positions and they have been seen to-day busily engaged throwing up dirt and strengthening all the crossings by additional works, though one would suppose, from the work they had previously executed, there was no room for more.

All I can say is that Hooker has disappointed the army and myself, in failing to show the nerve and coup d'oeil at the critical moment, which all had given him credit for before he was tried. It is another proof of what a sense of responsibility will do to modify a man's character, and should be a warning to all of us to be very cautious how we criticise our neighbors, or predict what we would do ourselves if placed in similar circumstances. My only fear is that Hooker, goaded by the attacks that are now made on him, may be induced to take some desperate step in the hope of retrieving his waning fortunes. At the same time, as I have already told you, he was fully aware when he ordered the withdrawal of the army, that he was running the risk, and great risk, of self-sacrifice. For he said he knew his personal interests were involved in advancing. I believe he acted sincerely, and for what he considered the interests of the army and the country, but I differed with him in judgment, and I fear events will confirm my view. I was clearly in favor of tempting the hazard of the die, and letting Washington take care of itself.

I am sorry for Hooker, because I like him and my relations have always been agreeable with him; but I cannot shut my eyes to the fact that he has on this occasion missed a brilliant opportunity of making himself. Our losses are terrible; they are said to exceed fifteen thousand men, greater than in any other battle or series of battles, greater than in the whole of the celebrated six days' fighting before Richmond, and greater than McClellan's Maryland campaign. This large loss, together with the loss of over twenty thousand nine-months' and two-years' men, will very materially reduce this army, and unless it be speedily reinforced will paralyze its movements.

Camp near Falmouth, Va., May 19, 1863

I am sorry to tell you I am at open war with Hooker. He yesterday came to see me and referred to an article in the *Herald*, stating that four of his corps commanders were opposed to the withdrawal of the army. He said this was not so, and that Reynolds and myself had determined him to withdraw. I expressed the utmost surprise at this statement; when he said that I had expressed the opinion that it was impracticable to withdraw the army, and therefore I had favored an advance, and as he knew it was perfectly practicable to withdraw, he did not consider my opinion as being in favor of an advance.

I replied to him that this was a very ingenious way of stating what I had said; that my opinion was clear and emphatic for an advance; that I had gone so far as to say that I would not be governed by any consideration regarding the safety of Washington, for I thought that argument had paralyzed this army too long.

He reiterated his opinion and said he should proclaim it. I answered I should deny it, and should call on those who were present to testify as to whether he or I was right. The fact is, he now finds he has committed a grave error, which at the time he was prepared to assume the responsibility of, but now desires to cast it off on to the shoulders of others; but I rather think he will find himself mistaken. At any rate, the entente cordiale is destroyed between us, and I don't regret it, as it makes me more independent and free.

Camp near Falmouth, Va., May 20, 1863
The battle of Chancellorsville was a miserable failure, in which Hooker disappointed me greatly. His plan was admirably designed, and the early part of it, entrusted to others, was well executed; but after he had assembled his army on the other side near Chancellorsville, instead of striking at once vigorously and instantly, before the enemy, who were surprised, could concentrate, he delayed; gave them thirty-six hours to bring up and dispose of their troops; permitted them to attack him, and after their doing so, failed to take advantage of their error in dividing and separating their forces, but allowed them to engage only about half his army and to unite their forces after driving back a portion of ours. He then assumed the defensive, doing nothing for two days, while we could hear Sedgwick's guns, and knew they were trying to crush him and must succeed. Finally he withdrew to this side, giving up all the advantages gained, and having to recross with all the obstacles and difficulties increased.

Notwithstanding these are my views, I have abstained from making them known to any one, out of consideration for Hooker, who has always pretended to be very friendly to me.

Camp near Falmouth, Va., May 23, 1863
The story of Hooker losing his head, and my saving the army, is a canard, founded on some plausible basis. When Hooker was obliged to give up Chancellorsville and draw in his lines, I fortunately had anticipated this, and was prepared with my troops to take up the new line in a very short time, and to receive within it the broken columns from the old line.

About this time Hooker, who had just been stunned by being struck with a pillar of a house, hit by a shot, felt himself fainting and had to dismount from his horse and lie on his back for ten or fifteen minutes. During this time he was constantly calling for me, and this operation above referred to was executed by me. Outsiders, particularly his staff, not knowing my previous preparations and expectation of having to do this, and seeing it so well and quickly done, were astonished, and gave me more credit than I was entitled to, and hence arose the story that I saved the army.

Hooker never lost his head, nor did he ever allow himself to be influenced by me or my advice. The objection I have to Hooker is that he did not and would not listen to those around him; that he acted deliberately on his own judgment, and in doing so, committed, as I think, fatal errors. If he had lost his head, and I had been placed in command, you may rest assured a very different result would have been arrived at, whether better or worse for us cannot be told now; but it certainly would have been more decisive one way or the other.

Soon after the action commenced, on the morning of the 3d of May, I received a severe contusion from a column of the building, near which I was standing, being thrown violently against me by a cannon shot. This rendered me insensible for half an hour or more. As soon as I had sufficiently recovered to mount my horse, I did so, under the impression that I was all right. In the effort of mounting the acute pain returned, and after riding a few steps I became faint, was taken from my horse, and again placed in the hands of the medical director. I may have been disqualified for command by this accident an hour or an hour and a half, during which time Major General Couch exercised my office.

—MAJOR-GENERAL JOSEPH HOOKER, IN HIS
TESTIMONY TO CONGRESS

"THE WHEEL OF FORTUNE"

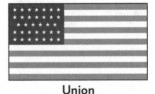

Union

Major-General Winfield Scott Hancock (See biography, page 116.)

Hancock explained where he felt matters went wrong in his testimony to Congress's investigating committee.

I consider the mistake in the matter was in ever stopping at Chancellorsville at all. There was the cause of the whole trouble. General Hooker did not arrive there until Thursday night, about the same time we did. If his troops had marched on even on Thursday afternoon, and opened Banks's ford, we would then have been within three miles of Fredericksburg, and would have been practically connected with the force under General Sedgwick, although separated by the town of Fredericksburg. There, no doubt, was the mistake. That movement might have been made on Thursday afternoon, or even on Friday morning.

General Lee had evidently been deceived by the movements of General Hooker, and had sent his troops down the river, below Fredericksburg, and had not been able to get them back in time to have resisted such a movement. I believe if we had not stopped at Chancellorsville, but had marched right down to Banks's ford, the whole movement would have been a perfect success. The mistake was, that when we had started to fight an offensive fight, we stopped and fought a defensive one before the concentration was complete.

Question: What do you say as to the original plan, as you understand it?

Answer: The original plan was full of risk, I think. To separate the army by so great a distance in the immediate presence of so wide-awake an enemy as we had was a movement very full of risk. A river was between us—picketed by us—and the country was wooded, so as to screen the movement, and it had been so secretly conducted that it was really a success up to the time that we changed the plan of the whole operation. No matter whether it was full of risk or not, it had succeeded up to that time.

In a letter to his wife, Hancock wrote:

I do not know what will be the next turn of the wheel of Fortune, or what Providence has in store for this unhappy army. I have had the blues ever since I returned from the campaign. I will send you a more complete account of this battle soon. We get the Chronicle and Inquirer daily: they are filled with inaccuracies. We are not allowed to have the New York papers. I am told that some of the New York papers recommend General —— and General —— for the command of the Army. That would be too much. I should ask to be relieved at once. I cannot stand any more inflictions of this kind.

I have not recovered from our last failure, which should have been a brilliant victory. Hooker

had two large corps (Meade's and Reynolds's), which had not been engaged. He was implored to put them into action at 10 o'clock on Sunday, when the enemy had, apparently, used up all their troops. He would not do it. Now the blame is to be put on Sedgwick for not joining us; as if it were possible to do so with one corps, when we had six corps, and this force was not considered strong enough to attempt to unite with Sedgwick, without risk to the command.

But it seems that Providence for some wise purpose intended our defeat. The day before the fight Hooker said to a general officer, "God Almighty could not prevent me from winning a victory to-morrow."

> *I always dreaded going to the army of the Potomac. After the battle of Gettysburg I was told I could have the command; but I managed to keep out of it. I had seen so many generals fall, one after another, like bricks in a row, that I shrank from it.*
>
> —General Ulysses S. Grant

Pray, could we expect a victory after that? He also told Mr. Lincoln that he would either win a victory or be in hell. The President told him to "carry plenty of water along."

Hooker's day is over. I have been approached again in connection with the command of the Army of the Potomac. Give yourself no uneasiness under no conditions would I accept the command. I do not belong to that class of generals whom the Republicans care to bolster up. I should be sacrificed.

THE SIEGE OF VICKSBURG

WARREN COUNTY, MISSISSIPPI
MAY 18–JULY 4, 1863

COMMANDERS

Union
Maj. Gen. Ulysses S. Grant

Confederate
Lieut. Gen. John C. Pemberton

PARTICIPANTS

35,000 (initial force)
75,278 (after reinforcements of June 14)
(Army of the Tennessee)

30,581 (Pemberton, Army of Mississippi)
26,000 (Johnston, Department of the West, rescue
  army not engaged)

CASUALTIES

Union
763 killed
3,746 wounded
162 POWs/MIA

Confederate
3,202 killed or wounded
29,495 POWs

VICTORY: UNION

OVERVIEW

The capture of Vicksburg, Mississippi, in the western theater allowed the Union to gain control of the Mississippi River. A vital transportation route extremely important to both North and South, it was also an important part of Winfield Scott's Anaconda Plan for suffocating the South with the blockade. Controlling the Mississippi effectively cut the South in half, separating the eastern portion from the three states that provided many of its supplies (Louisiana, Arkansas, and Texas).

Early in 1863 Grant established a base of operations on the Mississippi at Mulliken's Bend, roughly ten miles northwest of heavily fortified Vicksburg. He spent a couple of futile months trying to open waterways for Admiral Porter's boats and ironclads. Giving up, Porter finally ran the gauntlet of

Vicksburg's batteries, then ferried Grant's troops across the Mississippi at Bruinsburg, about fifteen miles southwest of Vicksburg. Grant then had to get between the two Confederate armies of Lieutenant-General John Pemberton and General Joseph Johnston to prevent them from uniting against him. He chased Pemberton into Vicksburg and then laid siege to the city.

Grant attempted to break through the city's defenses with two assaults, but both failed. He decided to starve Pemberton's army into surrender. He also tried to wear the Confederates out by bombarding the city. While he didn't have any siege guns, Admiral Porter did lend him some of the large naval guns. With Grant to the east and Porter's boats on the Mississippi to the west, the city was pounded by shot and shell.

"The mortar boats," wrote Porter, "were kept at work for forty days, night and day, throwing shells into every part of Vicksburg and its works, some of them even reaching the trenches in the rear of the city." In his dispatch on the day Vicksburg surrendered, Porter noted, "The mortars have fired seven thousand mortar-shells, and the gunboats four thousand five hundred. Four thousand five hundred shots have been fired from naval guns on shore, and we have supplied over six thousand to the different army corps."

In addition, Grant's army had its own field artillery firing into the city.

After a month and a half, conditions in Vicksburg were wretched. People resorted to eating mules, dogs, and their own shoe leather. About half of Pemberton's men had incapacitating scurvy, dysentery, and other diseases, putting him under great pressure to surrender.

Johnston's army was too small and ill-equipped to take on Grant, especially after Grant received reinforcements greater than Johnston's entire force. Johnston had about 26,000 men to take on Grant's 75,000. Still, he was preparing to attack, but the siege ended before he was ready.

Pemberton surrendered on July 4, thinking that Grant would give him better terms on the holiday. The surrender, coming as it did at the same time as the Union victory at Gettysburg, tremendously boosted the North's morale, landing a huge blow to the South. With the fall of Vicksburg, the Confederates' final foothold on the Mississippi— Port Hudson—surrendered without a fight, giving up an additional 6,000 prisoners.

Grant suddenly achieved international fame— but events could have easily gone another way. When Grant first described his plans to Sherman, the latter strongly opposed them because they violated one of the basic principles of war: Maintain and protect your supply line. Grant proposed to charge into Confederate territory without any supply line. He figured the area around Vicksburg was the South's breadbasket and his men could forage for what they needed there, which they did. Grant was also entering Confederate territory with a huge river at his back—which had caused the Army of the Potomac considerable trouble—while going up against Confederates entrenched in strongly fortified positions. But the country desperately needed a major victory, and Grant felt he couldn't withdraw his men in order to establish a supply depot at Memphis. Public opinion was already going against the war. If he retreated to start a new line of attack, he surmised that the public would be so discouraged that he would no longer receive new recruits or supplies and the Union cause would be lost. He determined to take the chance and do his best. Setting aside his reservations, Sherman was ready to forge ahead with him.

Grant knew Halleck would hate the idea, just as Sherman had, so he very carefully didn't let the

War Department know what he was doing. When they found out, Halleck tried to put a stop to it—but it was too late. Fortunately for Grant and the Union, his audacious plan worked. Vicksburg could be called Grant's "perfect battle."

LOST OPPORTUNITIES

Confederate

General Joseph Johnston (See biography, page 46.)

Jefferson Davis, in *The Rise and Fall of the Confederate Government*, blamed Johnston for the loss of Vicksburg. In response, Johnston wrote an article in *The North American Review* placing the blame back on Jefferson Davis and on Lieutenant-General John Pemberton.

In the first half of July, 1862, General Halleck was ordered to Washington as general-in-chief. Before leaving Corinth he left General Grant in command of those holding in subjection northeastern Mississippi and southern West Tennessee. They numbered about forty-two thousand present for duty by Mr. Davis's estimate. Their wide dispersion put them at the mercy of any superior or equal force, such as the Confederacy could have brought against them readily; but this opportunity, such a one as has rarely occurred in war, was put aside by the Confederate Government, and the army which, properly used, would have secured to the South the possession of Tennessee and Mississippi was employed in a wild expedition into Kentucky, which could have had only the results of a raid.

Mr. Davis extols the strategy of that operation, which, he says, "manoeuvred the foe out of a large and to us important territory." This advantage, if it could be called so, was of the briefest. For this "foe" drove us out of Kentucky in a few weeks, and recovered permanently the "large and to us important territory."

General Grant was then in northern Mississippi, with an army formed by uniting the detachments that had been occupying Corinth and various points in southern West Tennessee. He was preparing for the invasion of Mississippi, with the special object of gaining possession of Vicksburg. To oppose him, Lieutenant-General Pemberton, who commanded the Department of Mississippi and East Louisiana, had an active army of 23,000 effective infantry and artillery, and above 6,000 cavalry, most of it irregular. There were also intrenched camps at Vicksburg and Port Hudson, each held by about six thousand men, protecting batteries of old smooth bore guns, which, it was hoped, would prevent the Federal war vessels from occupying the intermediate part of the Mississippi. Lieutenant-General Holmes was then encamped near Little Rock with an army of above fifty thousand men. There were no Federal forces in Arkansas at the time, except one or two garrisons.

In all the time to which the preceding relates I had been out of service from the effects of two severe wounds received in the battle of Seven Pines [on June 1, 1862, when a bullet hit his shoulder and fragments from an exploding shell wounded his chest and thigh]. On the 12th of November, 1862, I reported myself fit for duty. The Secretary of War replied that I would be assigned to service in Tennessee and Mississippi in a few days. Thinking myself authorized to make suggestions in relation to the warfare in which I was to be engaged, I proposed to the Secretary, in his office, that, as the Federal forces about to invade Mississippi were united in that State, ours available for its defense should be so likewise; therefore General Holmes should be ordered to unite his forces with General Pemberton's without delay.

As a reply, he read me a letter of late date from himself to General Holmes, instructing that officer to make the movement just suggested, and then a note from the President directing him to countermand his order to General Holmes. A few days after this, General Randolph resigned the office of Secretary of War—unfortunately for the Confederacy.

On the 24th of November Mr. Seddon, who had succeeded General Randolph as Secretary of War, assigned me to the command of the departments of General Bragg and Lieutenant-Generals E. Kirby Smith and Pemberton, each to command his department under me. In acknowledging this order, I again suggested the transfer of the army in Arkansas to Mississippi. The suggestion was not adopted or noticed.

On the 21st and 22d Mr. Davis inspected the water-batteries and land defenses of Vicksburg, which were then very extensive, but slight—the usual defect of Confederate engineering. He also conferred with the commander, Major-General Martin L. Smith, and me, in reference to the forces required to hold that place and Port Hudson, and at the same time to oppose General Grant in the field. We agreed (General Smith and I) that at least twenty thousand more troops were necessary, and I again urged him to transfer the troops in Arkansas to Mississippi. In a friendly note to General Holmes, which I was permitted to read, Mr. Davis pointed out to him that he would benefit the service by sending twenty thousand men into Mississippi, but gave him no order; consequently no troops came.

Thus an army outnumbering that which General Grant was then commanding was left idle, while preparations were in progress, near it, for the conquest of a portion of the Confederacy so important as the valley of the Mississippi.

The detaching of almost a fourth of General Bragg's army to Mississippi, while of no present value to that department, was disastrous to that of Tennessee, for it caused the battle of Murfreesboro. General Rosecrans was, of course, soon informed of the great reduction of his antagonist's strength, and marched from Nashville to attack him. The battle, that of Murfreesboro' or Stone's River, occurred on the 31st of December, 1862, and the 2d of January, 1863, and was one of the most obstinately contested and bloody of the war, in proportion to the numbers engaged. The result of this action compelled the Confederate army to fall back and place itself behind Duck River, at Manchester, Tullahoma, and Shelbyville.

Early in December, Grant projected an enterprise against Vicksburg under Sherman's command. He directed that officer to embark at Memphis with about 30,000 men, descend the river with them to the neighborhood of the place, and with the cooperation of Admiral Porter's squadron proceed to reduce it.

I immediately wrote to General Pemberton that, if invested in Vicksburg, he must ultimately surrender; and that, instead of losing both troops and place, he must save the troops by evacuating Vicksburg and marching to the north-east. The question of obeying this order was submitted by him to a council of war, which decided that "it was impossible to withdraw the troops from that position with such morale and material as to be of further service to the Confederacy." This allegation was refuted by the courage, fortitude, and discipline displayed by that army in the long siege.

The so-called siege of Vicksburg was little more than a blockade. But one vigorous assault was made, which was on the third day.

He [Davis] accuses me of producing "confusion and consequent disasters" by giving a written order to Lieutenant-General Pemberton, which he terms opening correspondence. But as that order, dated May 13th, was disobeyed, it certainly produced neither confusion nor disaster. But "consequent disaster" was undoubtedly due to the disobedience of that order, which caused the battle of Champion's Hill.

When that order was written, obedience to it, which would have united all our forces, might have enabled us to contend with General Grant on equal terms, and perhaps to win the campaign. Strange as it may now seem, Mr. Davis thought so at the time.

A proper use of the available resources of the Confederacy would have averted the disasters referred to by Mr. Davis. If, instead of being sent on the wild expedition into Kentucky, General Bragg had been instructed to avail himself of the dispersed condition of the Federal troops in northern Mississippi and west Tennessee, he might have totally defeated the forces with which General Grant invaded Mississippi three months later. Those troops were distributed in Corinth, Jackson, Memphis, and intermediate points, while his own were united, so that he could have fought them in detail, with as much certainty of success as can be hoped for in war. And such success would have prevented the military and naval combination which gave the enemy control of the Mississippi and divided the Confederacy, and would have given the Confederacy the ascendency on that frontier.

I do not know that there was any better than Joe Johnston. I have had nearly all of the Southern generals in high command in front of me, and Joe Johnston gave me more anxiety than any of the others. I was never half so anxious about Lee. By the way, I saw in Joe Johnston's book that when I was asking Pemberton to surrender Vicksburg, he was on his way to raise the siege. I was very sorry. If I had known Johnston was coming, I would have told Pemberton to wait in Vicksburg until I wanted him, awaited Johnston's advance, and given him battle. He could never have beaten that Vicksburg army, and thus I would have destroyed two armies perhaps. Pemberton's was already gone, and I was quite sure of Johnston's. I was sorry I did not know Johnston was coming until it was too late. Take it all in all, the South, in my opinion, had no better soldier than Joe Johnston—none at least that gave me more trouble.

—General Ulysses S. Grant

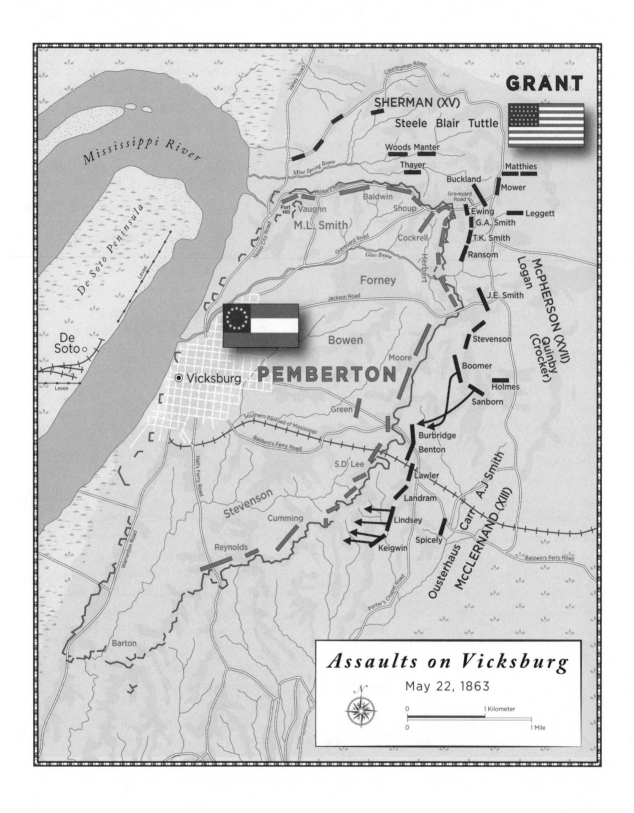

GRANT

SHERMAN (XV)
Steele Blair Tuttle

Woods Manter

Thayer
Buckland
Matthies
Mower

Baldwin
Shoup
Ewing
Leggett
G.A. Smith
T.K. Smith

Fort
Hill
Vaughn
M.L. Smith
Graveyard Road
Ransom

Cockrell
Herbert

Glass Bayou

Forney
J.E. Smith

Jackson Road
Stevenson

McPHERSON (XVII)
Logan
Quinby
(Crocker)

Boomer

Bowen
Holmes

Moore
Sanborn

Green
Burbridge

Benton

S.D. Lee
Lawler

Landram
A.J. Smith

Stevenson
Lindsey
Carr

Cumming
Keigwin
Spicely

Reynolds
Ousterhaus

McCLERNAND (XIII)
Baldwin's Ferry Road

Barton

Mississippi River

De Soto Peninsula

Levee

De
Soto

Levee

Mint Spring Bayou

Military Road

Valley Road

Countryman Road

Yazoo City Road

Graveyard Road

⊙ Vicksburg **PEMBERTON**

Southern Railroad of Mississippi

Baldwin's Ferry Road

Hall's Ferry Road

Warrenton Road

Porter's Chapel Road

Assaults on Vicksburg
May 22, 1863

0 _____ 1 Kilometer
0 _____ 1 Mile

It is evident, and was so then, that the three bodies of Confederate troops in Mississippi in July, 1862, should have been united under General Bragg. The army of above 65,000 men so formed could not have been seriously resisted by the Federal forces.

Even after this failure the Confederates were stronger to repel invasion than the Federals to invade. By uniting their forces in Arkansas with those in Mississippi, an army of above 70,000 men would have been formed, to meet General Grant's of 43,000. In all human probability such a force would have totally defeated the invading army, and not only preserved Mississippi but enabled us to recover Tennessee.

But if there were some necessity known only to the President to keep the Confederate troops then in Arkansas on that side of the Mississippi, he could have put General Pemberton on at least equal terms with his antagonist, by giving him the troops in April actually sent to him late in May. This would have formed an army of above fifty thousand men. General Grant landed two corps, less than 30,000 men, on the 30th of April and 1st and 2d of May; and it was not until the 8th of May that the arrival of Sherman's corps increased his force to about 43,000 men. The Confederate reinforcements could have been sent as well early in April as late in May; and then, without bad generalship on our part, the chances of success would have been in our favor, decidedly.

RUNNING THE GAUNTLET

Union

Admiral David Dixon Porter (*See biography, page 14.*)

The Army had already moved on the 10th of April, 1863, and that night was selected for the naval vessels to pass the batteries of Vicksburg.

Orders had been given that the coal in the furnaces should be well ignited, so as to show no smoke, that low steam should be carried, that not a wheel was to turn except to keep the vessel's bow down river, and to drift past the enemy's works fifty yards apart.

Most of the vessels had a coal barge lashed to them on the side away from the enemy, and the

wooden gun-boat *General Price*, was lashed to the off side of the iron-clad *Lafayette*.

When all was ready the signal was made to get under way and the squadron started. The *Benton*, passed the first battery without receiving a shot, but as she came up with the second, the railroad station on the right bank of the river was set on fire, and tar barrels were lighted all along the Vicksburg shore, illuminating the river and showing every object as plainly as if it was daylight. Then the enemy opened his batteries all along the line, and the sharpshooters in rifle-pits along the levee commenced operations at the same instant. The fire was returned with spirit by the vessels as they drifted on, and the sound of falling buildings as the shells burst within them attested the efficiency of the gun-boats' fire.

The vessels had drifted perhaps a mile when a shell exploded in the cotton barricades of the transport *Henry Clay*, and almost immediately the vessel was in a blaze; another shell soon after bursting in her hull, the transport went to pieces and sank. The *Forest Queen*, another transport, was also disabled by the enemy, but she was taken in tow by the *Tuscumbia* and conveyed safely through.

The scene while the fleet was passing the batteries was grand in the extreme, but the danger to the vessels was more apparent than real. Their weak points on the sides were mostly protected by heavy logs which prevented many shot and shells going through the iron. Some rents were made but the vessels stood the ordeal bravely and received no damage calculated to impair their efficiency.

The enemy's shot was not well aimed; owing to the rapid fire of shells, shrapnel, grape and canister from the gun-boats, the sharpshooters were glad to lay low, and the men at the great guns gave up in disgust when they saw the fleet drift on apparently unscathed.

They must have known that Vicksburg was doomed, for if the fleet got safely below the batteries their supplies of provisions from Texas would be cut off and they would have to depend on what they could receive from Richmond. General Steele had been sent up to the Steele's Bayou region to destroy all the provisions in that quarter, and Pemberton knew that if Grant's Army once got below Vicksburg it would eat up everything in the way of food between Warrenton and Bruinsburg.

Although the squadron was under fire from the time of passing the first battery until the last vessel got by, a period of two hours and thirty minutes, the vessels were struck in their hulls but sixty-eight times by shot and shells, and only fifteen men were wounded. At 2.30 a.m., all the vessels were safely anchored at Carthage, ten miles below Vicksburg, where was encamped the advanced division of the Army under General McClernand.

There was still work for the Navy to do in the Yazoo, while General Grant was starving the Confederates out in Vicksburg. The enemy now had to subsist on what provisions they had on hand, which was not much, and unless relieved by a superior force, a month more or less would bring about a surrender.

On the 19th of June, General Grant intended to open a general bombardment on the city at 4 a.m. and continue it until 10 o'clock. At the appointed time the bombardment commenced all along the army line and was joined on the water side by every gun-boat, the guns on scows and the mortars, until the earth fairly shook with the thundering noise. The gun-boats spread themselves all along in front of the city—cross firing on everything in the shape of a battery—but there was no response whatever—the works were all deserted.

After the fire was all over on the Union side, the city of Vicksburg was as quiet as the grave— not a soul could be seen. The women had all taken refuge in the shelters built in the hillsides, and every man that could hold a musket or point a bayonet was in the trenches. There they would stay for days and nights, lying in the mud and having what food they could get served out to them there.

IRONCLADS AND SUBMARINES

The Civil War was fought in the midst of the Industrial Revolution, when tremendous technological advancements were taking place. As such, many consider the Civil War the first modern war.

The world was moving into a state of rapid change. Gas lighting for streetlights and homes was beginning to appear. The manufacturing boom, with the formation of corporations like Bethlehem Steel—in 1857 in Pennsylvania—led to the development of mass production, which in turn enabled the war effort to produce large quantities of munitions. Steam engines—particularly useful in hauling troops, supplies, artillery, and ammunition, both by railroads and steamships—had become common. The Union's Army of the Potomac alone consumed 600 tons of food, supplies, and forage every day, much of which had to be transported to it in the South.

Advances in naval weapons and ammunition led to the ironclads. In the years before the war, eighteen- and twenty-four-pound guns were replaced by thirty-two- and sixty-eight-pounders, while ammunition evolved from solid shot to explosive and incendiary shells. These new armaments could do considerable damage to a wooden ship.

The Confederacy quickly realized it needed ironclads to break the Union blockade, while the Union needed some to protect its fleet. The first American ironclad used in battle[9] was the Confederate ram CSS *Manassas* at the Battle of the Head of Passes in the Mississippi River Delta on October 12, 1861. The Union finished its first ironclad at the same time the Confederates finished their second. These two very different-looking ironclads clashed at the Battle of Hampton Roads, Virginia, on March 9, 1862.

The Confederate ship was previously known as the USS *Merrimack*. The Union scuttled it, so when repairing it the Confederates added an iron casement on top with sloping sides to protect the crew and their guns. Most of the later Confederate ironclads were of this type. The Confederate navy rechristened this ironclad ram the CSS *Virginia*, and it sank two Union ships and disabled a third the day before the USS *Monitor* arrived.

The *Monitor* had a very unusual design, with a flat deck that rose only about a foot above the waterline. It was designed to be a river battery but saw service at sea. It had only two guns, both of large caliber, mounted side by side in a revolving twenty-foot-wide turret. Its design was completely innovative. The navy called it the "iron pot." One soldier fairly accurately described it as looking like a giant floating pumpkin seed with a round cheese box on top. At 172 feet long, it was smaller than the 275-foot *Virginia* but a lot more maneuverable. The Union had a lot riding on this odd ship, for if it had lost to the *Virginia*, the Union probably would have had to mine the Potomac River to keep the Confederates from sailing up it and shelling the White House.

The battle between the two ironclads came to a draw, but it clearly demonstrated that all other types of warships in the world were suddenly obsolete. Just days after the news reached England, the British Royal Navy canceled all its contracts for wooden ships, calling it madness to put any traditional ship into "an engagement with that little *Monitor*."

---

9   The Koreans may have had an ironclad turtle ship in the 16th century, but that's hotly debated. The French had ironclad gun batteries on barges that they used to bombard Kinburn in 1855 during the Crimean War. Both France and England had ironclads before the Confederates launched the CSS *Manassas*.

The Confederacy had a total of about thirty-seven ironclads in its navy, while the Union had sixty-eight ironclads—forty-nine of them monitors—along with sixty tinclads, which were riverboats with thin sheet-metal armor. The Union also had timberclads, which used wood for armor, and cottonclads, which used bales of cotton. Like the *Virginia*, most of the South's ironclads were rams with a pointed, reinforced extension on the bow that could sink ships by ramming into them.

Some of the *Monitor*'s protection came from being mostly underwater, since water greatly slows projectiles. Confederate engineers put this science to use by making submarine-shaped steamboats that maintained little more than their smokestack above the waterline. These were called torpedo boats because they were armed with a sixty- to seventy-pound "torpedo" or mine at the end of a spar. They rammed the mine into a ship below its waterline, attaching it to the ship by a barb on the tip of the spar. Then they pulled back until a trigger line attached to the mine became taut, detonating the mine. Powered with smokeless coal and used mainly on dark nights—making them doubly difficult to see—their main targets were ironclads. The Confederates had at least two of these torpedo boats and two other regular boats armed with spar mines. The Union developed two torpedo boats late in the war as well. These boats were first used off the coast of Charleston, South Carolina, on the night of October 5, 1863, when the fifty-foot CSS *David* torpedo boat with a crew of four exploded its mine, damaging but not sinking the casement ironclad steamship USS *New Ironsides*.

Taking the idea of the torpedo boats a step further, the Confederates built what we now would call submarines but which they called diving torpedo boats.[10] These arguably take second place as the most innovative invention of the war, right behind the *Monitor*. They seem to have built at least eight of them, although only two and possibly a third saw battle. Work on submarines was secretive, and records are incomplete, so there were probably other subs in use during the war.

Extremely unsafe, these early subs often sank. At least fifteen crewmen were killed in accidents, but the Confederates sent down divers in suits with large copper helmets to bring the subs back up, and they tried again. After the CSS *H. L. Hunley* submarine sank two or three times during testing, Beauregard quipped darkly: "'Tis more dangerous to those who use it than to enemy."

Also known as "the Cigar Boat" and "the Fish Boat," the *Hunley*, a forty-foot-long cylindrical vessel, had a propeller hand-cranked by a crew of eight men—one who also steered—and fore and aft hand-pumped ballast tanks enabling the sub to submerge and surface. Two short conning towers had escape hatches and small, two-inch-diameter viewing windows, four in the front tower and two in the back. It could dive for thirty minutes before needing to surface for air. The sub was armed with a 135-pound spar mine and was the first submarine to sink a ship in battle.

On the night of February 17, 1864, the *Hunley* exploded its mine, destroying the rear quarter of the ironclad USS *Housatonic*. The ship went down in five minutes, killing five of its crew. The *Hunley* was returning to port when it sank for the last time, once again killing its eight-man crew and proving Beauregard right.

On January 28, 1865, the seven-man, thirty-foot CSS *Saint Patrick* attacked USS *Octorara* in Mobile Bay, but its mine failed to explode. It was scuttled when the war ended. The *Saint Patrick*

---

10   The first American sub to be used in combat was the one-man *Turtle*, partially financed by George Washington and unsuccessfully used in New York Harbor in 1776 during the Revolutionary War.

used steam power on the surface and was hand-cranked when underwater. Some consider it a David-class torpedo boat because of its smokestack, but it seems to have been able to submerge, so others classify it as a sub. Whether the smokestack could go all the way under remains unknown. Circumstantial evidence indicates that a similar sub, the CSS *Captain Pierce*, sank the monitor-class ironclad USS *Tecumseh*, but the official story is that the *Tecumseh* hit a mine.

As with many new weapons, the opposition didn't like it. A Union commander of the blockade said he thought they should hang captured submariners "for using an engine of war not recognized by civilized nations." Others called it "unchivalrous." But that didn't stop the North from building its own subs.

Designed by a French inventor, the forty-seven-foot USS *Alligator* was rowed by a series of oars with a twenty-two-man crew. Interestingly, this sub had an air-purifying system, a diver's chamber, and air compressors for air renewal. The compressors also pumped air to a diver who could leave the sub to attach a limpet mine to the target ship, which would then be electrically detonated.

The *Alligator* was launched on May 1, 1862, its first mission to destroy a bridge over the Appomattox River and clear obstructions in the James River, but the rivers were too shallow for the sub to submerge. Union strategists wanted to use it against the CSS *Virginia II*, but tests determined the sub to be unsafe. The propulsion system changed from oars to a screw propeller, which only required an eight-man crew. President Lincoln witnessed a demonstration of the sub's capabilities, but less than a month later, in April 1863, it was lost at sea off Cape Hatteras, North Carolina.

Speculators attempted to interest the Union navy in a twenty-nine-foot sub called *The Intelligent Whale*, but the Navy refused to buy it, nor was it completed until after the war. Another sub, the *Explorer*, was pressurized with an open bottom for divers, but the government wasn't interested, so a pearl-diving company bought it.

ASSAULT OR SIEGE

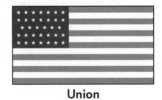

Union

General Ulysses S. Grant (See biography, page 54.)

We were now assured of our position between [the Confederate armies of] Johnston and Pemberton, without a possibility of a junction of their forces. Pemberton might have made a night march and, by moving north on the west side, have eluded us and finally returned to Johnston. But this would have given us Vicksburg. It would have been his proper move, however, and the one Johnston would have made had he been in Pemberton's place. In fact it would have been in conformity with Johnston's orders to Pemberton.

On the 19th [May 1863] there was constant skirmishing with the enemy while we were getting into better position. The enemy had been much demoralized by his defeats at Champion's Hill and the Big Black, and I believed he would not make much effort to hold Vicksburg. Accordingly, at two o'clock I ordered an assault. It resulted in securing more advanced positions for all our troops where they were fully covered from the fire of the enemy.

I now determined on a second assault [on the 22nd]. Johnston was in my rear, only fifty miles away, with an army not much inferior in numbers to the one I had with me, and I knew he was being reinforced. There was danger of his coming to the assistance of Pemberton, and after all he might defeat my anticipations of capturing the garrison if, indeed, he did not prevent the capture of the city. The immediate capture of Vicksburg would save sending me the reinforcements which were so much wanted elsewhere, and would set free the army under me to drive Johnston from the State. But the first consideration of all was—the troops believed they could carry the works in their front,

and would not have worked so patiently in the trenches if they had not been allowed to try.

The attack was ordered to commence on all parts of the line at ten o'clock a.m. on the 22d with a furious cannonade from every battery in position. The attack was gallant, and portions of each of the three corps succeeded in getting up to the very parapets of the enemy and in planting their battle flags upon them; but at no place were we able to enter. General McClernand reported that he had gained the enemy's intrenchments at several points, and wanted reinforcements. I occupied a position from which I believed I could see as well as he what took place in his front, and I did not see the success he reported. But his request for reinforcements being repeated I could not ignore it, and sent him Quinby's division of the 17th corps. Sherman and McPherson were both ordered to renew their assaults as a diversion in favor of McClernand, This last attack only served to increase our casualties without giving any benefit whatever.

I now determined upon a regular siege—to "outcamp the enemy," as it were, and to incur no more losses. The experience of the 22d convinced officers and men that this was best, and they went to work on the defences and approaches with a will.

MCCLERNAND AND THE SECOND ASSAULT

Union

General William Tecumseh Sherman (See biography, page 4.)

After our men had been fairly beaten back from off the parapet, and had got cover behind the spurs of ground close up to the rebel works, General Grant came to where I was, on foot, having left his horse some distance to the rear. I pointed out to him the rebel works, admitted that my assault had failed, and he said the result with McPherson and McClernand was about the same.

While he was with me, an orderly or staff-officer came and handed him a piece of paper, which he read and handed to me. I think the writing was in pencil, on a loose piece of paper, and was in General McClernand's handwriting, to the effect that "his troops had captured the rebel parapet in his front," that "the flag of the Union waved over the stronghold of Vicksburg," and asking him (General Grant) to give renewed orders to McPherson and Sherman to press their attacks on their respective fronts, lest the enemy should concentrate on him (McClernand).

General Grant said, "I don't believe a word of it"; but I reasoned with him, that this note was official, and must be credited, and I offered to renew the assault at once with new troops. He said he would instantly ride down the line to McClernand's front, and if I did not receive orders to the contrary, by 3 o'clock p.m., I might try it again. Mower's fresh brigade was brought up under cover, and, punctually at 3 p.m., hearing heavy firing down

along the line to my left, I ordered the second assault. It was a repetition of the first, equally unsuccessful and bloody. It also transpired that the same thing had occurred with General McPherson, who lost in this second assault some most valuable officers and men, without adequate result; and that General McClernand, instead of having taken any single point of the rebel main parapet, had only taken one or two small outlying lunettes open to the rear, where his men were at the mercy of the rebels behind their main parapet, and most of them were actually thus captured. This affair caused great feeling with us, and severe criticisms on General McClernand, which led finally to his removal from the command of the Thirteenth Corps, to which General Ord succeeded.

The immediate cause, however, of General McClernand's removal was the publication of a sort of congratulatory order addressed to his troops, first published in St. Louis, in which he claimed that he had actually succeeded in making a lodgment in Vicksburg, but had lost it, owing to the fact that McPherson and Sherman did not fulfill their parts of the general plan of attack. This was simply untrue. The several assaults made May 22d, on the lines of Vicksburg, had failed, by reason of the great strength of the position and the determined fighting of its garrison.

FORCING A SURRENDER

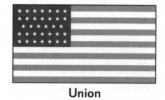

Union

General Ulysses S. Grant (See biography, page 54.)

We were now looking west, besieging Pemberton, while we were also looking east to defend ourselves against an expected siege by Johnston. But as against the garrison of Vicksburg we were as substantially protected as they were against us. Where we were looking east and north we were strongly fortified, and on the defensive. Johnston evidently took in the situation and wisely, I think, abstained from making an assault on us because it would simply have inflicted loss on both sides without accomplishing any result. We were strong enough to have taken the offensive against him; but I did not feel disposed to take any risk of losing our hold upon Pemberton's army, while I would have rejoiced at the opportunity of defending ourselves against an attack by Johnston.

From the 23d of May the work of fortifying and pushing forward our position nearer to the enemy had been steadily progressing. At three points on the Jackson road, in front of Leggett's brigade, a sap [i.e., a deep trench] was run up to the enemy's parapet, and by the 25th of June we had it undermined and the mine charged. The enemy had countermined, but did not succeed in reaching our mine. At this particular point the hill on which the rebel work stands rises abruptly. Our sap ran close up to the outside of the enemy's parapet. In fact this parapet was also our protection. The soldiers of the two sides occasionally conversed pleasantly

across this barrier; sometimes they exchanged the hard bread of the Union soldiers for the tobacco of the Confederates; at other times the enemy threw over hand-grenades, and often our men, catching them in their hands, returned them.

Our mine had been started some distance back down the hill; consequently when it had extended as far as the parapet it was many feet below it. This caused the failure of the enemy in his search to find and destroy it. On the 25th of June at three o'clock, all being ready, the mine was exploded. A heavy artillery fire all along the line had been ordered to open with the explosion. The effect was to blow the top of the hill off and make a crater where it stood.

The breach was not sufficient to enable us to pass a column of attack through. In fact, the enemy having failed to reach our mine had thrown up a line farther back, where most of the men guarding that point were placed. There were a few men, however, left at the advance line, and others working in the countermine, which was still being pushed to find ours. All that were there were thrown into the air, some of them coming down on our side, still alive.

As soon as the explosion took place the crater was seized by two regiments of our troops who were near by, under cover, where they had been placed for the express purpose. The enemy made a desperate effort to expel them, but failed, and soon retired behind the new line. From here, however, they threw hand-grenades, which did some execution. The compliment was returned by our men, but not with so much effect. The enemy could lay their grenades on the parapet, which alone divided the contestants, and roll them down upon us; while from our side they had to be thrown over the parapet, which was at considerable elevation.

During the night we made efforts to secure our position in the crater against the missiles of the enemy, so as to run trenches along the outer base of their parapet, right and left; but the enemy continued throwing their grenades, and brought boxes of field ammunition [shells], the fuses of which they would light with port-fires, and throw them by hand into our ranks.

We found it impossible to continue this work. Another mine was consequently started which was exploded on the 1st of July, destroying an entire rebel redan [a V-shaped projection from the line], killing and wounding a considerable number of its occupants and leaving an immense chasm where it stood. No attempt to charge was made this time, the experience of the 25th admonishing us. Our loss in the first affair was about thirty killed and wounded. The enemy must have lost more in the two explosions than we did in the first. We lost none in the second.

From this time forward the work of mining and pushing our position nearer to the enemy was prosecuted with vigor, and I determined to explode no more mines until we were ready to explode a number at different points and assault immediately after.

The picket lines were so close to each other that the men could converse. On the 21st of June I was informed, through this means, that Pemberton was preparing to escape, by crossing to the Louisiana side under cover of night; that

he had employed workmen in making boats for that purpose; that the men had been canvassed to ascertain if they would make an assault on the "Yankees" to cut their way out; that they had refused, and almost mutinied, because their commander would not surrender and relieve their sufferings, and had only been pacified by the assurance that boats enough would be finished in a week to carry them all over. The rebel pickets also said that houses in the city had been pulled down to get material to build these boats with. Afterwards this story was verified: on entering the city we found a large number of very rudely constructed boats.

All necessary steps were at once taken to render such an attempt abortive.

On the night of the 1st of July, Johnston was between Brownsville and the Big Black, and wrote Pemberton from there that about the 7th of the month an attempt would be made to create a diversion to enable him to cut his way out. Pemberton was a prisoner before this message reached him.

I rode into Vicksburg with the troops, and went to the river to exchange congratulations with the navy upon our joint victory. At that time I found that many of the citizens had been living under ground.

The ridges upon which Vicksburg is built are composed of a deep yellow clay of great tenacity. Many citizens secured places of safety for their families by carving out rooms in these embankments. A door-way in these cases would be cut in a high bank starting from the level of the road or street, and after running in a few feet a room of the size required was carved out of the clay, the dirt being removed by the door-way. In some instances I saw where two rooms were cut out, for a single family, with a door-way in the clay wall separating them. Some of these were carpeted and furnished with considerable elaboration. In these the occupants were fully secure from the shells of the navy, which were dropped into the city night and day without intermission.

> One man had his head blown off while in the act of picking up his child. Many strange escapes and incidents are spoken of—so many that they have not been specially noticed. One shell fell and exploded between two officers as they were riding together on the street, and lifted both horses and riders into the air without hurting either man or beast. One woman had just risen from her chair when a shell came through the roof, took her seat and shattered the house without injuring the lady; and a hundred others of similar cases. A little girl, the daughter of Mr. Jones, was sitting at the entrance of a cave, when a Parrott shell entered the portal and took her head right off.
>
> —FROM THE DIARY OF A VICKSBURG CITIZEN

The men of the two armies fraternized as if they had been fighting for the same cause. When they passed out of the works they had so long and so gallantly defended, between lines of their late antagonists, not a cheer went up, not a remark was made that would give pain. Really, I believe there was a feeling of sadness just then in the breasts of most of the Union soldiers at seeing the dejection of their late antagonists.

Having cleaned up about Vicksburg and captured or routed all regular Confederate forces for more than a hundred miles in all directions, I felt that the troops that had done so much should be allowed to do more before the enemy could recover from the blow he had received, and while important points might be captured without

bloodshed. I suggested to the General-in-chief the idea of a campaign against Mobile, starting from Lake Pontchartrain.

Halleck disapproved of my proposition to go against Mobile, so that I was obliged to settle down and see myself put again on the defensive as I had been a year before in west Tennessee. It would have been an easy thing to capture Mobile at the time I proposed to go there. Having that as a base of operations, troops could have been thrown into the interior to operate against General Bragg's army. This would necessarily have compelled Bragg to detach in order to meet this fire in his rear. If he had not done this the troops from Mobile could have inflicted inestimable damage upon much of the country from which his army and Lee's were yet receiving their supplies.

The General-in-chief having decided against me, the depletion of an army, which had won a succession of great victories, commenced, as had been the case the year before after the fall of Corinth when the army was sent where it would do the least good.

In a private letter in 1884, Grant wrote:

The fact is, General Pemberton, being a Northern man commanding a Southern army, was not at the same liberty to surrender an army that a man of Southern birth would be. In adversity or defeat he became an object of suspicion, and felt it. [General John] Bowen was a Southern man all over, and knew the garrison of Vicksburg had to surrender or be captured, and knew it was best to stop further effusion of blood by surrendering. He did all he could to bring about that result.

It was Bowen that proposed that he and A. J. Smith should talk over the matter of the surrender and submit their views. Neither Pemberton nor

I objected, but we were not willing to commit ourselves to accepting such terms as they might propose. In a short time those officers returned. Bowen acted as spokesman; what he said was substantially this: The Confederate army was to be permitted to march out with the honors of war, carrying with them their arms, colors, and field-batteries. The National troops were then to march in and occupy the city, and retain the siege-guns, small-arms not in the hands of the men, all public property remaining.

Of course I rejected the terms at once. I did agree, however, before we separated, to write Pemberton what terms I would give. I was very glad to give the garrison of Vicksburg the terms I did. There was a cartel in existence at that time which required either party to exchange or parole all prisoners either at Vicksburg or at a point on the James River within ten days after captures or as soon thereafter as practicable. This would have used all the transportation we had for a month. The men had behaved so well that I did not want to humiliate them. I believed that consideration for their feelings would make them less dangerous foes during the continuance of hostilities, and better citizens after the war was over.

In a conversation that later appeared in print with Grant's corrections and approval, he said:

War has responsibilities that are either fatal to a commander's position or very successful. I often go over our war campaigns and criticise what I did, and see where I made mistakes. Information now and then coming to light for the first time shows me frequently where I could have done better. I don't think there is one of my campaigns with which I have not some fault to find, and which, as I see now, I could not have improved, except perhaps Vicksburg. I do not see how I could have improved that.

When I determined on that campaign, I knew, as well as I knew anything, that it would not meet with the approval of the authorities in Washington. I knew this because I knew Halleck, and that he was too learned a soldier to consent to a campaign in violation of all the principles of the art of war. But I felt that every war I knew anything about had made laws for itself, and early in our contest I was impressed with the idea that success with us would depend upon our taking advantage of new conditions. No two wars are alike, because they are generally fought at different periods, under different phases of civilization.

To take Vicksburg, according to the rules of war as laid down in the books, would have involved a new campaign, a withdrawal of my forces to Memphis, and the opening of a new line of attack. The North needed a victory. We had been unfortunate in Virginia, and we had not gained our success at Gettysburg. Such a withdrawal as would have been necessary—say to Memphis, would have had all the effects, in the North, of a defeat.

I talked it over with Sherman. I told him it was necessary to gain a success in the south-west, that the country was weary and impatient, that the disasters in Virginia were weakening the government, and that unless we did something, there was no knowing what, in its despair, the country might not do. Lee was preparing to invade Maryland and Pennsylvania, as he did. Sherman said that the sound campaign was to return to Memphis, establish that as a base of supplies, and move from there on Vicksburg, building up the road as we advanced and never uncovering that base.

I felt that what was wanted was a forward movement to a victory that would be decisive. In a popular war we had to consider political exigencies.

You see there was no general in our army who had won that public confidence which came to many of them afterward. We were—all of us, more or less—on probation. Sherman contended that the risk of disaster in the proposed movement was so great that even for my own fame I should not undertake it; that if I failed the administration, about which I was worrying so much, would root me up and throw me away as a useless weed. I thought that war anyhow was a risk; that it made little difference to the country what was done with me. I might be killed or die from fever. The more I thought of it the more I felt that my duty was plain. I felt, however, that to carry out my move fully I must have it developed before it could be stopped from Washington, before orders could come—as they did in fact come—that would have rendered it impossible.

Instead of making a report to Washington of what had been done thus far, I hurried into the interior and developed my movement. You know the theory of the campaign was to throw myself between Johnston and Pemberton, prevent their union, beat each army separately if I could, and take Vicksburg.

An officer came into my lines from Banks's army, then investing Port Hudson. This officer was a brigadier-general, in a high state of excitement, a small and impressive man, so overcome with the sense of his tremendous responsibility that he seemed to stand on his toes to give it emphasis. He had the order from Halleck for me to withdraw at once with my force and join Banks. This order was so important that he, a general officer, had come all the way to bring it and to escort me, if necessary, to Port Hudson. I acknowledged the order, but said I was there in front of the enemy

and engaged, and could not withdraw; that even General Halleck, under the circumstances, would not expect me to do so.

The little brigadier, standing on his toes, became more and more emphatic. I pointed out that we were not only engaged with the enemy, but winning a victory, and that General Halleck never intended his order to destroy a victory.

If the Vicksburg campaign, meant anything, in a military point of view, it was that there are no fixed laws of war which are not subject to the conditions of the country, the climate, and the habits of the people. The laws of successful war in one generation would insure defeat in another.

Pemberton could not have held Vicksburg a day longer than he did. But desperate as his condition was, he did not want to surrender it. He knew that, as a Northern man by birth, he was under suspicion; that a surrender would be treated as disloyalty, and rather than incur that reproach he was willing to stand my assault. But as I learned afterward his officers, and even his men, saw how mad would have been such a course, and he reluctantly accepted the inevitable.

I could have carried Vicksburg by assault, and was ready when the surrender took place. But if Pemberton had forced this, had compelled me to throw away lives uselessly, I should have dealt severely with him. It would have been little less than murder, not only of my men but his own. I would severely punish any officer who, under such circumstances, compelled a wanton loss of life. War is war, and murder is murder, and Vicksburg was so far reduced, and its condition so hopeless when it surrendered, that the loss of another life in defending it would have been criminal.

THE BATTLE OF GETTYSBURG

ADAMS COUNTY, PENNSYLVANIA
JULY 1–3, 1863

COMMANDERS

Confederate
Gen. Robert E. Lee

Union
Maj. Gen. George Meade

PARTICIPANTS

71,699 (Army of Northern Virginia)

93,921 (Army of the Potomac)

CASUALTIES

Union
4,708 killed
12,693 wounded
5,830 POWs/MIA

Confederate
3,155 killed
14,531 wounded
5,369 POWs/MIA

VICTORY: UNION

OVERVIEW

The most famous battle of the Civil War, Gettysburg didn't end the hostilities, nor was there any territory to be gained by either side. Neither side was seeking or protecting a key location—no fuel depot, fort, crossroads, or bridge. It was just a place where two armies happened to meet. They could have thrashed it out somewhere else just as easily. The main objective of each army was to attack the other and to inflict as much damage as possible.

The battle's primary significance was psychological. Historians see it as the turning point of

the war, the point at which momentum shifted from the Confederacy to the Union. Pickett's men made their mad dash through a horrendous hail of gunfire to cross Union lines and reach what later became known as the high-water mark of the Confederacy. The point at which Pickett's brave men were stopped in their tracks is when the tide of the Confederacy crested and then began to recede. The Confederates never quite recovered from this defeat, combined with their surrender at Vicksburg on July 4 as well as the Union's success with the

Tullahoma campaign (or Middle Tennessee campaign), which concluded on July 3. Lee and the South continued to fight, though their spirits were dampened and Lee's confidence was shaken. He never launched another offensive battle, restricting his army to defensive engagements only.

The Battle of Gettysburg holds another claim to fame: It was the largest battle ever fought in North America—both in the number of men who fought and in the number of men who died.

Both sides had a very real chance to bring the war to a swift conclusion. If the Confederates had acted differently, they could have trapped the Union army or had it on the run in disarray. Lee might have even been able to capture Washington, D.C., and force the United States to recognize the independence of the Confederate States. On the other hand, if the Union forces had been able to pursue and attack the fleeing Confederates after the battle, they might have secured Lee's surrender or at least inflicted enough damage to his army that he couldn't have continued.

Many events of the battle could have gone differently over those tumultuous three days. But much lay beyond the immediate control of the commanders—the artillery unexpectedly runs out of ammunition; the cavalry can't be reached when needed; a division takes too long to march to a required destination; an important commander falls in battle. These commanders were making decisions with very limited access to the facts, and much of what we know today about the battle was unknown to them at the time. They had to plan for countless possibilities easily forgotten in hindsight.

Following the battle, recriminations flew on both sides. Lee and Longstreet had to explain what went wrong. Since Lee was held in such high regard, much of the blame unjustly fell on Longstreet's shoulders. On the Union side, even though Meade saved Washington and ended the Confederates' second invasion of the North, he was heavily criticized for having "allowed" Lee to get away—perhaps through no fault of his own. Either way, the chances for ending the war slipped away, and fighting raged for two more bloody years.

GENERAL LONGSTREET'S SPY

Confederate

Lieutenant-General James Longstreet (See biography, page 48.)

On the 9th of May I joined General Lee at his headquarters at Fredericksburg. At our first meeting we had very little conversation; General Lee merely stated that he had had a severe battle [Chancellorsville], and the army had been very much broken up. He regarded the wound accidently inflicted on [Stonewall] Jackson as a terrible calamity. Although we felt the immediate loss of Jackson's services, it was supposed he would rally and get well. He lingered for several days, one day reported better and the next worse, until at last he was taken from us to the shades of Paradise. The shock was a very severe one to men and officers, but the full extent of our loss was not felt until the remains of the beloved general had been sent home. The dark clouds of the future then began to lower above the Confederates.

General Lee at that time was confronted by two problems: one, the finding a successor for Jackson, another, the future movements of the Army of Northern Virginia. After considering the matter fully he decided to reorganize his army, making three corps instead of two. I was in command of the First Corps, and he seemed anxious to have a second and third corps under the command of Virginians. To do so was to overlook the claims of other generals who had been active and very efficient in the service. He selected General Ewell to command the Second, and General A. P. Hill for the Third Corps. General Ewell was entitled to command by reason of his rank, services, and ability. Next in rank was a North Carolinian, General D. H. Hill, and next a Georgian, General Lafayette McLaws, against whom was the objection that they were not Virginians.

While General Lee was reorganizing his army he was also arranging the new campaign. Grant had laid siege to Vicksburg, and Johnston was concentrating at Jackson to drive him away. Rosecrans was in Tennessee and Bragg was in front of him. The force Johnston was concentrating at Jackson gave us no hope that he would have sufficient strength to make any impression upon Grant, and even if he could, Grant was in position to reënforce rapidly and could supply his army with greater facility. Vicksburg was doomed unless we could offer relief by strategic move. I proposed

to send a force through east Tennessee to join Bragg and also to have Johnston sent to join him, thus concentrating a large force to move against Rosecrans, crush out his army, and march against Cincinnati. That, I thought, was the only way we had to relieve Vicksburg. General Lee admitted the force of my proposition, but finally stated that he preferred to organize a campaign into Maryland and Pennsylvania, hoping thereby to draw the Federal troops from the southern points they occupied.

One mistake of the Confederacy was in pitting force against force. The only hope we had was to outgeneral the Federals. We were all hopeful and the army was in good condition, but the war had advanced far enough for us to see that a mere victory without decided fruits was a luxury we could not afford. Our numbers were less than the Federal forces, and our resources were limited while theirs were not. The time had come when it was imperative that the skill of generals and the strategy and tactics of war should take the place of muscle against muscle. Our purpose should have been to impair the *morale* of the Federal army and shake Northern confidence in the Federal leaders.

Before the war Henry Thomas Harrison was a small-time actor whose short stature caused him some difficulty in landing roles. Longstreet called him a scout, but he was actually a spy—a role in which his acting abilities must have come in very handy. Information he gathered by mingling among Union troops directly led Lee's army to Gettysburg. Without Harrison the battle would have been fought elsewhere.

Longstreet talked about Harrison in three different places—a newspaper article, a magazine article, and his memoirs. Each source provides information not found in the others. The extract below combines selections from all accounts into one narrative. The main discrepancy among them is that the magazine article sets the night of Harrison's arrival back in camp as June 28, while the other two give it as the twenty-ninth, which is what appears below.

Before we left Fredericksburg for the campaign into Maryland and Pennsylvania, I called up my scout, Harrison, and, giving him all the gold he thought he would need, told him to go to Washington City and remain there until he was in possession of information which he knew would be of value to us, and directed that he should then make his way back to me and report. As he was leaving, he asked where he would find me. That was information I did not care to impart to a man who was going directly to the Federal capital. I answered that my command was large enough to be found without difficulty.

We had reached Chambersburg on the 27th of June and were remaining there to give the troops rest. We had not heard from the enemy for several days, and General Lee was in doubt as to where he was; indeed, we did not know that he had yet left Virginia.

After due preparation for our march of the 29th, all hands turned in early for a good night's rest. My mind had hardly turned away from the cares and labors of the day, when I was aroused by some one beating on the pole of my tent. It proved to be Assistant Inspector-General [Maj. John] Fairfax. A young man had been arrested by our outlying pickets under suspicious circumstances. He was looking for General Longstreet's head-quarters, but his comfortable apparel and well-to-do, though travel-stained, appearance caused doubt in the minds of the guards of his being a genuine Confederate who could be trusted about head-quarters. So he was sent up under a file of

men to be identified. He proved to be Harrison, the valued scout.

He told me he had been to Washington and had spent his gold freely, drinking in the saloons and getting upon confidential terms with army officers. In that way he had formed a pretty good idea of the general movements of the Federal army and the preparation to give us battle. He had walked through the lines of the Union army during the night of the 27th and the 28th, secured a mount at dark of the latter day to get in as soon as possible, and brought information of the location of two corps of Federals at night of the 27th, and approximate positions of others. General Hooker had crossed the Potomac on the 25th and 26th of June.

After questioning him sufficiently to find that he brought very important information, Colonel Sorrell brought him to my headquarters and awoke me. He gave the information that the enemy had crossed the Potomac, marched northwest, and that the head of his column was at Frederick City, on our right. He said there were three corps near Frederick when he passed there, one to the right and one to the left, but he did not succeed in getting the position of the other. This information proved more accurate than we could have expected if we had been relying upon our cavalry.

I felt that this information was exceedingly important, and might involve a change in the direction of our march. General Lee had already issued orders that we were to advance toward Harrisburg. He [Harrison] was sent under care of Colonel Fairfax to make report of his information at general head-quarters. General Lee declined, however, to see him, though he asked Colonel Fairfax as to the information that he brought, and, on hearing it, expressed want of faith in reports of scouts, in which Fairfax generally agreed, but suggested that in this case the information was so near General Longstreet's ideas of the probable movements of the enemy that he gave credit to it. I also sent up a note suggesting a change of direction of the head of our column east. This I thought to be the first and necessary step towards bringing the two armies to such concentration east as would enable us to find a way to draw the enemy into battle, in keeping with the general plan of campaign, and at the same time draw him off from the travel of our trains.

There were seven corps of the Army of the Potomac afield. We were informed on the 28th of the approximate positions of five of them—three near Frederick and two near the base of South Mountain. The others, of which we had no definite information, we now know were the Sixth (Sedgwick's), south of Frederick and east of the Monocacy, and the Twelfth, towards Harper's Ferry.

On the 26th, General Hooker thought to use the Twelfth Corps and the garrison of Harper's Ferry to strike the line of our communication, but General Halleck forbade the use of the troops of that post, when General Hooker asked to be relieved of the responsibility of command, and was succeeded by General Meade on the night of the 27th.

If General Hooker had been granted the authority for which he applied, he would have struck our trains, exposed from Chambersburg to the Potomac without a cavalryman to ride and report the trouble. General Stuart was riding around Hooker's army, General Robertson was in Virginia, General Imboden at Hancock, and Jenkins's cavalry was at our front with General Ewell.

By the report of the scout we found that the march of Ewell's east wing had failed of execution and of the effect designed, and that heavy columns of the enemy were hovering along the east base of the mountain.[11]

I followed him [Harrison to see Lee] myself early in the morning. I found General Lee up, and asked him if the information brought by the scout might not involve a change of direction of the head of our column to the right. He immediately acquiesced in the suggestion, possibly saying that he had already given orders to that effect. The movement toward the enemy was begun at once.

The two armies were then near each other, the Confederates being north and west of Gettysburg, and the Federals south and south-east of that memorable field. On the 30th of June we turned our faces toward our enemy and marched upon Gettysburg. The Third Corps, under Hill, moved out first and my command followed. We then found ourselves in a very unusual condition: we were almost in the immediate presence of the enemy with our cavalry gone. We knew nothing of Meade's movements further than the report my scout had made. We did not know, except by surmise, when or where to expect to find Meade, nor whether he was lying in wait or advancing. The Confederates moved down the Gettysburg road on June 30th, encountered the Federals on July 1st, and a severe engagement followed. The Federals were driven entirely from the field and forced back through the streets of Gettysburg to Cemetery Hill.

When Lee began his invasion, Hooker, commander of the Union's Army of the Potomac, wanted to

---

11 Lee had hoped that sending Ewell to Harrisburg and Early to Wrightsville would force the Union to spread out the Army of the Potomac to protect Washington, D.C., and Baltimore while drawing Grant and the Union's Army of the Tennessee away from their siege of Vicksburg, but this didn't happen. Still, Lee was successful in drawing the Union army out of Virginia and into Pennsylvania.

seize Richmond, but Lincoln said no, insisting that Hooker had to protect Washington, D.C., and Baltimore, while also pursuing and attacking Lee. Lincoln realized that delivering a major defeat to Lee's army would likely end the war, while taking Richmond probably wouldn't, especially with Lee threatening to take Washington. Lincoln was losing confidence in Hooker, so when Hooker got into a minor dispute with army headquarters and asked to resign, Lincoln replaced him with Meade—just three days before the Battle of Gettysburg.

ESPIONAGE

Washington, D.C., was very poorly situated for the war. Some sixty miles south of the Mason-Dixon Line, it lies directly across the Potomac from Virginia, with Richmond, the Confederate capital, just a hundred miles away. When the cotton states seceded, the Union capital contained many Southern sympathizers. Some went to the Confederacy, but many stayed. As such, the Confederacy began the war with agents already in place scattered throughout the federal government. Conversely, the Union had very few agents in Richmond, and some of those were rounded up pretty quickly.

The Union was slow to enter the spy game, but the Confederates were right on top of it. When Virginia seceded less than a week after the capture of Fort Sumter, Governor John Letcher already was thinking along these lines. He asked Thomas Jordan—who soon rose to brigadier general—to set up a spy network. Their first spy was Rose O'Neal Greenhow, a forty-four-year-old widow, who circulated freely within Washington's high society.

Greenhow openly supported the South, but that didn't prevent her from becoming romantically involved with the chairman of the Committee on Military Affairs, Senator Henry Wilson, later vice president under Grant, and with Senator Joseph Lane, also a member of that committee. She was also friends with Colonel Erasmus Keyes (Winfield Scott's military secretary) and Union major general John Dix. She used a simple cipher to encode the reports she sent to her controller, Jordan, using his cover name of Thomas Rayford.

One of her reports revealed the size of the Union army that Confederate general G. T. Beauregard was about to fight at the First Battle of Manassas. That information enabled him to obtain reinforcements that greatly contributed to the Confederates' victory. The Union captured evidence of her activities and put her under house arrest for ten months, but she kept trying to smuggle out messages, so she was imprisoned and eventually released and exiled to Richmond.

The South also had eighteen-year-old Belle Boyd, who passed information to Stonewall Jackson. She was caught and also banished to Richmond. The North had Elizabeth Van Lew, who led a ring of more than a dozen spies and couriers in Richmond, in addition to running an underground network aiding escaped Union POWs. Some of her agents were her black servants—slaves whom she had essentially freed, although not legally because by Virginia law within a year they would then be exiled from the state. She also wrote her reports in code, often using invisible ink. She was Grant's most valuable spy, particularly in the last year of the war.

Female spies were less likely to be suspected and, if caught, received lighter sentences. The men were usually hanged. General Braxton Bragg sentenced Harriet Wood to death near the end of the war, but before she was executed he retreated and left her behind. Also an actress—and better known by her stage name, Pauline Cushman—Wood was awarded the rank of brevet major after the war.

Quite a few spies were former slaves. Allan Pinkerton recruited some whom he sent back to Richmond undercover. Harriet Tubman, best known as a conductor on the Underground Railroad who smuggled about 300 escaped slaves to freedom in the North, also did espionage work. Early in 1863 Union officers recruited her as a covert operative to lead a cell of fellow ex-slaves in mapping uncharted areas, locating underwater river mines, and gathering intel.

Of course, not all spies were women. While at least eighteen are known, no doubt many are unknown. There were hundreds of undercover operatives in the war. Most are forgotten, and many remained secret to avoid retaliation after the war.

Some, however, boldly donned the enemy's uniform. Wild Bill Hickok, who served as a Union scout and spy in Missouri and Arkansas, is said to have spent some of his time undercover wearing a Confederate uniform.

At sunset on June 9, 1863, Confederate spies twenty-five-year-old Colonel W. Orton "Lawrence" Williams and his twenty-one-year-old cousin, Lieutenant Walter Peters, rode into a Union headquarters post at Franklin, Tennessee, wearing Union uniforms and claiming to be Colonel Austin and Major Dunlap of the inspector general's office. Handing over the proper paperwork, they explained that they were there to inspect the post and its defenses. After they left, the commander of the post grew suspicious and had them brought back under guard. Their true identities soon came to light, and they were hanged the next morning. Lee knew Orton Williams before the war, and even three years after the execution he said, "My blood boils at the thought of the atrocious outrage"—although he probably would have done the same in the reverse situation.

It appears that John Wilkes Booth was also a Confederate spy. The Confederates used a Vigenère square to encode and decode secret messages. One of these ciphers was in Booth's waistcoat pocket when he was killed, and another was in his trunk in a hotel room. His sister said that Booth told her he was a spy, and a Confederate agent claimed he had met with Booth in Canada, when Booth was there in October 1864 to discuss a plot to blow up federal buildings and to kidnap Lincoln.

THE FIRST DAY OF BATTLE

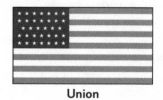

Union

Major-General Winfield Scott Hancock (See biography, page 116.)

On the morning of July 1, in accordance with orders from General Meade, the Second corps marched from Uniontown to Taneytown, where it arrived about 11 a.m. The troops were immediately massed, and I reported in person at headquarters of the Army of the Potomac, which were then at that point. While there, General Meade informed me of his plan for the coming battle. He stated, in general terms, that his intention was to fight on Pipe creek [about six miles west of Westminster, Maryland]; that he had not examined the ground, but, judging from his maps, it was the strongest position he could find; that the Engineers were examining and mapping it, and that he had made an order for the movement to occupy that line.

Shortly afterward General Meade received information that Reynolds [commander of the left wing of the Army of the Potomac] was engaged with the enemy at Gettysburg. Subsequently, at about 1 p.m., he heard that Reynolds was either killed or mortally wounded. General Meade came immediately to my headquarters and told me to assume command of the corps on that field the First and Eleventh, and the Third which was at Emmettsburg.[12]

Having been informed of General Meade's intentions to form his forces for the coming conflict on the line of Pipe creek, these orders required me not only to assume command of the troops at the front, but also to examine the ground at Gettysburg, and if I thought the position there a better one to fight a battle under existing circumstances, I was so to advise him and he would order his whole army up.

The moment these instructions were given me I started at a very rapid pace for the battlefield, which was distant about thirteen miles. On the way we met an ambulance containing the dead body of the heroic Reynolds.

Owing to the peculiar formation of the country, or the direction of the wind at the time, it was not until we had come within a few miles of the field that we heard the roar of the conflict then going on. I hurried to the front, and saw our troops retreating in disorder and confusion from the town, closely followed by the enemy. General [Oliver] Howard was on the crest of Cemetery hill, apparently endeavoring to stop the retreat of his troops, many of whom were passing over the hill and down the Baltimore pike. A portion of Steinwehr's division of Howard's corps, which had been stationed on Cemetery hill by order of General Reynolds, was still in position there, and had thus far taken no part in the battle.

---

12 Meade wanted Hancock to command the corps until Major-General Henry Slocum could take over. Slocum's vacillations and delays earned him the derisive nickname "Slow Come."

As soon as I arrived on the field, at about 3:30 p.m., I rode directly to the crest of the hill where General Howard stood, and said to him that I had been sent by General Meade to take command of all the forces present. As it was necessary at once to establish order in the confused mass of his troops on Cemetery hill and the Baltimore pike, I lost no time in conversation, but at once rode away and bent myself to the pressing task of making such dispositions as would prevent the enemy from seizing that vital point.

I then rode on to place the First corps further to the left, in order that we should cover the whole of Cemetery hill, only a small portion of which was occupied when I arrived upon the field. Seeing the importance of the point, I immediately sent Wadsworth's division and a battery to occupy Culp's hill.

I attach an extract giving a striking description of these occurrences at the time I took command of the left wing at Gettysburg, written by the late Brigadier-General C. H. Morgan, United States Army, then my chief of staff, who accompanied me to the battlefield from Taneytown:

Buford's cavalry was holding the front in the most gallant manner; the horse holders in some instances voluntarily giving up their horses to retreating infantrymen and going themselves to the skirmish line. General Buford himself was on Cemetery hill with General Warren, where General Hancock met them for a moment. Generals Howard, Buford, and Warren all assisted in forming the troops. By threats and persuasion the tide flowing along the Baltimore turnpike was diverted, and lines of battle formed behind the stone walls on either side of the road. To show the disorder into which General Howard's troops had been thrown by the unequal conflict they had waged during the day, it is only necessary to mention that 1,500 fugitives were collected by the provost guard of the Twelfth corps some miles in rear of the field.

The lines having been so established as to deter the enemy from further advance, General Hancock despatched his senior aide, Major Mitchell, with a verbal message to General Meade, that General Hancock could hold Cemetery hill until nightfall, and that he considered Gettysburg the place to fight the coming battle.

After turning over command to Slocum, Hancock returned to his own command. The following day he was called on to take over the command of Major-General Daniel Sickles after a cannonball shattered Sickles's leg.

"HOLD THAT GROUND AT ALL HAZARDS"

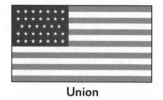

Union

Major-General Joshua Chamberlain

Brevet Major-General Joshua Chamberlain fought in twenty Civil War battles and many other skirmishes. He was wounded six times and cited for bravery four, in addition to receiving the Medal of Honor, the United States' highest military honor, awarded for acts of bravery and heroism, by the president, in the name of Congress.

Born and raised in Maine, Chamberlain was a professor at the Bangor Theological Seminary when the Civil War began. After telling his students that the Union cause was just and that they should follow their hearts, he was placed on leave. He volunteered, becoming a lieutenant colonel in the Twentieth Maine Volunteer Infantry Regiment, and three years later Grant made him a brigadier general with a battlefield promotion, and then Lincoln promoted him to brevet major general.

Colonel Joshua Chamberlain, commander of the Twentieth Maine Infantry, received the Medal of Honor for "daring heroism and great tenacity in holding his position on the Little Round Top against repeated assaults, and carrying the advance position on the Great Round Top" on the second day of battle at Gettysburg. Chamberlain's description of what happened comes from his official report.

Field near Emmitsburg, July 6, 1863

Lieut. George B. Herendeen, A. A. A. G., Third Brig., First Div., Fifth Army Corps

Sir: In compliance with the request of the colonel commanding the brigade, I have the honor to submit a somewhat detailed report of the operations of the Twentieth Regiment Maine Volunteers in the battle of Gettysburg, on the 2d and 3d instant.

Having acted as the advance guard, made necessary by the proximity of the enemy's cavalry, on the march of the day before, my command on reaching Hanover, Pa., just before sunset on that day, were much worn, and lost no time in getting ready for an expected bivouac. Rations were scarcely issued, and the men about preparing supper, when rumors that the enemy had been encountered that day near Gettysburg absorbed every other interest, and very soon orders came to march forthwith to Gettysburg.

My men moved out with a promptitude and spirit extraordinary, the cheers and welcome they received on the road adding to their enthusiasm. After an hour or two of sleep by the roadside just before daybreak, we reached the heights southeasterly of Gettysburg at about 7 a.m., July 2.

Massed at first with the rest of the division on the right of the road, we were moved several times

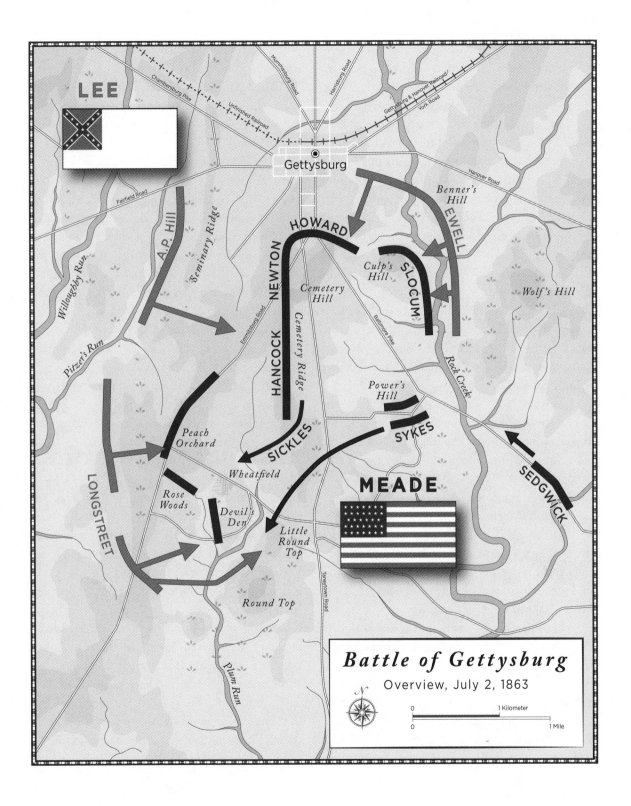

LEE

Gettysburg

Chambersburg Pike

Unfinished Railroad

Mummasburg Road

Harrisburg Road

Gettysburg & Hanover Railroad/
York Road

Hanover Road

Fairfield Road

A.P. Hill

Seminary Ridge

Willoughby Run

Pitzer's Run

HOWARD

NEWTON

Cemetery
Hill

Emmitsburg Road

Cemetery Ridge

HANCOCK

Benner's
Hill

EWELL

Culp's
Hill

SLOCUM

Wolf's Hill

Baltimore Pike

Rock Creek

Power's
Hill

SYKES

SEDGWICK

LONGSTREET

Peach
Orchard

SICKLES

Wheatfield

Rose
Woods

Devil's
Den

Little
Round
Top

MEADE

Round Top

Taneytown Road

Plum Run

Battle of Gettysburg
Overview, July 2, 1863

N

0   1 Kilometer

0   1 Mile

farther toward the left. Although expecting every moment to be put into action and held strictly in line of battle, yet the men were able to take some rest and make the most of their rations.

Somewhere near 4 p.m. a sharp cannonade, at some distance to our left and front, was the signal for a sudden and rapid movement of our whole division in the direction of this firing, which grew warmer as we approached. Passing an open field in the hollow ground in which some of our batteries were going into position, our brigade reached the skirt of a piece of woods, in the farther edge of which there was a heavy musketry fire, and when about to go forward into line we received from Colonel Vincent, commanding the brigade, orders to move to the left at the double-quick, when we took a farm road crossing Plum Run in order to gain a rugged mountain spur called Granite Spur, or Little Round Top.

The enemy's artillery got range of our column as we were climbing the spur, and the crashing of the shells among the rocks and the tree tops made us move lively along the crest. One or two shells burst in our ranks. Passing to the southern slope of Little Round Top, Colonel Vincent indicated to me the ground my regiment was to occupy, informing me that this was the extreme left of our general line, and that a desperate attack was expected in order to turn that position, concluding by telling me I was to "hold that ground at all hazards." This was the last word I heard from him.

The line faced generally toward a more conspicuous eminence southwest of ours, which is known as Sugar Loaf, or Round Top. Between this and my position intervened a smooth and thinly wooded hollow. My line formed, I immediately detached Company B, Captain Morrill commanding, to extend from my left flank across this hollow as a line of skirmishers, with directions to act as occasion might dictate, to prevent a surprise on my exposed flank and rear.

The artillery fire on our position had meanwhile been constant and heavy, but my formation was scarcely complete when the artillery was replaced by a vigorous infantry assault upon the center of our brigade to my right, but it very soon involved the right of my regiment and gradually extended along my entire front. The action was quite sharp and at close quarters.

We opened a brisk fire at close range, which was so sudden and effective that they soon fell back among the rocks and low trees in the valley, only to burst forth again with a shout, and rapidly advanced, firing as they came. They pushed up to within a dozen yards of us before the terrible effectiveness of our fire compelled them to break and take shelter.

They renewed the assault on our whole front, and for an hour the fighting was severe. Squads of the enemy broke through our line in several places, and the fight was literally hand to hand. The edge of the fight rolled backward and forward like a wave. The dead and wounded were now in our front and then in our rear. Forced from our position, we desperately recovered it, and pushed the enemy down to the foot of the slope. The intervals of the struggle were seized to remove our wounded (and those of the enemy also), to gather ammunition from the cartridge-boxes of disabled friend or foe on the field, and even to secure better muskets than the Enfields, which we found did not stand service well. Rude shelters were thrown up of the loose rocks that covered the ground.

The enemy seemed to have gathered all their energies for their final assault. We had gotten our thin line into as good a shape as possible, when a strong force emerged from the scrub wood in the valley and, opening a heavy fire, the first line came on as if they meant to sweep everything before them. We opened on them as well as we could with our scanty ammunition snatched from the field.

It did not seem possible to withstand another shock like this now coming on. Our loss had been severe. One-half of my left wing had fallen, and a third of my regiment lay just behind us, dead or badly wounded. At this moment my anxiety was increased by a great roar of musketry in my rear, on the farther or northerly slope of Little Round Top, apparently on the flank of the regular brigade, which was in support of Hazlett's battery on the crest behind us. The bullets from this attack struck into my left rear, and I feared that the enemy might have nearly surrounded the Little Round Top, and only a desperate chance was left for us. My ammunition was soon exhausted. My men were firing their last shot and getting ready to "club" their muskets.

It was imperative to strike before we were struck by this overwhelming force in a hand-to-hand fight, which we could not probably have withstood or survived. At that crisis, I ordered the bayonet. The word was enough. It ran like fire along the line, from man to man, and rose into a shout, with which they sprang forward upon the enemy, now not 30 yards away. The effect was surprising; many of the enemy's first line threw down their arms and surrendered. An officer fired his pistol at my head with one hand, while he handed me his sword with the other. Holding fast by our right, and swinging forward our left, we made an extended "right wheel," before which the enemy's second line broke and fell back, fighting from tree to tree, many being captured, until we had swept the valley and cleared the front of nearly our entire brigade.

Having thus cleared the valley and driven the enemy up the western slope of the Great Round Top, not wishing to press so far out as to hazard the ground I was to hold by leaving it exposed to a sudden rush of the enemy, I succeeded (although with some effort to stop my men, who declared they were "on the road to Richmond") in getting the regiment into good order and resuming our original position.

Four hundred prisoners, including two field and several line officers, were sent to the rear. These were mainly from the Fifteenth and Forty-seventh Alabama Regiments, with some of the Fourth and Fifth Texas. One hundred and fifty of the enemy were found killed and wounded in our front.

We went into the fight with 386, all told—358 guns. Every pioneer and musician who could carry a musket went into the ranks. Even the sick and foot-sore, who could not keep up in the march, came up as soon as they could find their regiments, and took their places in line of battle, while it was battle, indeed. Some prisoners I had under guard, under sentence of court-martial, I was obliged to put into the fight, and they bore their part well, for which I shall recommend a commutation of their sentence.

The loss, so far as I can ascertain it, is 136—30 of whom were killed, and among the wounded are many mortally.

On the 4th, we made a reconnaissance to the front, to ascertain the movements of the enemy, but finding that they had retired, at least beyond Willoughby's Run, we returned to Little Round Top, where we buried our dead in the place where we had laid them during the fight, marking each grave by a head-board made of ammunition boxes, with each dead soldier's name cut upon it. We also buried 50 of the enemy's dead in front of our position of July 2. We then looked after our wounded, whom I had taken the responsibility of putting into the houses of citizens in the vicinity of Little Round Top, and, on the morning of the 5th, took up our march on the Emmitsburg road.

I have the honor to be, your obedient servant, Joshua L. Chamberlain, Colonel, Commanding Twentieth Maine Volunteers

The Confederates against whom Chamberlain held his ground were the Fifteenth Alabama Infantry Regiment led by Colonel William Oates, whose brother died in the battle. They were one of five regiments comprising Brigadier-General Evander Law's brigade under Major-General John Bell Hood.

After the war, Oates served seven terms in the U.S. House of Representatives and became governor of Alabama. In 1898, during the Spanish-American War, this former Confederate colonel became a brigadier general in the U.S. Army.

With a withering and deadly fire pouring in upon us from every direction, it seemed that the entire command was doomed to destruction. While one man was shot in the face, his right hand or left hand comrade was shot in the side or back. Some were struck simultaneously with two or three balls from different directions. Captains Hill and Park suggested that I should order a retreat; but this seemed impracticable. My dead and wounded were then greater in number than those still on duty. Of 644 men and 42 officers, I had lost 343 men and 19 officers. The dead literally covered the ground. The blood stood in puddles on the rocks. The ground was soaked with the blood of as brave men as ever fell on the red field of battle.

—COLONEL WILLIAM OATES

General John Bell Hood (See biography, page 84.)

GENERAL LEE'S ORDERS

Confederate

New Orleans, La., June 28th, 1875
General James Longstreet:

You are correct in your assumption that I failed to make a report of the operations of my division around Suffolk, Va., and of its action in the battle of Gettysburg, in consequence of a wound which I received in this engagement. In justice to the brave troops under my command at this period, I should here mention another cause for this apparent neglect of duty on my part. Before I had recovered from the severe wound received at Gettysburg, your corps (excepting Pickett's Division) was ordered to join General

Bragg, in the West, for battle against Rosecranz[13]; my old troops—with whom I had served so long—were thus to be sent forth to another Army—quasi, I may say, among strangers—to take part in a great struggle; and upon an appeal from a number of the brigade and regimental officers of my division, I consented to accompany them, although I had but the use of one arm. This movement to the West soon resulted in the battle of Chickamauga, where I was again so seriously wounded as to cause the loss of a limb. Thus, the gallantry of these troops, as well as the admirable conduct of my division at Gettysburg, I have left unrecorded.

With this apology for seeming neglect, I will proceed to give a brief sketch, from memory, of the events forming the subject of your letter:

I arrived with my staff in front of the heights of Gettysburg shortly after daybreak on the morning of the 2d of July. My division soon commenced filing into an open field near me, where the troops were allowed to stack arms and rest until further orders. A short distance in advance of this point, and during the early part of that same morning, we were both engaged in company with Generals Lee and A P. Hill, in observing the position of the Federals. General Lee—with coat buttoned to the throat, sabre-belt buckled round the waist, and field glasses pending at his side—walked up and down in the shade of the large trees near us, halting now and then to observe the enemy. He seemed full of hope, yet, at times, buried in deep thought. Colonel Freemantle, of England, was ensconced in the forks of a tree not far off, with glass in constant use, examining the lofty position of the Federal Army.

General Lee was, seemingly, anxious you should attack that morning. He remarked to me, "The enemy is here, and if we do not whip him, he will whip us." You thought it better to await the arrival of Pickett's Division—at that time still in the rear—in order to make the attack; and you said to me, subsequently, whilst we were seated together near the trunk of a tree: "The General is a little nervous this morning; he wishes me to attack; I do not wish to do so without Pickett. I never like to go into battle with one boot off."

Thus passed the forenoon of that eventful day, when in the afternoon—about 3 o'clock—it was decided to no longer await Pickett's Division, but to proceed to our extreme right and attack up the Emmetsburg road. This movement was accomplished by throwing out an advanced force to tear down fences and clear the way. The instructions I received were to place my division across the Emmetsburg road, form line of battle, and attack. Before reaching this road, however, I had sent forward some of my picked Texas scouts to ascertain the position of the enemy's extreme

Little Round Top with Big Round Top in the background immediately after the battle.

---

13 The Confederates appear to have misspelled his name on purpose as a propaganda ploy to make him seem like a foreigner, as there were many Europeans fighting for the Union. They also spelled it Rosencranz.

left flank. They soon reported to me that it rested upon [Big] Round Top Mountain; that the country was open, and that I could march through an open woodland pasture around Round Top, and assault the enemy in flank and rear; that their wagon trains were packed in rear of their line, and were badly exposed to our attack in that direction.

I found that in making the attack according to orders, viz.: up the Emmetsburg road, I should have been the first to encounter and drive off this advanced line of battle; secondly, at the base and along the slope of the mountain, to confront immense boulders of stone, so massed together as to form narrow openings, which would break our ranks and cause the men to scatter whilst climbing up the rocky precipice. I found, moreover, that my division would be exposed to a heavy fire from the main line of the enemy in position on the crest of the high range, of which Round Top was the extreme left, and, by reason of the concavity of the enemy's main line, that we would be subject to a destructive fire in flank and rear, as well as in front; and deemed it almost an impossibility to clamber along the boulders up this steep and rugged mountain, and, under this number of cross fires, put the enemy to flight. I knew that if the feat was accomplished, it must be at a most fearful sacrifice of as brave and gallant soldiers as ever engaged in battle.

I was in possession of these important facts so shortly after reaching the Emmetsburg road, that I considered it my duty to report to you, at once, my opinion that it was unwise to attack up the Emmetsburg road, as ordered, and to urge that you allow me to turn Round Top, and attack the enemy in flank and rear. Accordingly, I despatched a staff officer, bearing to you my request to be allowed to make the proposed movement on account of the above stated reasons. Your reply was quickly received, "General Lee's orders are to attack up the Emmetsburg road." I sent another officer to say that I feared nothing could be accomplished by such an attack, and renewed my request to turn Round Top. Again your answer was, "General Lee's orders are to attack up the Emmetsburg road."

During this interim I had continued the use of the batteries upon the enemy, and had become more and more convinced that the Federal line extended to Round Top, and that I could not reasonably hope to accomplish much by the attack as ordered. In fact, it seemed to me the enemy occupied a position by nature so strong—I may say impregnable—that, independently of their flank fire, they could easily repel our attack by merely throwing and rolling stones down the mountain side, as we approached.

A third time I despatched one of my staff to explain fully in regard to the situation, and suggest that you had better come and look for yourself. I selected, in this instance, my adjutant-general, Colonel Harry Sellers, whom you know to be not only an officer of great courage, but also of marked ability. Colonel Sellers returned with the same message, "General Lee's orders are to attack up the Emmetsburg road." Almost simultaneously, Colonel Fairfax, of your staff, rode up and repeated the above orders.

> My men had to climb up, catching to the bushes and crawling over the immense boulders, in the face of an incessant fire of their enemy, who kept falling back, taking shelter and firing down on us from behind the rocks and crags that covered the mountain side thicker than grave stones in a city cemetery.
> —COLONEL WILLIAM OATES, DESCRIBING HIS ASCENT ON BIG ROUND TOP

After this urgent protest against entering the battle at Gettysburg, according to instructions—which protest is the first and only one I ever made during my entire military career—I ordered my line to advance and make the assault.

As my troops were moving forward, you rode up in person; a brief conversation passed between us, during which I again expressed the fears above mentioned, and regret at not being allowed to attack in flank around Round Top. You answered to this effect, "We must obey the orders of General Lee." I then rode forward with my line under a heavy fire. In about twenty minutes, after reaching the peach orchard, I was severely wounded in the arm [by a shell that exploded overhead], and borne from the field.

With this wound terminated my participation in this great battle. As I was borne off on a litter to the rear, I could but experience deep distress of mind and heart at the thought of the inevitable fate of my brave fellow-soldiers, who formed one of the grandest divisions of that world-renowned army; and I shall ever believe that had I been permitted to turn Round Top Mountain, we would not only have gained that position, but have been able finally to rout the enemy.

I am, respectfully, yours,

J. B. Hood

Hood's wounded arm didn't need amputating, but he was never able to use it after that.

A CAVALRY BATTLE

Confederate

Major-General J. E. B. Stuart

James Ewell Brown Stuart—nicknamed "Jeb" because of his initials—became one of the Civil War's most famous cavalry officers, known as the Knight of the Golden Spurs.

Stuart was born on a Virginia farm near the North Carolina border. His father had served a term in the U.S. House of Representatives, and while at West Point young Stuart befriended Robert E. Lee's family, often socializing with them before he graduated in 1854.

When Colonel Lee was assigned to put down John Brown's raid at Harper's Ferry, Stuart accompanied him as aide-de-camp. He had just been promoted to captain at age twenty-eight when the war began. He resigned to join Virginia's volunteers. Lee assigned him to the infantry under Colonel Stonewall Jackson, who instead placed him in charge of the Army of the Shenandoah's cavalry. Stuart was soon promoted to brigadier general, showing a particular talent for reconnaissance. He also adopted the flashy appearance of a cavalier, wearing a gray cape with red silk lining, a yellow sash, a flower in his lapel, cologne, and an ostrich-plumed hat cocked to one side.

During the Seven Days Battles of the Peninsula campaign, when McClellan marched up the Virginia Peninsula toward Richmond, Lee asked Stuart to determine whether the Union's right flank was vulnerable. Setting off with 1,200 men, he rode all the way around McClellan's forces—a journey of 150 miles—returning three days later with 165 captured soldiers, 260 horses and mules, and a variety of supplies and ordnance. This feat was particularly ironic since the commander of McClellan's cavalry was Colonel Philip St. George Cooke—Stuart's own father-in-law. Stuart instantly became a hero throughout the South, and he has since been described as "the greatest cavalryman ever foaled in America."

After Gettysburg many criticized Stuart and the cavalry for taking off and not remaining in contact with Lee. Doing so hindered Lee, depriving him of extended reconnaissance, leaving him blind as he searched for the Union army pursuing him. On the other hand, Lee's orders to Stuart were general, giving him considerable leeway. Stuart thought it more useful to hinder the Union army by harassing their supply lines and disrupting their communications with Washington, D.C., and U.S. Army headquarters. By the time he reached Gettysburg, it was late in the day on July 2.

On the third, Lee wanted Stuart to protect their left flank while trying to swing behind Union lines. This move resulted in a fight in which Stuart and about 3,500 men went up against Custer with 3,250 men.

Hdqrs. Second Corps, Army of Northern Virginia,
August 20, 1863

Col. R. H. Chilton, Chief of Staff, Army of Northern Virginia.

My advance reached Gettysburg July 2, just in time to thwart a move of the enemy's cavalry upon our rear by way of Hunterstown, after a fierce engagement, a series of charges compelling the enemy to leave the field and abandon his purpose.

On the morning of July 3, pursuant to instructions from the commanding general (the ground along our line of battle being totally impracticable for cavalry operations), I moved forward to a position to the left of General Ewell's left, and in advance of it, where a commanding ridge completely controlled a wide plain of cultivated fields stretching toward Hanover, on the left, and reaching to the base of the mountain spurs, among which the enemy held position. My command was increased by the addition of Jenkins' brigade, who here in the presence of the enemy allowed themselves to be supplied with but 10 rounds of ammunition, although armed with the most approved Enfield musket. I moved this command and W. H. F. Lee's secretly through the woods to a position, and hoped to effect a surprise upon the enemy's rear, but Hampton's and Fitz. Lee's brigades, which had been ordered to follow me, unfortunately debouched [emerged] into the open ground, disclosing the movement, and causing a corresponding movement of a large force of the enemy's cavalry.

The enemy had deployed a heavy line of sharpshooters, and were advancing toward our position, which was very strong. Our artillery had, however, left the crest, which it was essential for it to occupy, on account of being of too short range to compete with the longer range guns of the enemy, but I sent orders for its return. Jenkins' brigade was chiefly employed dismounted, and fought with decided effect until the 10 rounds were expended, and then retreated, under circumstances of difficulty and exposure which entailed the loss of valuable men.

The left, where Hampton's and Lee's brigades were, by this time became heavily engaged as dismounted skirmishers. My plan was to employ the enemy in front with sharpshooters, and move a command of cavalry upon their left flank from the position lately held by me, but the falling back of Jenkins' men caused a like movement of those on the left, and the enemy, sending forward a squadron or two, were about to cut off and capture a portion of our dismounted sharpshooters. To prevent this, I ordered forward the nearest cavalry regiment (one of W. H. F. Lee's) quickly to charge this force of cavalry. It was gallantly done, and about the same time a portion of General Fitz. Lee's command charged on the left, the First Virginia Cavalry being most conspicuous.

In these charges, the impetuosity of those gallant fellows, after two weeks of hard marching and hard fighting on short rations, was not only extraordinary, but irresistible. The enemy's masses vanished before them like grain before the scythe, and that regiment elicited the admiration of every beholder, and eclipsed the many laurels already won by its gallant veterans. Their impetuosity carried them too far, and the charge being very much prolonged, their horses, already jaded by hard marching, failed under it. Their movement was too rapid to be stopped by couriers, and the enemy perceiving it, were turning upon them with fresh horses.

The First North Carolina Cavalry and Jeff Davis Legion were sent to their support, and gradually this hand-to-hand fighting involved the greater portion of the command till the enemy were driven from the field, which was now raked by their artillery, posted about three-quarters of a mile off, our officers and men behaving with the greatest heroism throughout. Our own artillery commanding the same ground, no more hand-to-hand fighting occurred, but the wounded were removed and the prisoners (a large number) taken to the rear.

The enemy's loss was unmistakably heavy; numbers not known. Many of his killed and wounded fell into our hands. That brave and distinguished officer, Brigadier-General Hampton, was seriously wounded twice in this engagement.

Grateful to the Giver of all good for the attainment of such results with such small comparative losses, I have the honor to be, most respectfully, your obedient servant,

J. E. B. Stuart, Major-General

A Brilliant Charge

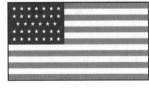

Union

Major-General George Armstrong Custer (See biography, page 3.)

In his official report, Custer described the same engagement on July 3 from the Union side, although it sounds considerably different. Custer led two charges, each time yelling, "Come on, you Wolverines!" In each charge the horse Custer was riding was shot from beneath him.

An entire brigade of the enemy's cavalry, consisting of four regiments, appeared just over the crest in our front. They were formed in column of regiments. To meet this overwhelming force I had but one available regiment, the First Michigan cavalry, and the fire of battery M, Second regular artillery. I at once ordered the First to charge, but learned at the same moment that similar orders had been given by Brigadier-General Gregg. The First was formed in column of battalions.

Upon receiving the order to charge, Colonel Town, placing himself at the head of his command, ordered the "trot" and sabres to be drawn. In this manner this gallant body of men advanced to the attack of a force outnumbering them five to one. In addition to this numerical superiority, the enemy had the advantage of position, and were exultant over the repulse of the Seventh Michigan cavalry. All these facts considered, would seem to render success on the part of the First impossible.

Not so, however. Arriving within a few yards of the enemy's column, the charge was ordered, and with a yell that spread terror before them, the First Michigan cavalry, led by Colonel Town, rode upon the front rank of the enemy, sabring all who came within reach.

For a moment, but only a moment, that long, heavy column stood its ground, then unable to with stand the impetuosity of our attack, it gave way into a disorderly rout, leaving vast numbers of their dead and wounded in our possession, while the First, being masters of the field, had the proud satisfaction of seeing the much vaunted "chivalry" seek safety in headlong flight.

I cannot find language to express my high appreciation of the gallantry and daring displayed by the officers and men of the First Michigan cavalry. They advanced to the charge of a vastly superior force with as much order and precision as if going upon parade; and I challenge the annals of warfare to produce a more brilliant or successful charge of cavalry than the one just recounted.

FROM SEMINARY RIDGE TO CEMETERY RIDGE

Confederate

Lieutenant-General James Longstreet (See biography, page 48.)

Gettysburg lies partly between Seminary Ridge on the west and Cemetery Ridge on the south-east, a distance of about fourteen hundred yards dividing the crests of the two ridges. As General Lee rode to the summit of Seminary Ridge [on July 1] and looked down upon the town he saw the Federals in full retreat and concentrating on the rock-ribbed hill that served as a burying-ground for the city.

He sent orders to Ewell to follow up the success if he found it practicable and to occupy the hill on which the enemy was concentrating. As the order was not positive, but left discretion with General

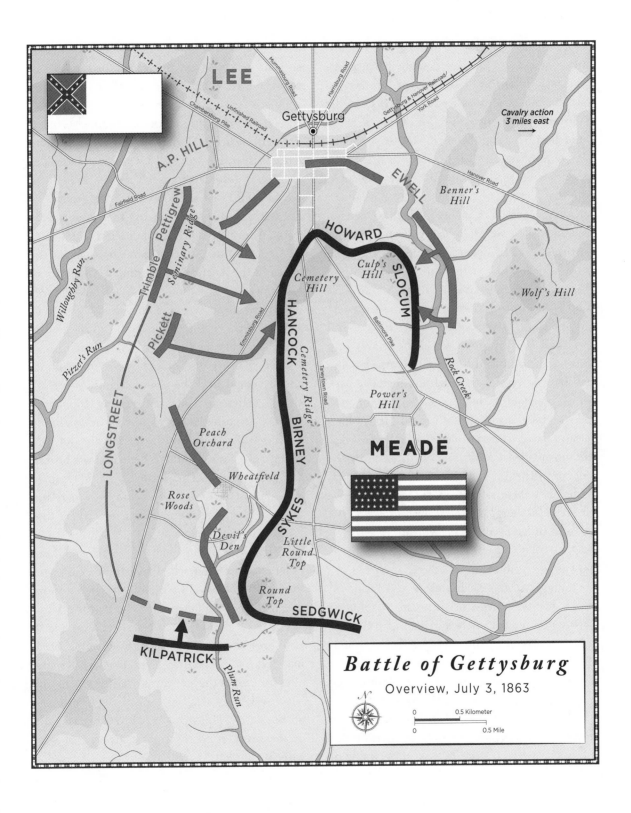

LEE

Gettysburg

Mummasburg Road
Harrisburg Road
Gettysburg & Hanover Railroad/
York Road

Chambersburg Pike
Unfinished Railroad

Cavalry action
3 miles east

A.P. HILL

EWELL

Fairfield Road

Hanover Road

Benner's
Hill

Pettigrew

HOWARD

Trimble

Seminary Ridge

Culp's
Hill

SLOCUM

Cemetery
Hill

Wolf's Hill

Willoughby Run

Pickett

HANCOCK

Emmitsburg Road

Baltimore Pike

Pitzer's Run

Cemetery Ridge

Power's
Hill

Rock Creek

LONGSTREET

BIRNEY

Taneytown Road

Peach
Orchard

MEADE

Wheatfield

Rose
Woods

SYKES

Devil's
Den

Little
Round
Top

Round
Top

SEDGWICK

KILPATRICK

Plum Run

Battle of Gettysburg

Overview, July 3, 1863

N

0   0.5 Kilometer

0   0.5 Mile

Ewell, the latter thought it better to give his troops a little rest and wait for more definite instructions.

I was following Hill's Corps as fast as possible, and as soon as I got possession of the road went rapidly forward to join General Lee. I found him watching the enemy on the opposite hill. He pointed out their position to me. I took my glasses and made as careful a survey as I could from that point.

After five or ten minutes I turned to General Lee and said, "If we could have chosen a point to meet our plans of operation, I do not think we could have found a better one than that upon which they are now concentrating. All we have to do is to throw our army around by their left, and we shall interpose between the Federal army and Washington. We can get a strong position and wait, and if they fail to attack us we shall have everything in condition to move back to-morrow night in the direction of Washington, selecting beforehand a good position into which we can place our troops to receive battle next day. Finding our object is Washington or that army, the Federals will be sure to attack us. When they attack, we shall beat them, as we proposed to do before we left Fredericksburg, and the probabilities are that the fruits of our success will be great."

"No," said General Lee; "the enemy is there, and I am going to attack him there."

I suggested that such a move as I proposed would give us control of the roads leading to Washington and Baltimore, and reminded General Lee of our original plans. If we had fallen behind Meade and had insisted on staying between him and Washington, he would have been compelled to attack and would have been badly beaten.

General Lee answered, "No; they are there in position, and I am going to whip them or they are going to whip me." I saw he was in no frame of mind to listen to further argument at that time, so I did not push the matter, but determined to renew the subject the next morning. It was then about 5 o'clock in the afternoon.

On the morning of the 2d I joined General Lee and again proposed the move to Meade's left and rear. He was still unwilling to consider the proposition, but soon left me and rode off to see General Ewell and to examine the ground on our left with a view to making the attack at that point. After making the examination and talking to General Ewell, he determined to make the attack by the right, and, returning to where I was, announced his intention of so doing. His engineer officers had been along the line far enough to find a road by which the troops could move and be concealed from the Federal signal stations.

As soon as the troops were in position, and we could find the points against which we should march and give the guiding points, the advance was ordered—at half-past 3 o'clock in the afternoon. The attack was made in splendid style by both divisions, and the Federal line was broken by the first impact. They retired, many of them, in the direction of Round Top behind bowlders and fences, which gave them shelter, and where they received reinforcements.

This was an unequal battle. General Lee's orders had been that when my advance was made, the Second Corps (Ewell), his left, should move and make a simultaneous attack; that the Third Corps (Hill) should watch closely and engage so as to prevent heavy massing in front of me. Ewell made no move at all until about 8 o'clock at night, after the heat of the battle was over, his line having been broken by a call for one of his brigades to go else where. Hill made no move whatever, save of the brigades of his right division that were covering our left.

When the battle of the 2d was over, General Lee pronounced it a success, as we were in possession of ground from which we had driven the Federals and had taken several field-pieces. The conflict had been fierce and bloody, and my troops had driven back heavy columns and had encountered a force three or four times their number, but we had accomplished little toward victorious results. Our success of the first day had led us into battle on the 2d, and the battle on the 2d was to lead us into the terrible and hopeless slaughter on the 3d.

The position of the Federals was quite strong, and the battle of the 2d had concentrated them so that I considered an attack from the front more hazardous than the battle on the 2d had been. The Federals were concentrated, while our troops were stretched out in a long, broken—and thus a weak—line. However, General Lee hoped to break through the Federal line and drive them off. I was disappointed when he came to me on the morning of the 3d and directed that I should renew the attack against Cemetery Hill, probably the strongest point of the Federal line. For that purpose he had already ordered up Pickett's division, which had been left at Chambersburg to guard our supply trains.

In the meantime the Federals had placed batteries on Round Top, in position to make a raking fire against troops attacking the Federal front. Meade knew that if the battle was renewed it would be virtually over the same ground as my battle of the 2d. I stated to General Lee that I had been examining the ground over to the right, and was much inclined to think the best thing was to move to the Federal left.

"No," he said; "I am going to take them where they are on Cemetery Hill. I want you to take Pickett's division and make the attack. I will reënforce you by two divisions (Heth's under Pettigrew and Pender's under Trimble) of the Third Corps."

"That will give me fifteen thousand men," I replied. "I have been a soldier, I may say, from the ranks up to the position I now hold. I have been in pretty much all kinds of skirmishes, from those of two or three soldiers up to those of an army corps, and I think I can safely say there never was a body of fifteen thousand men who could make that attack successfully."

The general seemed a little impatient at my remarks, so I said nothing more. As he showed no indication of changing his plan, I went to work at once to arrange my troops for the attack. The artillery combat was to begin with the rapid discharge of two field-pieces as our signal. As soon as the orders were communicated along the line, I sent Colonel E. P. Alexander (who was commanding a battalion of artillery and who had been an engineer officer) to select carefully a point from which he could observe the effect of our batteries. When he could discover the enemy's batteries silenced or crippled, he should give notice to General Pickett, who was ordered, upon receipt of that notice, to move forward to the attack.

When I took Pickett to the crest of Seminary Ridge and explained where his troops should be sheltered, and pointed out the direction General Lee wished him to take and the point of the Federal line where the assault was to be made, he seemed to appreciate the severity of the contest upon which he was about to enter, but was quite hopeful of success.

Upon receipt of notice, he was to march over the crest of the hill down the gentle slope and up the rise opposite the Federal stronghold. The distance was about fourteen hundred yards, and for most of the way the Federal batteries would have a raking fire from Round Top, while the sharp-shooters, artillery, and infantry would subject the assaulting column to a terrible and destructive fire. With my knowledge of the situation, I could see the desperate and hopeless nature of the charge and the cruel slaughter it would cause. My heart was heavy when I left Pickett. I rode once or twice along the ground between Pickett and the Federals, examining the positions and studying the matter over in all its phases so far as we could anticipate.

About 1 o'clock everything was in readiness. The signal guns broke the prevailing stillness, and immediately 150 Confederate cannon burst into a deafening roar, which was answered by a thunder almost as great from the Federal side. The great artillery combat proceeded. The destruction was, of course, not great; but the thunder on Seminary Ridge, and the echo from the Federal side, showed that both commanders were ready. The armies seemed like mighty wild beasts growling at each other and preparing for a death struggle. For an hour or two the fire was continued, and met such steady response on the part of the Federals, that it seemed less effective than we had anticipated.

I felt that my men were to be sacrificed, and that I should have to order them to make a hopeless charge. I had instructed General Alexander, being unwilling to trust myself with the entire responsibility, to carefully observe the effect of the fire upon the enemy, and when it began to tell to notify Pickett to begin the assault. I was so much impressed with the hopelessness of the charge, that I wrote the following note to General Alexander: "If the artillery fire does not have the effect to drive off the enemy or greatly demoralize him, so as to make our efforts pretty certain, I would prefer that you should not advise General Pickett to make the charge. I shall rely a great deal on your judgment to determine the matter, and shall expect you to let Pickett know when the moment offers."

To my note the General replied as follows: "I will only be able to judge the effect of our fire upon the enemy by his return fire, for his infantry is but little exposed to view, and the smoke will obscure the whole field. If, as I infer from your note, there is an alternative to this attack, it should be carefully considered before opening our fire, for it will take all of the artillery ammunition we have left to test this one thoroughly; and, if the result is unfavorable, we will have none left for another effort; and, even if this is entirely successful, it can only be so at a very bloody cost."

I still desired to save my men, and felt that if the artillery did not produce the desired effect, I would be justified in holding Pickett off. I wrote this note to Colonel Walton at exactly 1.30 p.m. "Let the batteries open. Order great precision in firing. If the batteries at the peach orchard cannot be used against the point we intend attacking, let them open on the enemy at Rocky Hill."

The cannonading which opened along both lines was grand. In a few moments a courier brought a note to General Pickett (who was standing near me) from Alexander, which, after reading, he handed to me. It was as follows: "If you are coming at all, you must come at once, or I cannot give you proper support; but the enemy's fire has not slackened at all; at least eighteen guns are still firing from the cemetery itself."

After I had read the note, Pickett said to me: "General, shall I advance?"

My feelings had so overcome me that I would not speak, for fear of betraying my want of confidence to him. I bowed affirmation, and turned to mount my horse. Pickett immediately said: "I shall lead my division forward, sir."

Colonel Alexander had set aside a battery of seven guns to advance with Pickett, but General Pendleton, from whom they were borrowed, recalled them just before the charge was ordered. Colonel Alexander told me of the seven guns which had been removed, and that his ammunition was so low he could not properly support the charge. I ordered him to stop Pickett until the ammunition could be replenished, and he answered, "There is no ammunition with which to replenish." In the hurry he got together such guns as he could to move with Pickett.

It has been said that I should have exercised discretion and should not have sent Pickett on his charge. It has been urged that I had exercised discretion on previous occasions. It is true that at times when I saw a certainty of another direction, I did not follow the orders of my general, but that was when he was not near and could not see the situation as it existed. When your chief is away, you have a right to exercise discretion; but if he sees everything that you see, you have no right to disregard his positive and repeated orders. I never exercised discretion after discussing with General Lee the points of his orders, and when, after discussion, he had ordered the execution of his policy. I had offered my objections to Pickett's battle and had been over ruled, and I was in the immediate presence of the commanding general when the order was given for Pickett to advance.

That day at Gettysburg was one of the saddest of my life. I foresaw what my men would meet and would gladly have given up my position rather than share in the responsibilities of that day. It was thus I felt when Pickett at the head of 4,900 brave men marched over the crest of Seminary Ridge and began his descent of the slope. As he passed me he rode gracefully, with his jaunty cap raked well over on his right ear and his long auburn locks, nicely dressed, hanging almost to his shoulders. He seemed rather a holiday soldier than a general at the head of a column which was about to make one of the grandest, most desperate assaults recorded in the annals of wars.

Armistead and Garnett, two of his brigadiers, were veterans of nearly a quarter of a century's service. Their minds seemed absorbed in the men behind, and in the bloody work before them. Intervening were several fences, a field of corn, a little swale running through it and then a rise from that point to the Federal stronghold. As soon as Pickett passed the crest of the hill, the Federals had a clear view and opened their batteries, and as he descended the eastern slope of the ridge his troops received a fearful fire from the batteries in front and from Round Top. The troops marched steadily, taking the fire with great coolness. As soon as they passed my batteries I ordered my artillery to turn their fire against the batteries on our right then raking my lines. They did so, but did not force the Federals to change the direction of their fire and relieve our infantry. As the troops were about to cross the swale I noticed a considerable force of Federal infantry moving down as though to flank the left of our line. I sent an officer to caution the division commanders to guard against that move, at the same time sending another staff-officer with similar orders so as to feel assured the order would be delivered. Both officers came back bringing their saddles, their horses having been shot under them.

After crossing the swale, the troops kept the same steady step, but met a dreadful fire at the hands of the Federal sharpshooters; and as soon as the field was open the Federal infantry poured down a terrific fire which was kept up during the entire assault. The slaughter was terrible, the enfilade fire of the batteries on Round Top being very destructive. At times one shell would knock down five or six men.

I dismounted to relieve my horse and was sitting on a rail fence watching very closely the movements of the troops. Colonel Fremantle, who had taken a position behind the Third Corps where he would be out of reach of fire and at the same time have a clear view of the field, became so interested that he left his position and came with speed to join me. Just as he came up behind me, Pickett had reached a point near the Federal lines. A pause was made to close ranks and mass for the final plunge. The troops on Pickett's left, although advancing, were evidently a little shaky. Colonel Fremantle, only observing the troops of Pickett's command, said to me, "General, I would not have missed this for anything in the world." He believed it to be a complete success.

I was watching the troops supporting Pickett and saw plainly they could not hold together ten minutes longer. I called his attention to the wavering condition of the two divisions of the Third Corps, and said they would not hold, that Pickett would strike and be crushed and the attack would be a failure. As Pickett's division concentrated in making the final assault, Kemper fell severely wounded. As the division threw itself against the Federal line Garnett fell and expired. The Confederate flag was planted in the Federal line, and immediately Armistead fell mortally wounded at the feet of the Federal soldiers. The wavering divisions then seemed appalled, broke their ranks, and retired. Immediately the Federals swarmed around Pickett, attacking on all sides, enveloped and broke up his command, having killed and wounded more than two thousand men in about thirty minutes. They then drove the fragments back upon our lines.

As they came back I fully expected to see Meade ride to the front and lead his forces to a tremendous counter-charge. Sending my staff-officers to assist in collecting the fragments of my command, I rode to my line of batteries, knowing they were all I had in front of the impending attack, resolved to drive it back or sacrifice my last gun and man. The Federals were advancing a line of skirmishers which I thought was the advance of their charge. As soon as the line of skirmishers came within reach of our guns, the batteries opened again and their fire seemed to check at once the threatened advance. After keeping it up a few minutes the line of skirmishers disappeared, and my mind was relieved of the apprehension that Meade was going to follow us.

General Lee came up as our troops were falling back and encouraged them as well as he could; begged them to re-form their ranks and reorganize their forces, and assisted the staff-officers in bringing them all together again. It was then he used the expression that has been mentioned so often, "It was all my fault; get together, and let us do the best we can toward saving that which is left us."

PICKETT'S CHARGE

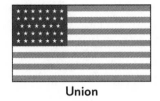

Union

Major-General Winfield Scott Hancock (See biography, page 116.)

Hancock wrote his official account of Pickett's Charge while convalescing from a wound sustained near the end of that battle. Hancock commanded First, Second, and Third Corps, situated in the center of the Union line, from Cemetery Ridge to Cemetery Hill. It was into the middle of Hancock's men that Pickett and his soldiers charged. Hancock's close friend Brigadier-General Lewis Armistead, commander of one of Pickett's brigades, was one of those who charged right at him.

The early morning passed in comparative quiet along our front, but the heavy and continued firing on the right indicated that the efforts of the enemy were being directed on the Twelfth Corps. Trifling affairs occurred at intervals between the enemy's skirmishers and our own, and the artillery of the corps was frequently and successfully engaged with that of the enemy.

From 11 a.m. until 1 p.m. there was an ominous stillness. About 1 o'clock, apparently by a given signal, the enemy opened upon our front with the heaviest artillery fire I have ever known. Their guns were in position at an average distance of about 1,400 yards from my line, and ran in a semicircle from the town of Gettysburg to a point opposite Round Top Mountain. Their number is variously estimated at from one hundred and fifteen to one hundred and fifty. The air was filled with projectiles, there being scarcely an instant but that several were seen bursting at once.

No irregularity of ground afforded much protection, and the plain in rear of the line of battle was soon swept of everything movable. The infantry troops maintained their position with great steadiness, covering themselves as best they might by the temporary but trifling defenses they had erected and the accidents of the ground. Scarcely a straggler was seen, but all waited the cessation of the fierce cannonade, knowing well what it foreshadowed. The artillery of the corps, imperfectly supplied with ammunition, replied to the enemy most gallantly, maintaining the unequal contest in a manner that reflected the highest honor on this arm of the service. Brown's battery (B, First Rhode Island), which had suffered severely on the 2d, and expended all of its canister on that day, retired before the cannonading ceased, not being effective for further service. The remaining batteries continued their fire until only canister remained to them, and then ceased.

After an hour and forty-five minutes, the fire of the enemy became less furious, and immediately their infantry was seen in the woods beyond the Emmitsburg road, preparing for the assault. A strong line of skirmishers soon advanced (followed by two deployed lines of battle), supported at different points by small columns of infantry. Their lines were formed with a precision and steadiness that extorted the admiration of the witnesses of that memorable scene. Their line of battle thus covered a front of not more than two of the small and incomplete divisions of the corps. The whole attacking force is estimated to have exceeded 15,000 men.

No attempt was made to check the advance of the enemy until the first line had arrived within about 700 yards of our position, when a feeble fire of artillery was opened upon it, but with no material effect. The column pressed on, coming within musketry range without receiving immediately our fire, our men evincing a striking disposition to withhold it until it could be delivered with deadly effect.

Two regiments of Stannard's Vermont Brigade, which had been posted in a little grove in front of and at a considerable angle with the main line, first opened with an oblique fire upon the right of the enemy's column. They still pressed on, however, without halting to return the fire. The rifled guns of our artillery, having fired away all their canister, were now withdrawn, or left on the ground inactive, to await the issue of the struggle between the opposing infantry.

Arrived at between 200 and 300 yards, the troops of the enemy were met by a destructive fire from the divisions of Gibbon and Hays, which they promptly returned, and the fight at once became fierce and general. Mowed down by canister from Woodruff's battery, and by the fire from two regiments judiciously posted by General Hays in his extreme front and right, and by the fire of different lines in the rear, the enemy broke in great disorder, leaving fifteen colors and nearly 2,000 prisoners in the hands of this division.

When the enemy's line had nearly reached the stone wall, led by General Armistead, the most of that part of Webb's brigade posted here abandoned their position, but fortunately did not retreat entirely. They were, by the personal bravery of General Webb and his officers, immediately formed behind the crest before referred to, which was occupied by the remnant of the brigade.

Emboldened by seeing this indication of weakness, the enemy pushed forward more pertinaciously, numbers of them crossing over the breastwork abandoned by the troops. The fight here became very close and deadly. The enemy's battle-flags were soon seen waving on the stone wall. The men of all the brigades had in some measure lost their regimental organization, but individually they were firm. The ambition of individual commanders to promptly cover the point penetrated by the enemy, the smoke of battle, and the intensity of the close engagement, caused this confusion. The point, however, was now covered. In regular formation our line would have stood four ranks deep.

The colors of the different regiments were now advanced, waving in defiance of the long line of battle-flags presented by the enemy. The men pressed firmly after them, under the energetic commands and example of their officers, and after a few moments of desperate fighting the enemy's troops were repulsed, threw down their arms, and sought safety in flight or by throwing themselves on the ground to escape our fire. The battle-flags were ours and the victory was won.

During the artillery barrage earlier in the afternoon, Hancock rode along the line on his horse to encourage his men—exposing himself to danger. He was still on horseback during Pickett's Charge. At one point he rode over to talk with Brigadier-General George Stannard, who commanded the Second Vermont Brigade. As he was leaving, he was struck. Stannard's aide, Lieut. George Benedict, wrote of it in a letter a few days later:

Just after General Stannard had ordered the Thirteenth and Sixteenth Vermont regiments out on Pickett's flank, General Hancock, followed by a single mounted orderly, rode down to speak to General Stannard. Lieutenant George W. Hooker and myself were standing near the General's side. The din of artillery and musketry was deafening at the time, and I did not hear the words that passed between the two generals. But my eyes were upon Hancock's striking figure—I thought him the most striking man I ever saw on horseback, and magnificent in the flush and excitement of battle—when he uttered an exclamation and I saw that he was reeling in his saddle.

Hooker and I with a common impulse sprang toward him, and caught him as he toppled from his horse into our outstretched arms. General Stannard bent over him as we laid him upon the ground, and opened his clothing where he indicated by a movement of his hand that he was hurt, a ragged hole, an inch or more in diameter, from which the blood was pouring profusely, was disclosed in the upper part and on the side of his thigh. He was naturally in some alarm for his life.

"Don't let me bleed to death," he said, "Get something around it quick."

Stannard had whipped out his handkerchief, and as I helped to pass it around General Hancock's leg, I saw that the blood, being of dark color and not coming in jets, could not be from an artery, and I said to him: "This is not arterial blood, General; you will not bleed to death."

From my use of the surgical term he took me for a surgeon, and replied, with a sigh of relief: "That's good; thank you for that, Doctor." We tightened the ligature by twisting it with the barrel of a pistol, and soon stopped the flow of blood. Major Mitchell of Hancock's staff rode up as we were at work over the general, and uttering an exclamation of pain as he saw the condition of his chief, turned and darted away after a surgeon. One came in fifteen minutes, and removing the handkerchief thrust his forefinger to the knuckle into the wound and brought out from it an iron nail bent double. "This is what hit you, General," he said, holding up the nail, "and you are not so badly hurt as you think."

Hancock was shot while facing Pickett's attacking men. A bullet had passed through the pommel of his saddle, carrying the nail and splinters of wood into his thigh. Six weeks later, after the wound had healed externally, he was still suffering from severe pain. Surgeons reopened the wound, dug down eight inches to the bone, and found the Minié ball and a round plug of wood.

After he was hit, Hancock wouldn't allow his men to carry him from the field. He continued directing his troops until the fighting had settled down. Years later he recalled:

I was shot from my horse when leaving the Vermont position by its right. Lying on my back and looking through the remains of a very low, disintegrated stone wall, I could observe the operations of the enemy and give directions accordingly; and the Vermont troops, obeying my orders, proceeded close to my left, along that wall, towards the right.

On March 22, 1864, Hancock testified to Congress's Committee on the Conduct of the War, providing insight into what he thought they should have done differently at Gettysburg.

I think it was probably an unfortunate thing that I was wounded at the time I was, and equally unfortunate that General Gibbon was also wounded, because the absence of a prominent commander, who knew the circumstances thoroughly, at such a moment as that, was a great disadvantage. I think that our lines should have advanced immediately, and I believe we should have won a great victory. I was very confident that the advance would be made.

General Meade told me before the fight that if the enemy attacked me he intended to put the 5th and 6th corps on the enemy's flank; I therefore, when I was wounded, and lying down in my ambulance and about leaving the field, dictated a note to General Meade, and told him if he would put in the 5th and 6th corps I believed he would win a great victory.

I asked him afterwards, when I returned to the army, what he had done in the premises. He said he had ordered the movement, but the troops were slow in collecting, and moved so slowly that nothing was done before night, except that some of the Pennsylvania reserves went out and met Hood's division, it was understood, of the enemy, and actually overthrew it, assisted, no doubt, in some measure, by their knowledge of their failure in the assault.

There were only two divisions of the enemy on our extreme left, opposite Round Top, and there was a gap in their line of one mile that their assault had left, and I believe if our whole line had advanced with spirit, it is not unlikely that we would have taken all their artillery at that point. I think that was a fault; that we should have pushed the enemy there, for we do not often catch them in that position; and the rule is, and it is natural, that when you repulse or defeat an enemy you should pursue him; and I believe it is a rare thing that one party beats another and does not pursue him, and I think that on that occasion it only required an order and prompt execution.

NOT BAGGING THE CONFEDERATE ARMY

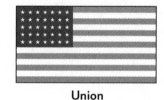

Union

Major-General George Meade (See biography, page 92.)

Even though the Union won, Meade suffered criticism for not pursuing Lee before the Confederates retreated back across the Potomac. Meade believed the Confederate force outnumbered his by about 10,000 men, which played a role in his decision. In reality, Meade's army outnumbered Lee's by about 20,000, but Meade's men had just fought the largest battle of the Civil War. They were exhausted, in disarray, and low on ammunition and supplies. Still, if he had sent them after Lee, he probably would have achieved the major victory Lincoln wanted.

Meade wrote to his wife telling her of the battle:

Hdqrs. Army of the Potomac, Gettysburg, Pa.,
July 5, 1863

I hardly know when I last wrote to you, so many and such stirring events have occurred. It was a grand battle, and is in my judgment a most decided victory, though I did not annihilate or bag the Confederate Army.

This morning they retired in great haste into the mountains, leaving their dead unburied and their wounded on the field. They awaited one day, expecting that, flushed with success, I would attack them when they would play their old game of shooting us from behind breastworks—a game we played this time to their entire satisfaction.

The men behaved splendidly; I really think they are becoming soldiers. They endured long marches, short rations, and stood one of the most terrific cannonadings I ever witnessed. At one time things looked a little blue; but I managed to get up reinforcements in time to save the day. The army are in the highest spirits, and of course I am a great man. The most difficult part of my work is acting without correct information on which to predicate action.

Meade meant that his men considered him great at that moment. Three days later he wrote to his wife again:

I see also that the papers are making a great deal too much fuss about me. I claim no extraordinary merit for this last battle, and would prefer waiting a little while to see what my career is to be before making any pretensions.

Meade has been criticised for not having destroyed Lee after Gettysburg, and the country seemed to share that disappointment after the battle. I have never thought it a fair criticism. Meade was new to his army, and did not feel it in his hand. If he could have fought Lee six months later, or if Sherman or Sheridan had commanded at Gettysburg, I think Lee would have been destroyed. Meade was certainly among the heroes of the war, and his name deserves all honor. I had a great fondness for him. No general ever was more earnest. As a commander in the field, he had only one fault—his temper. A battle always put him in a fury. He raged from the beginning to the end. His own staff officers would dread to bring him a report of anything wrong. Meade's anger would overflow on the heads of his nearest and best friends. Under this harsh exterior Meade had a gentle, chivalrous heart, and was an accomplished soldier and gentleman.

—General Ulysses S. Grant on Meade's
performance

Almost all of Lee's men made it across the Potomac before Meade launched a final assault, capturing 2,000 Confederates. While President Lincoln was pleased with the battle's outcome, he expressed disappointment that Lee's army got away. Halleck relayed the president's reaction to Meade, who took it as personal criticism and offered to resign. Halleck reassured Meade that there was no need, though Lincoln and Halleck had been pushing Meade to attack before Lee's men could withdraw.

TAKING THE BLAME

Confederate

Lieutenant-General James Longstreet (See biography, page 48.)

Camp Culpeper Court-House, July 24th, 1863
To A. B. Longstreet, LL.D., Columbus, Ga.

My Dear Uncle: As to our late battle I cannot say much. I have no right to say anything, in fact, but will venture a little for you, alone. If it goes to aunt and cousins it must be under promise that it will go no further. The battle was not made as I would have made it. My idea was to throw ourselves between the enemy and Washington, select a strong position, and force the enemy to attack us. So far as is given to man the ability to judge, we may say, with confidence, that we should have destroyed the Federal army, marched into Washington and dictated our terms, or, at least, held Washington, and marched over as much of Pennsylvania as we cared to, had we drawn the enemy into attack upon our carefully-chosen position in its rear.

General Lee chose the plans adopted; and he is the person appointed to choose and to order. I consider it a part of my duty to express my views to the commanding general. If he approves and adopts them, it is well; if he does not, it is my duty to adopt his views, and to execute his orders as faithfully as if they were my own.

As we failed, I must take my share of the responsibility. In fact, I would prefer that all the blame should rest upon me. As General Lee is our commander, he should have the support and influence we can give him. If the blame, if there is any, can be shifted from him to me, I shall help him and our cause by taking it. I desire, therefore, that all the responsibility that can be put upon me shall go there, and shall remain there. The truth will be known in time, and I leave that to show how much of the responsibility of Gettysburg rests on my shoulders.

Most affectionately yours,

J. Longstreet

Longstreet did take the blame for many years, occasionally from those who probably deserved some of it themselves and may have been trying to deflect it. But Longstreet gradually came to see that being the punching bag was more difficult than he thought and somewhat pointless once the war was over, so he tried to set the record straight—at least, as he perceived it. Doing so stirred considerable controversy, since most Southerners didn't want to hear anything bad said about General Lee.

After Lee's death, Longstreet revealed, "In a letter written to me by General Lee, in January, 1864, he says: 'Had I taken your advice at Gettysburg, instead of pursuing the course I did, how different all might have been.'" Longstreet also explained:

The cause of the battle was simply General Lee's determination to fight it out from the position in which he was at that time. He did not feel that he was beaten on the second day, but that he was the victor, and still hoped he would be able to dislodge Meade; but he made a mistake in sending such a small number of men to attack a formidable force in a position of great natural strength, reënforced by such temporary shelter as could be collected and placed in position to cover the troops. Lee's hope in entering the campaign was that he would be in time to make a successful battle north of the Potomac, with such advantages as to draw off the army at Vicksburg as well as the Federal troops at other points.

I do not think the general effect of the battle was demoralizing, but by a singular coincidence our army at Vicksburg surrendered to Grant on the 4th, while the armies of Lee and Meade were lying in front of each other, each waiting a movement on the part of the other, neither victor, neither vanquished. This surrender, taken in connection with the Gettysburg defeat, was, of course, very discouraging to our superior officers, though I do not know that it was felt as keenly by the rank and file.

For myself, I felt that our last hope was gone, and that it was now only a question of time with us. When, however, I found that Rosecrans was moving down toward Georgia against General Bragg, I thought it possible we might recover some of our lost prospects by concentrating against Rosecrans, destroying his army, and advancing through Kentucky.

DEALING WITH THE LOSS

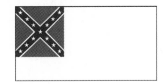

Confederate

General Robert E. Lee (See biography, page 9.)

Camp Culpeper 31 July '63
His Excy Jeffn Davis, President Confed. States

Mr President: Your note of the 27th enclosing a slip from the Charleston Mercury relative to the battle of Gettysburg is recd—I much regret its general censure upon the operations of the army, as it is calculated to do us no good either at home or abroad. But I am prepared for similar criticism & as far as I am concerned the remarks fall harmless. To take notice of such attacks would I think do more harm than good, & would be just what is desired.

No blame can be attached to the army for its failure to accomplish what was projected by me, nor should it be censured for the unreasonable expectations of the public—I am alone to blame, in perhaps expecting too much of its prowess & valour. It however in my opinion achieved under the guidance of the Most High a general success, though it did not win a victory. I thought at the time that the latter was practicable. I still think if all things could have worked together it would have been accomplished. But with the knowledge I then had, & in the circumstances I was then placed, I do not know what better course I could have pursued. With my present knowledge, & could I have foreseen that the attack on the last day would have failed to drive the enemy from his position, I should certainly have tried some other course. What the ultimate result would have been is not so clear to me. Our loss has been very heavy, that of the enemy's is proportionally so. His crippled condition enabled us to retire from the Country, comparatively unmolested.

With prayers for your health & happiness, & the recognition by your gratified country of your great services.

I remain truly & sincerely yours

R. E. Lee

It is said that, years later at a meeting of the Southern Historical Society, someone asked Major-General Pickett, "George, you were there. Why did we lose the battle?" To which Pickett replied simply: "I always thought the Yankees had something to do with it."

THE BATTLE OF CHICKAMAUGA

CATOOSA AND WALKER COUNTIES, GEORGIA
SEPTEMBER 19–20, 1863

COMMANDERS

Confederate
Gen. Braxton Bragg

Union
Maj. Gen. William Rosecrans

PARTICIPANTS

About 68,000 (Army of Tennessee)
(22,297 engaged September 19)
(38,846 engaged September 20)

55,000 to 60,000 (Army of the Cumberland)

CASUALTIES

Confederate
2,312 killed
14,674 wounded
1,468 POWs/MIA

Union
1,657 killed
9,756 wounded
4,757 POWs/MIA

VICTORY: CONFEDERACY

OVERVIEW

When Vicksburg surrendered and the Union won at Gettysburg, Rosecrans completed his Tullahoma campaign in the western theater, successfully driving the Confederate Army of Tennessee under Bragg out of central Tennessee. Many historians count it a model campaign with skillful maneuvers and low casualties.

After regrouping, storing supplies, and preparing to pursue Bragg in the mountains of eastern Tennessee and northwestern Georgia, Rosecrans launched his Chickamauga campaign on August 15, 1863. About three weeks later Rosecrans divided his army into three and sent each by different routes, trying to sneak up on Bragg. When Bragg discovered Union troops at his rear, he headed out of Chattanooga and into Georgia. Rosecrans thought Bragg would flee, but Bragg determined to retake Chattanooga and staged a surprise for

Rosecrans. When Rosecrans discovered Bragg nearby, he quickly tried to consolidate his army. The two armies clashed at West Chickamauga Creek in Georgia, about a dozen miles south of Chattanooga, on September 19.

Rosecrans tried to close what he mistakenly thought was a gap in his line, but he ended up opening a huge gap right where Longstreet was about to attack—Longstreet and his corps having been sent from Lee's army to reinforce Bragg after Gettysburg. As a result, Longstreet charged right through the Union right flank, forcing Rosecrans and a third of his army to flee back to Chattanooga in disarray, while Union major general George Thomas and his four divisions held out until twilight before retiring, allowing most of Rosecrans's army to escape. Rosecrans was so shaken up that Lincoln told John Hay, his private secretary, that the major general was "confused and stunned like a duck hit on the head."

Bragg's men took the heights above Chattanooga and laid siege to Rosecrans. Secretary of War Stanton quickly sent Hooker and 15,000 men to assist Rosecrans, while Grant sent Sherman and 20,000 men. Halleck suggested that Grant go there himself. Grant replaced Rosecrans with Thomas and headed off to Chattanooga. On the way he met Rosecrans, who, he said, "made some excellent suggestions as to what should be done. My only wonder was that he had not carried them out."

The Battle of Chickamauga was the second-bloodiest battle of the war and the biggest Confederate victory in the western theater. It also featured considerable strife between the commanders of both sides and brought Bragg's army close to mutiny.

WOUNDED

Confederate

General John Bell Hood (See biography, page 84.)

When the Confederate Army fell back from Gettysburg, I followed our marching column in an ambulance, suffering very much from the wound received in my arm. In the same vehicle lay General Hampton, so badly wounded that he was unable to sit up, whereas I could not lie down. I remained for a period of one month under medical treatment.

About the 14th of September my division passed through the Capital, under orders to join General Bragg in the West for the purpose of taking part in battle against Rosecranz. Although I had but partially recovered, I determined to place my horse upon the train, and follow in their wake.

On my arrival upon the field I met for the first time after the charge at Gettysburg a portion of

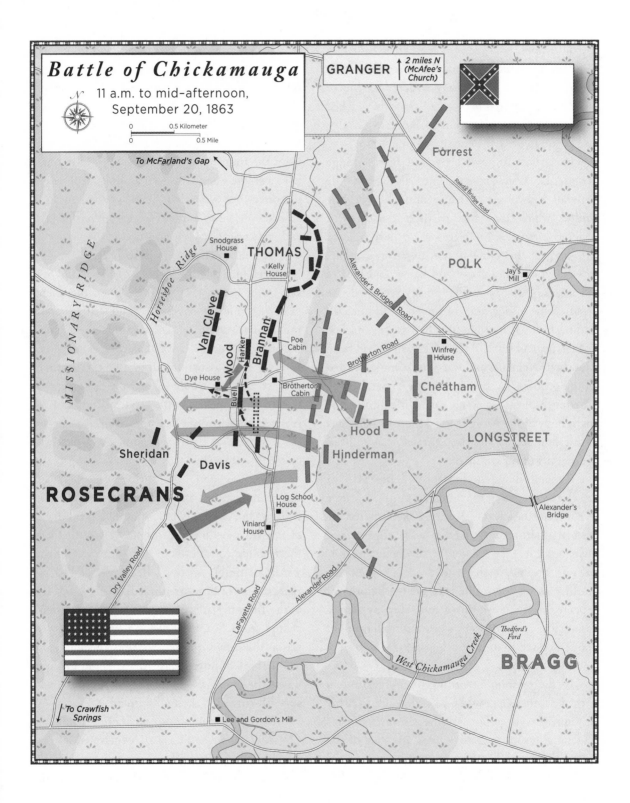

Battle of Chickamauga

11 a.m. to mid-afternoon,
September 20, 1863

N

0   0.5 Kilometer
0   0.5 Mile

To McFarland's Gap

GRANGER   2 miles N
(McAfee's
Church)

Forrest

To Crawfish Springs

MISSIONARY RIDGE

Horseshoe Ridge

Snodgrass House

THOMAS

Kelly House

Van Cleve

Wood

Harker

Brannan

Buell

Dye House

Poe Cabin

Brotherton Cabin

Sheridan

Davis

ROSECRANS

Log School House

Viniard House

LaFayette Road

Dry Valley Road

Alexander Road

Alexander's Bridge Road

Brotherton Road

POLK

Jay's Mill

Winfrey House

Cheatham

Hood

Hinderman

LONGSTREET

Alexander's Bridge

West Chickamauga Creek

Thedford's Ford

BRAGG

Lee and Gordon's Mill

Reed's Bridge Road

my old troops, who received me with a touching welcome. I assumed command in accordance with the instructions I had received, ordered the line to be broken by filing into the road, sent a few picked men to the front in support of Forrest's Cavalry, and began to drive the enemy at a rapid pace.

In a short time we arrived at Reid's bridge across the Chickamauga, and discovered the Federals drawn up in battle array beyond the bridge, which they had partially destroyed. I ordered forward some pieces of artillery, opened fire, and, at the same time, threw out flankers to effect a crossing above and below and join in the attack. Our opponents quickly retreated. We repaired the bridge, and continued to advance till darkness closed in upon us, when we bivouacked in line, near a beautiful residence which had been fired by the enemy, and was then almost burned to the ground. We had driven the Federals back a distance of six or seven miles. Meantime, the main body of the Army crossed the Chickamauga at different points, and concentrated that night in the vicinity of my command.

General Bragg having formed his plan of attack the following morning, I was given orders to continue the advance. We soon encountered the enemy in strong force, and a heavy engagement ensued. All that day we fought, slowly but steadily gaining ground. Fierce and desperate grew the conflict, as the foe stubbornly yielded before our repeated assaults; we drove him, step by step, a distance of fully one mile, when nightfall brought about a cessation of hostilities, and the men slept upon their arms.

In the evening, according to my custom in Virginia under General Lee, I rode back to Army headquarters to report to the Commander-in-Chief the result of the day upon my part of the line. I there met for the first time several of the principal officers of the Army of Tennessee. After

receiving orders from General Bragg to advance the next morning as soon as the troops on my right moved to the attack, I returned to the position occupied by my forces, and camped the remainder of the night with General [Simon] Buckner, as I had nothing with me save that which I had brought from the train upon my horse. Nor did my men have a single wagon, or even ambulance in which to convey the wounded. They were destitute of almost everything, I might say, except pride, spirit, and forty rounds of ammunition to the man.

General Longstreet joined the Army. I informed him that the feeling of officers and men was never better, that we had driven the enemy fully one mile the day before, and that we would rout him before sunset. This distinguished general instantly responded with that confidence which had so often contributed to his extraordinary success, that we would of course whip and drive him from the field. I could but exclaim that I was rejoiced to hear him so express himself, as he was the first general I had met since my arrival who talked of victory.

About 9 a.m. the firing on the right commenced; we immediately advanced and engaged the enemy, when followed a terrible roar of musketry from right to left. We wrestled with the resolute foe till about 2.30 p.m., when, from a skirt of timber to our left, a body of Federals rushed down upon the immediate flank and rear of the Texas brigade, which was forced to suddenly change front. Some confusion necessarily arose. I was at the time on my horse, upon a slight ridge about three hundred yards distant, and galloped down the slope, in the midst of the men, who speedily corrected their allignment.

With a shout along my entire front, the Confederates rushed forward, penetrated into the wood, over and beyond the enemy's breastworks, and thus achieved another glorious victory for our arms. About this time I was pierced with a Minié ball in the upper third of the right leg; I turned from my horse upon the side of the crushed limb and fell—strange to say, since I was commanding five divisions—into the arms of some of the troops of my old brigade, which I had directed so long a period, and upon so many fields of battle.

I was borne to the hospital of my old division, where a most difficult operation was performed.[14]

I then received intelligence from General Bragg that the enemy was contemplating a raid to capture me. I at once moved to Atlanta, and thence to Richmond. I remained in Richmond, and, having been blessed, with a good constitution, rapidly recovered from my wound. My restoration was so complete that I was enabled to keep in the saddle when on active duty. Often President Davis was kind enough to invite me to accompany him in his rides around Richmond, and it was thus I was for the first time afforded an opportunity to become well acquainted with this extraordinary man, and illustrious patriot and statesman of the South.

---

14 His leg was amputated just inches below his hip.

The Grit to Hold the Field

Union

General Philip Sheridan

General Sheridan commanded an infantry division in the western theater before becoming commander of the Army of the Potomac's Cavalry Corps, where he was noted for his use of scorched-earth tactics. His pursuit of General Lee's army played an important role in Lee's surrender.

Sheridan's father was an Irish-immigrant laborer on the canals and railroads. Sheridan variously said he was born in New York, Massachusetts, or Ohio, but he was raised in Ohio from infancy. He graduated from West Point in 1853 and was stationed in Texas and California in the infantry before heading to the Oregon and Washington Territories, where he took part in the Yakima War and Rogue River Wars. He was promoted to first lieutenant just before Fort Sumter and to captain right after. His role in the Civil War began as a staff officer auditing the accounts of the explorer, former U.S. senator, and presidential candidate Major-General John C. Frémont, accused of corruption but probably only guilty of bad bookkeeping.

Sheridan became a prominent cavalry commander later in the war, working closely with Grant, who said, "I believe General Sheridan has no superior as a general, either living or dead, and perhaps not an equal. He has judgment, prudence, foresight, and power to deal with the dispositions needed in a great war."

On another occasion, Grant added, "I rank Sheridan with Napoleon and Frederick and the great commanders in history. No man ever had such a faculty of finding out things as Sheridan, of knowing all about the enemy. He was always the best-informed man in his command as to the enemy. Then he had that magnetic quality of swaying men which I wish I had—a rare quality in a general."

When his army began to flee back to Chattanooga, Rosecrans decided that protecting his supplies and holding Chattanooga were more important than beating Bragg. The tactical defeat would have turned into a major strategic defeat. Still, he must have known that leaving the battlefield would look bad. As he moved out behind his line to the road to Rossville, he tried to speak to Sheridan.

General Rosecrans passed down the road behind my line and sent word that he wished to see me, but affairs were too critical to admit of my going to him at once, and he rode on to Chattanooga. It is to be regretted that he did not wait till I could join him, for the delay would have permitted him to see that matters were not in quite such bad shape as he supposed; still, there is no disguising the fact that at this juncture his army was badly crippled.

Shortly after my division had rallied on the low hills, I discovered that the enemy, instead of attacking me in front, was wedging in between my division and the balance of the army; in short, endeavoring to cut me off from Chattanooga. This necessitated another retrograde movement, which brought me back to the southern face of Missionary Ridge, where I was joined by Carlin's brigade of Davis's division.

Still thinking I could join General Thomas, I rode some distance to the left of my line to look for a way out, but found that the enemy had intervened so far as to isolate me effectually. I then determined to march directly to Rossville, and from there effect a junction with Thomas by the Lafayette road. I reached Rossville about 5 o'clock in the afternoon, bringing with me eight guns, forty-six caissons, and a long ammunition train, the latter having been found in a state of confusion behind the widow Glenn's when I was being driven back behind the Dry Valley road.

The head of my column passed through Rossville, appearing upon Thomas's left about 6 o'clock in the evening, penetrated without any opposition the right of the enemy's line, and captured several of his field-hospitals. As soon as I got on the field I informed Thomas of the presence of my command, and asked for orders. He replied that his lines were disorganized, and that it would be futile to attack; that all I could do was to hold on, and aid in covering his withdrawal to Rossville.

I accompanied him back to Rossville, and when we reached the skirt of the little hamlet General Thomas halted and we dismounted. Going into one of the angles of a worm fence near by I took a rail from the top and put it through the lower rails at a proper height from the ground to make a seat, and General Thomas and I sat down while my troops were moving by. The General appeared very much exhausted, seemed to forget what he had stopped for, and said little or nothing of the incidents of the day.

This was the second occasion on which I had met him in the midst of misfortune, for during the fight in the cedars at Stone River, when our prospects were most disheartening, we held a brief conversation respecting the line he was then taking up for the purpose of helping me. At other times, in periods of inactivity, I saw but little of him.

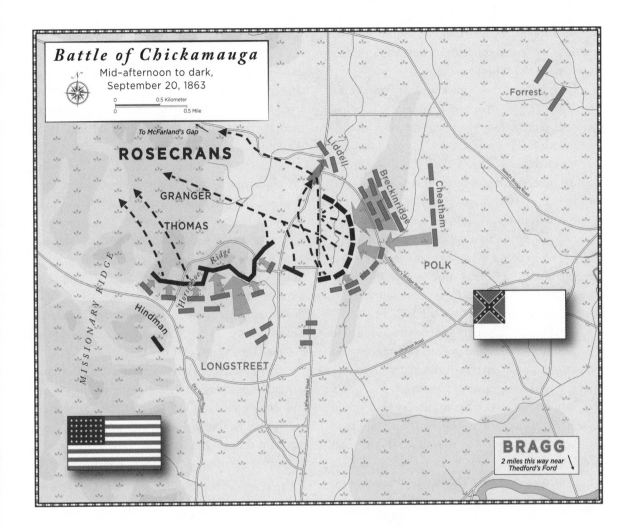

To McFarland's Gap

ROSECRANS

GRANGER

THOMAS

Liddell

Breckinridge

Cheatham

Reed's Bridge Road

MISSIONARY RIDGE

Horseshoe Ridge

Hindman

POLK

Alexander's Bridge Road

LONGSTREET

Dry Valley Road

LaFayette Road

Brotherton Road

BRAGG

*2 miles this way near
Thedford's Ford*

He impressed me now as he did in the cedars, his quiet, unobtrusive demeanor communicating a gloomy rather than a hopeful view of the situation. This apparent depression was due no doubt to the severe trial through which he had gone in the last forty-eight hours, which strain had exhausted him very much both physically and mentally. His success in maintaining his ground was undoubtedly largely influenced by the fact that two-thirds of the National forces had been sent to his succor, but his firm purpose to save the army was the main-stay on which all relied after Rosecrans left the field.

I mounted and rode off to supervise the encamping of my division, by no means an easy task considering the darkness, and the confusion that existed among the troops that had preceded us into Rossville.

I was very tired, very hungry, and much discouraged by what had taken place since morning. I had been obliged to fight my command under the most disadvantageous circumstances, disconnected, without supports, without even opportunity to form in line of battle, and at one time contending against four divisions of the enemy.

In this battle of Chickamauga, out of an effective strength of 4,000 bayonets, I had lost 1,517 officers and men, including two brigade commanders. This was not satisfactory indeed, it was most depressing and then there was much confusion prevailing around Rossville; and, this condition of things doubtless increasing my gloomy reflections, it did not seem to me that the outlook for the next day was at all auspicious, unless the enemy was slow to improve his present advantage. Exhaustion soon quieted all forebodings, though, and I fell into a sound sleep, from which I was not aroused till daylight.

On the morning of the 21st the enemy failed to advance, and his inaction gave us the opportunity for getting the broken and disorganized army into shape. It took a large part of the day to accomplish this, and the chances of complete victory would have been greatly in Bragg's favor if he could have attacked us vigorously at this time. But he had been badly hurt in the two days' conflict, and his inactivity on the 21st showed that he too had to go through the process of reorganization.

Indeed, his crippled condition began to show itself the preceding evening, and I have always thought that, had General Thomas held on and attacked the Confederate right and rear from where I made the junction with him on the Lafayette road, the field of Chickamauga would have been relinquished to us; but it was fated to be otherwise.

Rosecrans, [Alexander] McCook, and [Thomas] Crittenden passed out of the battle when they went back to Chattanooga, and their absence was discouraging to all aware of it. Doubtless this had much to do with Thomas's final withdrawal, thus leaving the field to the enemy, though at an immense cost in killed and wounded. The night of the 21st the army moved back from Rossville, and my division, as the rear-guard of the Twentieth Corps, got within our lines at Chattanooga about 8 o'clock the morning of the 22d.

Our unmolested retirement from Rossville lent additional force to the belief that the enemy had been badly injured, and further impressed me with the conviction that we might have held on. Indeed, the battle of Chickamauga was somewhat like that of Stone River, victory resting with the side that had the grit to defer longest its relinquishment of the field.

APPEAL TO THE PRESIDENT

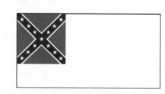

Confederate

Lieutenant-General Leonidas Polk

Many priests, ministers, and clergymen joined the militaries of both sides, although Lieutenant-General Polk—known as the Fighting Bishop—is probably the most famous.

Born in Raleigh, North Carolina, to a Revolutionary War colonel who was at Valley Forge with George Washington—and who had since become a wealthy landowner, public servant, and politician—Leonidas was cousin to James Polk, the eleventh president. After graduating from West Point in 1847 and being assigned to the artillery, he resigned five months later to enter a seminary, eventually becoming an Episcopal priest and then a bishop. By 1850 he was one of Tennessee's largest slaveholders, owning 215 slaves, and he may have ended up owning upward of 400. He helped found the University of the South in Tennessee, a liberal arts college and the official theological seminary for the Episcopal Church.

As the war was gearing up, his West Point classmate Jefferson Davis convinced him to become a major general in the Confederate army. He commanded a corps at Shiloh and at Perryville, and was injured four days after the latter when the Confederacy's largest cannon exploded as it was being fired, also blowing up a nearby magazine containing several hundred pounds of powder and killing eleven men. "My clothes were torn to pieces," he wrote, "and I was literally covered with dust and fragments of the wreck. I was only injured by the stunning effect of the concussion." He was confined to bed for several weeks with a ruptured eardrum.

Soon promoted to lieutenant general, he didn't get along well with some of his fellow commanders, particularly General Braxton Bragg, but he was extremely popular with his soldiers.

At Chickamauga both sides missed many opportunities. For the Confederates, in some cases Bragg's senior officers failed to carry out his orders to attack. Others came from Bragg's failure to act quickly. Much of Bragg's army consisted of reinforcements from other armies, and he hadn't had time to gain their respect. Bragg became increasingly furious when his orders were not carried out because of insubordination or other causes. After the battle he cracked down.

Bragg relieved three generals from command—Hindman, Polk, and D. H. Hill: Major-General Thomas Hindman for failing to attack at McLemore's Cove on September 10 when his force outnumbered the Union's three to one. Lieutenant-General Polk was relieved for refusing to attack on September 13 and for delaying the main attack at Chickamauga on September 20. Major-General D. H. Hill was removed a few weeks later for his involvement at McLemore's Cove, his role in delaying the attack on the twentieth, and for organizing a movement to have Bragg replaced. These disgruntled officers then roped Longstreet into the mess. They and many others were also upset that Bragg had failed to follow up their victory by pursuing and destroying Rosecrans's retreating army.

In Polk's case, he insisted that on the thirteenth he was the one who was about to be attacked and that he required reinforcements to defend himself. The attack never came, but the delay he caused gave Rosecrans time to consolidate his forces. Polk claimed his failure to attack on time on the twentieth resulted from an undelivered order to D. H. Hill. Polk insisted that it wasn't his fault and certainly didn't warrant his being relieved of duty, so he appealed to his close friend Jefferson Davis.

Atlanta, October 6, 1863

His Excellency, President Davis,

My dear Sir: I wrote you on the 27th ult., renewing the expression of my opinion of the incapacity of General Bragg for the responsible office of commander-in-chief of the Army of Tennessee, and asking that he should be replaced by General Lee or some other. It is proper to add that that letter was written after a meeting, by appointment, of Lieutenant-Generals Longstreet and Hill and myself, to consider what should be done in view of the palpable weakness and mismanagement manifested in the conduct of the military operations of this array.

It was agreed that I should address you, sir; and General Longstreet, the Secretary of War, on the other subject.

Three letters were written and forwarded, and, I need not add, after mature deliberation General Hill concurred in the necessity of the measure. As you may not have received these letters before leaving Richmond, I have deemed it proper to bring them to your notice.

Two days subsequent to my writing this letter to you, I received an order from General Bragg suspending me from my command and ordering me to this place. The order was based on alleged disobedience in not attacking the enemy at daylight on Sunday, the 20th. My explanation of that failure was furnished in a note, of which the accompanying is a copy. In this paper it will be perceived, 1st, that I directed a staff-officer of General Hill to say to the general I desired to see him at my headquarters, that he might receive his orders as to the operations of the following day; 2d, that the necessary orders were issued from my headquarters at 11.30 p.m. to General Hill and to Generals [Benjamin] Cheatham and [William] Walker, and dispatched by couriers. Cheatham and Walker received their orders. Hill could not be found by any courier, nor did Hill make his way to my headquarters.

These facts with others, you will observe, were embodied and presented to the commanding general in reply to a request for a written explanation of the failure. They were pronounced unsatisfactory, and the order for my suspension issued.

For the delay charged I cannot feel myself responsible, and it should be observed, by whomsoever caused, it did not occasion any failure in our success in the battle, for the enemy was clearly beaten at all points along my line and fairly driven from the field.

It will no doubt be affirmed that had the attack been made at daylight the enemy would have been overwhelmed, Chattanooga taken, etc., etc., and that all subsequent delays and miscarriages are to be set down to that account. To make this affirmation good it must be shown that at the close of the battle that night such a condition of things was developed as to make pursuit impossible, and that it was equally hopeless next morning.

This will not be pretended, inasmuch as the troops at the close of the fight were in the very highest spirits, ready for any service, and the moon, by whose guidance the enemy fled from the field, was as bright to guide us in pursuit as the enemy in flight. Besides, if the commander-in-chief, under a delusion he took no pains to dispel, thought the troops were fatigued, and chose to put off pursuit until the morning, why did he not attempt it then? Was it because he had made the discovery that the enemy had made his retreat into Chattanooga in good order, and there he was secure behind ample fortifications? Not at all, for he had no reason to believe that any material additions had been made to the work we had begun and left unfinished. And as to the order in which they entered into the town. General Forrest, who pressed them, in a dispatch from Missionary Ridge, dated between 8 and 9 a.m., Monday, and sent through me to the commanding general, informed him that the approaches to Chattanooga were covered with troops, wagons, and herds of cattle in great confusion, and urged him to press forward, saying that every hour would be worth to him a thousand men.

No, sir! General Bragg did not know what had happened. He let down as usual, and allowed the fruits of the great but sanguinary victory to pass from him by the most criminal incapacity; for there are positions in which "weakness is wickedness."

By that victory, and its heavy expenditure of the life-blood of the Confederacy, we bought and paid for the whole of the State of Tennessee to the Mississippi River, at the very least; and all that was wanted was to have gone forward and taken possession of it. It was but a repetition of our old story in the battles of the West, and the army and the country feel that they have a right to ask for a thorough investigation of the cause of such repeated and grievous failures, that the responsibility may be fixed where it properly belongs.

As to my own case, my experience in this army has taught me to expect such a movement at any time for the last two years. I am not, therefore, taken by surprise. I have respectfully asked of the Secretary of War a court of inquiry at the earliest moment.

I remain, respectfully, your obedient servant,

L. Polk, Lieutenant-General

"A DAMNED SCOUNDREL"

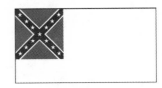

Confederate

Lieutenant-General Nathan Bedford Forrest (See biography, page 73.)

Forrest commanded cavalry and appreciated the value of rapid responses. After chasing the badly demoralized Union army back to within three miles of Chattanooga, he began firing his artillery on Union positions, while requesting that Bragg bring up the infantry. Instead, Bragg withdrew Forrest. Colonel R. B. Kyle, in conversation with President Davis, said that Forrest was furious that Bragg refused to follow up their victory, adding, "He urged that they move on in pursuit of the enemy at once, as their capture was certain. Bragg asked how he could move an army without supplies, as his men had exhausted them. Forrest's reply was: 'General Bragg, we can get all the supplies our army needs in Chattanooga.' Bragg made no reply, and Forrest rode away disgusted." Forrest was later recorded as asking in rage, "What does he fight battles for?"

Bragg had an ongoing feud with Forrest, and after Shiloh had transferred Forrest's cavalry to another commander, forcing Forrest to raise a new command. On September 28 Bragg essentially did it again by combining his two cavalry corps, effectively placing Forrest under the command of Major-General Joseph Wheeler—a man Forrest detested and wasn't about to serve. Forrest's chief surgeon, Dr. J. B. Cowan, accompanied Forrest when he stormed into Bragg's tent to dress down his commander. In a letter Cowan reported Forrest's heated words to Bragg:

You commenced your cowardly and contemptible persecution of me soon after the battle of Shiloh, and you have kept it up ever since. You did it because I reported to Richmond facts, while you reported damned lies. You robbed me of my command in Kentucky, and gave it to one of your personal favorites—men that I armed and equipped from the enemies of our country. In a spirit of revenge and spite, because I would not fawn upon you as others did, you drove me into West Tennessee in the winter of 1862, with a second brigade I had organized, with improper arms and without sufficient ammunition, although I had made repeated applications for the same. You did it to ruin me and my career.

When in spite of all this I returned with my command, well equipped by captures, you began your work of spite and persecution, and have kept it up. And now this second brigade, organized and equipped without thanks to you or the government, a brigade which has won a reputation for successful fighting second to none in the army, taking advantage of your position as the commanding general in order to further humiliate me, you have taken these brave men from me.

I have stood your meanness as long as I intend to. You have played the part of a damned scoundrel, and are a coward, and if you were any part of a man I would slap your jaws and force you to resent it.

You have threatened to arrest me for not obeying your orders promptly. I dare you to do it, and I say that if you ever again try to interfere with me or cross my path, it will be at the peril of your life.

ENTERING A HORNETS' NEST

Confederate

Lieutenant-General James Longstreet (See biography, page 48.)

After moving from Virginia to try to relieve our comrades of the Army of Tennessee, we thought that we had cause to complain that the fruits of our labor had been lost, but it soon became manifest that the superior officers of that army themselves felt as much aggrieved as we at the halting policy of their chief, and were calling in letters and petitions for his removal. A number of them came to have me write the President for them. As he had not called for my opinion on military affairs since the Johnston conference of 1862, I could not take that liberty, but promised to write to the Secretary of War and to General Lee, who I thought could excuse me under the strained condition of affairs.

About the same time they framed and forwarded to the President a petition praying for relief. It was written by General D. H. Hill (as he informed me since the war).

While the superior officers were asking for relief, the Confederate commander was busy looking along his lines for victims. Lieutenant-General Polk was put under charges for failing to open the battle of the 20th at daylight; Major-General Hindman was relieved under charges for conduct before the battle, when his conduct of the battle with other commanders would have relieved him of any previous misconduct, according to the customs of war, and pursuit of others was getting warm.

On the Union side the Washington authorities thought vindication important, and Major-Generals McCook and Crittenden, of the Twentieth and Twenty-first Corps, were relieved and went before a Court of Inquiry; also one of the generals of division of the Fourteenth Corps.

The President came to us on the 9th of October and called the commanders of the army to meet him at General Bragg's office. After some talk, in the presence of General Bragg, he made known the object of the call, and asked the generals, in turn, their opinion of their commanding officer, beginning with myself. It seemed rather a stretch of authority, even with a President, and I gave an evasive answer and made an effort to turn the channel of thought, but he would not be satisfied, and got back to his question. The condition of the army was briefly referred to, and the failure to make an effort to get the fruits of our success, when the opinion was given, in substance, that our commander could be of greater service elsewhere than at the head of the Army of Tennessee. Major-General Buckner was called, and gave opinion somewhat similar. So did Major-General Cheatham, who was then commanding the corps recently commanded by Lieutenant-General Polk, and General D. H. Hill, who was called last, agreed with emphasis to the views expressed by others.

The next morning the President called me to private conference, and had an all day talk. He thought to assign me to command, but the time had passed for handling that army as an independent force. Regarding this question, as considered in Virginia, it was understood that the assignment would be made at once, and in time for opportunity to handle the army sufficiently to gain the confidence of the officers and soldiers before offering or accepting battle. The action was not taken, a battle had been made and won, the army was then seriously entangled in a quasi siege, the officers and soldiers were disappointed, and disaffected in morale. General Grant was moving his army to reinforce against us, and an important part of the Union army of Virginia was moving to the same purpose.

In my judgment our last opportunity was lost when we failed to follow the success at Chickamauga, and capture or disperse the Union army, and it could not be just to the service or myself to call me to a position of such responsibility. The army was part of General Joseph E. Johnston's department, and could only be used in strong organization by him in combining its operations with his other forces in Alabama and Mississippi. I said that under him I could cheerfully work in any position. The suggestion of that name only served to increase his displeasure, and his severe rebuke.[15]

---

15 Davis had very strong feelings against Johnston.

> There has been much suffering among the men. They have for weeks been reduced to quarter rations, and at times so eager for food that the commissary store-rooms would be thronged, and the few crumbs which fell from broken boxes of hard-bread carefully gathered up and eaten. Men have followed the forage wagons and picked up the grains of corn which fell from them, and in some instances they have picked up the grains of corn from the mud where mules have been fed. The suffering among the animals has been intense. Hundreds of mules and horses have died of starvation.
>
> —FROM UNION BRIGADIER GENERAL JOHN BEATTY'S DIARY, DURING THE SIEGE

The interview was exciting, at times warm, but continued until Lookout Mountain lifted above the sun to excuse my taking leave. The President walked as far as the gate, gave his hand in his usual warm grasp, and dismissed me with his gracious smile; but a bitter look lurking about its margin, and the ground-swell, admonished me that clouds were gathering about head-quarters of the First Corps even faster than those that told the doom of the Southern cause.

A day or two after this interview the President called the commanders to meet him again at General Bragg's head-quarters. He expressed desire to have the army pulled away from the lines around Chattanooga and put to active work in the field. He had brought General Pemberton with him to assign to the corps left by General Polk, but changed his mind. General D. H. Hill was relieved of duty; after a time General Buckner took a leave of absence, and General [William] Hardee relieved General Cheatham of command of the corps left to him by General Polk.

The President left the army more despondent than he found it. General Pemberton's misfortune at Vicksburg gave rise to severe prejudice of the people and the army, and when the troops heard of the purpose of the President to assign him to command of Polk's corps, parts of the army were so near to mutiny that he concluded to call General Hardee to that command. A few days after he left us a severe season of rain set in, and our commander used the muddy roads to excuse his failure to execute the campaign that the President had ordered.

THE OTHER SIDE OF THE STORY

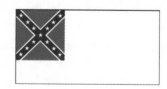

Confederate

General Braxton Bragg (See biography, page 72.)

Years later General Bragg gave his side of the story in a private letter to Maj. E. T. Sykes. His candid letter is considerably more revealing than the public record.

I reply to your questions.

1st. "Did not Genl. Polk delay moving on the morning of the second day at Chickamauga an hour or more after the appointed time, although the order for his movement was issued the night previous, thereby jeopardizing your plans, and for that reason was subsequently placed in arrest?"

This question is best answered by my official report. In addition to what is there said, I can now add that the Staff officer sent to Genl. Polk, Maj. Lee A. A. Genl. [Assistant Adjutant General], to urge his compliance with orders of the previous night reported to me that he found him at a Farm House three miles from the line of his troops, about one hour after sunrise, sitting on the gallery reading a newspaper and waiting, as he (the Genl.) said, for his breakfast. It was nine o'clock before I got him into position, and about ten before the attack was made. *Five precious hours*—in which our independence might have been won.

As soon as time would allow, Genl. Polk was called on for an explanation. The order given him the night before in the presence of several Generals was plain and emphatic and before he left me he was asked if he fully understood the order and replied in the affirmative. His explanation in writing was entirely unsatisfactory, as it placed the responsibility on a subordinate— Lieut. Genl. Hill—when he (Genl. Polk) was himself absent from the field and had not even attempted to execute his orders, nor informed me of their having been disobeyed. Breckinridge and Cheatham say in their reports, Polk told them during the night he had orders to attack at daylight—I have the correspondence, but cannot now lay my hands on it.

2d. Question, as to Hindman and McLemore's Cove.[16]

My report gives a full answer to this question, but not a complete history of the whole affair, as it was too bad to put before the country. Genl. Hill having failed in a querrulous, insubordinate spirit, to send [Major-General Patrick] Cleburn's Division to join Hindman, on the pretext that Cleburn was sick, I ordered Buckner with his Division to the duty, and went myself to Hill's Hd. Qrs., riding half the night. There I found Cleburn, who expressed surprise that Hill should have reported him sick and he moved with his Division next morning.

After Buckner joined Hindman, it will be seen, the latter became doubtful and dilatory and finally asked a change of orders. This produced loss of valuable time, and common sense teaches the importance in every moment of striking at a divided enemy. I was so greatly vexed that my deportment towards Gen. Hill and Maj. Nocquet during the conference was observed by my Staff and intimation given me of some harshness.

> I gave Genl [D. H.] Hill discretionary orders from Richmond to apportion his force to the strength of enemy and send what could be spared. He declined to act and requested positive orders. I gave such orders as I could at this distance. Now he objects. I cannot operate in this manner.
>
> —GENERAL ROBERT E. LEE IN A MAY 29, 1863,
> TELEGRAM TO PRESIDENT JEFFERSON DAVIS

---

16 Sykes's questions were: "What Federal command was it that

General Hindman was ordered to cut off in McLemore's Cove near Lafayette, Ga., a few days preceding the battle of Chickamauga? And did Hindman have more than his own division? And was he not suspended from command for his failure? Would not his success on that occasion have given you great advantage over the remainder of the enemy?"

3d Question.[17] As to Genl. D. H. Hill's critical, captious and dictatorial manner, &c., &c.

This manner of Hill, and his general deportment united to the fact, which came to my knowledge after Polk's suspension from command, that Polk did order two of his Division Commanders, in writing soon after sunrise to attack, and that Hill, being present in person countermanded the order, without notifying either Polk or myself, induced me to ask his suspension from command. And he was removed by the President before the Battle of Missionary Ridge. He had, however, greatly demoralized the troops he commanded, and sacrificed thousands at Chickamauga.

I have always believed our disasters at Missionary Ridge was due immediately to misconduct of a brigade of Buckner's troops from East Tennessee, commanded by Brig. Genl. Alex W. Reynolds, which first gave way and could not be rallied. But the other troops would have saved the day and repaired the small disaster but for the effect which had been produced by the treasonable act of Longstreet, Hill and Buckner in sacrificing the army in their effort to degrade and remove me for personal ends. Had I known at the time Polk and Hindman were suspended, of the conduct of Hill, especially of his suspending Polk's orders to attack at Chickamauga, and of Buckner's influencing Hindman to disobey me in McLemore's Cove, and of his mutinous conduct in getting up meetings in the army to ask my removal, I certainly should have arrested both of them.

Still, I am satisfied no good could have resulted. Our country was not prepared to sustain a military commander who acted on military principles, and no man could do his duty and sustain himself against the combined power of imbeciles, traitors, rogues and intriguing politicians.

Longstreet's disobedience of orders enabled the enemy under Hooker from Virginia, to pass Lookout Mountain, and join Grant in Chattanooga. That was the first step in our disaster, after the army had been practically purged. Thus I yielded my convictions to the President's policy and sent Longstreet instead of Breckinridge (my choice) to capture Burnside at Knoxville. This could have been done long before Sherman reached Grant with his twenty-five (25,000) thousand men, by due diligence. And my information was perfect and daily.

Had it been done, and those Fifteen (15,000) Thousand troops been returned and in place at Missionary Ridge, Grant would not have attacked us, and if he had, would certainly have been defeated unless aided by treason. Indeed he must have recrossed the mountains, for his troops could not be fed, and his animals were already starved. He could not move twenty (20) pieces of artillery. No man was ever under greater obligations to a traitor [meaning Grant to Longstreet]; no traitor has ever been more faithfully rewarded.

In writing you thus fully and freely I rely on you to use my facts only, not my comments—they are private and could not be made public—it would do more harm than good. It would, be said these are some of Bragg's prejudices. I acknowledge myself prejudiced. I always was prejudiced against every species of dishonest knavery and treacherous selfishness.

In our retreat from Missionary Ridge the enemy could make but feeble pursuit, for want of artillery horses.

At the Mountain gorge, near Ringgold, I believed he could be successfully repulsed, and

---

17 The questions were: "Was not General D. H. Hill's critical, captious and dictatorial manner one of the prime causes of the failure of the army to defeat General Grant at Mission Ridge? Or, was it as reported by you to the department at Richmond, in substance, attributable to the unaccountable and inexplicable conduct of a portion of our troops? And if attributable to the latter, what troops?"

the army quietly withdrawn. Genl. Cleburn, one of the best and truest officers in our cause, was placed at that point in command of the rear-guard. Late at night, hours after all the army was at rest, my information being all in, I called for a reliable, confidential Staff officer, and gave him verbal directions to ride immediately to Cleburn, about three (3) miles in my rear, at this mountain gorge, and give him my positive orders to hold his position up to a named hour the next day, and, if attacked, to defend the pass at every hazzard. The message was delivered at Cleburn's Camp fire. He heard it with surprise and expressed his apprehension that it would result in the loss of his command, as his information differed from mine, and he believed the enemy would turn his position and cut him off.

But said he, true soldier as he was, I always obey orders, and only ask as protection in case of disaster, that you put the order in writing. This was done as soon as material could be found, and the staff officer returned and reported the result of his mission. He had not reached me, however, before the attack in front, as I expected, was made. Cleburn gallantly met it, defeated the enemy under Hooker, drove him back, and then quietly followed the army without further molestation—mark the difference in conduct and results. A good soldier, by obedience, without substituting his own crude notions, defeats the enemy and saves an army from disaster.

I would add much more, but should exhaust your patience. Whiskey was a great element in our disasters. In the battle of Murfreesboro, Cheatham was so drunk on the field all the first day, that a staff officer had to hold him on his horse. After the army reached Tullahoma, I directed Genl. Polk, his Corps Commander, to notify him that I know of his conduct, and only overlooked it in consideration of other meritorious services—

Polk reported to me that he had done so, that Cheatham acknowledged the charge, expressed deep contrition, and pledged himself never to repeat the offense. Imagine my surprise at reading Genl. Polk's report of that battle some weeks after, to find that he commended Cheatham's conduct on that field above all others in his corps.

At Missionary Ridge, Breckinridge, as gallant and true a man as ever lived, was overcome in the same way, whilst in the active command of a corps, and was really unfit for duty, one of the many causes of our disaster. At night he came into my office, a little depot hut at Chickamauga station, where I sat up all night giving orders, soon sank down on the floor, dead drunk, and was so in the morning. I sent for the commander of the Rear Guard, Brig. Genl. Gist, of S. C, and told him not to leave Genl. B—and if necessary, to put him in a wagon and haul him off. But under no circumstances to allow him to give an order. At Dalton I relieved Genl. B of his command and he acknowledged the justice of it, but said it was the deepest mortification of his life. In France or Germany either of the men I have named, would have been shot in six hours. With us they pass for great heroes.

After conducting his investigation, President Davis sided with General Bragg, calling the complaints from the other generals "shafts of malice." Concerning his friend, Polk, he determined there was no basis for the court-martial that Bragg wanted nor the court of inquiry that Polk wanted. Instead, he reassigned Polk as commander of the Department of Mississippi and East Louisiana, saying this would be "the best evidence of my appreciation of your past service and expectations of your future career."

"The Battle Roared with Increasing Fury"

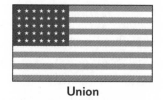

Union

Major-General William Rosecrans

William Rosecrans was born in Ohio, where his family had a farm, store, and tavern. Graduating from West Point in the same class as James Longstreet in 1842, he entered the Army Corps of Engineers as a brevet second lieutenant. About a year later he became a professor at West Point, teaching engineering. Health problems forced him to leave the army, and he went into mining. He did well, even patenting some inventions and becoming president of the Preston Coal Oil Company, until an oil lamp exploded and badly burned his face. It took him a year and a half to recover, at which point Fort Sumter was attacked.

He was initially aide-de-camp to McClellan, then commander of the Ohio volunteers. Briefly Rosecrans commanded an infantry regiment, in which served future presidents Rutherford B. Hayes and William McKinley, but he soon moved into the regular army as a brigadier general. After the First Battle of Manassas (First Bull Run), he became commander of what would become the Department of Western Virginia. In the western theater in 1862, he fought and won key battles in Mississippi, Tennessee, and Georgia.

Rosecrans was asked to run as Lincoln's vice president in 1864, but his telegram of acceptance never reached its destination. Some suspect that Secretary of War Edwin Stanton intercepted it.

[On September 20:] The battle roared with increasing fury, and approached from the left to the center. Two aides arrived successively within a few minutes, from General Thomas, asking for re-enforcements. The first was directed to say that General [James] Negley had already gone and should be near at hand at that time, and that [John] Brannan's reserve brigade was available. The other was directed to say that General [Horatio] Van Cleve would at once be sent to his assistance, which was accordingly done.

A message from General Thomas soon followed, that he was heavily pressed, informing me at the same time that General Brannan was

out of line, and General [Joseph] Reynolds' right was exposed. Orders were dispatched to General [Thomas] Wood to close up on Reynolds, and word was sent to General Thomas that he should be supported, even if it took away the whole corps of Crittenden and McCook. General [Jefferson C.] Davis was ordered to close on General Wood, and General McCook was advised of the state of affairs and ordered to close his whole command to the left with all dispatch.

General Wood, overlooking the direction to "close up" on General Reynolds, supposed he was to support him, by withdrawing from the line and passing to the rear of General Brannan, who, it appears, was not out of line, but was *en échelon*, and slightly in rear of Reynolds' right.[18] By this unfortunate mistake a gap was opened in the line of battle, of which the enemy took instant advantage, and striking Davis in flank and rear, as well as in front, threw his whole division in confusion.

The same attack shattered the right brigade of Wood before it had cleared the space. The right of Brannan was thrown back, and two of his batteries, then in movement to a new position, were taken in flank and thrown back through two brigades of Van Cleve, then on the march to the left, throwing his division into confusion from which it never recovered until it reached Rossville.

While the enemy poured in through this breach, a long line stretching beyond Sheridan's right was advancing. Sheridan's other two brigades made a gallant charge against the enemy's advancing column, but were thrown into disorder by the enemy's line advancing on their flank, and were likewise compelled to fall back, rallying on the Dry Valley road, and repulsing the enemy, but they were again compelled to yield to superior numbers and retired westward.

Thus Davis' two brigades, one of Van Cleve's, and Sheridan's entire division were driven from the field, and the remainder, consisting of the divisions of Baird, Johnson, Palmer, Reynolds, Brannan, and Wood, two of Negley's brigades and one of Van Cleve's, were left to sustain the conflict against the whole power of the rebel army, which, desisting from pursuit on the right, concentrated their whole efforts to destroy them.

At the moment of the repulse of Davis' division, I was standing in rear of his right, waiting the completion of the closing of McCook's corps to the left. Seeing confusion among Van Cleve's troops, and the distance Davis' men were falling back, and the tide of battle surging toward us, the urgency for Sheridan's troops to intervene became imminent, and I hastened in person to the extreme right, to direct Sheridan's movement on the flank of the advancing rebels. It was too late. The crowd of returning troops rolled back, and the enemy advanced.

Giving the troops directions to rally behind the ridge west of the Dry Valley road, I passed down it under a shower of grape, canister, and musketry, for 200 or 300 yards, and attempted to rejoin General Thomas and the troops sent to his support, by passing to the rear of the broken portion of our lines, but found the routed troops far toward the left, and hearing the enemy's advancing musketry and cheers, I became doubtful whether the left had held its ground, and started for Rossville.

On consultation and further reflection, however, I determined to send General [James A.] Garfield there, while I went to Chattanooga, to give orders for the security of the pontoon bridges at Battle Creek and Bridgeport, and to make preliminary dispositions either to forward ammunition and supplies, should we hold our ground, or to withdraw the troops into good position. General Garfield proceeded to the front, remained there until the close of the fight, and dispatched me the triumphant defense our troops there made against the assaults of the enemy.

The fight on the left, after 2 p.m., was that of the army. Never, in the history of this war at least, have troops fought with greater energy and determination. Bayonet charges, often heard of

---

18 The order, written down by one of Rosecrans's aides and sent without being reviewed, said to "close up" and "support." Rosecrans had just castigated Wood for not following orders promptly, so Wood wasn't about to argue. In order to close up on or support Reynolds, Wood had to get on the other side of Brigadier-General John Brannan's division. There wasn't room to close up, so he moved behind Reynolds as support.

but seldom seen, were repeatedly made by brigades and regiments in several of our divisions.

From 1 to half past 3 o'clock, the unequal contest was sustained throughout our line. Then the enemy in overpowering numbers flowed around our right, held by General Brannan, and occupied a low gap in the ridge of our defensive position, which commanded our rear. The moment was critical. Twenty minutes more and our right would have been turned, our position taken in reverse, and probably the army routed.

Fortunately, Major-General Granger, whose troops had been posted to cover our left and rear, with the instinct of a true soldier and a general, hearing the roar of battle on our left, determined to move to its assistance. General Granger discovered at once the peril and the point of danger—the gap. Quick as thought he directed his advance brigade upon the enemy. General Steedman, taking a regimental color, led the column. Swift was the charge and terrible the conflict, but the enemy was broken. A thousand of our brave men, killed and wounded, paid for its possession, but we held the gap.

Two divisions of Longstreet's corps confronted the position. Determined to take it, they successively came to the assault. A battery of six guns, placed in the gorge, poured death and slaughter into them. They charged to within a few yards of the pieces, but our grape and canister, and the leaden hail of our musketry, delivered in sparing but terrible volleys from cartridges taken in many instances from the boxes of their fallen companions, was too much even for Longstreet's men. About sunset they made their last charge, when our men, being out of ammunition, rushed on them with bayonet, and they gave way to return no more.

General Thomas, considering the excessive labors of the troops, the scarcity of ammunition, food, and water, and having orders from the general commanding to use his discretion, determined to retire on Rossville, where they arrived in good order. On the night of the 21st we withdrew from Rossville, took firm possession of the objective point of our campaign—Chattanooga—and prepared to hold it.

Before Congress's investigative committee, Rosecrans testified:

I desire to direct attention to the contrast in the manner in which our movement on Vicksburg and Missionary ridge were supported to show that the authorities at Washington by their action in these cases recognized the principle which was violated in the case of this movement, and thus bear testimony to the greatness of the mistake they made in not suitably supporting the movement of the army of the Cumberland in this great campaign.

I will also call the attention of the committee to the spirit of the report of the general-in-chief [Halleck], wherein he implies that the battle of Chickamauga was a consequence of a wild scheme of advance into Georgia undertaken by me without just warrant of prudence or authority.

The general is very much mistaken in this matter. I well remember my surprise on receiving the following from General Halleck, directing me to occupy Dalton, and the passes to the west of it, at the moment when every nerve was tense with energy and anxiety to get my troops out of those passes and concentrated on the Lafayette and Chattanooga road, twenty miles north of Dalton, in time to cover Chattanooga and prevent the enemy from tailing on and beating us in detail.

To meet controversy directly on this point, I will state that no "wild" or other scheme of advance into Georgia was ever entertained by me, nor anything beyond the capture and firm possession of Chattanooga contemplated, save a sharp pursuit moving lightly to injure the enemy should we find him hastily retreating in a condition to be injured north of Oostenaula.

The committee will observe from my official report that we began to cross the Tennessee on the 28th of August, and that, therefore, we were twenty-two days out from our depots; our army having to carry in that campaign ammunition for two great battles and twenty-five days' subsistence, which was done and pronounced by General Meigs [quartermaster general] to be not only the greatest operation in this war, but a great thing in any war.

Forgetting my past record, and influenced by the calumnies put in circulation, it has been thought that I needlessly or languidly forsook the field of battle on the 20th. When the breach on the right of our lines occurred at midday of the 20th, the train with all our spare subsistence and other supplies lay along the valley of Chattanooga creek, from near the front some four or five miles; and as the distance from the point where the enemy had penetrated our infantry lines to the flank and rear of the train was only three or four miles, they were in the most critical condition, and it became a matter of the utmost importance to put it out of the enemy's reach.

Nor was I unmindful of the consideration that, as the security of Chattanooga was the essential thing, my duty as commanding general required that I should look to the ground with a view to the eventualities of being driven from the field of battle, where we were so vastly outnumbered, and that I should make such dispositions as would enable us to hold that place and to subsist our troops until we could be re-enforced.

In General Grant's official report of the battle of Missionary ridge, I think—for I have not the document—there is an implication that when he assumed command there was great danger of my abandoning Chattanooga. Nothing could be more mistaken or unjust to me than such an impression. All my actions and sentiments were utterly at variance with the idea of giving up that point, which I had won, and the possession of which formed an epoch in the war.

REBEL YELL, YANKEE CHEER

During a saber or bayonet charge, the rebel yell instilled the Confederates with courage, while generating fear in their enemy. Union soldiers replied with their own battle cry, known as the Yankee cheer. While its name is a lot less familiar, it essentially remains with us today ("Hooray!"), while the precise sounds of the rebel yell died out after the war (vaguely surviving as "Yeehaw!").

According to legend, the rebel yell originated with Stonewall Jackson during the First Battle of Manassas (First Bull Run). In an 1866 biography of Jackson, R. L. Dabney described the event: "Riding up to the 2d regiment, he cried, 'Reserve your fire till they come within fifty yards, then fire and give them the bayonet; and, when you charge, yell like furies!' Like noble hounds unleashed, his men sprang to their feet, concentrating into that moment all the pent-up energies and revenge of the hours of passive suffering, delivered one deadly volley, and dashed upon the enemy."

Some describe the rebel yell as a high-pitched "Wa-woo woohoo! Wa-woo woohoo!"; others as "Ooo-eee!"; and then there were these variations: "Whooo-wow!"; "Yeeeow!"; "Yeee-ahhh!"; "Yuhhh-wooo-eee-UH!"; "Eee-YUH-haeeeooo!"; and "Rrr-yahhh-yip-yip-yip-yip-yip!"

Perhaps the yell evolved over the course of the war, or maybe the yell varied from brigade to brigade or from army to army. At any rate, it worked; the Union soldiers hated it. Author Ambrose Bierce, who experienced it as a Union lieutenant at the Battle of Chickamauga, described it as "the ugliest sound that any mortal ever heard," while war correspondent William Howard Russell reported that it was "a shrill ringing scream with a touch of the Indian war-whoop in it." Confederate colonel Keller Anderson, who also heard it at Chickamauga, said it was a "maniacal maelstrom of sound; that penetrating, rasping, shrieking, blood-curdling noise that could be heard for miles and whose volume reached the heavens—such an expression as never yet came from the throats of sane men, but from men whom the seething blast of an imaginary hell would not check while the sound lasted."

Of course, the Confederates thought their battle cry was stronger than the Union's, while the Union soldiers felt theirs had more volume and wasn't as high-pitched as the rebel yell.

Confederate colonel J. Harvie Dew, in Jeb Stuart's cavalry, gives us the best, most detailed description of the rebel yell and Yankee cheer from the battle on the plains at Brandy Station, Virginia, in the fall of 1863:

In a moment more one of the Federal regiments was ordered to charge, and down they came upon us in a body two or three times outnumbering ours. Then was heard their peculiar characteristic yell—"Hoo-ray! Hoo-ray! Hoo-ray!" etc. (This yell was called by the Federals a "cheer," and was intended for the word "hurrah," but that pronunciation I never heard in a charge. The sound was as though the first syllable, if heard at all, was "hoo," uttered with an exceedingly short, low, and indistinct tone, and the second was "ray," yelled with a long and high tone slightly deflecting at its termination. In many instances the yell seemed to be the simple interjection "heigh," rendered with the same tone which was given to "ray.")

In an instant every voice with one accord vigorously shouted that "Rebel yell," which was so often heard on the field of battle. "Woh-who—ey! who—ey! who—ey! Woh-who—ey! who-ey!" etc. (The best illustration of this "true yell" which can be given the reader is by spelling it as above, with directions to sound the first syllable "woh" short and low, and the second "who" with a very high and prolonged note deflecting upon the third syllable "ey.")

"Rosecrans Was Badly Defeated"

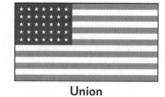

Union

General Ulysses S. Grant (See biography, page 54.)

Soon it was discovered in Washington that Rosecrans was in trouble and required assistance. The emergency was now too immediate to allow us to give this assistance by making an attack in rear of

Bragg upon Mobile. It was therefore necessary to reinforce directly, and troops were sent from every available point.

Rosecrans had very skilfully manoeuvred Bragg south of the Tennessee River, and through and beyond Chattanooga. If he had stopped and intrenched, and made himself strong there, all would have been right and the mistake of not moving earlier partially compensated. But he pushed on, with his forces very much scattered, until Bragg's troops from Mississippi began to join him. Then Bragg took the initiative. Rosecrans had to fall back in turn, and was able to get his army together at Chickamauga, some miles south-east of Chattanooga, before the main battle was brought on.

The battle was fought on the 19th and 20th of September, and Rosecrans was badly defeated, with a heavy loss in artillery and some sixteen thousand men killed, wounded and captured. The corps under Major-General George H. Thomas stood its ground, while Rosecrans, with Crittenden and McCook, returned to Chattanooga. Thomas returned also, but later, and with his troops in good order. Bragg followed and took possession of Missionary Ridge, overlooking Chattanooga. He also occupied Lookout Mountain, west of the town, which Rosecrans had abandoned, and with it his control of the river and the river road as far back as Bridgeport. The National troops were now strongly intrenched in Chattanooga Valley, with the Tennessee River behind them and the enemy occupying commanding heights to the east and west, with a strong line across the valley from mountain to mountain, and with Chattanooga Creek, for a large part of the way, in front of their line.

On the 29th Halleck telegraphed me the above results, and directed all the forces that could be spared from my department to be sent to Rosecrans. Long before this dispatch was received Sherman was on his way, and McPherson was moving east with most of the garrison of Vicksburg.

A retreat at that time would have been a terrible disaster. It would not only have been the loss of a most important strategic position to us, but it would have been attended with the loss of all the artillery still left with the Army of the Cumberland and the annihilation of that army itself, either by capture or demoralization.

The first time I saw Mr. Stanton was in the West. I had come from Cairo, had reached Indianapolis, changed cars for Louisville, and was just on the point of starting, when a messenger informed me that Mr. Stanton and Governor Brough of Ohio had just arrived at the station from another direction. Mr. Stanton immediately joined me, and we went on to Louisville together. He gave me my new command, to take the army and relieve Rosecrans. Stanton being a little fatigued went to bed, while I went to the theater.

As I was strolling back messengers began to hail me. Stanton was anxious to see me as something terrible had happened. I hastened to the Secretary, not knowing what had taken place. On the way I reproached myself with having attended the theater, while there was no knowing what terrible things had happened in my absence. When I reached Stanton's room, I found the Secretary in his night garments in great distress. He had received a dispatch from the Assistant Secretary of War telling him that Rosecrans had given orders to his army to retreat, and that such a retreat would be disastrous not only to that campaign but to the Union. I saw the situation at once, and wrote several dispatches.

> Amid all this the practical incapacity of the general commanding is astonishing, and it often seems difficult to believe him of sound mind. His imbecility appears to be contagious, and it is difficult for any one to get anything done. If the army is finally obliged to retreat, the probability is that it will fall back like a rabble, leaving its artillery, and protected only by the river behind it. If, on the other hand, we regain control of the river and keep it, subsistence and forage can be got here, and we may escape with no worse misfortune than the loss of 12,000 animals.
>
> —Assistant Secretary of War Charles Dana's dispatch to Stanton from Chattanooga on October 18

My first was a dispatch to General Rosecrans relieving him of his command and taking command of the army myself. My second dispatch was to General Thomas, directing him to take command of the army until I reached head-quarters, and also ordering General Thomas to hold his position at any and all hazards against any force. A reply came from General Thomas that he would hold his position until he and his whole army starved.

I hurried down to the front, and on my way at one of the stations met Rosecrans. He was very cheerful, and seemed as though a great weight had been lifted off his mind, and showed none of the feeling which might have been expected in meeting the general who had been directed to supersede him. I remember he was very fluent and eager in telling me what I should do when I reached the army.

When I arrived at head-quarters, I found the army in a sad condition. The men were badly fed and badly clothed. We had no communications open for supplies. Cattle had to be driven a long way over the mountains, and were so thin when they came into the lines that the soldiers used to call it "beef dried on the hoof."

I opened communications with our supplies, or, as they called it, opened the "cracker lines." Rosecrans's plan [of retreating], which was checked before put in execution by my order, would have been most disastrous—nothing could have been more fatal. He would have lost his guns and his trains, and Bragg would have taken Nashville. By opening our lines, and feeding our men, and giving them good clothing, our army was put into good condition. Then, when Sherman reached me, I attacked Bragg, and out of that attack came Mission Ridge. Rosecrans was a great disappointment to us all—to me especially.

While Bragg was dealing with the rebellion of his officers, Grant replaced Rosecrans. Bragg reduced his force by sending Longstreet to conduct his Knoxville campaign against Burnside's Army of the Ohio, while the Grant's Army of the Cumberland at Chattanooga was receiving reinforcements. Bragg was now facing Grant, Sherman, Hooker, and Thomas.

After a series of battles around Chattanooga in November 1863, Union forces drove Bragg into Alabama. Confederates, thrilled by their victory at Chickamauga, mourned their defeat at Chattanooga and the Union's control over Tennessee. It also enabled Sherman to use Chattanooga the following year as his supply base for his Atlanta campaign.

Bragg tendered his resignation, and was disappointed when Davis accepted it. Johnston replaced him, fighting against Sherman during the Atlanta campaign. On the Union side Rosecrans was transferred to command the Department of Missouri.

THE BATTLE OF THE CRATER

ALSO KNOWN AS THE BATTLE OF THE MINE
PETERSBURG, VIRGINIA
JULY 30, 1864

COMMANDERS

Union
Lieut. Gen. Ulysses S. Grant
Maj. Gen. George Meade
Maj. Gen. Ambrose Burnside

Confederate
Gen. Robert E. Lee
Gen. G. T. Beauregard
Maj. Gen. Bushrod Johnson

PARTICIPANTS

8,500 (Ninth Corps)

4,000 (elements of the Army
of Northern Virginia)

CASUALTIES

Union
504 killed
1,881 wounded
1,413 POWs/MIA

Confederate
361 killed
727 wounded
403 POWs/MIA

VICTORY: CONFEDERACY

OVERVIEW

It was a good idea badly executed. The plan was to blow a huge hole in General Lee's line and charge through it, driving the Confederates out of Petersburg, Virginia. This was during the "siege" of Petersburg, although it wasn't really a siege. Petersburg and neighboring Richmond weren't cut off from communication and supplies from the rest of the Confederacy, as a siege normally entails. It was actually trench warfare.

Following his success with the battles of Chattanooga, Grant was promoted to lieutenant general, becoming the second person, after George Washington, to hold this rank—Winfield Scott having held the rank of brevet lieutenant general. With the promotion, Grant replaced Halleck as general in chief, which put him in charge of all the Union's armies. Halleck became Grant's chief of staff, managing Washington, while Grant managed the field.

The power of the Confederacy was waning, but it still had a lot of fight left in it. Grant launched a surprise attack on Petersburg, a major cog in the supply line linking Richmond and Lee's army to the rest of the South. Lee quickly sprang to its defense, and the two armies built fortifications from south of Petersburg up along its eastern side, covering more than twenty-five miles. Complex systems of trenches defended the men from snipers, while bomb shelters, then known as "bomb-proofs," protected the soldiers from artillery. The Union launched attacks on June 9 and from June 15 to 18, but they failed.

Burnside had control of a southern portion of the Union line just south of Petersburg. One of his men suggested digging a mine across no-man's land about fifty feet beneath one of the Confederate salients, which are outward projections of fortification that enable defenders to more easily shoot attackers at fortification walls. This particular salient was essentially a fort armed with four artillery guns and about 350 Confederate soldiers. The idea was to load the mine with gunpowder, as Grant did at Vicksburg, and blow it up along with the salient. Then attacking soldiers could charge through the Confederate line into Petersburg.

For the plan to work, Burnside had to get his men across 100 yards of open ground to the explosion crater, and then get them through or around the crater and across another 500 yards to the crest of a hill, where they could look across a valley at Petersburg less than a mile away. Getting his men to the crest as rapidly as possible was the key to the whole operation. Unfortunately, the plan started going wrong for Burnside from the start, and it snowballed from there.

Grant staged a brilliant feint that caused Lee to move all his available troops to Richmond, leaving just enough behind to man Petersburg's fortifications. The attack was supposed to begin at 3:30 a.m. on July 30, but Burnside had trouble getting his subterranean bomb to detonate. His men finally succeeded at 4:44 a.m. The mine, filled with 320 kegs (8,000 pounds) of powder, blew up, throwing about 100,000 cubic feet of earth, the salient, guns, and men manning the fort a hundred feet into the air. Confederate major general Bushrod Johnson reported 278 of his men killed in the explosion, with another 76 missing. Years later Colonel Fitz William McMaster reported 56 known dead, with 260 missing.

The corps of Burnside and Major-General Edward Ord had to pass down a single covered walkway to get across their own line into no-man's land in front of the huge crater. This walkway bottlenecked their movement, and as they got through, most of the men stopped inside the crater. Soldiers at that time were trained to fight in formation. When out of formation they quickly became confused and had difficulty taking orders. Some made it beyond the crater into a labyrinth of Confederate rifle pits, trenches, and bunkers. By 6 a.m. the Confederates had established heavy cross fire both in front of and behind the crater. Rifle fire swept the top of the crater and mortars rained down into it.

Then the African American soldiers of the Fourth Division went in. While most of the previous attackers were still in the crater, somehow they made it between 300 and 400 yards beyond the crater, but they were sent in too late and met strong resistance, forcing them to retreat. As the men of the Fourth Division were pushed back toward the captured rifle pits, they saw other men fleeing from the Confederate assault, so they kept going until they reached the Union trenches. Colonel H. G. Thomas, who commanded a brigade of African American troops, said, "It is but justice to the line officers to say, that more than two-thirds of them were shot; and to the colored troops, that the white troops were running back just ahead of them." The resulting stampede of about 2,000 men occurred just before 9 a.m. Seizing the advantage, some of the Confederates moved up to about twenty-five yards from the crater.

About an hour later, on receiving telegrams that their assaults were being repulsed, Grant and Meade called off the attack. It took until noon for most of the men to get back through the bottleneck. This is when the Union suffered most of its losses. Just before noon Burnside sent the evacuation order into the crater. The Confederates launched two more assaults, regaining the crater and their original line at 2 p.m. Because of the bottleneck, only around 8,500 of the 40,000 to 50,000 Union troops lined up for battle even made it across the Union line.

Burnside, a munitions manufacturer before the war, had focused his attention on the mine, disregarding orders for other preparations. Later he insisted that he didn't want to tip off the Confederates to the pending attack. From

Northern newspapers, deserters, and prisoners, the Confederates knew of the mine, but they didn't know when it was to go off, so Beauregard had additional trenches and works constructed in preparation for the attack.

Burnside was also terrible at reporting to Major-General Meade, often ignoring Meade's frantic demands for information. When he responded, he did so with minimal information that didn't reveal much. Grant had to make several visits to the Union trenches to determine how matters were progressing.

Meade, technically in charge of the battle, was about three-quarters of a mile away, where he received telegraphic communications from all along the line. He couldn't tell what was happening and feared that if he went to the front he'd miss an important communication from another part of the field. He tried to send orders based on the snippets of information he did receive, but these orders just made things worse.

The battle became a major fiasco for the Union and a minor incident for the Confederacy. As a result, the ongoing standoff between the armies of Grant and Lee remained in a stalemate for eight more months.

The Long Delay

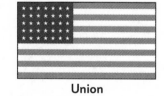

Union

Major-General Joshua Chamberlain (See biography, page 174.)

Evil-minded people were trying to make our men believe that Grant and Lincoln were making this

long delay in front of Petersburg in order to secure their continuance in office. But this was an outrage

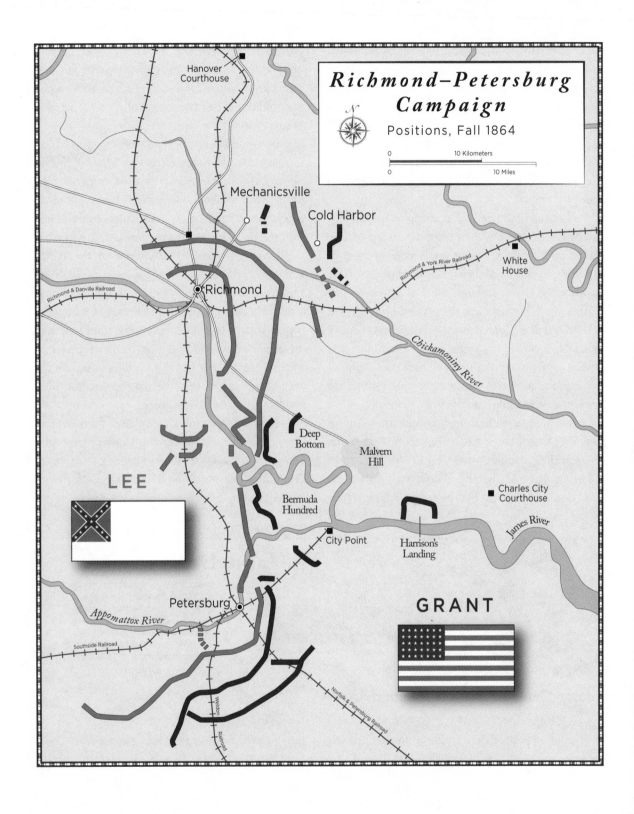

Richmond–Petersburg Campaign

Positions, Fall 1864

N

0 ____ 10 Kilometers

0 ____ 10 Miles

Hanover Courthouse

Mechanicsville

Cold Harbor

Richmond & York River Railroad

White House

Richmond

Richmond & Danville Railroad

Chickahominy River

Deep Bottom

Malvern Hill

LEE

Bermuda Hundred

Charles City Courthouse

City Point

Harrison's Landing

James River

Petersburg

GRANT

Appomattox River

Southside Railroad

Weldon Railroad

Norfolk & Petersburg Railroad

upon those noble characters, and an insult to the common sense of every man among us. We knew that the surest way for our high officials to hold their place was by no means to court delay, but to strike a quick, bold blow at the enemy.

Grant's change of base from the Rappahannock to the James, and his immediate objective from the front of Richmond to its rear by way of Petersburg, called for no adverse criticism. Although technically a change of base, it was not a change in his grand purpose—"to fight it out on this line if it takes all summer." That meant there was to be no retreating. And this might justly be considered a master stroke of grand tactics in the continuous movement to turn Lee's right, and also cut his communications.

When we understood the purpose of this move we believed it to be good tactics, and we took it up with hope and cheer. Our army was skilfully withdrawn from the front of a watchful and active enemy, and the main body of our army was before Petersburg before Lee knew it had crossed the James.

The first blow was well delivered; but a series of shortcomings, for which it must be said neither the men nor their immediate commanders were responsible, brought all to nought. Successive assaults on the enemy's lines were made as corps after corps extended leftward; but gallant fighting left little to show but its cost.

By this time it was too late; all Lee's army were up and entrenched. We encountered a far outnumbering force of veteran troops well entrenched and a cross-fire of twenty guns in earthworks planted with forethought and skill. Desperate valor could accomplish nothing but its own demonstration. Our veterans were hurled back over the stricken field, or left upon it—I, too, proud witness and sharer of their fate. I am not of Virginia blood; she is of mine. So ended the evening of the second day. And the army sat down to that ten months' symposium, from which twenty thousand men never rose.

As for Grant, he was like Thor, the hammerer; striking blow after blow, intent on his purpose to beat his way through, somewhat reckless of the cost. Yet he was the first one of our commanders who dared to pursue his policy of delay without apology or fear of overruling. He made it a condition of his acceptancy of the chief command that he should not be interfered with from Washington. That gave him more freedom and "discretion" than any of his predecessors. He had somehow, with all his modesty, the rare faculty of controlling his superiors as well as his subordinates. He outfaced Stanton, captivated the President, and even compelled acquiescence or silence from that dread source of paralyzing power—the Congressional Committee on the conduct of the war.

The Government and the country had to exercise patience—with us no doubt, and even with General Grant.

TRENCH WARFARE

The Civil War transformed warfare in many ways. With many new innovations and rapid improvements in weaponry, commanders had a difficult time adjusting tactics to keep up. For much of the war, officers maintained control over their men by marching them around in formation. When they lost formation, the officers tended to lose control until they were able to re-form. Often soldiers didn't know what the objective was. They were trained to obey commands. When their officer was wounded or killed, they usually didn't know what to do, leading to many inglorious, disorderly retreats.

When attacking, they used the old Napoleonic tactic of charging in a tight group, the idea being that if you bunch enough men together and they run really fast, enough of the attackers will reach the enemy to stick them with bayonets or for attacking cavalry to kill the defenders with sabers. This strategy worked when the defenders were armed with muzzle-loading, smooth-bore muskets, but as firearms and ammunition improved, soldiers loaded and fired faster, and their guns shot farther and more accurately, doing more damage. Early in the war a formation could march toward a defensive position and not sustain many casualties until the last hundred yards. Then they increased their march to quick time for their bayonet charge, receiving two or three volleys from the defenders before engaging in hand-to-hand combat. Oddly, they didn't charge at double-quick time.

Just by adding rifling to muskets and cannon, defenders could fire up to eighteen effective volleys starting at a distance of 1,000 yards. Charging while exposed into weapons such as these resulted in particularly bloody repulses, such as Marye's Heights, Cold Harbor, and Pickett's Charge. The introduction of repeating rifles and machine guns made these charges even worse. Since it was difficult to get close enough to use sabers and bayonets, these began to fade from use, and hand-to-hand combat became relatively rare. Of around 250,000 wounded treated at Union hospitals, only 922 suffered from saber or bayonet wounds. Still, it took many senseless slaughters before the generals realized they had to change their tactics—but even then they didn't know what to do.

When frontal assaults no longer worked, two armies suddenly found themselves facing each other in a stalemate. Snipers picked off anyone in an exposed position, so they began digging foxholes, rifle pits, and trenches to protect themselves. Thus trench warfare was born.

Lee, an engineer, put such emphasis on digging in and creating extensive systems of fortifications as defensive positions early in the war that he soon became known derisively as the "King of Spades," but it helped him succeed. Sandbags and gabions—large baskets filled with rocks or dirt—created or reinforced walls. Bomb shelters provided further protection with a thick roof of logs and dirt. Networks of trenches usually ran for miles.

Prior to trench warfare, using available protective cover or crawling along the ground was considered cowardly and dishonorable. Suddenly maintaining cover and the use of camouflage became a requirement. Trench periscopes allowed men to spy over trenches without exposure.

Different weapons were used to strike at hidden opponents. Trench mortars lobbed shells high into the air so they could drop down into trenches. Hand grenades flew across no-man's land into opposing trenches. Snipers constantly scanned the opposing line for anything exposed.

Defenses were needed in case the enemy suddenly launched a surprise attack by going over the top, so defenders placed a variety of obstacles in front of their trenches. A fraise resembled a knocked-over picket fence, with a row of sharpened stakes tied or wired together and angled to point toward the enemy. A cheval-de-frise, primarily a barrier against cavalry, consisted of a central log through which stakes alternated at right angles so, endwise, they formed a row of X's. The abatis, sometimes called a fraise or cheval-de-frise, was a barricade of cut-down trees laid in front of a trench with sharpened branches pointed toward the enemy.

Fortifications generally consisted of one or more rows of abatis or similar barriers along with rifle pits for skirmishers and pickets connected by trenches. Behind this usually lay a two- to six-foot-deep ditch. Behind that, four to eight feet from ground level, rose a rampart or embankment of dirt faced with a wall of logs or stone, topped with logs or sandbags, with gaps for firing through. On the back of the rampart, if it was higher than four feet, was a step on which men could stand when firing over the parapet. Behind all this ran a covered walkway to protect soldiers passing to the rear. Batteries and forts often looked down on the trenches. And all of this was repeated by the enemy along their line.

Such fortifications were difficult to overcome. Unless they could be breached or flanked, the confrontation essentially became a siege or near siege—a battle of attrition in which each side slowly ground away at the other until one finally gave out.

PLAN OF ATTACK

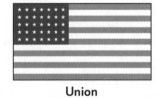

Union

General Ulysses S. Grant (See biography, page 54.)

On the 25th of June General Burnside had commenced running a mine from about the centre of his front under the Confederate works confronting him. He was induced to do this by Colonel Pleasants, of the Pennsylvania Volunteers, whose regiment was mostly composed of miners, and who was himself a practical miner. Burnside had submitted the scheme to Meade and myself, and we both approved of it, as a means of keeping the men occupied. His position was very favorable for carrying on this work, but not so favorable for the operations to follow its completion. The position of the two lines at that point were only about a hundred yards apart with a comparatively deep ravine intervening. In the bottom of this ravine the work commenced.

The position was unfavorable in this particular: that the enemy's line at that point was re-entering [recessed], so that its front was commanded by their own lines both to the right and left. Then, too, the ground was sloping upward back of the Confederate line for a considerable distance, and it was presumable that the enemy had, at least, a detached work on this highest point.

On the 17th of July several deserters came in and said that Lee was coming out to make an attack upon us—the object being to put us on the defensive so that he might detach troops to go to Georgia where the army Sherman was operating against was said to be in great trouble. I concluded to do something in the way of offensive movement myself, having in view something of the same object that Lee had had.

I had other objects in view, however, besides keeping Lee where he was. The mine was constructed and ready to be exploded, and I wanted to take that occasion to carry Petersburg if I could. It was the object, therefore, to get as many of Lee's troops away from the south side of the James River as possible. Accordingly, on the 26th, we commenced a movement with Hancock's corps and Sheridan's cavalry to the north side.

The plan, in the main, was to let the cavalry cut loose and destroy as much as they could of the Virginia Central Railroad, while, in the mean time, the infantry was to move out so as to protect their rear and cover their retreat back when they should have got through with their work. We were successful in drawing the enemy's troops to the north side of the James as I expected. The mine was ordered to be charged, and the morning of the 30th of July was the time fixed for its explosion. I gave Meade minute orders on the 24th directing how I wanted the assault conducted, which orders he amplified into general instructions for the guidance of the troops that were to be engaged.

Meade's instructions, which I, of course, approved most heartily, were all that I can see now was necessary. The only further precaution which he could have taken, and which he could not foresee, would have been to have different men to execute them.

The gallery to the mine was over five hundred feet long from where it entered the ground to the point where it was under the enemy's works, and with a cross gallery of something over eighty feet running under their lines. Eight chambers had been left, requiring a ton of powder each to charge them.

On the 29th Hancock and Sheridan were brought back near the James River with their troops. Under cover of night they started to recross the bridge at Deep Bottom, and to march directly for that part of our lines in front of the mine.

[General Gouverneur] Warren was to hold his line of intrenchments with a sufficient number of men and concentrate the balance on the right next to Burnside's corps, while Ord, now commanding the 18th corps, temporarily under Meade, was to form in the rear of Burnside to support him when he went in. All were to clear off the parapets and the abatis in their front so as to leave the space as open as possible, and be able to charge the moment the mine had been sprung and Burnside had taken possession. Burnside's corps was not to stop in the crater at all but push on to the top of the hill, supported on the right and left by Ord's and Warren's corps.

Warren and Ord fulfilled their instructions perfectly so far as making ready was concerned. Burnside seemed to have paid no attention whatever to the instructions, and left all the obstruction in his own front for his troops to get over in the best way they could. The four divisions of his corps were commanded by Generals [Robert] Potter, [Orlando] Willcox, [James] Ledlie and [Edward] Ferrero. The last was a colored division; and Burnside selected it to make the assault. Meade interfered with this. Burnside then took Ledlie's division—a worse selection than the first could have been.[19] In fact, Potter and Willcox were the only division commanders Burnside had who were equal to the occasion.

---

19 Grant said this not so much about the men but because division commanders Brigadier-Generals Ledlie and Ferrero remained in a bunker near the Union line during the battle.

> The crater presented an obstacle of fearful magnitude. I suppose it was a hole of about 200 feet in length, by perhaps 50 or 60 feet in width, and nearly 30 feet in depth. The sides of it were composed of jagged masses of clay projecting from loose sand. It was an obstacle which it was perfectly impossible for any military organization to pass over intact, even if not exposed to fire.
>
> —Lieutenant-Colonel Charles Loring, assistant inspector general of Burnside's corps, testifying before the Congressional Committee

> Having occasion to be down in the gallery the greater part of the time, I was in it at about 5 a.m. the 30th instant, when I was startled by the sound of a very heavy explosion and thrown from my feet by the shock, the ground or rather gallery heaved and waved as if from an earthquake. After recovering from our surprise I took the three men out, who were at work in the mine, and on reaching the outside saw that the works had been utterly destroyed for a distance of 100 or 150 yards as near as I could judge.
>
> —Sergeant A. H. Smyth, working in one of the Confederate mine shafts trying to locate the Union's mine

---

A Most Unfortunate Operation

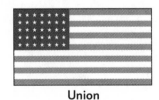

Union

Major-General George Meade (See biography, page 92.)

As soon as the mine was sprung, the 1st division 9th corps, Brigadier-General Ledlie commanding, mixed forward and occupied the crater without opposition. No advance, however, was made from the crater to the ridge, some 400 yards beyond; Brigadier-General Ledlie giving as a reason for not pushing forward, that the enemy could occupy the crater in his rear, he seeming to forget that the rest of his corps and all the 18th corps were waiting to occupy the crater and follow him.

> The earth around us trembled and heaved so violently that I was lifted to my feet. Then the earth along the enemy's lines opened, and fire and smoke shot upward seventy-five or one hundred feet. The air was filled with earth, cannon, caissons, sand-bags and living men, and with everything else within the exploded fort. I gave the command 'Forward,' but at the outset a serious difficulty had to be surmounted. Our own works, which were very high at this point, had not been prepared for scaling. But scale them in some way we must, and ladders were improvised by the men placing their bayonets between the logs in the works and holding the other end at their hip or on shoulders, thus forming steps over which men climbed. Our colors were the first to be planted on the ruined fort. Nearly all who were within it were killed or buried alive. We succeeded in taking out many—some whose feet would be waving above their burial-place; others, having an arm, hand, or head only, uncovered; others, alive but terribly shaken.
>
> —Brevet Major Charles Houghton

Brigadier-Generals Potter and Wilcox, commanding 2d and 3d divisions, 9th corps, advanced simultaneously with Ledlie, and endeavored to occupy parts of the enemy's line on Ledlie's right and left, so as to cover those flanks, respectively, but on reaching the enemy's line Ledlie's men were found occupying the vacated parts, both to the right and left of the crater, in consequence of which the men of the several divisions got mixed up, and a scene of disorder and confusion commenced, which seems to have continued to the end of the operations.

In the mean time, the enemy rallying from the confusion incident to the explosion, began forming his infantry in a ravine to the right, and planting his artillery both on the right and left of the crater. Seeing this, Potter was enabled to get his men out of the crater and enemy's line, and had formed them for an attack on the right, when he received an order to attack the crest of the ridge. Notwithstanding he had to change front in the presence of the enemy, he succeeded not only in doing so, but, as he reports, advancing to within a few yards of the crest, which he would have taken if he had been supported.

This was after 7 a.m., more than two hours after Ledlie had occupied the crater, and yet he had made no advance. He, however, states that he was forming to advance when the 4th division, (colored troops,) General Ferrero commanding, came rushing into the crater, and threw his men into confusion. The 4th division passed beyond the crater, and made an assault, when they encountered a heavy fire of artillery and infantry, which threw them into inextricable confusion, and they retired in disorder through the troops in the crater, and back into our lines. In the mean time, in ignorance of what was occurring, I sent orders to Major-General Ord, commanding 18th corps, who was expected to follow the 9th, to advance at once on the right of the 9th, and independently of the latter. To this General Ord replied, the only debouches were choked up with the 9th corps, which had not all advanced at this time.

He, however, pushed on a brigade of Turner's division over the 9th corps parapets, and directed it to charge the enemy's line on the right, where it was still occupied. While it was about executing this order, the disorganized 4th division (colored) of the 9th corps came rushing back and carrying everything with them, including Turner's brigade.

By this time—between 8 and 9 a.m.—the enemy, seeing the hesitation and confusion on our part, having planted batteries on both flanks in ravines where our artillery could not reach them, opened a heavy fire, not only on the ground in front of the crater, but between it and our lines, their mortars at the same time throwing shells into the dense mass of our men in the crater and adjacent works.

In addition to this artillery fire, the enemy massed his infantry and assaulted the position. Although the assault was repulsed and some heroic fighting was done, particularly on the part of Potter's division and some regiments of the 18th corps, yet the exhaustion incident to the crowding of the men and the intense heat of the weather,

added to the destructive artillery fire of the enemy, produced its effect, and report was brought to me that our men were retiring into our old lines. Being satisfied the moment for success had passed, and that any further attempt would only result in useless sacrifice of life, with the concurrence of the lieutenant general commanding, who was present, I directed the suspension of further offensive movements, and the withdrawal of the troops in the crater when it could be done with security, retaining the position till night if necessary. It appears that when this order reached the crater, 12.20, the greater portion of those that had been in were out; the balance remained for an hour and a half repulsing an attack of the enemy, but on the enemy threatening a second attack, retreating in disorder, losing many prisoners. This terminated this most unfortunate and not very creditable operation.

THE ORDER TO WITHDRAW

 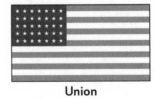

Union

Major-General Ambrose Burnside (See biography, page 122.)

Between half past nine and ten o'clock I received two despatches from General Meade with reference to withdrawal. I was very much concerned in reference to the matter, because, although we had met with some reverses, I could not help feeling myself that we could hold the position which we occupied, if we could not gain more ground. In fact I was under the impression at the time that we were gaining ground in the

direction of the enemy's rifle pits to the right and left, and I felt that if troops were put in on our left flank, that then we would have been enabled to establish ourselves on the enemy's line, which, of course, would have made our position secure. However, that is simply a matter of opinion, upon which the commanding general had to decide.

I also felt that if we could gain no more ground, we could run out lines at an angle to the crater, and establish a salient upon the enemy's lines, which would be of material advantage to us in future operations, particularly in making him vacate that part of the line which is now opposite my front, and in fact, as I had not given up all hopes of carrying the crest even, if a positive and decided effort were made by all the troops.

But feeling disinclined to withdraw the troops, I got on my horse and rode over to General Meade's headquarters, which were at my permanent headquarters. He and General Grant were there together. General Ord and I entered the tent, and General Meade questioned General Ord as to the practicability of his troops being withdrawn. I made the remark that none of General Ord's troops were in the enemy's line, and he would have no trouble in withdrawing; that none but the troops of the ninth corps were in the line, and I thought that my opinion on that subject would probably be a proper one to be received, and I stated that I did not think that we had fought long enough that day that I felt that the crest could still be carried if a decided effort were made to carry it. To that I received the reply that the order was final, or something to that effect.

This order, I consider, materially affected the result of our withdrawal, inasmuch as the enemy's forces upon our right and left were entirely unoccupied, and thereby had an opportunity of concentrating upon us during the withdrawal. It could hardly have been expected that the withdrawal could have been made without disaster after all offensive operations had ceased on the right and left, and the supporting force withdrawn from the rear. My only hope was that the force in the crater would be able to hold the position until a covered way could be dug from our advanced line out to the crater, a distance of a little over a hundred yards. This covered way had been commenced both in the crater, and on our advanced line, and I instructed General Ferrero to push it forward as rapidly as possible, with such of his troops as had been driven back and collected in the advanced line.

The communication between the advanced line and the crater was almost entirely cut off; and although the distance was so short, only about a hundred yards, it was next to an impossibility for messengers to reach the crater, much less to send in ammunition and water. The men had become very much exhausted with the heat and labors of the day.

> The sun was pouring its fiercest heat down upon us and our suffering wounded. No air was stirring within the crater. It was a sickening sight: men were dead and dying all around us; blood was streaming down the sides of the crater to the bottom, where it gathered in pools for a time before being absorbed by the hard red clay.
>
> —Brevet Major Charles Houghton

"THE SADDEST AFFAIR I HAVE WITNESSED"

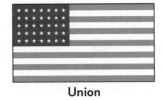

Union

General Ulysses S. Grant (See biography, page 54.)

City Point, Va., August 1, 1864
Major-General Halleck, Washington, D.C.

The loss in the disaster of Saturday last foots up about 3,500, of whom 450 men were killed and 2,000 wounded. It was the saddest affair I have witnessed in the war. Such opportunity for carrying fortifications I have never seen and do not expect again to have. The enemy with a line of works five miles long had been reduced by our previous movements to the north side of James River to a force of only three divisions. This line was undermined and blown up, carrying a battery and most of a regiment with it. The enemy were taken completely by surprise and did not recover from it for more than an hour.

The crater and several hundred yards of the enemy's line to the right and left of it and a short detached line in front of the crater were occupied by our troops without opposition. Immediately in front of this and not 150 yards off [in reality, 500 yards], with clear ground intervening, was the crest of the ridge leading into town, and which, if carried, the enemy would have made no resistance, but would have continued a flight already commenced. It was three hours from the time our troops first occupied their works before the enemy took possession of this crest. I am constrained to believe that had instructions been promptly obeyed that

Petersburg would have been carried with all the artillery and a large number of prisoners without a loss of 300 men. It was in getting back to our lines that the loss was sustained. The enemy attempted to charge and retake the line captured from them and were repulsed with heavy loss by our artillery; their loss in killed must be greater than ours, whilst our loss in wounded and captured is four times that of the enemy.

U. S. Grant, Lieutenant-General

Addenda
City Point, August 2, 1864—9.30 p.m.
Major-General Halleck, Chief of Staff:

I have the honor to request that the President may direct a court of inquiry, to assemble without delay at such place as the presiding officer may appoint, to examine into and report upon the facts and circumstances attending the unsuccessful assault on the enemy's position in front of Petersburg on the morning of July 30, 1864, and also to report whether, in their judgment, any officer or officers are censurable for the failure of the troops to carry into successful execution the orders issued for the occasion, and I would suggest the following detail: Maj. Gen. W. S. Hancock, Brig. Gen. E. B.

Ayres, Brig. Gen. N. A. Miles, Volunteer service: Col. E. Schriver, inspector-general and recorder.

U. S. Grant, Lieutenant-General

There was some delay about the explosion of the mine. When it did explode it was very successful. Instantly one hundred and ten cannon and fifty mortars, which had been placed in the most commanding positions, commenced playing. Ledlie's division marched into the crater immediately on the explosion, but most of the men stopped there in the absence of any one to give directions; their commander having found some safe retreat to get into before they started. There was some delay on the left and right in advancing, but some of the troops did get in and turn to the right and left, carrying the rifle-pits as I expected they would do.

There had been great consternation in Petersburg, as we were well aware, about a rumored mine that we were going to explode. They knew we were mining, and they had failed to cut our mine off by countermining, though Beauregard had taken the precaution to run up a line of intrenchments to the rear of that part of their line fronting where they could see that our men were at work. We had learned through deserters who had come in that the people had very wild rumors about what was going on on our side. They said that we had undermined the whole of Petersburg; that they were resting upon a slumbering volcano and did not know at what moment they might expect an eruption. I somewhat based my calculations upon this state of feeling, and expected that when the mine was exploded the troops to the right and left would flee in all directions, and that our troops, if they moved promptly, could get in and strengthen themselves before the enemy had come to a realization of the true situation.

It was just as I expected it would be. We could see the men running without any apparent object except to get away. It was half an hour before musketry firing, to amount to anything, was opened upon our men in the crater. It was an hour before the enemy got artillery up to play upon them; and it was nine o'clock before Lee got up reinforcements from his right to join in expelling our troops.

The effort was a stupendous failure. It cost us about four thousand men, mostly, however, captured; and all due to inefficiency on the part of the corps commander [Burnside] and the incompetency of the division commander [Brigadier-General Ledlie] who was sent to lead the assault.

I am satisfied that if the troops had been properly commanded, and been led in accordance with General Meade's order, we would have captured Petersburg with all the artillery and a good portion of its support, without the loss of 500 men. There was a full half hour, I think, when there was no fire against our men, and they could have marched past the enemy's intrenchments just as they could in the open country.

But that opportunity was lost in consequence of the division commanders not going with their men, but allowing them to go into the enemy's intrenchments and spread themselves there, without going on further, thus giving the enemy time to collect and organize against them.

I blame myself a little for one thing. General Meade made his orders most perfectly. I do not think that now, knowing all the facts, I could improve upon his order. But I was informed of this fact: that General Burnside, who was fully alive to the importance of this thing, trusted to the pulling of straws which division should lead. It happened to fall on what I thought was the worst commander in his corps. I knew that fact before the mine was exploded, but did nothing in regard to it. That is the only thing I blame myself for. I knew the man was the one that I considered the poorest division commander that General Burnside had—I mean General Ledlie.

If they had marched through to the crest of that ridge they would then have taken everything in rear. I do not think there would have been any opposition at all to our troops had that been done. I think we would have cut off entirely those of the enemy to our right, while those on the left would have tried to make their escape across the Appomattox.

General Burnside wanted to put his colored division in front, and I believe if he had done so it would have been a success. Still I agreed with General Meade in his objection to that plan. General Meade said that if we put the colored troops in front, (we had only that one division,) and it should prove a failure, it would then be said, and very properly, that we were shoving those people ahead to get killed because we did not care anything about them. But that could not be said if we put white troops in front. That is the only point General Meade changed after he had given his orders to General Burnside. It was then that General Burnside left his three division commanders to toss coppers or draw straws which should and which should not go in front.

THE COURT OF INQUIRY

Union

Major-General Winfield Scott Hancock (*See biography, page 116.*)

After losing the battle, Meade and Burnside blamed each other for the failure. The generals recommended by Grant conducted the court of inquiry ordered by President Lincoln, with Hancock presiding. After collecting testimony, reports, and dispatches from Grant on down, the court determined the following:

The causes of failure are:

1. The injudicious formation of the troops in going forward, the movement being mainly by flank instead of extended front. General Meade's order indicated that columns of assault should be employed to take Cemetery hill, and that proper passages should be prepared for those columns. It is the opinion of the court that there were no proper columns of assault. The troops should have been formed in the open ground in front of the point of attack parallel to the line of the enemy's works. The evidence shows that one or more columns might have passed over at, and to the left of the crater without any previous preparation of the ground.

2. The halting of the troops in the crater instead of going forward to the crest, when

there was no fire of any consequence from the enemy.

3. No proper employment of engineer officers and working parties, and of materials and tools for their use, in the 9th corps.

4. That some parts of the assaulting columns were not properly led.

5. The want of a competent common head at the scene of the assault, to direct affairs as occurrences should demand.[20]

Had not failure ensued from the above causes and the crest been gained, the success might have been jeoparded by the failure to have prepared in season proper and adequate debouches through the 9th corps' lines for troops, and especially for field artillery, as ordered by Major-General Meade.

The court further cited the failures of five officers, primarily Burnside, saying:

1. Major-General A. E. Burnside, United States volunteers, he having failed to obey the orders of the commanding general:

1. In not giving such formation to his assaulting column as to insure a reasonable prospect of success;

2. In not preparing his parapets and abatis for the passage of the columns of assault;

3. In not employing engineer officers who reported to him to lead the assaulting columns with working parties, and not causing to be provided proper materials necessary for crowning the crest when the assaulting columns should arrive there;

4. In neglecting to execute Major-General Meade's orders, respecting the prompt advance of General Ledlie's troops from the crater to the crest; or, in default of accomplishing that, not causing those troops to fall back and give place to other troops more willing and equal to the task, instead of delaying until the opportunity passed away, thus affording time for the enemy to recover from his surprise, concentrate his fire, and bring his troops to operate against the Union troops assembled uselessly in the crater.

Notwithstanding the failure to comply with orders, and to apply proper military principles, ascribed to General Burnside, the court is satisfied he believed that the measures taken by him would insure success.

Congress's Committee on the Conduct of the War investigated further, taking statements from and questioning many of the same witnesses, along with a few more. The committee included transcripts of Hancock's court in its record and placed all blame on Meade.

Your committee cannot, from all the testimony, avoid the conclusion that the first and great cause of disaster was the change made on the afternoon preceding the attack, in the arrangement of General Burnside to place the division of colored troops in the advance. The reasons assigned by General Burnside for not taking one of his divisions of white troops for that purpose are fully justified by the result of the attack. Their previous arduous labors, and peculiar position, exposed continually to the enemy's fire, had, as it were, trained them in the habit of seeking shelter; and, true to that training, they sought shelter the first opportunity that presented itself after leaving our lines. And it is but reasonable to suppose that

---

20 This is one of several condemnations of Meade, although he wasn't specifically named.

the immediate commander of a corps is better acquainted with the condition and efficiency of particular divisions of his corps than a general further removed from them.

The conduct of the colored troops, when they were put into action, would seem to fully justify the confidence that General Burnside reposed in them. And General Grant himself, in his testimony, expresses his belief that if they had been placed in the advance, as General Burnside desired, the assault would have been successful, although at the time the colored troops were ordered in the white troops already in were in confusion, and had failed in the assault upon the crest beyond the crater, and the fire of the enemy had become exceedingly destructive. The colored troops advanced in good order, passed through the enemy's lines and beyond our disorganized troops there, and, stopping but a short time to re-form, made the charge as directed. But the fire of the enemy was too strong, and some others of our troops hurrying back through their lines, they were thrown into confusion and forced to retire.

Your committee desire to say that, in the statement of facts and conclusions which they present in their report, they wish to be distinctly understood as in no degree censuring the conduct of the troops engaged in this assault.

In conclusion they, your committee, must say that, in their opinion, the cause of the disastrous result of the assault of the 30th of July last is mainly attributable to the fact that the plans and suggestions of the general who had devoted his attention for so long a time to the subject, who had carried out to a successful completion the project of mining the enemy's works, and who had carefully selected and drilled his troops for the purpose of securing whatever advantages might be attainable from the explosion of the mine, should have been so entirely disregarded by a general who had evinced no faith in the successful prosecution of that work, had aided it by no countenance or open approval, and had assumed the entire direction and control only when it was completed, and the time had come for reaping any advantages that might be derived from it.

Burnside was charged with not following orders and was relieved of duties. Meade never called him back up.

General Edward Ferrero (seated on the left) with his staff and a sentry at Petersburg in August 1864. Ferrero was the commander of a division of African-American soldiers.

SHERMAN'S MARCH TO THE SEA

ALSO KNOWN AS THE SAVANNAH CAMPAIGN IN GEORGIA
CENTRAL GEORGIA
NOVEMBER 15–DECEMBER 21, 1864

COMMANDERS

Union
Maj. Gen. William Tecumseh Sherman

Confederate
Gen. G. T. Beauregard
Lieut. Gen. William Hardee

PARTICIPANTS

62,000 (Army of the Tennessee and Army of Georgia)

15,000 (Department of South Carolina, Georgia, and Florida)

CASUALTIES

Union
103 killed
428 wounded
278 MIA

Confederate
At least 700 killed/wounded
1,338 POWs

VICTORY: UNION

OVERVIEW

Sherman's March to the Sea is famous and important, not because it represented a great battle, siege, or surrender, but because it applied a new strategy and had a clear psychological impact. From Sherman's point of view, compared to the rest of the war, it was a walk to the beach. He had very little opposition, and what little presented itself largely fell away before him.

The war was dragging on, and people were tired of it—most just wanted it to stop. Many in the North wanted to punish the South for all the lives lost. Grant was bogged down in a stalemate with Lee at Petersburg; Sheridan was in a similar situation with John Bell Hood at Atlanta; and Lincoln was pushing for decisive moves. Meanwhile, the South was getting desperate. Both the Union and the Confederacy were gradually introducing principles from the military doctrine of total war. Normally battles take place between soldiers, and both sides make efforts to keep civilians out of it. In total war the line blurs as one army tries to damage the infrastructure supporting the enemy.

Grant was already doing his best to cut Lee's supply lines by attacking the South's railroads. Sherman wanted to take it one step further and disrupt the farms and factories supplying the Confederate armies. He wanted to cripple the Confederacy's ability to fight.

Over the course of the war, the Confederates had launched several invasions of Maryland and Pennsylvania, threatening Washington, D.C., by passing through Virginia's Shenandoah Valley. Jubal Early did this in July 1864, coming within five miles of Lincoln's residence just outside the nation's capital. Putting a stop to this, Grant implemented a scorched-earth policy and authorized Major-General David Hunter and the Army of the Shenandoah to destroy what they could in the valley to deprive Early of food. In retaliation, Early tried to ransom Chambersburg, Pennsylvania, for $100,000 in gold or $500,000 in greenbacks. When the townspeople didn't pay, the Confederates set the town on fire, destroying more than 500 buildings—two-thirds of the town.

The presidential election was about to take place, and the Democrats had just nominated McClellan on an antiwar platform. Lincoln, his popularity waning, thought he was going to lose unless he landed a major Union victory. Sherman's four-month siege of Atlanta—a major freight hub where the Confederates also manufactured munitions and other military supplies—came to an end when Hood finally felt he could no longer hold the city. It was the victory Lincoln needed.

In Atlanta, before he left, Hood ordered his corps to destroy everything of use to the Union army. Sherman couldn't hold the city, so he continued the job, making it totally unusable to the Confederacy by setting it afire, avoiding churches and hospitals. Some 3,000 to 5,000 buildings burned, and only 400 survived.

Hood headed for Tennessee intending to attack Sherman's supply line, thereby drawing him away from Georgia—but it didn't work. Defying standard military principles, Sherman split his army, sending half under Major-General George Thomas to deal with Hood. Then, echoing Grant's abandonment of communication and supply lines when he laid siege to Vicksburg, Sherman did the same, heading away from Hood toward Savannah.

Sherman's primary mission was to destroy the railroad, but without a supply line he also needed to feed his army. Dividing his army into four columns and spreading out—with up to twenty miles between columns—he had his men fan out further, gathering all the food, wagons, and livestock they could and destroying what they couldn't take. Other crews destroyed railroad tracks. They marched along at a comfortable pace until they reached Savannah, cutting a 66-mile-wide and 285-mile-long swath of destruction through the heart of Georgia, showing that nowhere in the South was safe from the ravages of the war.

The march had a tremendous psychological effect in the North and South, in opposite ways, which was completely unexpected to both Sherman and Grant, who saw the move as the destruction of another railroad. It cemented Sherman's reputation as a hero in the North and a devil in the South. Many Southerners despise him to this day.

Lieutenant-General William Hardee—author of the textbook on military tactics at West Point and at the Virginia Military Institute—led the Confederate force remaining in Georgia after Hood's departure. After Chickamauga, Hardee helped talk Davis into replacing Bragg. Although

Davis disliked Joseph Johnston, he placed him at the head of Bragg's army to defend Georgia against Sherman. Then, deciding that Johnston's methods of maneuvering, establishing defenses, and pulling back weren't aggressive enough, Davis replaced Johnston with Hood. Hardee thought Hood too reckless and asked Davis for a transfer, which is how he ended up in Savannah facing Sherman.

The Confederacy's strength was failing, and most of its men were serving with Hood, headed for Tennessee. With only about 15,000 men against Sherman's 62,000, Hardee couldn't do much. His cavalry skirmished around the edge of Sherman's army, while others tried to slow him down by destroying bridges, cutting down trees to block roads, and burning what might be of use to Sherman. It did little to deter him.

"MAKING GEORGIA HOWL"

Union

General William Tecumseh Sherman (See biography, page 4.)

More than a month before Sherman began his march, he wrote this dispatch outlining his intentions:

Hdqrs. Military Division of the Mississippi, In the Field, Allatoona, Ga., October 9, 1864
Lieutenant-General Grant, City Point, Va.:

It will be a physical impossibility to protect the roads, now that Hood, Forrest, and Wheeler, and the whole batch of devils, are turned loose without home or habitation. I think Hood's movements indicate a diversion to the end of the Selma and Talladega Railroad at Blue Mountain, about sixty miles southwest of Rome, from which he will threaten Kingston, Bridgeport, and Decatur, Ala. I propose we break up the railroad from Chattanooga, and strike out with wagons for Milledgeville, Millen, and Savannah.

Until we can repopulate Georgia, it is useless to occupy it, but the utter destruction of its roads, houses, and people will cripple their military resources. By attempting to hold the roads we will lose 1,000 men monthly, and will gain no result. I can make the march, and make Georgia howl. We have over 8,000 cattle and 3,000,000 of bread, but no corn; but we can forage in the interior of the State.

W. T. Sherman, Major-General,
Commanding

GENERAL JOHNSTON, GENERAL HOOD

Union

General Ulysses S. Grant (*See biography, page 54.*)

Here Grant explained the situation that led to the march, along with the different tactics used by Johnston and adopted-Texan John Bell Hood.

The possession of Atlanta by us narrowed the territory of the enemy very materially and cut off one of his two remaining lines of roads from east to west.

A short time after the fall of Atlanta Mr. Davis visited Palmetto and Macon and made speeches at each place. He spoke at Palmetto on the 20th of September, and at Macon on the 22d. Inasmuch as he had relieved Johnston and appointed Hood, and Hood had immediately taken the initiative, it is natural to suppose that Mr. Davis was disappointed with General Johnston's policy.

My own judgment is that Johnston acted very wisely: he husbanded his men and saved as much of his territory as he could, without fighting decisive battles in which all might be lost. As Sherman advanced [toward Atlanta], his army became spread out, until, if this had been continued, it would have been easy to destroy it in detail. I know that both Sherman and I were rejoiced when we heard of the change. Hood was unquestionably a brave, gallant soldier and not destitute of ability; but unfortunately his policy was to fight the enemy

wherever he saw him, without thinking much of the consequences of defeat.

In his speeches Mr. Davis denounced General Johnston in unmeasured terms, even insinuating that their loyalty to the Southern cause was doubtful. I think Davis did him a great injustice in this particular. I had known the general before the war and strongly believed it would be impossible for him to accept a high commission for the purpose of betraying the cause he had espoused.

Then, as I have said, I think that his policy was the best one that could have been pursued by the whole South—protract the war, which was all that was necessary to enable them to gain recognition in the end. The North was already growing weary, as the South evidently was also, but with this difference. In the North the people governed, and could stop hostilities whenever they chose to stop supplies. The South was a military camp, controlled absolutely by the government with soldiers to back it, and the war could have been protracted, no matter to what extent the discontent reached, up to the point of open mutiny of the soldiers themselves.

Mr. Davis's speeches were frank appeals to the people of Georgia and that portion of the South to come to their relief. He tried to assure his frightened hearers that the Yankees [Sherman's men] were rapidly digging their own graves; that measures were already being taken to cut them off [by Hood] from supplies from the North; and that with a force in front, and cut off from the rear, they must soon starve in the midst of a hostile people.

When Hood was forced to retreat from Atlanta he moved to the south-west and was followed by a portion of Sherman's army. He soon appeared upon the railroad in Sherman's rear, and with his whole army began destroying the road. At the same time also the work was begun in Tennessee and Kentucky. He ordered Forrest (about the ablest cavalry general in the South) north for this purpose; and Forrest and Wheeler carried out their orders with more or less destruction, occasionally picking up a garrison. Forrest indeed performed the very remarkable feat of capturing, with cavalry, two gunboats and a number of transports, something the accomplishment of which is very hard to account for.

Sherman was obliged to push on with his force and go himself with portions of it hither and thither, until it was clearly demonstrated to him that with the army he then had it would be impossible to hold the line from Atlanta back and leave him any force whatever with which to take the offensive. Had that plan been adhered to, very large reinforcements would have been necessary.

Hood had about thirty-five to forty thousand men, independent of Forrest, whose forces were operating in Tennessee and Kentucky, as Mr. Davis had promised they should. This part of Mr. Davis's military plan was admirable, and promised the best results of anything he could have done, according to my judgment.

About this time Beauregard arrived upon the field, not to supersede Hood in command, but to take general charge over the entire district in which Hood and Sherman were, or might be, operating. He made the most frantic appeals to the citizens for assistance to be rendered in every way: by sending reinforcements, by destroying supplies on the line of march of the invaders, by destroying the bridges over which they would have to cross, and by, in every way, obstructing the roads to their front. But it was hard to convince the people of the propriety of destroying supplies which were so much needed by themselves, and each one hoped that his own possessions might escape.

Atlanta was destroyed so far as to render it worthless for military purposes before starting, Sherman himself remaining over a day to superintend the work, and see that it was well done. Sherman's orders for this campaign were perfect. Before starting, he had sent back all sick, disabled and weak men, retaining nothing but the hardy, well-inured soldiers to accompany him on his long march in prospect. His artillery was reduced to sixty-five guns. The ammunition carried with them was two hundred rounds for musket and gun. Small rations were taken in a small wagon train, which was loaded to its capacity for rapid movement. The army was expected to live on the country, and to always keep the wagons full of forage and provisions against a possible delay of a few days.

A "WILD ADVENTURE"

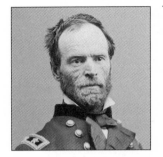

Union

General William Tecumseh Sherman (See biography, page 4.)

Sherman's general orders for the campaign specified these rules for foraging:

IV. The army will forage liberally on the country during the march. To this end, each brigade commander will organize a good and sufficient foraging party, under the command of one or more discreet officers, who will gather, near the route traveled, corn or forage of any kind, meat of any kind, vegetables, corn-meal, or whatever is needed by the command, aiming at all times to keep in the wagons at least ten days' provisions for the command and three days' forage [for animals]. Soldiers must not enter the dwellings of the inhabitants, or commit any trespass, but during a halt or a camp they may be permitted to gather turnips, potatoes, and other vegetables, and to drive in stock in sight of their camp. To regular foraging parties must be intrusted the gathering of provisions and forage at any distance from the road traveled.

V. To army corps commanders alone is intrusted the power to destroy mills, houses, cotton-gins, &c., and for them this general principle is laid down: In districts and neighborhoods where the army is unmolested no destruction of such property should be permitted; but should guerrillas or bushwhackers molest our march, or should the inhabitants burn bridges, obstruct

roads, or otherwise manifest local hostility, then army commanders should order and enforce a devastation more or less relentless according to the measure of such hostility.

VI. As for horses, mules, wagons, &c., belonging to the inhabitants, the cavalry and artillery may appropriate freely and without limit, discriminating, however, between the rich, who are usually hostile, and the poor or industrious, usually neutral or friendly. Foraging parties may also take mules or horses to replace the jaded animals of their trains, or to serve as pack-mules for the regiments or brigades. In all foraging, of whatever kind, the parties engaged will refrain from abusive or threatening language, and may, where the officer in command thinks proper, give written certificates of the facts, but no receipts, and they will endeavor to leave with each family a reasonable portion for their maintenance.

Sherman described the beginning of his famous march:

It surely was a strange event—two hostile armies [Sherman's and Hood's] marching in opposite directions, each in the full belief that it was achieving a final and conclusive result in a great war; and I was strongly inspired with the feeling that the movement on our part was a direct attack upon the rebel army and the rebel capital at Richmond, though a full thousand miles of hostile country intervened, and that, for better or worse, it would end the war.

I reached Atlanta during the afternoon of the 14th [of November, 1864], and found that all preparations had been made—Colonel Beckwith, chief commissary, reporting one million two hundred thousand rations in possession of the troops, which was about twenty days' supply, and he had on hand a good supply of beef-cattle to be driven along on the hoof. Of forage, the supply was limited, being of oats and corn enough for five days, but I knew that within that time we would reach a country well stocked with corn, which had been gathered and stored in cribs, seemingly for our use, by Governor Brown's militia.

> Our armies are devastating the land, and it is sad to see the destruction that attends our progress—we cannot help it. Farms disappear, houses are burned and plundered, and every living animal killed and eaten. General officers make feeble efforts to stay the disorder, but it is idle.
>
> —MAJOR-GENERAL SHERMAN IN A LETTER TO HIS BROTHER, SENATOR JOHN SHERMAN, ON JANUARY 25, 1863, ALMOST TWO YEARS BEFORE HIS MARCH TO THE SEA

Colonel Poe, United States Engineers, of my staff, had been busy in his special task of destruction [of Atlanta]. He had a large force at work, had leveled the great depot, round-house, and the machine-shops of the Georgia Railroad, and had applied fire to the wreck. One of these machine-shops had been used by the rebels as an arsenal, and in it were stored piles of shot and shell, some of which proved to be loaded, and that night was made hideous by the bursting of shells, whose fragments came uncomfortably near Judge Lyon's house, in which I was quartered.

> I know that in Washington I am incomprehensible because at the outset of the war I would not go it blind and rush headlong into a war unprepared and with an utter ignorance of its extent and purpose. I was then construed unsound; and now that I insist on war pure and simple, with no admixture of civil compromises, I am supposed vindictive.
>
> —GENERAL WILLIAM TECUMSEH SHERMAN

The fire also reached the block of stores near the depot, and the heart of the city was in flames all night, but the fire did not reach the parts of Atlanta where the court-house was, or the great mass of dwelling-houses.

About 7 a.m. of November 16th we rode out of Atlanta by the Decatur road and reaching the hill, just outside of the old rebel works, we naturally paused to look back upon the scenes of our past battles. We stood upon the very ground whereon was fought the bloody battle of July 22d, and could see the copse of wood where McPherson fell. Behind us lay Atlanta, smouldering and in ruins, the black smoke rising high in air, and hanging like a pall over the ruined city. Away off in the distance, on the McDonough road, was the rear of Howard's column, the gun-barrels glistening in the sun, the white-topped wagons stretching away to the south; and right before us the Fourteenth Corps, marching steadily and rapidly, with a cheery look and swinging pace.

There was a "devil-may-care" feeling pervading officers and men, that made me feel the full load of responsibility, for success would be accepted as a matter of course, whereas, should we fail, this "march" would be adjudged the wild adventure of a crazy fool.

The first night out we camped by the road-side near Lithonia. Stone Mountain, a mass of granite, was in plain view, cut out in clear outline against the blue sky[21]; the whole horizon was lurid with the bonfires of rail-ties, and groups of men all night were carrying the heated rails to the nearest trees, and bending them around the trunks. The best and easiest way is the one I have described, of heating the middle of the iron-rails on bonfires made of the cross-ties, and then winding them around a telegraph-pole or the trunk of some convenient sapling.[22]

---

21 This became the South's version of Mt. Rushmore, with the carved images of Davis, Lee, and Stonewall Jackson on horseback.

22 These twisted rails became known as "Sherman's neckties."

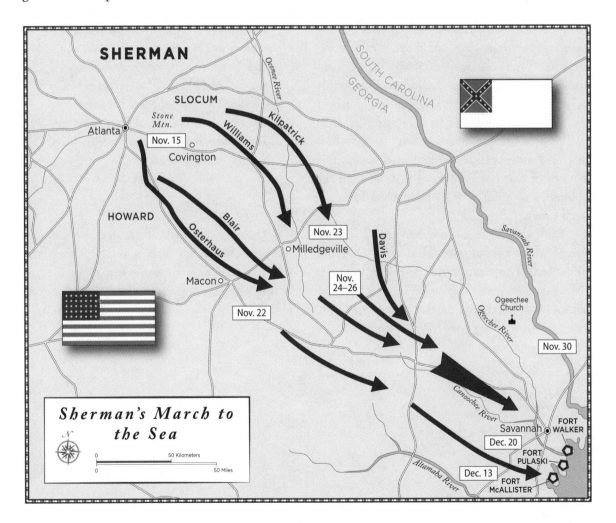

Sherman's March to the Sea

The next day we passed through the handsome town of Covington, the soldiers closing up their ranks, the color-bearers unfurling their flags, and the bands striking up patriotic airs. The white people came out of their houses to behold the sight, in spite of their deep hatred of the invaders, and the negroes were simply frantic with joy.

The skill and success of the men in collecting forage was one of the features of this march. Each brigade commander had authority to detail a company of foragers, usually about fifty men, with one or two commissioned officers selected for their boldness and enterprise. This party would proceed on foot five or six miles from the route traveled by their brigade, and then visit every plantation and farm within range. They would usually procure a wagon or family carriage, load it with bacon, corn-meal, turkeys, chickens, ducks, and every thing that could be used as food or forage, and would deliver to the brigade commissary the supplies thus gathered by the way. Although this foraging was attended with great danger and hard work, there seemed to be a charm about it that attracted the soldiers, and it was a privilege to be detailed on such a party.

Daily they returned mounted on all sorts of beasts, which were at once taken from them and appropriated to the general use; but the next day they would start out again on foot, only to repeat the experience of the day before. No doubt, many acts of pillage, robbery, and violence, were committed by these parties of foragers, usually called "bummers"; for I have since heard of jewelry taken from women, and the plunder of articles that never reached the commissary; but these acts were exceptional and incidental. I never heard of any cases of murder or rape.

> The people at the South became so frantic at this time at the successful invasion of Georgia that they even liberated the State convicts under promise from them that they would serve in the army. I have but little doubt that the worst acts that were attributed to Sherman's army were committed by these convicts, and by other Southern people who ought to have been under sentence—such people as could be found in every community, North and South—who took advantage of their country being invaded to commit crime. They were in but little danger of detection, or of arrest even if detected.
>
> —GENERAL ULYSSES S. GRANT

This system of foraging was simply indispensable to our success. By it our men were well supplied with all the essentials of life and health, while the wagons retained enough in case of unexpected delay, and our animals were well fed.

Trying to Stop Sherman

Confederate

General G. T. Beauregard (See biography, page 19.)

Everyone feared Sherman might be heading for them, while of course Sherman tried to mask his intentions. Besieged by calls for help and advice from all over his district, Beauregard headed to see Bragg in Augusta, and then intended to go to Savannah to see Hardee, and to continue on to Charleston.

Augusta, Ga., Dec. 6th, 1864
To his Excellency Jefferson Davis, President of the Confederate States:

Sir: Your letter of the 30th, acknowledging the receipt of my telegram of the 24th of November, was received by me on the road from Macon to this place.

With the limited reliable means at our command I believe that all that could be has been done, under existing circumstances, to oppose the advance of Sherman's forces towards the Atlantic coast. That we have not, thus far, been more successful, none can regret more than myself, but he will doubtless be prevented from capturing Augusta, Charleston, and Savannah, and he may yet be made to experience serious loss before reaching the coast.

I telegraphed to Lieutenant-General Taylor, at Selma, Ala., to call on Governor Watts, of Alabama, and Governor Clarke, of Mississippi, for all the State troops that they could furnish. I also telegraphed to General Cobb to call upon Governor Brown, of Georgia, and Governor Bonham, of South Carolina, for all the State troops that could be collected.[23]

> If the roads that General Sherman must travel to get to Charleston or Savannah can be thoroughly ploughed and the trees felled over them, I think that General Sherman will not be able to get to his destination in fifty days, as the Northern papers expect; and it is not thought to be possible that he can collect more than fifty days' rations before reaching the coast. If the parties are properly organized, I think that they might destroy or injure all of the roads so as to break down General Sherman's animals, and result in the capture of most of his forces.
>
> —Lieutenant-General Longstreet to General Lee on November 24, 1864

On my arrival at Corinth, on the 18th of November, having been informed that Sherman had commenced his movement, I issued all necessary orders to meet the emergency, including

---

23 These militias consisted primarily of the elderly and boys. Most men between the ages of seventeen and fifty had already been drafted into the Confederate army.

an order to General Hood to send one division of cavalry (Jackson's) to reinforce Wheeler; but this order was suspended by him, his objection being that his cavalry could not be reduced without endangering the success of his campaign in Tennessee, and that General Wheeler already had thirteen brigades under his command. I finally instructed him to send only one brigade, if he contemplated taking the offensive at once, as already had been decided upon. I then left Corinth for Macon, where I arrived on the 24th of November.

In October last, when passing through Georgia to assume command of the Military Division of the West, I was informed by Governor Brown that he could probably raise, in case of necessity, about six thousand men, which, I supposed, might be doubled in a levy en masse.

General Cobb informed me at the same time that at Augusta, Macon, and Columbus he had about six thousand five hundred local troops, and that he hoped shortly to have collected at his reserve and convalescent camps, near Macon, two thousand five hundred more. Of these nine thousand men he supposed about one-half, or five thousand, could be made available as movable troops for an emergency.

To oppose the advance of the enemy from Atlanta the State of Georgia would thus have probably seventeen thousand men, to which number must be added the thirteen brigades of Wheeler's cavalry, amounting to about seven thousand men. The troops which could have been collected from Savannah, South Carolina, and North Carolina, before Sherman's forces could reach the Atlantic coast, would have amounted, it was supposed, to about five thousand men.

Thus, it was a reasonable supposition that about twenty-nine or thirty thousand men could be collected in time to defend the State of Georgia, and insure the destruction of Sherman's army, estimated by me at about thirty-six thousand effectives of all arms, their cavalry, about four thousand strong, being included in this estimate.

Under these circumstances, after consultation with General Hood, I concluded to allow him to prosecute with vigor his campaign into Tennessee and Kentucky, hoping that by defeating Thomas's army and such other forces as might hastily be sent against him he would compel Sherman, should he reach the coast of Georgia or South Carolina, to repair at once to the defence of Kentucky, and perhaps Ohio, and thus prevent him from reinforcing Grant. Meanwhile, supplies might be sent to Virginia from Middle and East Tennessee, thus relieving Georgia from the present constant drain upon its limited resources.

I remain, very respectfully, your obedient servant,

G. T. Beauregard, General

JOURNEY TO THE SEA

Union

General William Tecumseh Sherman (See biography, page 4.)

Sherman soon arrived at Milledgeville, at that time the capital of Georgia.

Orders were made for the total destruction of the arsenal and its contents, and of such public buildings as could be easily converted to hostile uses. But little or no damage was done to private property, and General Slocum, with my approval, spared several mills, and many thousands of bales of cotton, taking what he knew to be worthless bonds that the cotton should not be used for the Confederacy. Meantime the right wing continued its movement along the railroad toward Savannah, tearing up the track and destroying its iron.

General Wheeler, with his division of rebel cavalry, had succeeded in getting ahead of us between Milledgeville and Augusta; and General W. J. Hardee had been dispatched by General Beauregard from Hood's army to oppose our progress directly in front. He had, however, brought with him no troops, but relied on his influence with the Georgians (of whose State he was a native) to arouse the people, and with them to annihilate Sherman's army!

On the 24th we renewed the march, and I accompanied the Twentieth Corps, which took the direct road to Sandersville, which we reached simultaneously with the Fourteenth Corps, on the 26th. A brigade of rebel cavalry was deployed

before the town, and was driven in and through it by our skirmishline. I myself saw the rebel cavalry apply fire to stacks of fodder standing in the fields at Sandersville, and gave orders to burn some unoccupied dwellings close by. On entering the town, I told certain citizens (who would be sure to spread the report) that, if the enemy attempted to carry out their threat to burn their food, corn, and fodder, in our route, I would most undoubtedly execute to the letter the general orders of devastation made at the outset of the campaign. With this exception, and one or two minor cases near Savannah, the people did not destroy food, for they saw clearly that it would be ruin to themselves.

On the 5th of December, I reached Ogeechee Church, about fifty miles from Savannah, and found there fresh earthworks, which had been thrown up by [Confederate Major-General Lafayette] McLaws' division; but he must have seen that both his flanks were being turned, and prudently retreated to Savannah without a fight.[24]

All the columns then pursued leisurely their march toward Savannah, corn and forage

---

24 After Longstreet relieved McLaws of his command, McLaws was transferred to fight Sherman in Georgia.

becoming more and more scarce, but rice-fields beginning to occur along the Savannah and Ogeechee Rivers, which proved a good substitute, both as food and forage.

The weather was fine, the roads good, and every thing seemed to favor us. Never do I recall a more agreeable sensation than the sight of our camps by night, lit up by the fires of fragrant pine-knots. The trains were all in good order, and the men seemed to march their fifteen miles a day as though it were nothing. No enemy opposed us, and we could only occasionally hear the faint reverberation of a gun to our left rear, where we knew that General Kilpatrick was skirmishing with Wheeler's cavalry, which persistently followed him. But the infantry columns had met with no opposition whatsoever.

On the 8th, as I rode along, I found the column turned out of the main road, marching through the fields. Close by, in the corner of a fence, was a group of men standing around a handsome young officer, whose foot had been blown to pieces by a torpedo [land mine] planted in the road. He was waiting for a surgeon to amputate his leg, and told me that he was riding along with the rest of his brigade-staff of the Seventeenth Corps, when a torpedo trodden on by his horse had exploded, killing the horse and literally blowing off all the flesh from one of his legs. I saw the terrible wound, and made full inquiry into the facts.

There had been no resistance at that point, nothing to give warning of danger, and the rebels had planted eight-inch shells in the road, with friction-matches to explode them by being trodden on. This was not war, but murder, and it made me very angry. I immediately ordered a lot of rebel prisoners to be brought from the provost-guard, armed with picks and spades, and made them march in close order along the road, so as to explode their own torpedoes, or to discover and dig them up. They begged hard, but I reiterated the order, and could hardly help laughing at their stepping so gingerly along the road, where it was supposed sunken torpedoes might explode at each step, but they found no other torpedoes till near Fort McAllister.

During the next two days, December 9th and 10th, the several corps reached the defenses of Savannah, completely investing the city. Wishing to reconnoitre the place in person, I rode forward by the Louisville road, into a dense wood of oak, pine, and cypress, left the horses, and walked down to the railroad-track, at a place where there was a side-track, and a cut about four feet deep.

From that point the railroad was straight, leading into Savannah, and about eight hundred yards off were a rebel parapet and battery. I could see the cannoneers preparing to fire, and cautioned the officers near me to scatter, as we would likely attract a shot. Very soon I saw the white puff of smoke, and, watching close, caught sight of the ball as it rose in its flight, and, finding it coming pretty straight, I stepped a short distance to one side, but noticed a negro very near me in the act of crossing the track at right angles. Some one called to him to look out; but, before the poor fellow understood his danger, the ball (a thirty-two-pound round shot) struck the ground, and rose in its first ricochet, caught the negro under the right jaw, and literally carried away his head, scattering blood and brains about.

A soldier close by spread an overcoat over the body, and we all concluded to get out of that railroad-cut.

I gave General [William] Hazen, in person, his orders to march rapidly down the right bank of the Ogeechee, and without hesitation to assault and carry Fort McAllister by storm. I knew it to be strong in heavy artillery, as against an approach from the sea, but believed it open and weak to the rear. I explained to General Hazen, fully, that on his action depended the safety of the whole army, and the success of the campaign. The Second of the Fifteenth Corps [was] the same old division which I had commanded at Shiloh and Vicksburg, in which I felt a special pride and confidence.

Fort McAllister had the rebel flag flying, and occasionally sent a heavy shot back across the marsh to where we were, but otherwise every thing about the place looked as peaceable and quiet as on the Sabbath.

I expected the fort to be carried before night, I received by signal the assurance of General Hazen that he was making his preparations, and would soon attempt the assault. The sun was rapidly declining, and I was dreadfully impatient. At that very moment some one discovered a faint cloud of smoke, and an object gliding, as it were, along the horizon above the tops of the sedge toward the sea, which little by little grew till it was pronounced to be the smoke-stack of a steamer coming up the river. "It must be one of our squadron!" Soon the

flag of the United States was plainly visible, and our attention was divided between this approaching steamer and the expected assault.

When the sun was about an hour high, another signal-message came from General Hazen that he was all ready, and I replied to go ahead, as a friendly steamer was approaching from below.

Soon we made out a group of officers on the deck of this vessel, signaling with a flag, "Who are you?"

The answer went back promptly, "General Sherman."

Then followed the question, "Is Fort McAllister taken?"

"Not yet, but it will be in a minute!"

Almost at that instant of time, we saw Hazen's troops come out of the dark fringe of woods that encompassed the fort, the lines dressed as on parade, with colors flying, and moving forward with a quick, steady pace. Fort McAllister was then all alive, its big guns belching forth dense clouds of smoke, which soon enveloped our assaulting

This is what Sherman's men saw as they charged to capture Fort McAllister. This photograph was taken in mid-December 1864.

line. One color went down, but was up in a moment. On the lines advanced, faintly seen in the white, sulphurous smoke; there was a pause, a cessation of fire; the smoke cleared away, and the parapets were blue with our men, who fired their muskets in the air, and shouted so that we actually heard them, or felt that we did. Fort McAllister was taken, and the good news was instantly sent by the signal-officer to our navy friends on the approaching gunboat.

After supper, we all walked down to the fort, nearly a mile from the house where we had been, entered Fort McAllister, held by a regiment of Hazen's troops, and the sentinel cautioned us to be very careful, as the ground outside the fort was full of torpedoes.

Indeed, while we were there, a torpedo exploded, tearing to pieces a poor fellow who was hunting for a dead comrade. Inside the fort lay the dead as they had fallen, and they could hardly be distinguished from their living comrades, sleeping soundly side by side in the pale moonlight.

Sherman turned his attention to Savannah, held by Hardee and approximately 10,000 soldiers. Greatly outnumbered, Hardee had Sherman's army on three sides except to the east, and the town had about 25,000 citizens that had to be fed. Grant wanted Sherman to help him with the continuing siege of Petersburg, so if Sherman was going to take Savannah, he had to do it quickly.

Sherman sent Hardee the following note:

A view of Fort McAllister in December 1864. Sherman's men finished dismantling and destroying the fort on December 29, before heading north to the Carolinas.

In the Field, near Savannah, Dec. 17th, 1864
General William J. Hardee, Comdg. Confederate Forces in Savannah, Ga.:

General, You have doubtless observed from your status at Roseden that sea-going vessels now come through Ossabaw Sound and up Ogeechee to the rear of my army, giving me abundant supplies of all kinds, and more especially heavy ordnance, necessary to the reduction of Savannah. I have already received guns that can cast heavy and destructive shot as far as the heart of the city. Also, I have for some days held and controlled every avenue by which the people and garrison of Savannah can be supplied.

I am therefore justified in demanding the surrender of Savannah and its dependent forts, and shall wait a reasonable time your answer before opening with heavy ordnance.

Should you entertain the proposition, I am prepared to grant liberal terms to the inhabitants and garrison. But should I be forced to resort to assault, or to the slower and surer process of starvation, I shall then feel justified in resorting to the harshest measures, and shall make little effort to restrain my army, burning to avenge a great national wrong they attach to Savannah and other large cities which have been so prominent in dragging our country into civil war. I enclose you a copy of General Hood's demand for the surrender of the town of Resaca, Ga., to be used by you for what it is worth.

I have the honor to be, your obedient servant, W. T. Sherman, Major-General, U. S. A.

Hood's demand at Resaca said, "If the place is carried by assault, no prisoners will be taken."
Hardee responded:

Headquarters, Departments S. C., Ga., and Fla.,
Savannah, Ga., Dec. 17th, 1864
Major-Genl. W. T. Sherman, Comdg. Federal Forces near Savannah, Ga.:

General, I have to acknowledge receipt of a communication from you of this date, in which you demand "the surrender of Savannah and its dependent forts," on the ground that you "have received guns that can cast heavy and destructive shot into the heart of the city," and for the further reason that you have, "for some days, held and controlled every avenue by which the people and garrison can be supplied." You add, that should you be "forced to resort to assault, or to the slower and surer process of starvation, you will then feel justified in resorting to the harshest measures, and will make little effort to restrain your army," etc., etc.

The position of your forces, a half-mile beyond the outer line for the land defence of Savannah, is, at the nearest point, at least four miles from the heart of the city.[25] That and the interior line are both intact.

Your statement that you have for some days held and controlled every avenue by which the people and garrison can be supplied is incorrect. I am in free and in constant communication with my Department.[26]

Your demand for the surrender of Savannah and its dependent forts is refused.

With respect to the threats conveyed in the closing paragraphs of your letter of what may be expected in case your demand is not complied with, I have to say that I have hitherto conducted

---

25 It was actually three miles.

26 He wasn't.

the military operations intrusted to my direction in strict accordance with the rules of civilized warfare, and I should deeply regret the adoption of any course by you that may force me to deviate from them in future.

I have the honor to be, very respectfully, your obdt. servt.,

W. J. Hardee, Lieut.-General

During the night Hardee and his men sneaked out of the city on the east side and escaped through the swamps.

Sherman wrote in his official report:

I was very much disappointed that Hardee had escaped with his garrison, and had to content myself with the material fruits of victory without the cost of life which would have attended a general assault. Suffice here to state that the important city of Savannah, with its valuable harbor and river, was the chief object of the campaign. With it we acquire all the forts and heavy ordnance in its vicinity, with large stores of ammunition, shot and shells, cotton, rice, and other valuable products of the country. We also gain locomotives and cars, which, though of little use to us in the present condition of the railroads, are a serious loss to the enemy; as well as four steam-boats gained, and the loss to the enemy of the iron-clad Savannah, one ram, and three transports, blown up or burned by them the night before.

Formal demand having been made for the surrender, and having been refused, I contend that everything within the line of intrenchments belongs to the United States, and I shall not hesitate to use it, if necessary, for public purposes. But inasmuch as the inhabitants generally have manifested a friendly disposition, I shall disturb them as little as possible.

Our former labors in North Georgia had demonstrated the truth that no large army, carrying with it the necessary stores and baggage, can overtake and capture an inferior force of the enemy in his own country. Therefore no alternative was left me but the one I adopted—namely, to divide my forces, and with the one part act offensively against the enemy's resources, while with the other I should act defensively, and invite the enemy to attack, risking the chances of battle. In this conclusion I have been singularly sustained by the results. General Hood, who had moved to the westward near Tuscumbia [in Alabama], with a view to decoy me away from Georgia, finding himself mistaken, was forced to choose either to pursue me, or to act offensively against the other part left in Tennessee. He adopted the latter course; and General Thomas has wisely and well fulfilled his part of the grand scheme in drawing Hood well up into Tennessee until he could concentrate all his own troops and then turn upon Hood, as he has done, and destroy or fatally cripple his army.

I was thereby left with a well-appointed army to sever the enemy's only remaining railroad communications eastward and westward, for over 100 miles. We have also consumed the corn and fodder in the region of country thirty miles on either side of a line from Atlanta to Savannah, as also the sweet potatoes, cattle, hogs, sheep and poultry, and have carried away more than 10,000 horses and mules, as well as a countless number of their slaves. I estimate the damage done to the State of Georgia and its military resources at $100,000,000; at least, $20,000,000 of which has inured to our advantage, and the remainder is simple waste and destruction. This may seem a hard species of warfare, but it brings the sad realities of war home to those who have been directly or indirectly instrumental in involving us in its attendant calamities.

Here terminated the "March to the Sea". I only regarded the march from Atlanta to Savannah as a "shift of base," as the transfer of a strong army, which had no opponent, and had finished its then work, from the interior to a point on the sea-coast, from which it could achieve other important results. I considered this march as a means to an end, and not as an essential act of war. Still, then, as now, the march to the sea was generally regarded as something extraordinary, something anomalous, something out of the usual order of events; whereas, in fact, I simply moved from Atlanta to Savannah, as one step in the direction of Richmond, a movement that had to be met and defeated, or the war was necessarily at an end.

After Sherman captured Fort McAllister, he received his mail from the navy, and one of the letters from Grant ordered him to move his army by ships to Petersburg to assist in the siege. When Grant heard that Sherman had captured Savannah, he realized what a huge impact Sherman's march had had and gave him free rein to do whatever he wanted. Sherman chose to continue marching up through the Carolinas.

> Hardee reported the Salkehatchie swamps [in South Carolina] as absolutely impassable; but when I heard that Sherman was marching through those very swamps at the rate of thirteen miles a day, making corduroy road every foot of the way, I made up my mind there had been no such army since the days of Julius Caesar.
>
> —General Joseph Johnston, quoted in the New York Times after the war

INNOVATIVE WEAPONS

Armaments evolved rapidly throughout the war. At its start many soldiers were armed with muskets. Rifles replaced these, their grooved barrels causing the bullet to spin, increasing accuracy and giving them a longer range, making them effective at more than half a mile. Carbines, with their shorter barrels, weren't as accurate at longer ranges, but they proved easier to handle in combat situations. Minié balls—not balls at all but shaped like modern bullets—made small-arms fire deadlier. Heavy artillery also improved. Breechloaders replaced muzzle-loaders, increasing the rate of fire.

The Spencer repeating rifle had a magazine, allowing it to be reloaded by cocking a lever, particularly useful for the cavalry. It could fire its seven rounds in twenty-one seconds. Two of Custer's cavalry regiments field-tested the rifle at the Battle of Gettysburg. Custer wrote in his official report that the Spencer repeating rifle, "in the hands of brave, determined men ... is, in my estimation, the most effective fire-arm that our cavalry can adopt." The sixteen-round, lever-action Henry repeating rifle also proved popular—although the men had to buy their own since it wasn't issued by the army.

The Agar gun, probably the first machine gun used in action, was called the "coffee mill gun" because of its hand crank and hopper that gravity-fed cartridges into the top of the gun. Several were used at the Battle of Gaines' Mill in June 1862. The Gatling gun was similar but only saw limited use near the end of the war on gunboats and at Petersburg in 1864. It was hand-cranked with a hopper and six revolving barrels to help keep it cool. It could fire 600 rounds a minute, making wholesale slaughter easy and efficient.

Both sides tested new weapons to give them an advantage. Grant wrote of a new Confederate weapon tested at Vicksburg: "The enemy used in their defence explosive musket-balls, no doubt thinking that, bursting over our men in the trenches, they would do some execution; but I do not remember a single case where a man was injured by a piece of one of these shells. When they were hit and the ball exploded, the wound was terrible. In these cases a solid ball would have hit as well. Their use is barbarous, because they produce increased suffering without any corresponding advantage to those using them."

Lee had a Brooke naval rifle, which fired thirty-two-pound explosive shells, mounted on a railroad flatcar that he used at the Battle of Savage's Station in June 1862. This 7,200-pound cannon didn't do much damage, but the scream of its shells terrified Union soldiers.

The Confederates used naval mines, called "torpedoes," in harbors and rivers to keep Union gunships away. Occasionally the powder got damp, so they didn't always function well. It was these to which Rear Admiral David Farragut referred when famously (quoted as) saying, "Damn the torpedoes! Full speed ahead!" at the Battle of Mobile Bay in August 1864 after a mine sank one of his ironclads.[27]

A war correspondent for the New York Tribune colorfully described these mines: "Any quantity of torpedoes had been sunk in the river, but they were as harmless as a pretty school-girl who does the tragedy at a literary exhibition. About one hundred of these submarine failures were piled up on the banks, with accompanying buoys and anchors, and they looked as innocent as unrewarded virtue."

Despite malfunctions, they worked well enough that the Union had to invent minesweepers with projecting booms that triggered the mines or pushed them aside. Other ships had what were called "cowcatchers" for mine removal. Confederate contact mines sank twenty-two Union vessels and damaged another twelve, while Union mines sent six Confederate ships to the bottom.

Both sides seem to have tested actual torpedoes. Confederate documents state that as early as November 1862 they were testing rocket-powered torpedoes in Mobile Bay, Alabama, and that engineer Colonel E. H. Angamar was developing a rocket-powered boat from which the torpedoes could be launched. Actually it was two boats. One boat took the rocket boat out to sea, aimed it, and then launched it. By July 1863 the boats were completed, and Angamar was formulating a plan to attack the Union fleet outside Mobile Bay. What happened next is unknown; the records are silent on the matter.

In the fall of 1862, the Union tested two rocket-powered torpedoes near Washington, D.C., in the Potomac River. The first plunged down into the mud and exploded. The second shot off at a sixty-degree angle, accidentally blowing up the schooner Diana. If the Diana hadn't been there, it would have sunk the much larger steamer State of Georgia. A month later a third torpedo was tested. It went about five feet before flying out of the water, briefly touching the surface twenty feet out, sailing through the air for a hundred yards, and plunging back into the river. Failing to see the weapon's potential, the navy canceled the project.

During the evacuation of Yorktown in May 1862, the Confederates introduced land mines—also called torpedoes, as by Sherman on his march—deploying them in roads and near wells. Though the practice was considered barbaric at the time, Union officers used Confederate prisoners to clear them. Estimates put the number of planted Confederate land mines at fewer than 2,000.

---

27 If he said this at all, his words most likely were: "Damn the torpedoes! Four bells. Captain Drayton, go ahead! Jouett, full speed!"—but the paraphrased version has a better ring to it.

In one of many instances of sabotage, the Confederates created small iron bombs resembling lumps of coal. These were tossed into U.S. Navy coal piles and exploded in the ships' furnaces. Porter issued orders in March 1864 that if anyone was caught with one of these bombs, he was to be shot immediately. Porter later wrote, "In devices for blowing up vessels the Confederates were far ahead of us, putting Yankee ingenuity to shame."

On August 9, 1864, a Confederate secret agent named John Maxwell put a time bomb in a box marked "candles" and got it aboard an ammunition barge at Grant's headquarters and supply depot during the Petersburg siege. The bomb, containing twelve to fifteen pounds of explosives, set off the ammunition, vaporizing the barge, and blowing up another barge and a building on the wharf, killing at least 43 people—probably many more—and wounding 126.

Hand grenades and flamethrowers date back to Greco-Roman times, but new versions were developed during the Civil War. The Union threw many Ketchum grenades at the Confederates during the siege of Port Hudson, Louisiana, from May to July of 1863. A Ketchum grenade resembled an elongated opium poppy pod with a dart's tail and weighed three to five pounds. Many failed to detonate, so the Confederates threw them back. The Confederates' grenades were small black iron balls with fuses. They used these at Vicksburg. Union soldiers were sometimes able to throw these back as well.

The Union used incendiary shells on Charleston in January 1864 and at Petersburg that July. In November, Alfred Burney demonstrated a flamethrower to generals that included Grant, Meade, and Benjamin Butler. Butler ordered eight of them, along with 1,500 gallons of flammable liquid, and received them in February 1865, but it is not known whether they were used in the war.

Many ideas and inventions weren't used. In May 1862 a schoolteacher named John Doughty sent Lincoln a letter urging him to use chlorine gas against the Confederates. Such chemical warfare is now considered a war crime.

"CRUELTY AND SEVERITY"

Union

General Ulysses S. Grant (See biography, page 54.)

The details of the march, the conduct, the whole glory, belong to Sherman. My objection to Sherman's plan at the time, and my objection now, was his leaving Hood's army in his rear. I always wanted the march to the sea, but at the same time I wanted Hood.

If Hood had been an enterprising commander, he would have given us a great deal of trouble. Probably he was controlled from Richmond. As it was he did the very thing I wanted him to do. If I had been in Hood's place I would never have gone near Nashville. I would have gone to Louisville, and on north until I came to Chicago. What was the use of his knocking his head against the stone walls of Nashville? If he had gone north, Thomas never would have caught him. We should have had to raise new levies. I was never so anxious during the war as at that time.

I urged Thomas again and again to move. Finally I issued an order relieving him, and not satisfied with that I started west to command his army, and find Hood. So long as Hood was loose the whole West was in danger. When I reached Washington, I learned of the battle of Nashville. The order superseding Thomas was recalled, and I sent Thomas a dispatch of congratulation.

I was reading the other day a lament about the cruelty and severity shown by the Northern troops during the war. I was a good deal annoyed by the statement, because it was contrary to the truth. The Northern troops were never more cruel than the necessities of the war required.

At no time do I remember giving an order for the destruction of property, save when we occupied Jackson [Mississippi]. Before leaving Jackson, [Confederate general] Joe Johnston had given orders for the destruction of stores. I found a cotton-mill at work making goods for the Confederate army with the trade-mark C. S. A. on them. Here was an active mill providing goods for the enemy. I went in with Sherman, and when I saw what was going on, I said, "I guess we shall have to burn this."

The Southerners never hesitated to burn if it suited their purpose. They burned Chambersburg, for instance, which was a most wanton piece of destruction. They put York under contribution, and the York people are paying interest on the amount to this day [1879]. They set fire to Richmond when their cause was gone irretrievably, and when every dollar fired was a dollar wantonly wasted. They set fire to Columbia. In fact, whenever our armies entered a town, it was very frequently their first duty to take care of Southern property which had been set fire to by Southern armies. Then the Southerners tried to burn New York City, and made raids upon St. Alban's.[28] In fact, I think our treatment of the South, and all the consequences, personal and otherwise, arising out of the Rebellion, was magnanimous.

---

28 At St. Albans, Vermont, on October 19, 1864, raiders from one of the Confederacy's espionage headquarters in Canada apparently planned to burn down the governor's mansion, rob three banks, and then set the village on fire. They only succeeded in robbing two banks and killing one civilian before fleeing back to Canada. They were captured in Canada, but a judge there released them. Two more times Canadian authorities arrested five of the men, but each time judges released them. The Confederate government was allowed to keep the stolen money, while the Canadian government reimbursed the banks.

On November 25, 1864, soon after the presidential election, Confederate saboteurs from Canada set fire to a number of New York City hotels and landmarks, hoping the city would go up in flames, but the New York fire departments quickly extinguished the fires. Most of the saboteurs fled back to Canada. These would be considered acts of terrorism today since they were directed at civilians.

THE BATTLE OF APPOMATTOX COURT HOUSE

APPOMATTOX COUNTY, VIRGINIA
APRIL 9, 1865

COMMANDERS

Union
Maj. Gen. Philip Sheridan

Confederate
Gen. Robert E. Lee

PARTICIPANTS

110,000 (Army of the Potomac and the Army of the James; 63,285 engaged in battle)

29,000 (Army of Northern Virginia; 9,992 engaged in battle)

CASUALTIES

Union
164 killed/wounded

Confederate
Approximately 500 killed/wounded
28,356 paroled

VICTORY: UNION

OVERVIEW

After nearly ten months the Siege of Petersburg was nearing its end. Lee tried to force Grant to contract his lines by staging an attack on Fort Stedman, but the battle only weakened Lee's right flank. Then Sheridan defeated Pickett on April 1, 1865, in the Battle of Five Forks. That loss convinced Lee to abandon Petersburg and Richmond. His right flank was about to give way, and he knew he'd quickly be overwhelmed by Grant's much larger force. He determined the best course was to retreat to the west, then south, to join forces with General Johnston in Greensboro, North Carolina.

The Union broke through his right flank on April 2. By that evening Lee's army of about 54,000 men was on the move. Petersburg surrendered the morning of April 3, followed by Richmond that evening. Before President Davis left, he ordered all supplies of use to the Union destroyed—inadvertently setting Richmond afire. Grant immediately took off after Lee with about 110,000 men.

On April 4 Lee arrived at Amelia Court House—about forty miles west of Petersburg—where he expected to find supplies that he had ordered, but nothing was there. His men, worn out from fighting and marching, now had nothing to eat. He lost twenty-four hours while his men fanned out through the countryside scrounging food. On the fifth he moved toward the Richmond & Danville Railroad, where he encountered Sheridan's cavalry, which prevented him from using the railroad for transportation or for bringing up supplies from Danville.

Nothing could be found in the countryside, so he headed toward Appomattox Station, about fifty miles west of Amelia Court House, to meet three wagon trains from Lynchburg and perhaps to send his men south by rail to North Carolina. On April 6 Custer captured and burned 400 supply wagons, while Sheridan's men captured almost an eighth of Lee's army, including Lieutenant-General Richard Ewell and eight other generals, along with 180 of their supply wagons. Lee's army was reduced to two corps under Generals Longstreet and John Brown Gordon. On April 8, before Lee arrived at Appomattox Station, about five miles south of Appomattox Court House, Custer swooped in and captured the four large railroad trains of supplies there. Lee's next move would have been to continue twenty miles west to Lynchburg.

Some of the Union infantry pressed on, marching overnight, while Lee camped for the night near Appomattox Court House. He awoke to find Sheridan and Major-General John Griffin's Twenty-fourth Corps on his south side and Meade on his northeast. He could have tried to retreat toward Lynchburg, but he had received several notes from "Unconditional Surrender" Grant indicating that the Union was willing to offer favorable terms. While Grant is often given credit for being lenient to Lee, it was actually Lincoln who set the generous terms of surrender beforehand.

While Lee was weighing his options, Gordon informed him that the men were so worn out they wouldn't be able to fight without help from Longstreet's division, which was defending the other end of Lee's army. As his final battle geared up, Lee called a truce, and on April 9 surrendered to Grant.

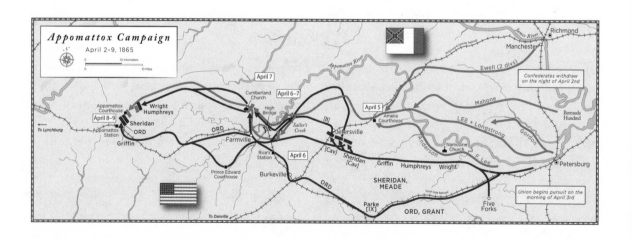

PREPARATIONS WITH SHERIDAN

Union

General Ulysses S. Grant (See biography, page 54.)

My anxiety for some time before Richmond fell was lest Lee should abandon it. My pursuit of Lee was hazardous. I was in a position of extreme difficulty. You see I was marching away from my supplies, while Lee was falling back on his supplies. If Lee had continued his flight another day I should have had to abandon the pursuit, fall back to Danville, build the railroad, and feed my army. So far as supplies were concerned, I was almost at my last gasp when the surrender took place.

When I returned to Washington [after Lee's surrender], Lincoln said, "General, I half suspected that movement of yours would end the business, and wanted to ask you, but did not like to."

Of course, I could not have told him, if he had asked me, because the one thing a general in command of an army does not know, is what the result of a battle is until it is fought. I never would have risked my reputation with Mr. Lincoln by any

danger of his life, I would have laughed at him.[29]

"As we reached the edge of the city, the sidewalks were lined on both sides of the streets with black and white alike—all looking with curious, eager faces at the man who held their destiny in his hand; but there was no anger in any one's face; the whole was like a gala day, and it looked as if the President was some expected guest who had come to receive great honors.

"Judging from present appearances, they certainly were not grieving over the loss of the Government which had just fled. There was nothing like taunt or defiance in the faces of those who were gazing from the windows or craning their necks from the sidewalks to catch a view of the President."

"What a careless thing it was to be going about with the President without a guard to protect him! I never thought of any danger to him at the time. Our people were not given to assassination, and if any one had told me that the President stood in

29   Lincoln wanted to see the Confederate capital, so—accompanied by his son Tad, Admiral Porter, a captain, a bodyguard, and a guard of just twelve marines— he entered the city mere hours after the Confederates left with the Union Army close behind. Disembarking from a boat, they walked past Libby Prison where Union prisoners-of-war were held, to President Davis's mansion, then to the State-House where the Confederate Congress had held its sessions. They were mobbed by crowds the entire way. Though Lincoln towered over everyone, no one tried to harm him. Lincoln knew some people wanted to kill him—someone had put a bullet through his hat just eight months earlier—but he tried to play down the danger and make like everything was normal. Most seemed thrilled to see him, particularly the former slaves.

such prophecies. As a matter of fact, however, my own mind was pretty clear as to what the effect of the movement would be. I was only waiting for Sheridan to finish his raid around Lee to make it.

When Sheridan arrived from that raid, and came to my quarters, I asked him to take a walk. As we were walking, I took out his orders and gave them to him. They were orders to move on the left and attack Lee. If the movement succeeded, he was to advance. If it failed, he was to make his way into North Carolina and join Sherman.

When Sheridan read this part, he was, as I saw, disappointed. His countenance fell. He had just made a long march, a severe march, and now the idea of another march into North Carolina would disconcert any commander—even Sheridan. He, however, said nothing.

I said: "Sheridan, although I have provided for your retreat into North Carolina in the event of failure, I have no idea that you will fail, no idea that you will go to Carolina. I mean to end this business right here."

Sheridan's eyes lit up, and he said, with enthusiasm, "That's the talk. Let us end the business here."

A White Flag

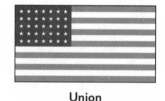

Union

General Philip Sheridan (*See biography, page 203.*)

When Lee awoke on April 9, he found the Union army unexpectedly in front of him. Two days earlier, after receiving a note from Grant, he didn't want to talk of surrender, but now he began considering it. Without food he knew he couldn't continue much longer. He decided it was the best course, and while the Battle of Appomattox was beginning, he sent out white flags in several directions to call a truce in preparation for his meeting with Grant to finalize terms. Sheridan didn't know any of this, of course, and was preparing to attack the Army of Northern Virginia.

A move on the enemy's left was ordered, and every guidon [unit pennant] was bent to the front. As the cavalry marched along parallel with the Confederate line, and in toward its left, a heavy fire of artillery opened on us, but this could not check us at such a time, and we soon reached some high ground about half a mile from the Court House, and from here I could see in the low valley beyond the village the bivouac undoubtedly of Lee's army. The troops did not seem to be disposed in battle order, but on the other side of the bivouac was a line of battle—a heavy rear-guard—confronting, presumably, General Meade.

I decided to attack at once, and formations were ordered at a trot for a charge by Custer's and Devin's divisions down the slope leading to the camps. Custer was soon ready, but Devin's division being in rear its formation took longer, since he had to shift further to the right; Devin's preparations were, therefore, but partially completed when an aide-de-camp galloped up to me with the word from Custer, "Lee has surrendered; do not charge; the white flag is up."

The enemy perceiving that Custer was forming for attack, had sent the flag out to his front and stopped the charge just in time. I at once sent word of the truce to General Ord, and hearing nothing more from Custer himself, I supposed that he had gone down to the Court House to join a mounted group of Confederates that I could see near there, so I, too, went toward them, galloping down a narrow ridge, staff and orderlies following; but we had not got half way to the Court House when, from a skirt of timber to our right, not more than three hundred yards distant, a musketry fire was opened on us. This halted us, when, waving my hat, I called out to the firing party that we were under a truce, and they were violating it.

This did not stop them, however, so we hastily took shelter in a ravine so situated as to throw a ridge between us and the danger. We traveled in safety down this depression to its mouth, and thence by a gentle ascent approached the Court House. I was in advance, followed by a sergeant carrying my battle-flag.

When I got within about a hundred and fifty yards of the enemy's line, which was immediately in front of the Court House, some of the Confederates leveled their pieces at us, and I again

halted. Their officers kept their men from firing, however, but meanwhile a single-handed contest had begun behind me, for on looking back I heard a Confederate soldier demanding my battle-flag from the color-bearer, thinking, no doubt, that we were coming in as prisoners. The sergeant [Sheridan's] had drawn his sabre and was about to cut the man down, but at a word from me he desisted and carried the flag back to my staff, his assailant quickly realizing that the boot was on the other leg.

These incidents determined me to remain where I was till the return of a staff-officer whom I had sent over to demand an explanation from the group of Confederates for which I had been heading. He came back in a few minutes with apologies for what had occurred, and informed me that General Gordon and General Wilcox were the superior officers in the group. As they wished me to join them I rode up with my staff, but we had hardly met when in front of [General Wesley] Merritt firing began.

At the sound I turned to General Gordon, who seemed embarrassed by the occurrence, and remarked: "General, your men fired on me as I was coming over here, and undoubtedly they are treating Merritt and Custer the same way. We might as well let them fight it out."

He replied, "There must be some mistake."

I then asked, "Why not send a staff-officer and have your people cease firing; they are violating the flag."

He answered, "I have no staff-officer to send."

Whereupon I said that I would let him have one of mine, and calling for Lieutenant Vanderbilt Allen, I directed him to carry General Gordon's orders to General Geary, commanding a small brigade of South Carolina cavalry, to discontinue firing. Allen dashed off with the message and soon delivered it, but was made a prisoner, Geary saying, "I do not care for white flags: South Carolinians never surrender."

By this time Merritt's patience being exhausted, he ordered an attack, and this in short order put an end to General Geary's last ditch absurdity, and extricated Allen from his predicament.

When quiet was restored Gordon remarked: "General Lee asks for a suspension of hostilities pending the negotiations which he is having with General Grant."

WAITING FOR GRANT

Confederate

Lieutenant-General James Longstreet (See biography, page 48.)

Captain Sims, through some informality, was sent to call the truce. The firing ceased. General Custer rode to Captain Sims to know his authority, and, upon finding that he was of my staff, asked to be conducted to my head-quarters, and down they came in fast gallop, General Custer's flaxen locks flowing over his shoulders, and in brusk, excited manner, he said, "In the name of General Sheridan I demand the unconditional surrender of this army."

He was reminded that I was not the commander of the army, that he was within the lines of the enemy without authority, addressing a superior officer, and in disrespect to General Grant as well as myself; that if I was the commander of the army I would not receive the message of General Sheridan.

He then became more moderate, saying it would be a pity to have more blood upon that field. Then I suggested that the truce be respected, and said, "As you are now more reasonable, I will say that General Lee has gone to meet General Grant, and it is for them to determine the future of the armies."

He was satisfied, and rode back to his command.

General Grant rode away from the Army of the Potomac on the morning of the 9th to join his troops near Appomattox Court-House, so General Lee's note was sent around to him. When advised of the change, General Lee rode back to his front to await there the answer to his note. While waiting, General Lee expressed apprehension that his refusal to meet General Grant's first proposition might cause him to demand harsh terms.

> *General, unless he offers us honorable terms, come back and let us fight it out!*
>
> —LIEUTENANT-GENERAL JAMES LONGSTREET'S WORDS
> TO LEE AS HE RODE OFF FOR HIS MEETING WITH
> GRANT, ACCORDING TO BRIGADIER-GENERAL E. P.
> ALEXANDER, LONGSTREET'S CHIEF OF ARTILLERY

I assured him that I knew General Grant well enough to say that the terms would be such as he would demand under similar circumstances, but he yet had doubts. The conversation continued in broken sentences until the bearer of the return despatch approached. As he still seemed apprehensive of humiliating demands, I suggested that in that event he should break off the interview and tell General Grant to do his worst. The thought of another round seemed to brace him, and he rode with Colonel Marshall, of his staff, to meet the Union commander.

General Grant was found prepared to offer as liberal terms as General Lee could expect, and, to obviate a collision between his army of the rear with ours, ordered an officer sent to give notice of the truce.

Soon after General Lee's return ride his chief of ordnance reported a large amount of United States currency in his possession. In doubt as to the proper disposition of the funds, General Lee sent the officer to ask my opinion. As it was not known or included in the conditions of capitulation, and was due (and ten times more) to the faithful troops, I suggested a pro rata distribution of it.

The officer afterwards brought three hundred dollars as my part. I took one hundred, and asked to have the balance distributed among Field's division, the troops most distant from their homes.

The commissioners appointed to formulate details of the capitulation were assigned a room in the McLean residence. The way to it led through the room occupied as General Grant's head-quarters.

As I was passing through the room, as one of the commissioners, General Grant looked up, recognized me, rose, and with his old-time cheerful greeting gave me his hand, and after passing a few remarks offered a cigar, which was gratefully received.

GUERRILLAS

Guerrilla groups were fighting the Civil War well before the war began and after it ended. Before the war, guerrilla activity almost became a war in itself during the Bleeding Kansas years, sometimes called the Border War. It began with the Kansas-Nebraska Act of 1854. In 1820 proslavery and antislavery politicians established the Missouri Compromise, which allowed Missouri to become a slave state but prohibited the institution in the rest of the former Louisiana Territory north of parallel 36° 30' north. The Kansas-Nebraska Act nullified this arrangement, allowing the inhabitants of each state or territory to decide for themselves whether to become a free state or slave state. This put the Kansas Territory up for grabs, the result of which would have a huge impact on the struggle for dominance between Democrats and Republicans.

Both preservationist and abolitionist forces flooded into Kansas. Twice when they held elections, thousands of armed "border ruffians" flooded into the territory from Missouri. Through voter fraud, both elections went proslavery. At about the same time, Reverend Henry Ward Beecher was collecting money to buy Sharps rifles to send to abolitionists in Kansas; the guns were called "Beecher's Bibles."

When a proslavery farmer murdered a Free-Soiler in a land dispute, reprisals began flying back and forth. About 1,500 proslavery men raided an arsenal and, led by the sheriff, laid siege to the Free-Soil town of Lawrence. Abolitionist John Brown led the defense. The attack wasn't made, although five months later the sheriff returned to arrest some Lawrence citizens for establishing an illegal state government—and was nonfatally shot for his trouble. The sheriff returned again with a posse of about 750 proslavery men, many from Missouri and some from the proslavery Law and Order Party. They arrested three Free-Soil leaders and sacked the town. The only death was one of the sheriff's men, struck by falling masonry. In retaliation John Brown, his four sons, and two others murdered five proslavery men with swords in what became known as the Pottawatomie Massacre.

John Brown later gained fame for his ill-planned raid on the federal arsenal at Harper's Ferry, Virginia (now West Virginia), in 1859, hoping to start a slave uprising. A detachment of U.S. marines headed by Colonel Robert E. Lee, accompanied by Lieutenant Jeb Stuart, captured him and twenty insurgents. Brown and six of his raiders were tried and found guilty of treason. John Wilkes Booth, among others, witnessed Brown's hanging.

Missouri, the northernmost slave state, was deeply divided, and people began murdering their neighbors solely because of their political views. For protection, men throughout the region formed themselves into private militias. When the war began, these vigilante groups became semiofficial guerrillas. As self-established irregulars, they answered only to themselves and rarely received orders from the military. Without specific objectives they focused on killing, punishing, and looting civilians while occasionally engaging in sabotage. Most guerrillas were between the ages of seventeen and twenty-five, brave, reckless, and ruthless. They terrorized and plundered, which was how they financed themselves. Anyone with criminal tendencies found the groups extremely attractive. Those siding with the South were "bushwhackers," while Unionists were known as "jayhawkers." They sometimes fought the soldiers of the opposing side and each other when they crossed paths, but generally they focused on civilians.

Jesse James, his brother Frank, and Cole Younger were bushwhackers throughout the war. Mark Twain served in a bushwhacker militia for two weeks before heading to Nevada, disillusioned. Soon after the war began, Buffalo Bill Cody joined the Red Legs, a band of jayhawkers. Cody soon left what he called "the enterprise of crippling the Confederacy by appropriating the horses of non-combatants" and became a Union soldier and scout.

On the Union side, Charles Jennison's militia had the worst reputation. Jennison's Jayhawkers plundered and burned Dayton, Missouri, on January 1, 1861. All of the town's forty-seven buildings and homes were destroyed, except for one owned by a pro-Union man. On September 23, 1861, U.S. Senator James Lane's Kansas Brigade of jayhawkers sacked Osceola, Missouri, population 3,000. After plundering it, they burned it to the ground and executed nine of its citizens.

In February 1862 the Union tried to rein in the jayhawkers by making them part of the military and establishing martial law. Jennison's Jayhawkers became part of the Union army as the Seventh Kansas Volunteer Cavalry and Jennison became its colonel. Lane's Kansas Brigade became the Third, Fourth, and Fifth Kansas Volunteers, with Lane as its brigadier general.

While both sides committed atrocities, some of the worst were by William "Bloody Bill" Anderson and William Quantrill, the two most notorious Confederate guerrillas. In retaliation for the earlier jayhawker attacks, Quantrill's bushwhackers, along with Frank James and Cole Younger, raided the town of Lawrence on August 21, 1863, hoping to find Senator (and Brigadier-General) Lane, but he escaped by running off through a cornfield in his nightshirt. Quantrill's men robbed two banks, looted the town, set it on fire, and then murdered all the men and boys of gun-bearing age. Estimates of the dead range from 100 to more than 200, with the higher number more likely. It became known as the Lawrence Massacre, one of the worst atrocities of the war.

In response, Brigadier-General Thomas Ewing, in command of the district, ordered that the four Missouri counties bordering Kansas be evacuated, evicting thousands from their homes.

On September 27, 1864, Bloody Bill Anderson's bushwhackers, along with Jesse James, were looting Centralia, Missouri, when a train pulled into the station. His men found twenty-three Union soldiers on board. All were on leave and unarmed, and some were wounded. In what became known as the Centralia Massacre, Anderson, Frank James, and others robbed the train and killed all but one of the soldiers, along with some passengers who tried to hide their valuables. After scalping the soldiers to decorate their saddles and bridles, they set fire to the train and sent it rolling toward its next destination.

While guerrilla activity was widespread, the worst hot spots were in the Kansas-Missouri area and along eastern Tennessee and Kentucky.

After the war Grant explained how he dealt with guerrillas: "I told the inhabitants of Mississippi, when I was moving to Holly Springs, that if they allowed their sons and brothers to remain within my lines and receive protection, and then during the night sneak out and burn my bridges and shoot officers, I would desolate their country for forty miles around every place where it occurred. This put an end to bridge-burning. This was necessary, because I could not fight two armies—an army in front under military conditions, and a secret army hid behind every bush and fence."

When the war ended, the guerrillas faded into the woodwork. Some bushwhackers joined the burgeoning Ku Klux Klan, while others continued their activities in small gangs. Frank and Jesse James, along with the Younger brothers, claimed they were continuing the fight by robbing only Northern banks and businesses. On at least one occasion they robbed a train wearing Klan garb. The number of robberies they committed remains unknown, although it is estimated the gang stole between $82,000 and $450,000—roughly $11 million to $69 million today.

Many Southerners viewed the bushwhackers as heroes, and some newspapers painted the James-Younger gang's crimes as a continuation of their guerrilla activities, using them to rally against the excesses of the Reconstruction. Helped by many Southerners, Jesse James eluded the authorities for fifteen years, becoming one of the war's last rebels.

THE SURRENDER

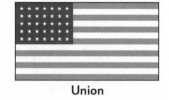

Union

General Ulysses S. Grant (See biography, page 54.)

On the night before Lee's surrender, I had a wretched headache—headaches to which I have been subject—nervous prostration, intense personal suffering. But, suffer or not, I had to keep moving. I saw clearly, especially after Sheridan had cut off the escape to Danville, that Lee must surrender or break and run into the mountains—break in all directions and leave us a dozen guerilla bands to fight.

The object of my campaign was not Richmond, not the defeat of Lee in actual fight, but to remove him and his army out of the contest, and, if possible, to have him use his influence in inducing the surrender of Johnston and the other isolated armies. You see, the war was an enormous strain upon the country. Rich as we were I do not now see how we could have endured it another year, even from a financial point of view.

So with these views I wrote Lee, and opened the correspondence with which the world is familiar. Lee does not appear well in that correspondence, not nearly so well as he did in our subsequent interviews, where his whole bearing was that of a patriotic and gallant soldier, concerned alone for the welfare of his army and his state.

I received word that Lee would meet me at a point within our lines near Sheridan's head-quarters. I had to ride quite a distance through a muddy country. I remember now that I was concerned about my personal appearance. I had an old suit on, without my sword, and without any distinguishing mark of rank except the shoulder-straps of a lieutenant-general on a woolen blouse. I was splashed with mud in my long ride. I was afraid Lee might think I meant to show him studied discourtesy by so coming—at least I thought so. But I had no other clothes within reach, as Lee's letter found me away from my base of supplies.

I kept on riding until I met Sheridan. The General, who was one of the heroes of the campaign, and whose pursuit of Lee was perfect in its generalship and energy, told me where to find Lee. I remember that Sheridan was impatient when I met him, anxious and suspicious about the whole business, feared there might be a plan to escape, that he had Lee at his feet, and wanted to end the business by going in and forcing an absolute surrender by capture. In fact, he had his troops ready for such an assault when Lee's white flag came within his lines.

I went up to the house where Lee was waiting. I found him in a fine, new, splendid uniform, which only recalled my anxiety as to my own clothes while on my way to meet him. I expressed my regret that I was compelled to meet him in so unceremonious a manner, and he replied that the only suit he had available was one which had been sent him by some admirers in Baltimore, and which he then wore for the first time.

We spoke of old friends in the army. I remembered having seen Lee in Mexico. He was so much higher in rank than myself at the time that I supposed he had no recollection of me. But he said he remembered me very well. We talked of old times and exchanged inquiries about friends. Lee then broached the subject of our meeting. I told him my terms, and Lee, listening attentively, asked me to write them down. I took out my "manifold" order-book and pencil and wrote them down. General Lee put on his glasses and read them over. The conditions gave the officers their side-arms, private horses, and personal baggage. I said to Lee that I hoped and believed this would be the close of the war; that it was most important that the men should go home and go to work, and the government would not throw any obstacles in the way. Lee answered that it would have a most happy effect, and accepted the terms.

I handed over my penciled memorandum to an aide to put into ink, and we resumed our conversation about old times and friends in the armies. Various officers came in—Longstreet, Gordon, Pickett, from the South; Sheridan, Ord, and others from our side. Some were old friends— Longstreet and myself, for instance, and we had a general talk. Lee no doubt expected me to ask for his sword, but I did not want his sword. It would only have gone to the Patent Office to be worshiped by the Washington rebels.

There was a pause, when General Lee said that most of the animals in his cavalry and artillery were owned by the privates, and he would like to know, under the terms, whether they would be regarded as private property or the property of the government. I said that under the terms

of surrender they belonged to the government. General Lee read over the letter and said that was so. I then said to the general that I believed and hoped this was the last battle of the war; that I saw the wisdom of these men getting home and to work as soon as possible, and that I would give orders to allow any soldier or officer claiming a horse or a mule to take it.

General Lee showed some emotion at this—a feeling which I also shared—and said it would have a most happy effect. The interview ended, and I gave orders for rationing his troops.

What General Lee's feelings were I do not know. As he was a man of much dignity, with an impassible face, it was impossible to say whether he felt inwardly glad that the end had finally come, or felt sad over the result, and was too manly to show it. Whatever his feelings, they were entirely concealed from my observation; but my own feelings, which had been quite jubilant on the receipt of his letter, were sad and depressed. I felt like anything other than rejoicing at the downfall of a foe who had fought so long and valiantly, and had suffered so much for a cause, though that cause was, I believe, one of the worst for which a people ever fought, and one for which there was the least excuse. I do not question, however, the sincerity of the great mass of those who were opposed to us.

When news of the surrender first reached our lines our men commenced firing a salute of a hundred guns in honor of the victory. I at once sent word, however, to have it stopped. The Confederates were now our prisoners, and we did not want to exult over their downfall. I determined to return to Washington at once, with a view to putting a stop to the purchase of supplies, and what I now deemed other useless outlay of money. Before leaving, however, I thought I would like to see General Lee again; so next morning I rode out beyond our lines towards his headquarters, preceded by a bugler and a staff-officer carrying a white flag.

Lee soon mounted his horse, seeing who it was, and met me. We had there between the lines, sitting on horseback, a very pleasant conversation of over half an hour, in the course of which Lee said to me that the South was a big country and that we might have to march over it three or four times before the war entirely ended, but that we would now be able to do it as they could no longer resist us. He expressed it as his earnest hope, however, that we would not be called upon to cause more loss and sacrifice of life; but he could not foretell the result.

I then suggested to General Lee that there was not a man in the Confederacy whose influence with the soldiery and the whole people was as great as his, and that if he would now advise the surrender of all the armies I had no doubt his advice would be followed with alacrity. But Lee said, that he could not do that without consulting the [Confederate] President first. I knew there was no use to urge him to do anything against his ideas of what was right.

I was accompanied by my staff and other officers, some of whom seemed to have a great desire to go inside the Confederate lines. They finally asked permission of Lee to do so for the purpose of seeing some of their old army friends, and the permission was granted. They went over, had a very pleasant time with their old friends, and brought some of them back with them when they returned.

When Lee and I separated he went back to his lines and I returned to the house of Mr. McLean.

> The enemy was more than five times our numbers. If we could have forced our way one day longer, it would have been at a great sacrifice of life, and at its end I did not see how a surrender could have been avoided. We had no subsistence for man or horse, and it could not be gathered in the country. The supplies ordered to Pamplin's Station from Lynchburg could not reach us, and the men, deprived of food and sleep for many days, were worn out and exhausted.
>
> —General Robert E. Lee, explaining why he surrendered

Lee's great blunder was in holding Richmond. He must have been controlled by Davis, who, taking the gambler's desperate view of the situation, staked the Confederacy on one card. It must have been that Davis felt that the moral effect of the fall of Richmond would have been equal to the fall of the South. Or it may be, as I have sometimes thought, that Lee felt that the war was over; that the South was fought out; that any prolongation of the war would be misery to both the North and the South. After I crossed the James, the holding of Richmond was a mistake. Nor have I ever felt that the surrender at Appomattox was an absolute military necessity. I think that in holding Richmond, and even in consenting to that surrender, Lee sacrificed his judgment as a soldier to his duty as a citizen and the leader of the South. I think Lee deserves honor for that, for if he had left Richmond when Sherman invaded Georgia, it would have given us another year of war.

Because the federal government didn't recognize the secession as legitimate, it never viewed the Confederacy as an actual government. From the U.S. point of view, the Southern states remained part of the Union while under the temporary and illegal control of rebels. When General Johnston contacted Major-General Sherman to negotiate an armistice between the two countries, Sherman said it was impossible. In the eyes of the federal government, there was no such thing as the Confederate government; therefore the United States couldn't negotiate with it.

The surrender of the Confederacy's primary fighting force, the Army of Northern Virginia, effectively ended the war, though some sporadic fighting continued for another two months. Johnston surrendered his 98,270 men to Sherman on April 26. The last Confederate cabinet meeting took place on May 5. When Jefferson Davis was captured on May 10, President Andrew Johnson immediately declared that armed resistance had ended. On June 23 Brigadier-General Stand Watie was the final Confederate general to surrender.

"MORNING DAWNED"

Union

Major-General Joshua Chamberlain (See biography, page 174.)

Major-General Joshua Chamberlain described the effect of the news that Lee wanted to surrender.

Everybody seemed acquiescent and for the moment cheerful—except Sheridan. He did not like the cessation of hostilities, and did not conceal his opinion. His natural disposition was not sweetened by the circumstance that he was fired on by some of the Confederates as he was coming up to the meeting under the truce. He is for unconditional surrender, and thinks we should have banged right on and settled all questions without asking them.

One o'clock came; no answer from Lee. Nothing for us but to shake hands and take arms to resume hostilities. As I turned to go, General Griffin said to me in a low voice, "Prepare to make, or receive, an attack in ten minutes!" It was a sudden change of tone in our relations, and brought a queer sensation. Where my troops had halted, the opposing lines were in close proximity. The men had stacked arms and were resting in place.

It did not seem like war we were to recommence, but willful murder. But the order was only to "prepare," and that we did. Our troops were in good position, my advanced line across the road, and we stood fast intensely waiting. I had mounted, and sat looking at the scene before me, thinking of all that was impending and depending, when I felt coming in upon me a strange sense of some presence invisible but powerful—like those unearthly visitants told of in ancient story, charged with supernal message. Disquieted, I turned about, and there behind me, riding in between my two lines, appeared a commanding form, superbly mounted, richly accoutred, of imposing bearing, noble countenance, with expression of deep sadness overmastered by deeper strength. It is no other than Robert E. Lee! And seen by me for the first time within my own lines.

I sat immovable, with a certain awe and admiration. He was coming, with a single staff officer, for the great appointed meeting which was to determine momentous issues. Not long after, by another in-leading road, appeared another form, plain, unassuming, simple, and familiar to our eyes, but to the thought as much inspiring awe as Lee in his splendor and his sadness. It is Grant! He, too, came with a single aide, a staff officer of Sheridan's who had come out to meet him. Slouched hat without cord; common soldier's blouse, unbuttoned, on which, however, the four stars; high boots, mud-splashed to the top; trousers tucked inside; no sword, but the sword-hand deep in the pocket; sitting in his saddle with the ease of a born master, taking no notice of anything, all his faculties gathered into intense thought and mighty calm.

He seemed greater than I had ever seen him,—a look as of another world about him. No wonder I forgot altogether to salute him. Anything like that would have been too little.

He rode on to meet Lee at the Court House.[30] But the final word is not long coming now. Staff officers are flying, crying "Lee surrenders!"

---

30 Wilmer McLean's house in the small community called Appomattox Court House.

They [the Confederates] had a supper that night, which was something of a novelty. For we had divided rations with our old antagonists now that they were by our side as suffering brothers. In truth, Longstreet had come over to our camp that evening with an unwonted moisture on his martial cheek and compressed words on his lips: "Gentlemen, I must speak plainly; we are starving over there. For God's sake! can you send us something?"

We were men; and we acted like men, knowing we should suffer for it ourselves. We were too short-rationed also, and had been for days, and must be for days to come. But we forgot Andersonville and Belle Isle [notorious POW prisons] that night, and sent over to that starving camp share and share alike for all there; nor thinking the merits of the case diminished by the circumstance that part of these provisions was what Sheridan had captured from their trains the night before.

Late that night I was summoned to headquarters, where General Griffin informed me that I was to command the parade on the occasion of the formal surrender of the arms and colors of Lee's army. He said the Confederates had begged hard to be allowed to stack their arms on the ground where they were, and let us go and pick them up after they had gone; but that Grant did not think this quite respectful enough to anybody, including the United States of America; and while he would have all private property respected, and would permit officers to retain their side-arms, he insisted that the surrendering army as such should march out in due order, and lay down all tokens of Confederate authority and organized hostility to the United States, in immediate presence of some representative portion of the Union Army. Griffin added in a significant tone that Grant wished the ceremony to be as simple as possible, and that nothing should be done to humiliate the manhood of the Southern soldiers.

Morning dawned; and then, in spite of all attempts to restrain it, came the visiting and sightseeing. Our camp was full of callers before we were up. They stood over our very heads now—the men whose movements we used to study through field-glasses, or see close at hand framed in fire.

We woke, and by force of habit started at the vision. But our resolute and much-enduring old antagonists were quick to change their mood when touched by appealing sentiment; they used their first vacation to come over and see what we were really made of, and what we had left for trade.

Food was what was most needed; but was precisely what we also most lacked. Such as we parted with was not for sale, or barter; this went for "old times"—old comradeship across the lines. But tobacco, pipes, knives, money—or symbols of it—shoes—more precious still; and among the staff, even saddles, now and then, and other more trivial things that might serve as souvenirs, made an exchange about as brisk as the bullets had done a few days ago.

The authorities in charge had to interpose and forbid all visiting. It was now the morning of the 12th of April. I had been ordered to have my lines formed for the ceremony at sunrise. It was a chill gray morning, depressing to the senses. But our hearts made warmth.

We formed along the principal street, from the bluff bank of the stream to near the Court House on the left—to face the last line of battle, and receive the last remnant of the arms and colors of that great army which ours had been created to confront for all that death can do for life.

On our part not a sound of trumpet more, nor roll of drum; not a cheer, nor word nor whisper of vain-glorying, nor motion of man standing again at the order, but an awed stillness rather, and breath-holding, as if it were the passing of the dead!

As each successive division masks our own, it halts, the men face inward towards us across the road, twelve feet away; then carefully "dress" their line, each captain taking pains for the good appearance of his company, worn and half starved as they were. The field and staff take their positions in the intervals of regiments; generals in rear of their commands. They fix bayonets, stack arms; then, hesitatingly, remove cartridge-boxes and lay them down. Lastly—reluctantly, with agony of expression—they tenderly fold their flags, battle-worn and torn, blood-stained, heart-holding colors, and lay them down; some frenziedly rushing from the ranks, kneeling over them, clinging to them, pressing them to their lips with burning tears.

And only the Flag of the Union greets the sky!

What visions thronged as we looked into each other's eyes! Here pass the men of Antietam, the Bloody Lane, the Sunken Road, the Cornfield, the Burnside-Bridge; the men whom Stonewall Jackson on the second night at Fredericksburg begged Lee to let him take and crush the two corps of the Army of the Potomac huddled in the streets in darkness and confusion; the men who swept away the Eleventh Corps at Chancellorsville; who left six thousand of their companions around the bases of Culp's and Cemetery Hills at Gettysburg; these survivors of the terrible Wilderness, the Bloody-Angle at Spottsylvania, the slaughter pen of Cold Harbor, the whirlpool of Bethesda Church!

Here comes Cobb's Georgia Legion, which held the stone wall on Marye's Heights at Fredericksburg, close before which we piled our dead for breastworks so that the living might stay and live. Here too come Gordon's Georgians and Hoke's North Carolinians, who stood before the terrific mine explosion at Petersburg, and advancing retook the smoking crater and the dismal heaps of dead—ours more than theirs—huddled in the ghastly chasm.

Now the sad great pageant—Longstreet and his men! What shall we give them for greeting that has not already been spoken in volleys of thunder and written in lines of fire on all the riverbanks of Virginia? Shall we go back to Gaines' Mill and Malvern Hill? Or to the Antietam of Maryland, or Gettysburg of Pennsylvania?—deepest graven of all.

With what strange emotion I look into these faces before which in the mad assault on Rives' Salient, June 18, 1864, I was left for dead under their eyes! It is by miracles we have lived to see this day—any of us standing here.

Now comes the sinewy remnant of fierce Hood's Division, which at Gettysburg we saw pouring through the Devil's Den, and the Plum Run gorge; turning again by the left our stubborn Third Corps, then swarming up the rocky bastions of Round Top, to be met there by equal valor, which changed Lee's whole plan of battle and perhaps the story of Gettysburg.

Ah, is this Pickett's Division?—this little group left of those who on the lurid last day of Gettysburg breasted level cross-fire and thunderbolts of storm, to be strewn back drifting wrecks, where after that awful, futile, pitiful charge we buried them in graves a furlong wide, with names unknown!

Thus, all day long, division after division comes and goes, surrendered arms being removed by our wagons in the intervals, the cartridge-boxes emptied in the street when the ammunition was found unserviceable, our men meanwhile resting in place.

ASSASSINATION

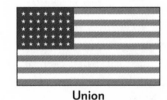

Union

General Ulysses S. Grant (See biography, page 54.)

Lincoln, I may almost say, spent the last days of his life with me. I often recall those days. I have no doubt that Lincoln will be the conspicuous figure of the war; one of the great figures of history. He was incontestably the greatest man I ever knew.

The darkest day of my life was the day I heard of Lincoln's assassination. I did not know what it meant. Here was the rebellion put down in the field, and starting up in the gutters; we had fought it as war, now we had to fight it as assassination. Lincoln was killed on the evening of the 14th of April. Lee surrendered on the 9th of April. I arrived in Washington on the 13th. I was busy sending out orders to stop recruiting, the purchase of supplies, and to muster out the army. Lincoln had promised to go to the theater, and wanted me to go with him. While I was with the President, a note came from Mrs. Grant saying she must leave Washington that night. She wanted to go to Burlington to see our children. Some incident of a trifling nature had made her resolve to leave that evening.

I was glad to have the note, as I did not want to go to the theater. So I made my excuse to Lincoln, and at the proper hour we started for the train. As we were driving along Pennsylvania Avenue, a horseman drove past us on a gallop, and back again around our carriage, looking into it.

Mrs. Grant said, "There is the man who sat near us at lunch to-day, with some other men, and tried to overhear our conversation."

He was so rude that we left the dining-room. Here he is now riding after us. I thought it was only curiosity, but learned afterward that the horseman was Booth. It seems I was to have been attacked, and Mrs. Grant's sudden resolve to leave deranged the plan.

A few days later I received an anonymous letter from a man, saying he had been detailed to kill me, that he rode on my train as far as Havre de Grace, and as my car was locked he could not get in. He thanked God he had failed. I remember the conductor locked our car, but how true the letter was I cannot say. I learned of the assassination as I was passing through Philadelphia. I turned around, took a special train, and came on to Washington. It was the gloomiest day of my life.

THE WAR ENDS

APRIL 9, 1865
LAST SHOTS FIRED IN JUNE 1865

CASUALTIES

Between 650,000 and 850,000 soldiers died in the war.

About 50,000 civilians also died.

Union
364,511 confirmed dead from all causes
(140,414 killed in action)
281,881 wounded
194,743 POWs/MIA
200,000 to 280,000 deserters (one-third returned)

Confederate
More than 260,000 dead from all causes
(72,524 killed in action)
More than 137,000 wounded
214,865 POWs/MIA
More than 100,000 deserters (many returned)

1 in every 4 soldiers killed or wounded.

1 in every 3 soldiers killed or wounded.

VICTORY: UNION

General Robert E. Lee (See biography, page 9.)

FAREWELL TO THE ARMY OF NORTHERN VIRGINIA

Confederate

This was the last order issued to the Army of Northern Virginia:

Hdqrs. Army of Northern Virginia, April 10, 1865

After four years' of arduous service, marked by unsurpassed courage and fortitude, the Army of Northern Virginia has been compelled to yield to overwhelming numbers and resources. I need not tell the survivors of so many hard-fought battles, who have remained steadfast to the last, that I have consented to this result from no distrust of them; but, feeling that valour and devotion could accomplish nothing that could compensate for the loss that would have attended the continuation of the contest, I have determined to avoid the useless sacrifice of those whose past services have endeared them to their countrymen.

By the terms of the agreement, officers and men can return to their homes and remain there until exchanged. You will take with you the satisfaction that proceeds from the consciousness of duty faithfully performed; and I earnestly pray that a merciful God will extend to you his blessing and protection. With an increasing admiration of your constancy and devotion to your country, and a grateful remembrance of your kind and generous consideration of myself, I bid you an affectionate farewell.

R. E. Lee, General

YOUR FINAL ORDERS

Confederate

Lieutenant-General Nathan Bedford Forrest (See biography, page 73.)

Headquarters Forrest's Cavalry Corps, Gainesville, Ala., May 9, 1865

Soldiers:

By an agreement made between Lieutenant-General Taylor, commanding the Department of Alabama, Mississippi, and East Louisiana, and Major-General Canby, commanding U.S. forces, the troops of this department have been surrendered. I do not think it proper or necessary at this time to refer to the causes which have reduced us to this extremity, nor is it now a matter of material consequence to us how such results

were brought about. That we are beaten is a self-evident fact, and any further resistance on our part would be justly regarded as the very height of folly and rashness.

The armies of Generals Lee and Johnston having surrendered, you are the last of all the troops of the C. S. Army east of the Mississippi River to lay down your arms. The cause for which you have so long and so manfully struggled, and for which you have braved dangers, endured privations and sufferings, and made so many sacrifices, is to-day hopeless. The Government which we sought to establish and perpetuate is at an end. Reason dictates and humanity demands that no more blood be shed.

Fully realizing and feeling that such is the case, it is your duty and mine to lay down our arms, submit to the "powers that be," and to aid in restoring peace and establishing law and order throughout the land. The terms upon which you were surrendered are favorable, and should be satisfactory and acceptable to all. They manifest a spirit of magnanimity and liberality on the part of the Federal authorities which should be met on our part by a faithful compliance with all the stipulations and conditions therein expressed. As your commander, I sincerely hope that every officer and soldier of my command will cheerfully obey the orders given and carry out in good faith all the terms of the cartel.

Those who neglect the terms and refuse to be paroled may assuredly expect when arrested to be sent North and imprisoned. Let those who are absent from their commands, from whatever cause, report at once to this place or to Jackson, Miss.; or, if too remote from either, to the nearest U.S. post or garrison for parole.

Civil war, such as you have just passed through, naturally engenders feelings of animosity, hatred, and revenge. It is our duty to divest ourselves of all such feelings, and so far as in our power to do so to cultivate friendly feelings toward those with whom we have so long contested and heretofore so widely but honestly differed. Neighborhood feuds, personal animosities, and private differences should be blotted out, and when you return home a manly, straightforward course of conduct will secure the respect even of your enemies.

Whatever your responsibilities may be to Government, to society, or to individuals, meet them like men. The attempt made to establish a separate and independent confederation has failed, but the consciousness of having done your duty faithfully and to the end will in some measure repay for the hardships you have undergone.

In bidding you farewell, rest assured that you carry with you my best wishes for your future welfare and happiness. Without in any way referring to the merits of the cause in which we have been engaged, your courage and determination as exhibited on many hard-fought fields has elicited the respect and admiration of friend and foe. And I now cheerfully and gratefully acknowledge my indebtedness to the officers and men of my command, whose zeal, fidelity, and unflinching bravery have been the great source of my past success in arms.

I have never on the field of battle sent you where I was unwilling to go myself, nor would I now advise you to a course which I felt myself unwilling to pursue. You have been good soldiers, you can be good citizens. Obey the laws, preserve your honor, and the Government to which you have surrendered can afford to be and will be magnanimous.

N. B. Forrest, Lieutenant-General

VISITING OLD FRIENDS

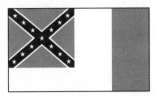

Confederate

Major-General George Pickett (See biography, page 11.)

When the war ended, Pickett and his wife fled the country, as did many other Confederate officers and politicians. They spent a year in exile in Canada living under the assumed name of Edwards to conceal their identities. When he finally returned to the United States, he visited some old friends.

[General Grant's surgeon George] Suckley and I arrived safely after an interesting but, to me, sad trip, because of the many sorrowful memories that it brought back. [Rufus] Ingalls [U.S. quartermaster general], bless his old loyal heart, met us at the train and took us up in the Quartermaster's carriage. It is the first time that I have ridden in one of Uncle Sam's vehicles since I changed colors and donned the gray, and now I ride, not as an owner but as a guest!

We had a fine steamed-oyster supper at Harvey's and told stories and talked of old times till after two o'clock.

After breakfast we went, as arranged, to see Grant. I just can't tell you, my darling, about that visit. You'll have to wait till I see you to tell you how the warm-hearted modest old warrior and loyal old friend met me how he took in his the hand of your heart-sore soldier poor, broken, defeated profession gone and looking at him for a moment without speaking, said slowly: "Pickett, if there is anything on the top of God's green earth that I can do for you, say so."

Just then his orderly apologetically brought in a card to him.

"Tell Sheridan to go to hell!"

While Sheridan was obeying Grant's order and going to his new station we three sat down and had a heart-to-heart conference. One listening would never have known that we had been on opposite sides of any question.

When I started to go Grant pulled down a cheque-book and said, "Pickett, it seems funny, doesn't it, that I should have any money to offer, but how much do you need?"

"Not any, old fellow, not a cent, thank you," I said. "I have plenty."

"But Rufus tells me that you have begun to build a house to take the place of the one old Butler burned and how can you build it without money; you do need some."

"I have sold some timber to pay for it," I told him, and to show my appreciation and gratitude unobserved I affectionately squeezed his leg, when he called out, "Rufus, it's the same old George Pickett; instead of pulling my leg he's squeezing it."

Grant is going to take Rufus, Suckley and myself to ride this afternoon to show me the changes since I was last here, years ago.

To-morrow, if all goes well, I'll start back to what is worth more to me than all I've lost, my precious wife, who was as queenly and gracious and glorious as Mrs. Edwards in one room in a boarding house in exile, as she was in Petersburg in a palatial home when her husband was the Department Commander and she had not only "vassals and slaves at her side," but the General Commanding and all his soldiers and our world at her feet.

Your Devoted Soldier

History Written in Blood

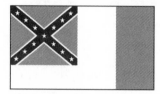

Confederate

Lieutenant-General James Longstreet (See biography, page 48.)

In glancing backward over the period of the war, and the tremendous and terrible events with which it was fraught, the reflection irresistibly arises, that it might perhaps have been avoided and without dishonor. The flag and the fame of the nation could have suffered no reproach had General Scott's advice, before the outbreak, been followed, "Wayward sisters, depart in peace."

The Southern States would have found their way back to the Union without war far earlier than they did by war. The reclaiming bonds would then have been those only of love, and the theory of government formulated by George Washington would have experienced no fracture. But the inflexible fiat of fate seemingly went forth for war; and so for four long years the history of this great nation was written in the blood of its strong men.

How We Could Have Won

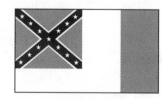

Confederate

General G. T. Beauregard (See biography, page 19.)

I was convinced that our success lay in a short, quick war of decisive blows, before the Federals, with their vast resources, could build up a great military power; to which end a concerted use of our forces, immediate and sustained, was necessary, so that, weaker though we were at all separate points, we might nevertheless strike with superior strength at some chosen decisive point, and after victory there, reach for victory now made easier elsewhere, and thus sum up success.

Instead of this, which in war we call concentration, our actual policy was diffusion, an inferior Confederate force at each separate point defensively confronting a superior Federal force; our power daily shrinking, that of the enemy increasing; and the avowed Federal policy of "attrition" of the bigger masses left free to grind the smaller, one by one, to naught. Out of this state we never emerged, when the direction of the government was, as almost always, necessary, excepting when "Richmond" was immediately in danger.

Thus, in the fall of 1861, about three months after the battle of Manassas, I proposed that the army should be raised to an effective of 60,000 men, by drawing 20,000 for the immediate enterprise from several points along the seaboard, not even at that time threatened, and from our advanced position be swiftly thrown across the Potomac at a point which I had carefully surveyed for that purpose, and moved upon the rear of Washington, thus forcing McClellan to a decisive engagement before his organization (new enlistments) was completed, and while our own army had the advantage of discipline and prestige seasoned soldiers, whose term, however, would expire in the early part of the coming summer.

This plan, approved by General Gustavus W. Smith (then immediately commanding General Johnston's own forces) as well as by General Johnston, was submitted to Mr. Davis in a conference at my headquarters, but rejected because he would not venture to strip those points of the troops we required.

Even if those points had been captured, though none were then even threatened, they must have reverted as a direct consequence to so decisive a success. I was willing, then, should it have come to that, to exchange even Richmond temporarily for Washington. Yet it was precisely from similar combinations and elements that the army was made up, to enable it next spring, under General Lee, to encounter McClellan's then perfectly organized army of 150,000 men at the very door of Richmond.

If that which was accepted as a last defensive resort against an overwhelming aggressive army had been used in an enterprising offensive against that same army while yet in the raw, the same venture had been made at less general risk, less cost of valuable lives, and with immeasurably greater certain results. The Federal Army of the Potomac would have had no chance meanwhile to become tempered to that magnificent military machine which, through all its defeats and losses, remained sound, and was stronger, with its readily assimilating new strength, at the end of the war than ever before; the pressure would have been lifted from Kentucky and Missouri, and we should have maintained what is called an active defensive warfare, that is, taken and kept the offensive against the enemy, enforcing peace.

No people ever warred for independence with more relative advantages than the Confederates; and if, as a military question, they must have failed, then no country must aim at freedom by means of war.

It is an extraordinary fact that during the four years of war Mr. Davis did not call the five Generals together into conference with a view to determining the best military policy or settling upon a decisive plan of operations involving the whole theater of war, though there was often ample opportunity for it. We needed for President either a military man of a high order, or a politician of the first class (such as Howell Cobb) without military pretensions.

The South did not fall crushed by the mere weight of the North; but it was nibbled away at all sides and ends because its executive head never gathered and wielded its great strength under the ready advantages that greatly reduced or neutralized its adversary's naked physical superiority. It is but another of the many proofs that timid direction may readily go with physical courage, and that the passive defensive policy may make a long agony, but can never win a war.

FAILURE OF THE RECONSTRUCTION

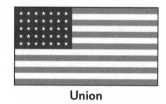

Union

General Ulysses S. Grant (See biography, page 54.)

The South has been in many ways a disappointment to me. I hoped a great deal from the South, but these hopes have been wrecked. I hoped that Northern capital would pour into the South, that Northern influence and Northern energy would soon repair all that war had wasted. But that never came. Northern capitalists saw that they could not go South without leaving self-respect at home, and they remained home. The very terms of the invitations you see in all the Southern papers show that. The editors say they are glad to have Northern men provided they do not take part in politics. Why shouldn't they take part in politics? They are made citizens for that. So long as this spirit prevails there will be no general emigration of Northern men to the South. I was disappointed, very much so. It would have been a great thing for the South if some of the streams of emigration from New England and the Middle States toward Iowa and Kansas had been diverted into the South. I hoped for different results, and did all I could to bring them around, but it could not be done.

Looking back over the whole policy of reconstruction, it seems to me that the wisest thing would have been to have continued for some time the military rule. Sensible Southern men see now that there was no government so frugal, so just and fair, as what they had under our generals. That would have enabled the Southern people to pull themselves together and repair material losses.

As to depriving them, even for a time, of suffrage, that was our right as a conqueror, and it was a mild penalty for the stupendous crime of treason. Military rule would have been just to all, to the negro who wanted freedom, the white man who wanted protection, the Northern man who wanted Union.

The trouble about military rule in the South was that our people did not like it. It was not in accordance with our institutions. I am clear now that it would have been better for the North to have postponed suffrage, reconstruction, State governments, for ten years, and held the South in a territorial condition.

But we made our scheme, and must do what we can with it. Suffrage once given can never be taken away, and all that remains for us now is to make good that gift by protecting those who have received it.

Apart from the triumph of the Union, and the emancipation of the slaves, one of the great results of the war was the position it gave us as a nation among the nations of the world. That I have seen every day during my residence abroad, and to me it is one of the most gratifying results of the war. That alone was worth making a great sacrifice for.

Forrest's Civil Rights Speech

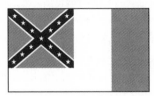

Confederate

Lieutenant-General Nathan Bedford Forrest (See biography, page 73.)

After the war Nathan Bedford Forrest associated himself with the first of the three incarnations of the Ku Klux Klan. As it expanded and tried to become a national organization, he became its first grand wizard. In a newspaper interview three years after the war, he described it as "a protective, political, military organization … Its objects originally were protection against Loyal Leagues and the Grand Army of the Republic; but … it was then made a political organization."

Apologists say he left the group because of its violence or perhaps because a federal grand jury had labeled it a "terrorist organization." It is possible that his views changed as he aged.

Forrest gave the following keynote speech to a large peace gathering in Memphis, Tennessee, on July 5, 1875, sponsored by the area's African American clubs and societies. Most Southerners didn't celebrate the Fourth of July for many years after the war, but as the centennial approached, it was making a slow comeback. This occasion was held on the day after the holiday, and several of the honored speakers were ex-Confederates, including Forrest and Gideon Pillow. The crowd gathered at the fairgrounds probably numbered more than 5,000. Before Forrest spoke, a woman approached him on the stand and presented him with a bouquet of flowers as an offering of peace.

Miss Lewis, ladies and gentlemen: I accept the flowers as a memento of reconciliation between the white and colored races of the Southern states. I accept them more particularly as it comes from a colored lady, for if there is any one on God's earth who loves the ladies I believe it is myself.

This day is a day that is proud to me, having occupied the position that I did for the past thirteen years [as a Confederate general], and been misunderstood by your race. This is the first opportunity I have had during that time to say that I am your friend. I am here a representative of the Southern people, one more slandered and maligned than any man in the nation. I will say to you and to the colored race that the men who bore arms and followed the flag of the Confederacy are, with very few exceptions, your friends.

I have an opportunity of saying what I have always felt that I am your friend, for my interests are your interests, and your interests are my interests. We were born on the same soil, breathe the same air, and live in the same land. Why, then, can we not live as brothers?

I will say that when the war broke out I felt it my duty to stand by my people. When the time came I did the best I could, and I don't believe I flickered. I came here with the jeers and sneers of some white people, who think that I am doing wrong. I believe I can exert some influence, and do much to assist the people in strengthening fraternal relations, and shall do all in my power to bring about harmony, peace and unity. It has always been my motto to elevate every man—to depress none. I want to elevate you to take positions in law offices, in stores, on farms, and wherever you are capable of going.

I have not said anything about politics today. I don't propose to say anything about politics, but I want you to do as I do—go to the polls and select the best men to vote for. You have a right to elect whom you please; vote for the man you think best, and I think, when that is done, that you and I are freemen. Do as you consider right and honest in electing men for office.

I did not come here to make you a long speech, although invited to do so by you. I am not much of a speaker, and my business prevented me from preparing myself. I came to meet you as friends, and welcome you to the white people. I want you to come nearer to us. When I can serve you I will do so. We have but one Union, one flag, one country; let us stand together. We may differ in color, but not in sentiment.

Use your best judgment in selecting men for office and vote as you think right.

Many things have been said about me which are wrong, and which white and black persons here, who stood by me through the war, can contradict. I have been in the heat of battle—oftener, perhaps, than any within the sound of my voice. Men have come to me to ask for quarter, both black and white, and I have shielded them. I have placed myself between them and the bullets of my men, and told them they should be kept unharmed. Do your duty as citizens. Go to work, be industrious, live honestly and act truly, and when you are oppressed I'll come to your relief.

I thank you, ladies and gentlemen, for this opportunity you have afforded me to be with you. I thank you for the flowers, and to assure you that I am with you in heart and in hand.

When Forrest spoke of being "one more slandered and maligned than any man in the nation," he was referring mainly to the Fort Pillow Massacre, in which Forrest's force of 1,500 to 2,500 Confederates attacked a garrison of 600 mostly African-American soldiers, murdering many unarmed men— including officers and civilians—as they tried to

surrender or well after they already had surrendered. Between 277 and 297 on the Union side died in the battle and massacre, while Forrest lost only 14. It is not known whether Forrest ordered his men to give no quarter, whether he allowed his men to do it, or whether he was unaware of what they were doing—but as the commander he was ultimately responsible, and he was heavily criticized for the massacre.

Some apologists compare Forrest's speech with a quotation of Lincoln's from before the war[31]. In the end, what you say is important, but what really matters is what you do. Lincoln ended legalized slavery. We can only hope Forrest meant what he said.

---

31 See page xviii.

REMEMBERING THE DEAD AT GETTYSBURG

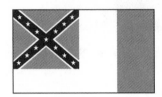

Confederate

Major-General George Pickett (See biography, page 11.)

In a letter to his wife, George Pickett—who led the most famous charge of the war—described attending a memorial service at Richmond's Hollywood Cemetery to honor those who had died at Gettysburg.

From the old Market to the Cemetery of Hollywood the streets, sidewalks, windows and housetops were crowded. There must have been twelve thousand people at Hollywood. Such a demonstration of devotion and sympathy was, I think, never before witnessed on earth.

Think of it, my darling, so penetrating, so universal a oneness of love and respect and reverence existed that there was a stillness, an awesomeness, save for those necessary sounds— the clanking of swords, the tramp of horses and the martial tread of men keeping time with funeral marches—the solemn requiem. No cheers, no applause, only loving greetings from tear-stained faces, heads bent in reverence, clasped hands held out to us as we passed along. As I saw once more the courage-lit faces of my brave Virginians, again I heard their cry—"We'll follow you, Marse George!"

From their eternal silence those who marched heroically to death looked down upon us yesterday and were sad. My darling, you cannot know—no, you cannot know!

As I clasped the hand of one after another of those who crowded around me I was greeted with the words—"My husband was killed at Gettysburg." "My son is lying there among the dead"—"My brother was with you there and he has just come back to me"—so many crushed hearts filling my heart with grief.

Among the guests were some of our West Point comrades whose only vocation, like mine, was war. Our tents are folded now and we parted, going off, each to his work; one to the farm, another to the trade; one to seek some position; one to one place, one to another; and I to return to my beautiful wife and my sick baby, my only joy and my life, knowing that what is best will come.

Your Devoted Soldier

LOOKING BACK ON THE STORM

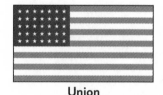

Union

Major-General Winfield Scott Hancock (*See biography, page 116.*)

The historian of the future undertakes an onerous task, a high responsibility, a sacred trust. Above all things, justice and truth should dwell in his mind and heart. Then, dipping his pen as it were in the crimson tide, the sunshine of heaven lighting his page, giving honor to whom honor is due, doing even justice to the splendid valor alike of friend and foe, he may tell the world how the rain descended in streams of fire, and the floods came in billows of rebellion, and the winds blew in blasts of fraternal execration, and beat upon the fabric of the Federal Union, and that it fell not, for, resting on the rights and liberties of the people, it was founded upon a rock.

ROLL CALL

CONFEDERATE STATES ARMY

Full Gen. Robert E. Lee

When the war ended, Robert E. Lee wasn't arrested. Some of his property was seized, and he lost the right to vote. His family mansion became Arlington National Cemetery, for which his family was later compensated. He spent the remainder of his life as president of Washington College in Lexington, Virginia, later renamed Washington and Lee University in his honor. He died of pneumonia in 1870, two weeks after suffering a stroke. He was sixty-three.

Lincoln had insisted that as part of the terms of surrender, everyone would be pardoned, but after his death, President Andrew Johnson changed this, establishing fourteen classes of people who needed his specific approval before they were pardoned. Lee took the Amnesty Oath and applied for a pardon, but it appears Secretary of State William Seward prevented it. Lee's U.S. citizenship wasn't restored until 105 years after his death.

Lieut. Gen. Thomas "Stonewall" Jackson

Lieutenant-General Stonewall Jackson was accidentally shot by his own men at Chancellorsville. After his left arm was amputated, he died of pneumonia in May 1863 at the age of thirty-nine.

Lieut. Gen. James Longstreet

After the war many Southerners considered Longstreet a pariah because—like John "the Gray Ghost" Mosby—he joined the Republican Party and supported the candidacy of Grant, his prewar friend, for president. Settling in New Orleans, he became partner in a cotton brokerage; president of the Great Southern and Western Fire, Marine, and Accident Insurance Company; president of the New Orleans and Northeastern Railroad; and surveyor of customs in New Orleans. He was also the adjutant general of the state militia and was placed in command of all of the militia and state police forces in New Orleans, given the rank of major general.

For his safety from anti-Reconstructionists, he moved his family back to where he grew up in Gainesville, Georgia. He then was appointed ambassador to the Ottoman Empire and served as U.S. commissioner of railroads. He died in 1904 of pneumonia, aged eighty-two.

Maj. Gen. George Pickett

After fleeing to Canada, Pickett returned to Norfolk, Virginia, in 1866, taking a job as an insurance agent. He died of scarlet fever in 1875 at age fifty.

Maj. Gen. J. E. B. Stuart

Stuart was shot at the Battle of Yellow Tavern, about six miles north of Richmond, on May 11, 1864, and died the following day. He was thirty-one years old. In the general orders announcing his death, Lee wrote, "Among the gallant soldiers who have fallen in this war, General Stuart was second to none in valour, in zeal, and in unflinching devotion to his country." Lieutenant-General Longstreet asserted, "His death was possibly a greater loss to the Confederate army even than that of the swift-moving General 'Stonewall' Jackson."

Full Gen. G. T. Beauregard

Settling in New Orleans after the war, Beauregard became chief engineer and general superintendent of the New Orleans, Jackson, & Great Northern Railroad. The following year he became the railroad's president. He was also the president of the New Orleans & Carrollton Street Railway, inventing a cable car system.

Both he and Jubal Early made considerable money overseeing the drawings of the Louisiana State Lottery several days a month. The lottery tickets were sold throughout the United States and abroad, generating considerable profits for the company that ran it, with the state receiving a set fee. The two former Confederate generals lent credibility to the lottery from 1877 until antigambling groups had it outlawed in 1893.

Beauregard also served in the Louisiana state militia as its adjutant general and was elected commissioner of public works in New Orleans. He was seventy-four when he died in his sleep from heart failure in 1893.

Lieut. Gen. Nathan Bedford Forrest

By the end of the war, Forrest said that he'd had thirty horses shot out from under him and had killed thirty-one men in hand-to-hand combat—adding, "I was a horse ahead at the end."

He returned to Memphis, Tennessee, but abolition put an end to his businesses as a slaveholder and dealer, so he took a job with the Marion & Memphis Railroad. He became president of the company, but it soon went bankrupt.

Meanwhile, Forrest famously joined the Ku Klux Klan, though he was not a founding member. He left the group in 1869. His descendants say that he ordered the group to disband, and it does appear that his views changed as he grew older. In 1877 he died at age fifty-six, reportedly from complications of diabetes.

Lieut. Gen. Jubal Early

Early met his final defeat in March 1865 at Waynesboro, Virginia. His men surrendered, while he and a few of his staff escaped. Lee then relieved Early of command, citing his need for someone who could "develop the strength and resources of the country, and inspire the soldiers with confidence."

When Lee surrendered the following month, Early fled through Texas to Mexico, disguised as a farmer. He ended up in Cuba, and then settled in Toronto, Canada, where he wrote his memoir on the final year of the war. He helped establish and promote "Lost Cause" propaganda that romanticized the Confederacy; portrayed noble Southern generals fighting immoral Northerners before inevitably succumbing to the North's overwhelming numbers, resources, wealth, and power; held that Northern aggression against the Southern way of life justified secession; and promoted a decidedly tinted view that the antebellum South was an idyllic paradise and that the war really wasn't about slavery, which was actually beneficial to the slaves, who remained loyal and faithful to their benevolent masters until Northern abolitionists corrupted them.

Early returned to Virginia in 1869 and resumed his law practice. He died in 1894 at age seventy-seven after falling down a flight of stairs.

Full Gen. John Bell Hood

Hood became a cotton broker in Louisiana and president of the Life Association of America insurance company. He fathered eleven children, including three pairs of twins. In the winter of 1878–79, yellow fever struck New Orleans, wiping out his insurance company and killing him at age forty-eight, along with his wife and eldest child. The ten orphans were scattered into foster care across five states in the North and South.

Full Gen. Braxton Bragg

The government had confiscated Bragg's plantation, making it a shelter for freed slaves, so he and his family lived at his brother's plantation in Alabama for a couple of years. He briefly worked a number of jobs, including as an insurance agent for Jefferson Davis's Carolina Life Insurance Company. One day in 1876, while walking along in Galveston, Texas, he fell, unconscious, and died a few minutes later at the age of fifty-nine.

Full Gen. Joseph Johnston

Like many other former officers, Johnston became a railroad executive and an insurance agent after the war. Once the restrictions preventing former Confederates from seeking political office had lifted, he served a single two-year term to the U.S. House of Representatives from Virginia.

He met Sherman a number of times after the war, as friends, and refused to allow anyone to say anything bad about Sherman in his presence. He died in 1891, aged eighty-four, from pneumonia contracted while acting as an honorary pallbearer at Sherman's funeral.

Photo by Mark Albertin

Lieut. Gen. Leonidas Polk

Polk, along with his 20,000 men, was sent to join forces with Joseph Johnston's Army of Tennessee to stop Sherman's march on Atlanta. While observing Union positions, Polk was killed at age fifty-eight in 1864 near Pine Mountain, Georgia, when a cannonball went through his left arm and chest and exited through his right arm, practically cutting the Fighting Bishop in half.

Greatly saddened by his death, President Davis wrote, "Since the calamitous fall of General Albert Sidney Johnston at Shiloh and of General T. J. Jackson at Chancellorsville, the country sustained no heavier blow than in the death of General Polk."

UNITED STATES ARMY

Full Gen. Ulysses S. Grant

Considered to be the great hero of the war, Grant became America's first full, or four-star, general. Officially his rank was General of the Army of the United States. He assisted in the Reconstruction and served two terms as president, during which time he helped protect the civil rights of African Americans and forced the first incarnation of the Ku Klux Klan to disband. Unfortunately, scandals involving corrupt appointees and friends marred his presidency. After leaving office, he traveled the world with his family for two years, after which he was swindled in a business deal and left destitute. Mark Twain came to his rescue by publishing his memoirs to great acclaim. In 1885, at age sixty-three, he died from throat cancer.

Fourteen years later Longstreet—a friend of Grant from West Point and after the war—spoke of fighting against him while at a dinner in the home of Grant's son in San Diego, California. "Thirty-odd years ago I first met General Grant in the Civil War at the Wilderness, and there received the wound that paralyzed my right arm. During the fiercest warfare this nation has seen, General Grant was the strongest obstacle that stood between me and my people and the consummation of the dearest hopes that they then cherished. Now, in this day of peace and union, with not a cloud upon the sky of a reunited country, in the presence of General Grant's descendants, under the roof of his namesake son, I want to drink this toast to the memory of Grant, revered alike by the brave men who fought with him and the equally brave men who fought him."

Forrest, not Grant's friend, said: "I regard him as a great military commander, a good man, honest and liberal. I am opposed to General Grant in everything, but I would do him justice."

Maj. Gen. George Armstrong Custer

After the war Custer went to fight in the Indian Wars. In Dakota Territory he suffered his disastrous defeat in the Battle of the Little Bighorn when he launched a surprise attack on a very large group of Sioux and Cheyenne villages, who greatly outnumbered his forces. He was killed at age thirty-six. The news of his death and the deaths of most of the Seventh Cavalry arrived during the nation's centennial celebrations on July 4, 1876. It was an inauspicious beginning for the nation's second century.

Full Gen. William Tecumseh Sherman

In 1866 Congress created the rank of General of the Army—four-star general—specifically for Grant. Sherman was then promoted to lieutenant general. Three years later when Grant became president, Sherman was promoted to Grant's former rank and position. Sherman commanded the army through most of the Indian Wars. In 1884 he retired and lived in New York City until his death. He was seventy-one when he died in 1891 a week after he caught a cold while attending an opera.

Maj. Gen. George McClellan

Lincoln replaced McClellan as commander of the Army of the Potomac in 1862. He ran a failed 1864 presidential campaign against Lincoln, losing in a landslide. After spending several years in Europe, he became chief engineer of New York City's Department of Docks, president of the Atlantic & Great Western Railroad, and governor of New Jersey. In 1885, at age fifty-eight, he died of a heart attack.

Full Gen. Philip Sheridan

When the war ended, Sheridan was given a large occupation force of 50,000 soldiers and assigned to protect Texas from Mexico, then under the puppet regime of Austrian Archduke Maximilian, who had declared himself emperor of Mexico. Sheridan played a major role in the Reconstruction as well as the Indian Wars. It was largely because of Sheridan's support that Custer was promoted to brevet major general. During the Indian Wars, Sheridan continued the Civil War's scorched-earth policies and nearly drove the buffalo to extinction.

In 1883 Sheridan took over from Sherman as commanding general and shortly before his death in 1888 was promoted to full general—the country's third four-star general, after Grant and Sherman. He died at age fifty-seven following a series of heart attacks.

Maj. Gen. Winfield Scott Hancock

After Lincoln's assassination Hancock supervised the execution of the conspirators. He was briefly assigned to the Indian Wars until President Johnson had him swap places with Sheridan, managing the Reconstruction in Louisiana and Texas, because of his pro-Southern sentiments. When Grant became president, Hancock found himself back in the Indian Wars in charge of Minnesota and the Montana and Dakota Territories.

In 1880 Hancock, a Democrat, ran for president against Congressman James Garfield and lost. He died in 1886 from an infection worsened by diabetes. He was sixty-one.

Maj. Gen. Joshua Chamberlain

After returning to Maine, Chamberlain was elected governor, serving four years before becoming president of Bowdoin College in Brunswick. He was wounded six times during the war, once very severely. At that time the mortality rate was so high for gut wounds that doctors usually just left these patients to die, but they operated on Chamberlain four times and were amazed when he survived. He lived for another fifty years, but the wound never fully healed and in 1914, at the age of eighty-five, he became the last Civil War veteran to die from wounds received during the war.

Maj. Gen. Ambrose Burnside

After the war ended, Burnside resigned from the army. He held a number of corporate directorships, including four railroad presidencies. Entering politics, he became governor of Rhode Island and a U.S. senator. In 1881 he died of angina at age fifty-seven.

Maj. Gen. Joseph Hooker

Hooker continued in the military until he had a stroke in 1868. He spent the remaining eleven years of his life in Ohio, dying in 1879 at age sixty-four during a visit to Long Island, New York. The cause of his death is unknown.

Maj. Gen. George Meade

When the war came to an end, Meade went on to command the Military Division of the Atlantic, the Department of the East, and the Department of the South, before becoming governor of the Reconstruction Third Military District in Atlanta. Complications from the wounds he received in the Battle of Glendale during the Peninsula campaign, combined with pneumonia, sent him to his grave in 1872 at the age of fifty-six.

Maj. Gen. William Rosecrans
Rosecrans worked in railroads and served for five months as U.S. minister to Mexico, until the newly elected President Grant replaced him. He served in Congress from 1881 to 1885 as a Democrat from California and from 1885 to 1893 as the register of the treasury. He died in 1898 in Redondo Beach, California. He had been recovering from pneumonia when he received news that his favorite grandson had died. His heath declined, and his family said he died from sorrow.

United States Navy

Full Adm. David Dixon Porter
Porter became the superintendent of the U.S. Naval Academy at Annapolis, Maryland, which he reformed, bringing to it professional standards that rivaled those of West Point. He eventually took over as full admiral from his adopted brother, but as the position was largely honorary, he was able to devote some of his time to writing history books and fiction. His health declined after he suffered a heart attack, and he died at the age of seventy-seven in 1891, just a day before his friend Sherman did.

CONCLUSION

THE STORM CLOUDS BEGIN TO CLEAR

> The real greatness in a battle is the fearless courage, the brave and heroic conduct, of the men under withering fire. It was the enlisted men who were the glory of the army. It was they, the rank and file, who stood in the front, closed the gaps, and were mowed down in swaths like grass by cannon and musket-balls.
> —HENRY W. ELSON IN THE PHOTOGRAPHIC HISTORY OF THE CIVIL WAR (1911)

The Civil War preserved the territorial integrity of the United States of America. President Lincoln's Emancipation Proclamation freed slaves in the Confederacy in 1863, while the Thirteenth Amendment to the Constitution ended legal slavery in 1865. Unfortunately, equality has come slowly, and still hasn't quite arrived. Part of the reason for this was the difficulty of Reconstruction, which likely resulted from Lincoln's untimely assassination. He wanted to reunite the country rapidly with a generous policy of reconciliation. For the South, which hated Lincoln throughout the war and considered him a tyrant, he was probably their best hope of a smooth integration back into the reunited country.

But the winds of war blow unpredictably. By killing Lincoln, John Wilkes Booth hoped to avenge the South. Instead, he caused it irreparable harm, contributing to wounds that remain today, and which may take yet another century to heal.

Lincoln's death placed the ineffectual Andrew Johnson—the only Southern senator not to quit the Union upon secession—in the presidency, enabling the Radical Republicans to gain control of Congress and push through their plan to punish the South. The failure of the Reconstruction resulted in widespread corruption; the rise of the Ku Klux Klan; the enactment of Jim Crow laws; the establishment of thousands of all-white "sundown towns" throughout the North, Midwest, and West; the lynching of at least 3,446 black and 1,297 white people, which continued until 1968; and many other evils, which still reverberate today.

Compare this to Britain, which abolished slavery in 1833 without much problem. Canada, Sweden, Denmark, Greece, Argentina, Peru, Venezuela, Chile, Bolivia, Mexico, and Tunisia also abolished slavery before the start of American Civil War. Slavery became tangled in politics and the issues of states' rights, self-determination, state government versus federal government, national integrity, national identity, patriotism, the use of armed force against fellow Americans, and ultimately the beating of a portion of the population into submission with military might.

The Civil War remains the worst disaster in U.S. history. More Americans died in this war than all of America's other wars combined. Good men—brothers and friends—fought on both sides. Of all Northern males aged twenty to forty-five, 10 percent died. Of all Southern white males aged eighteen to forty, 30 percent died. Two-thirds of the soldiers succumbed to disease. Altogether, the war wiped out about 3.7 percent of the total population—about 1,150,000 people. By the end of the war, 60 percent of the South's antebellum wealth had evaporated, while Northern wealth increased by 50 percent during the same period largely because of industrialization. From 1860 to 1870 the percentage of the nation's wealth in the South dropped from 30 to 12 percent. With the exception of Virginia, which has done well, the Southern states—with the addition of Montana and New Mexico—remain the poorest states in the Union today.

The Civil War transformed the nation. Before the war people considered themselves citizens of their home state first and of their country second, particularly in the South. Each state was seen as a separate entity, joined with other states to form the federal government. This was apparent when General Lee struggled with divided loyalties between the federal government and his home state, with loyalty to Virginia finally winning out. This was also apparent right before the Battle of Gettysburg, after Stonewall Jackson died, when Lee had to appoint three commanders and passed over two generals who had seniority because they were not Virginians.

The war changed all this. People were now Americans first, citizens of the United States. They resided in their states, but state took a back seat to country. The individual states lost considerable power and standing, while the federal government grew to tower over the states and became the dominant force that it is today.

Before the war each state assembled its own militias and volunteer armies. There were Illinois regiments and Florida regiments. Soldiers from a single town were able to serve and fight together. Even the U.S. Army was divided into the Army of the Potomac, the Army of the Tennessee, and a dozen or so regional armies. After the war state militias remained, but by 1903 they all fell under the National Guard of the United States as a single reserve military force. By World War II there was little sign of individual states; the military had become national.

This change of perception began in the North before the war, but it wasn't until after the war began that many Northerners realized that they were willing to die to keep the Southern states in the Union. Maintaining the integrity of the government suddenly became of paramount importance to them, with the Stars and Stripes a symbol of this.

Adam Goodheart describes in 1861: The Civil War Awakening how Northerners responded when Major Anderson defiantly moved from Fort Moultrie to Fort Sumter.

Before that day, the flag had served mostly as a military ensign or a convenient marking of American territory, flown from forts, embassies, and ships, and displayed on special occasions like the Fourth of July. But in the weeks after Major Anderson's surprising stand, it became something different. Suddenly the Stars and Stripes flew—as it does today, and especially as it did after September 11—from houses, from storefronts, from churches; above the village greens and college quads. For the first time American flags were mass-produced rather than individually stitched and even so, manufacturers could not keep up with demand. ... The abstraction of the Union cause was transfigured into a physical thing: strips of cloth that millions of people would fight for, and many thousands die for.

The Civil War also brought the introduction of income taxes. In 1861, to help pay for the war,

Lincoln established a flat 3 percent income tax for everyone making more than $800 a year (about $200,000 in today's dollars). The following year Congress changed it to a more complex progressive tax that placed a greater burden on the middle class. Today the middle class pays roughly 30 to 40 percent of their income in taxes, while the mega-rich generally pay nothing, or if they do pay tax, up to 22 percent.

What would the Founding Fathers—Washington, Jefferson, Franklin, and the rest—think if they could see how their country has evolved from a loose collection of former colonies to the superpower of today? Would they mourn the decrease in state sovereignty and individual freedoms? Would they have outlawed slavery then to spare the nation from suffering through the Civil War? Jefferson famously knew it was coming, and he surely wasn't the only one. What would the world be like if the war had never happened? Would the Confederacy still exist, or would there have been a peaceful reconciliation? Would the Southern states have given up slavery on their own, perhaps from external pressure and boycotts? Lee thought they would. How would all those who died in the war have changed the world?—legions of potential artists, business leaders, doctors, farmers, inventors, scientists, teachers, and writers, their lives cut short before they could make their contributions to society.

We can never know.

A girl in mourning holding photograph of her father in his cavalry uniform.

ACKNOWLEDGMENTS

I wish to express my appreciation to Elaine Molina; Martha and Jim Goodwin; Scott Stephens; Marty Goeller and Dorian Rivas; Terity, Natasha, and Debbie Burbach; Brandon, Alisha, and Kathy Hill; Jeff and Carol Whiteaker; Christopher, Doug, and Michelle Whiteaker; Gabriel, Aurelia, Elijah, Nina, and Justin Weinberger; Rachel and Roxanne Nunez; Anthony, Jayla, Sin, and Bobby Gamboa; Pat Egner; Baba and Mimi Marlene Bruner; Anne and Jerry Buzzard; Krystyne Göhnert; Eric, Tim, and Debbie Cissna; Norene Hilden; Doug and Shirley Strong; Barbara Main; Joanne and Monte Goeller; Irma and Joe Rodriguez; Danny and Mary Schutt; Les Benedict; Dr. Rich Sutton; SK Lindsey; Jeanne Sisson; Michael and Roz McKevitt; Dennis Kelly; and to my agent, Charlotte Cecil Raymond.

SOURCES

ABBREVIATED TITLES:

Beauregard, "Bull Run": Gen. G. T. Beauregard, "The Battle of Bull Run," The Century Illustrated Monthly Magazine 29, no. 1 (November 1884): 80–106.

Grant, Memoirs: Gen. Ulysses S. Grant, Personal Memoirs of U. S. Grant, vol. 1 (New York: Charles L. Webster & Co., 1885; 1892 printing).

Hancock, Reminiscences: Almira Hancock, Reminiscences of Winfield Scott Hancock (New York: Charles L. Webster & Co., 1887).

Hood, Advance: Gen. John Bell Hood, Advance and Retreat (published for the Hood Orphan Memorial Fund [by] G. T. Beauregard, 1880).

Johnson, Battles: Robert Underwood Johnson and Clarence Clough Buel, eds., Battles and Leaders of the Civil War, vol. 1 (New York: The Century Co., 1888).

Longstreet, "Fredericksburg": Lieut. Gen. James Longstreet, "The Battle of Fredericksburg," The Century Illustrated Monthly Magazine 32 (August 1886): 609–26.

Longstreet, "Campaign": Lieut. Gen. James Longstreet, "The Campaign of Gettysburg," The Philadelphia Weekly Times, 3 November 1877; Col. A. K. McClure, "Lee in Pennsylvania," The Annals of the War: Written by Leading Participants North and South (Philadelphia: The Times Publishing Co., 1879).

Longstreet, Manassas: Lieut. Gen. James Longstreet, From Manassas to Appomattox (Philadelphia: J. B. Lippincott Co., 1896).

McClellan, Story: Maj. Gen. George McClellan, McClellan's Own Story (New York: C. L. Webster, 1887).

Meade, Life: Maj. Gen. George Meade, The Life and Letters of George Gordon Meade, Major-General United States Army, vols. 1 and 2 (New York: Charles Scribner's Sons, 1913).

Moore, Rebellion: Frank Moore, The Rebellion Record, vols. 5 and 7 (New York: G. P. Putnam, 1864).

Pickett, Heart: George Pickett, The Heart of a Soldier: As Revealed in the Intimate Letters of Gnl George E. Pickett CSA (New York: Seth Moyle Inc., 1913). Note that there is considerable scholarly debate over whether Sallie fictionalized, rewrote, or heavily edited her husband's letters.

Computer analysis suggests the letters I've included are mostly authentic.

Porter, Incidents: Adm. David Dixon Porter, Incidents and Anecdotes of the Civil War (New York: D. Appleton and Co., 1885).

Porter, History: Adm. David Dixon Porter, The Naval History of the Civil War (New York: The Sherman Publishing Co., 1886).

Sherman, "Letters": Gen. William Tecumseh Sherman and Senator John Sherman, "Letters of Two Brothers", The Century Illustrated Monthly Magazine 45, no. 3 (January 1893): 425-40.

Sherman, Memoirs: Gen. William Tecumseh Sherman, Memoirs of General William T. Sherman, vols. 1 and 2 (New York: D. Appleton & Co., 1875).

Joint Committee, Conduct (1863): U.S. Congress Joint Committee on the Conduct of the War, Report of the Joint Committee on the Conduct of the War, 37th Congress, 3rd Session, vol. 1 (Washington: U.S. Government Printing Office, 1863).

Joint Committee, Conduct (1865): U.S. Congress Joint Committee on the Conduct of the War, Report of the Joint Committee on the Conduct of the War, at the Second Session Thirty-Eighth Congress, vols. 1 and 3 (Washington: U.S. Government Printing Office, 1865).

Joint Committee, Petersburg: U.S. Congress Joint Committee on the Conduct of the War, Report of the Committee on the Conduct of the War on the Attack on Petersburg, 38th Congress, 2d Session (Washington: U.S. Government Printing Office, 1865).

War Dept., OR: U.S. War Department, The War of the Rebellion, series I, various volumes (Washington: U.S. Government Printing Office, various years).

Young, World: John Russell Young, Around the World with General Grant, vol. 2 (New York: The American News Co., 1879). Gen. Grant reviewed, corrected, and approved all his interviews in this book.

INTRODUCTION

Stephens—The Rising Storm

Sherman, Memoirs, vol. 1, 149–50.

Box Quotation

Col. John "the Gray Ghost" Mosby, letter to Capt. Samuel
Chapman, 4 June 1907, The Gilder Lehrman Institute
of American History, New York. gilderlehrman.org/
collections/4420081c-eb80-4104-9f34-204723373231.

THE WAR BEGINS

Custer—Thoughts of War from West Point

Maj. Gen. George Armstrong Custer, "War Memoirs," The
Galaxy 21, no. 3 (March 1876): 322; 21, no. 4 (April 1876):
450–51, 453–54.

Sherman—From New Orleans to Washington, D.C.

Sherman, Memoirs, vol. 1, 152–53, 162–63, 166–68.

Early—Virginia Secedes

Lieut. Gen. Jubal Early and R. H. (Ruth Hairston) Early,
Autobiographical Sketch and Narrative of the War between the
States (Philadelphia: J. B. Lippincott Co., 1912), vii–ix.

Lee—Lee Resigns His Commission

Bio Box: Lee's reconnaissance patrol in Grant, Memoirs,
131–32.

Gen. Robert E. Lee, letter from Texas, 27 December 1856,
and letter to Gen. Scott, Memoirs of Robert E. Lee (New
York: J. M. Stoddard & Co., 1887), 83–84, 94.

Pickett—The Journey to Richmond

Bio Box: Maj. Gen. George McClellan quoted in LaSalle
Corbell Pickett, Pickett and His Men, 2d ed. (Atlanta: The
Foote & Davies Co., 1900), 422.

Maj. Gen. George Pickett, letters to his fiancée, Sallie;
Pickett, Heart, 34–37.

Box Quotation

Lieut. Gen. Thomas "Stonewall" Jackson quoted in William
A. Obenchain, "Stonewall Jackson's Scabbard Speech,"
Southern Historical Society Papers XVI (January–December
1888): 46.

THE BATTLE OF FORT SUMTER

Porter—Fort Sumter vs. Fort Pickens

Bio Box: Young, World, 2, 305.

Porter, Incidents, 13–16, 23.

Beauregard—The Bombardment of Fort Sumter

Brig. Gen. G. T. Beauregard, official report, 27 April 1861;
War Dept., OR, series I, vol. I, part I (1880): 30–35.

Brig. Gen. G. T. Beauregard, report, 17 April 1861; War Dept.,
OR, series I, vol. I, part I (1880): 28.

Box Quotation

Capt. James Chester, "Inside Sumter in '61"; Johnson,
Battles, vol. 1, 66.

Side Box—Lincoln's War Room

A. B. Chandler quoted in Col. Alexander K. McClure, "Abe"
Lincoln's Yarns and Stories (Chicago: The Educational Co.,
1901), 86–87.

THE FIRST BATTLE OF MANASSAS

Custer—Custer's First Two Days on Duty

Maj. Gen. George Armstrong Custer, "War Memoirs," The
Galaxy 21, no. 4 (April 1876): 457–60; 21, no. 5 (May 1876):
624, 627–32; 21, no. 6 (June 1876): 809.

Beauregard—The Confederate Battle Plan

Beauregard, "Bull Run," 80–81, 85–88, 91, 95–97.

Jackson—Turning the Tide

Lieut. Gen. Thomas "Stonewall" Jackson, letters to his wife,
22 July, 5 August, and 15 August 1861; Mary Anna Jackson,
Life and Letters of General Thomas J. Jackson (Stonewall
Jackson) (New York: Harper & Brothers, 1892), 177–80,
182–83.

Sherman—Confusion among the Federals

Col. William Tecumseh Sherman, official report, 25 July
1861, and dispatch, 22 July 1861; War Dept., OR, series I,
vol. II (1880): 370–71, 755.

Sherman, Memoirs, vol. 1, 188–91.

Beauregard—Analysis of the Battle

Beauregard, "Bull Run," 101–2.

**Johnston—The Impossibility of Invading Washington,
D.C.**

Bio Box: Sherman, Memoirs, vol. 1, 328, 407 (quoted in an
advertisement for Johnston's book).

Gen. Joseph Johnston, "Manassas to Seven Pines," The
Century Illustrated Monthly Magazine 30, no. 1 (May 1885):
103, 106.

Gen. Joseph Johnston, Narrative of Military Operations,
Directed, During the Late War Between the States (New York:
D. Appleton and Co., 1874), 57, 60–63, 64–65.

Longstreet—Mistakes and What Could Have Been

Longstreet, Manassas, 54–57, 59.

Johnston and Beauregard—A "Glorious Victory"

Brig. Gens. Joseph Johnston and G. T. Beauregard, congratulatory proclamation of Generals Johnston and
Beauregard, 25 July 1861; War Dept., OR, series I, vol. II
(1880): 574.

Box Quotations

Longstreet, Manassas, 48–49, 51–52.

Hunter McGuire, "General T. J. ('Stonewall') Jackson, Confederate States Army. His Career and Character," *Southern Historical Society Papers* XXV (January–December 1897): 94.

McClellan, Story, 364–65.

Side Box—Friendly Fire

Lieut. Gen. Leonidas Polk quoted in Lieut. Col. Arthur Fremantle, *Three Months in the Southern States. April-June, 1863* (New York: John Bradburn, 1864), 165–67.

THE BATTLE OF SHILOH

Grant—Fighting with Raw Recruits

Bio Box: Longstreet, Manassas, 17–18.

Gen. Ulysses S. Grant, "The Battle of Shiloh," *The Century Illustrated Monthly Magazine* 29, no. 4 (February 1885): 593–606, 608–13. Most of this was reprinted in Grant's memoirs.

Young, World, vol. 2, 469, 471, 473.

Sherman—The Extreme Fury of Battle

Sherman, Memoirs, vol. 1, 230, 244–46.

Brig. Gen. William Tecumseh Sherman, official report, 10 April 1862; War Dept., OR, series I, vol. X, part 1 (1880): 249–52.

Beauregard—Striking a Sudden Blow

Gen. G. T. Beauregard, official report, 11 April 1862; War Dept., OR, series I, vol. X, part 1 (1880): 385–88.

Gen. G. T. Beauregard, "The Shiloh Campaign," part 2, *The North American Review* 142, no. 351 (February 1886): 161–74.

Gen. G. T. Beauregard, "The Campaign of Shiloh"; Johnson, Battles, vol. 1, 589f.

Bragg—"Our Condition Is Horrible"

Maj. Gen. Braxton Bragg, dispatch, 8 April 1862; War Dept., OR, series I, vol. X, part 2 (1880): 398–99.

Forrest—"Recruits Wanted"

Bio Box: Nathan Bedford Forrest slavery ad; Julian Street, *American Adventures* (New York: The Century Co., 1917), 522.

Col. Nathan Bedford Forrest, recruiting ad; *Memphis Appeal*, May 18–29, 1862.

Box Quotations

Gen. William Tecumseh Sherman, speech before the Society of the Army of the Tennessee in Chicago, 9 September 1885, Gen. William Tecumseh Sherman, "An Unspoken Address to the Loyal Legion," *The North American Review* 142, no. 352 (March 1886): 306.

Gen. Ulysses S. Grant, "The Battle of Shiloh," *The Century Illustrated Monthly Magazine* 29, no. 4 (February 1885): 598.

Gen. William Tecumseh Sherman, letter to Allen Thorndike Rice, 2 January 1886, reprinted in "Sherman's Opinion of Grant," *The North American Review* 142, no. 351 (February 1886): 207.

Maj.-Gen. Braxton Bragg, official report, 30 April 1862; War Dept., OR, series I, vol. X, part 1 (1880): 470.

Side Box—Military Intelligence

Maj. Gen. William Tecumseh Sherman, letter to his brother, Senator John Sherman, 12 February 1863; Sherman, "Letters," 436.

THE BATTLE OF ANTIETAM

Overview

Maj. Gen. George McClellan, letter to his wife, 11 July 1862; Bruce Catton, *The Centennial History of the Civil War*, vol. 2, *Terrible Swift Sword* (New York: Doubleday, 1963), 347.

Maj. Gen. George McClellan, letter to his wife, 18 July 1862; McClellan, Story, 450–51.

Maj. Gen. George McClellan, letters to his wife, 10 and 20 August 1862; Stephen W. Sears, ed., *The Civil War Papers of George B. McClellan* (New York: Ticknor and Fields, 1989), 389, 397.

U.S. Congress Joint Committee on the Conduct of the War, *Report of the Operations of the Army of the Potomac* (New York: The Tribune Association, 1863), 18.

Pres. Lincoln to John Hay; William Roscoe Thayer, *John Hay*, vol. 1 (Boston: Houghton Mifflin Co., 1915), 128–29, 191.

Longstreet—The Invasion of Maryland

Lieut. Gen. James Longstreet, "The Invasion of Maryland," *The Century Illustrated Monthly Magazine* 32, no. 2 (August 1886): 309–15.

Lieut. Gen. James Longstreet, "to Keedysville, and on the march changed the order, making Sharpsburg the point of assembly" is from Longstreet, Manassas, 227.

McClellan—Rushing to Defend the North

Bio Box: Gen. Robert E. Lee quoted in Capt. Robert E. Lee, *Recollections and Letters of General Lee* (Westminster, UK: Archibald, Constable & Co., 1904), 416.

Maj. Gen. George McClellan, "From the Peninsula to Antietam," *The Century Illustrated Monthly Magazine* 32, no. 1 (May 1886): 129–30.

McClellan, Story, 586–88, 590–91.

Hood—"The Hardest Fought Battle"

Hood, Advance, 43–45.

Early—Fighting at the Dunkard Church

Lieut. Gen. Jubal Early and R. H. (Ruth Hairston) Early,
*Autobiographical Sketch and Narrative of the War between
the States* (Philadelphia: J. B. Lippincott Co., 1912), 143–48,
150–51, 152, 154, 159–60.

Longstreet—Holding the Line with Two Cannons

Lieut. Gen. James Longstreet, "The Invasion of Maryland,"
The Century Illustrated Monthly Magazine 32, no. 2 (August
1886): 312–14.

Longstreet, Manassas, 262–63.

Lee—Stragglers

Gen. Robert E. Lee, letter to President Davis, 21 September
1862; War Dept., OR, series I, vol. XIX, part 1 (1902): 143.

Meade—Battlefield Promotion

Bio Box: Grant, Memoirs, 538.

Maj. Gen. George G. Meade, letters to his wife, 18 and 20
September and 5 October 1862; Meade, Life, vol. 1, 310–12,
317–18.

Hooker—"A Great Battle Has Been Fought"

Bio Box: Grant, Memoirs, 539.

Maj. Gen. Joseph Hooker, dispatch, 17 September 1862;
Moore, Rebellion, vol. 5, 454.

McClellan—"A Masterpiece of Art"

Maj. Gen. George McClellan, official report, 4 August 1863;
War Dept., OR, series I, vol. XIX, part 1 (1902): 65.

Maj. Gen. George McClellan, dispatch to Gen. Halleck, 27
September 1862; War Dept., OR, series I, vol. XIX, part 1
(1902): 71.

Maj. Gen. George McClellan, letters to his wife, 18 and 20
September 1862; McClellan, Story, 612–13.

Pres. Abraham Lincoln, message to Maj. Gen. George
McClellan, 25 October 1862; Joint Committee, Conduct
(1863), vol. 1, 547.

Longstreet—What Might Have Been

Longstreet, Manassas, 288–89.

Box Quotations

Anonymous, "The Invasion of Maryland," *Harper's Weekly*,
September 27, 1862, 618.

Maj.-Gen. George McClellan, "From the Peninsula to
Antietam," *The Century Illustrated Monthly Magazine* 32, no.
1 (May 1886): 122.

Young, World, vol. 2, 214, 216–17.

Maj. Gen. William Tecumseh Sherman, letter to his brother,
Senator John Sherman, 22 September 1862; Sherman,
"Letters," 430–31.

Side Box—Aerial Reconnaissance

John Steiner, letters to Thaddeus Lowe; Col. Frederick S.
Haydon, *Aeronautics in the Union and Confederate Armies*,
vol. 1 (Baltimore: Johns Hopkins Press, 1941), 388.

The Battle of Fredericksburg

Longstreet—Preparation for Battle

Longstreet, "Fredericksburg," 609–11.

Hooker—Planning the Attack

Maj. Gen. Joseph Hooker, testimony at Fredericksburg, 20
December 1862; Joint Committee, Conduct (1863), vol. 1,
667.

Lee—The Union Army Enters the Town

Gen. Robert E. Lee, letter to his daughter Mary, 24
November 1862; Rev. J. William Jones, *Personal
Reminiscences, Anecdotes, and Letters of Gen. Robert E. Lee*
(New York: D. Appleton & Co., 1876), 393–94.

Gen. Robert E. Lee, final official report, 10 April 1863; War
Dept., OR, series I, vol. XXI (1888): 551.

Gen. Robert E. Lee, letter to his wife; Capt. Robert E. Lee,
Recollections and Letters of General Lee (Westminster, UK:
Archibald, Constable & Co., 1904), 86.

Gen. Robert E. Lee, report to the secretary of war, 14
December 1862; War Dept., OR, series I, vol. XXI (1888):
546–47.

Hood—Discussions with Lee and Stonewall Jackson

Hood, Advance, 49–51.

Meade—"I Should Have Been the Great Hero"

Maj. Gen. George Meade, letters to his wife, 16 and 20
December 1862; Meade, Life, vol. 1, 337–40.

Jackson—The Attack Had to Be Abandoned

Lieut. Gen. Thomas J. Jackson, official report, 31 January
1863; War Dept., OR, series I, vol. XXI (1888): 631–32.

Longstreet—Defending Marye's Heights

Longstreet, "Fredericksburg," 613–18.

Lieut. Gen. James Longstreet, official report, 20 December
1862; War Dept., OR, series I, vol. XXI (1888): 570.

Longstreet, Manassas, 313.

Hancock—Assaulting Marye's Heights

Bio Box: Grant, Memoirs, 539.

Maj. Gen. Winfield Scott Hancock, official report, 25 December 1862; War Dept., OR, series I, vol. XXI (1888): 227.

Hooker—Yet Another Futile Assault

Maj. Gen. Joseph Hooker, testimony at Fredericksburg, 20
December 1862; Joint Committee, Conduct (1863), vol. 1,
667–69, 671–72.

Sherman—McClernand and the Second Assault

Sherman, Memoirs, vol. 1, 326–28.

Grant—Forcing a Surrender

Grant, Memoirs, 549–55, 566–67, 570, 579.

Gen. Ulysses S. Grant, letter to Gen. Marcus J. Wright, 30 November 1884; Gen. Ulysses Grant, "General Grant on the Terms at Vicksburg," *The Century Illustrated Monthly Magazine* 34, no. 4 (August 1887): 617.

Young, World, vol. 2, 615–19, 623, 625–26.

Box Quotations

Young, World, vol. 2, 212–13.

Anonymous, "Diary of a Citizen in Vicksburgh during the Siege"; Moore, Rebellion, vol. 7, 170.

Side Box—Ironclads and Submarines

Gen. G. T. Beauregard, telegram to Lieut. George Dixon; Glen Oeland, "The H.L. Hunley: Secret Weapon of the Confederacy," *National Geographic* 202, no. 1 (July 2002): 90.

THE BATTLE OF GETTYSBURG

Longstreet—General Longstreet's Spy

Lieut. Gen. James Longstreet, "Lee's Invasion of Pennsylvania," *The Century Illustrated Monthly Magazine* 33, no. 4 (February 1887): 622–24.

Longstreet, Manassas, 346–48.

Longstreet, "Campaign," 419.

Hancock—The First Day of Battle

Maj. Gen. Winfield Scott Hancock, "Gettysburg," *The Galaxy* 22, no. 6 (December 1876): 821–23, 825, 828–29.

Chamberlain—"Hold That Ground at All Hazards"

Maj. Gen. Joshua Chamberlain, official report, 6 July 1863; War Dept., OR, series I, vol. XXVII, part I (1889): 622–26. Note: Maj. Gen. Chamberlain and his defense of Little Round Top on July 2, 1862, were dramatically portrayed in the movie Gettysburg, with Jeff Daniels as Chamberlain.

Col. William C. Oates, "Gettysburg—The Battle on the Right," *Southern Historical Society Papers* VI, no. 4 (October 1878): 177–78.

Hood—General Lee's Orders

Hood, Advance, 54–59.

Stuart—A Cavalry Battle

Maj. Gen. James Ewell Brown "Jeb" Stuart, official report, 20 August 1863; War Dept., OR, series I, vol. XXVII, part II (1889): pp. 687, 697–98, 710.

Custer—A Brilliant Charge

Brig. Gen. George Armstrong Custer, official report, 22 August 1863; Moore, Rebellion, vol. 7, 398.

Longstreet—From Seminary Ridge to Cemetery Ridge

Lieut. Gen. James Longstreet, "Lee's Right Wing at Gettysburg"; Johnson, Battles, vol. 1, 339–54.

Longstreet, "Campaign," 430–31.

Hancock—Pickett's Charge

Maj. Gen. Winfield Scott Hancock, official report, undated, but written sometime before 24 October 1863; War Dept., OR, series I, vol. XXVII, part I (1889): 372–74.

Lieut. George G. Benedict, letter dated 14 July 1863 to the Burlington Free Press; George Grenville Benedict, Army Life in Virginia (Burlington, VT: Free Press Association, 1895), 182–84.

Maj. Gen. Winfield Scott Hancock, letter to Brig. Gen. Francis A. Walker quoted in Steven J. Wright, "'Don't Let Me Bleed To Death': The Wounding of Maj. Gen. Winfield Scott Hancock," *Gettysburg Magazine* no. 6 (January 1, 1992): 87–92.

Hancock, Reminiscences, 69–70.

Maj. Gen. Winfield Hancock testimony; Joint Committee, Conduct (1865), vol. 1, 408–9.

Meade—Not Bagging the Confederate Army

Maj. Gen. George Meade, letter to his wife, 5 July 1863; Meade, Life, vol. 2, 125.

Longstreet—Taking the Blame

Lieut. Gen. James Longstreet, letter to uncle; Anonymous, "The Battle of Gettysburg," *The New York Times*, January 29, 1876, reprinted from the New Orleans Republican.

Gen. Lee quotation "Had I taken your advice …"; Longstreet, "Campaign," 434.

Lieut. Gen. James Longstreet, "Lee's Right Wing at Gettysburg"; Johnson, Battles, vol. 1, 350–54.

Lee—Dealing with the Loss

Gen. Robert E. Lee, report to Gen. S. Cooper, the adjutant and inspector general, 31 July 1863; War Dept., OR, series I, vol. XXVII, part II (1889): 305, 307–9.

Gen. Robert E. Lee, letter to Davis on newspaper article; War Dept., OR, series I, vol. XXVII, part III (1889): 108–10.

Box Quotations

Young, World, vol. 2, 299–300.

Col. William C. Oates, "Gettysburg—The Battle on the Right," *Southern Historical Society Papers* VI, no. 4 (October 1878): 174.

Side Box—Espionage

Hancock, Reminiscences, 90.

THE BATTLE OF CHICKAMAUGA

Overview

Pres. Abraham Lincoln quoted in John Hay's diary, 24 October 1863; John Hay and Clara Louise Hay, *Letters of John Hay and Extracts from Diary*, vol. 1 (Washington: n.p., 1908), 112.

Grant, *Memoirs*, 28.

Hood—Wounded

Hood, *Advance*, 60–65, 67.

Sheridan—The Grit to Hold the Field

Bio Box: Gen. Ulysses S. Grant quoted in George F. Hoar, "Some Political Reminiscences," *Scribner's Magazine* 25, no. 4 (April 1899): 462.

Bio Box: Young, *World*, vol. 2, 297.

Gen. Philip Sheridan, *Personal Memoirs of P. H. Sheridan, General, United States Army*, vol. 1 (New York: C. L. Webster & Co., 1888), 283–90.

Polk—Appeal to the President

Lieut. Gen. Leonidas Polk, letter to President Davis, 6 October 1863; War Dept., OR, series I, vol. XXX, part II (1890): 67–68.

Pres. Davis, letter to Lieut. Gen. Leonidas Polk, 29 October 1863; War Dept., OR, series I, vol. XXX, part II (1890): 70.

Forrest—"A Damned Scoundrel"

Col. R. B. Kyle to Pres. Jefferson Davis, quoted in John Allan Wyeth, *Life of Lieutenant-General Nathan Bedford Forrest* (New York: Harper & Bros., 1899), 267.

Dr. J. B. Cowan letter quoted in John Allan Wyeth, *Life of Lieutenant-General Nathan Bedford Forrest* (New York: Harper & Bros., 1899), 265–66. Oddly, some early and late pressings have this quotation and some don't.

Longstreet—Entering a Hornets' Nest

Longstreet, *Manassas*, 464–66, 468.

Bragg—The Other Side of the Story

Gen. Braxton Bragg, letter to Maj. E. T. Sykes, 8 February 1873; William Polk, *Leonidas Polk: Bishop and General*, vol. 2 (New York: Longmans, Green & Co., 1915), 308–13.

Rosecrans—"The Battle Roared with Increasing Fury"

Maj. Gen. William Rosecrans, official report, October 1863; War Dept., OR, series I, vol. XXX, part I (1890): 58–61.

Maj. Gen. William Rosecrans, testimony at Washington, D.C., 22 April 1865; Joint Committee, Conduct (1865), vol. 3, 29–33.

Grant—"Rosecrans Was Badly Defeated"

Grant, *Memoirs*, 21–24.

Young, *World*, vol. 2, 287–88.

Box Quotations

Brig. Gen. John Beatty, diary entry for 11 November 1863; John Beatty, *The Citizen-Soldier; or, Memoirs of a Volunteer* (Cincinnati: Wilstach, Baldwin & Co., 1879), 352–53.

Asst. Secretary of War Charles Dana, dispatch to Secretary of War Edwin Stanton; War Dept., OR, series I, vol. XXX, part I (1890): 221.

Gen. Robert E. Lee, telegram to Pres. Jefferson Davis, 29 May 1863; Robert E. Lee, *Lee's Dispatches* (New York: G. P. Putnam's Sons, 1915), 99.

Side Box—Rebel Yell, Yankee Cheer

R. L. Dabney, *Life and Campaigns of Lieut.-Gen. Thomas J. Jackson (Stonewall Jackson)*, (London: James Nesbit & Co., 1864), 259.

Ambrose Bierce, "A Little of Chickamauga," in *The Collected Works of Ambrose Bierce*, vol. 1 (New York: The Neale Publishing Co., 1909), 277.

Young, *World*, vol. 2, 26.

Col. Keller Anderson, *Memphis Appeal*, quoted in Lizzie Cary Daniel, *Confederate Scrap-book* (1893), 107.

J. Harvie Dew, "The Yankee and Rebel Yells," *The Century Illustrated Monthly Magazine* 43, no. 6 (April 1892): 953–55.

THE BATTLE OF THE CRATER

Overview

Maj. Gen. Grant, telegram to Maj. Gen. Meade, 1 August 1864; Joint Committee, Petersburg, 52.

Chamberlain—The Long Delay

Maj. Gen. Joshua Chamberlain, *The Passing of the Armies* (New York: G. P. Putnam's Sons, 1915), 25–27, 29.

Grant—Plan of Attack

Grant, *Memoirs*, 307–13.

Meade—A Most Unfortunate Operation

Maj. Gen. George Meade, official report, 16 August 1864; Joint Committee, Petersburg, 33–34.

Burnside—The Order to Withdraw

Maj. Gen. Ambrose Burnside, testimony before the congressional committee, 20 July 1864, and testimony at the Hancock inquiry, 10 August 1864; Joint Committee, Petersburg, 24, 165.

Grant—"The Saddest Affair I Have Witnessed"

Lieut. Gen. Ulysses S. Grant, dispatches to Maj. Gen. Halleck, 1 and 2 August 1864; War Dept., OR, series I, vol. XL, part I (1892): 17–18.

Grant, *Memoirs*, 313–15.

Lieut. Gen. Ulysses S. Grant, testimony before the congressional committee, 20 December 1864; Joint Committee, Petersburg, 123–25.

Hancock—The Court of Inquiry

Maj. Gen. Winfield Scott Hancock, opinion of the court, 9 September 1864; Joint Committee, Petersburg, 230–231.

Joint Committee, Petersburg, 8, 10.

Box Quotations

Lieut. Col. Charles Loring, testimony before the congressional committee, 20 December 1864; Joint Committee, Petersburg, 104–5.

Bvt. Maj. Charles H. Houghton, "In the Crater"; Johnson, Battles, vol. 4, 562.

Ibid., 562.

Sergt. A. H. Smyth, report, 30 July 1864; War Dept., OR, series I, vol. XL, part III (1892): 820.

SHERMAN'S MARCH TO THE SEA

Sherman—"Making Georgia Howl"

Maj. Gen. William Tecumseh Sherman, telegram to Lieut. Gen. Grant, 9 October 1864; War Dept., OR, series I, vol. XXXIX, part III (1892): 162.

Grant—General Johnston, General Hood

Grant, Memoirs, 344–47, 355–56, 358, 361.

Sherman—A "Wild Adventure"

Maj. Gen. William Tecumseh Sherman, telegram to Lieut. Gen. Grant, 9 October 1864; War Dept., OR, series I, vol. XXXIX, part III (1892): 713–14.

Sherman, Memoirs, vol. 2, 170, 177, 178–80, 182–83.

Beauregard—Trying to Stop Sherman

Gen. G. T. Beauregard, letter to Pres. Jefferson Davis, 6 December 1863; War Dept., OR, series I, vol. XLIV, part I (1893): 931–33.

Sherman—Journey to the Sea

Sherman, Memoirs, vol. 2, 190–91, 193–95, 196, 197–98, 199–200.

Maj. Gen. William Tecumseh Sherman, letter to Lieut. Gen. William Hardee, 17 December 1864, and Lieut. Gen. Hardee, letter to Maj. Gen. Sherman, 17 December 1864; Alfred Roman, The Military Operations of General Beauregard, vol. 2 (New York: Harper & Bros., 1883), 315–17.

Maj. Gen. William Tecumseh Sherman, official report, 1 January 1865; War Dept., OR, series I, vol. XLIV, part I (1893): 12–13.

Sherman, Memoirs, vol. 2, 220–21.

Grant—"Cruelty and Severity"

Young, World, vol. 2, 294–95, 307–8.

Box Quotations

Maj. Gen. William Tecumseh Sherman, letter to his brother, Senator John Sherman, 25 January 1863; Sherman, "Letters," 434.

Young, World, vol. 2, 470.

Gen. William Tecumseh Sherman, letter to Brig. Gen. J. A. Rawlins, 17 September 1863; Sherman, Memoirs, vol. 1, 342.

Longstreet, Manassas, 640–41.

Gen. Joseph Johnston quoted in The New York Times, October 12, 1901.

Side Box—Innovative Weapons

Brig. Gen. George Armstrong Custer, official report, 22 August 1863; Moore, Rebellion, vol. 7, 398.

Grant, Memoirs, 538.

Junius Henri Browne, Four Years in Secessia: Adventures Within and Beyond the Union Lines (Hartford, CT: O. D. Case and Co., 1865), 89–90.

Porter, Incidents, 266.

THE BATTLE OF APPOMATTOX COURT HOUSE

Grant—Preparations with Sheridan

Young, World, vol. 2, 460, 656–57.

Sheridan—A White Flag

Gen. Philip Sheridan, Personal Memoirs of P. H. Sheridan, General, United States Army, vol. 2 (New York: C. L. Webster & Co., 1888), 193–97.

Longstreet—Waiting for Grant

Longstreet, Manassas, 627–30.

Grant—The Surrender

Young, World, vol. 2, 455–58.

Grant, Memoirs, 489–90, 496–98.

Chamberlain—"Morning Dawned"

Maj. Gen. Joshua Chamberlain, The Passing of the Armies (New York: G. P. Putnam's Sons, 1915), 244–50, 258, 261–65.

Grant—Assassination

Young, World, vol. 2, 354–56.

Box Quotations

Porter, Incidents, pp. 289, 299–300.

Brig. Gen. E. P. Alexander, Military Memoirs of a Confederate: A Critical Narrative (New York: Charles Scribner's Sons, 1907), 609.

Gen. Robert E. Lee, report to Pres. Jefferson Davis, 12 April 1865; War Dept., OR, series I, vol. XLVI, part 1, section 2 (1894): 1267.

Side Box—Guerrillas

Young, World, vol. 2, 308–9.

The War Ends

Lee—Farewell to the Army of Northern Virginia

Gen. Robert E. Lee, General Orders No. 9, 10 April 1865; War Dept., OR, series I, vol. XLVI, part 2, section 2 (1894): 1267.

Forrest—Your Final Orders

Lieut. Gen. Nathan Bedford Forrest, farewell orders, 9 May 1865; War Dept., OR, series I, vol. XLIX, part 2 (1897): 1289–90.

Pickett—Visiting Old Friends

Maj. Gen. George Pickett, The Heart of a Soldier (New York: Seth Moyle Inc., 1913), 183–87. Note that there is considerable scholarly debate over whether Sallie fictionalized, rewrote, or heavily edited her husband's letters. Computer analysis suggests this letter is mostly authentic.

Longstreet—History Written in Blood

Longstreet, Manassas, 630.

Beauregard—How We Could Have Won

Beauregard, "Bull Run," 103–4, 106.

Grant—Failure of the Reconstruction

Young, World, vol. 2, 661–63.

Forrest—Forrest's Civil Rights Speech

Anonymous, "The Fourth," Memphis Daily Appeal 35, no. 139 (July 6, 1875): 1. With some corrections from the Memphis Daily Avalanche, July 6, 1875, as quoted in J. H. Segars and Charles Kelly Barrow, eds., Black Southerners in Confederate Armies: A Collection of Historical Accounts (Gretna, LA: Pelican Publishing, 2001; 2007 printing), 169–70.

Pickett—Remembering the Dead at Gettysburg

Maj. Gen. George Pickett, The Heart of a Soldier (New York: Seth Moyle Inc., 1913), 205–7. Note that there are scholars who suggest Sallie fictionalized or rewrote her husband's letters. Computer analysis suggests this letter is mostly authentic.

Hancock—Looking Back on the Storm

Maj. Gen. Winfield Scott Hancock, "Gettysburg," The Galaxy 22, no. 6 (December 1876): 831.

Roll Call

Stuart

Gen. Robert E. Lee, General Orders No. 44, 20 May 1864; War Dept., OR, series I, vol. XXXVI, part III (1891): 800.

Longstreet, Manassas, 573.

Polk

Jefferson Davis, The Rise and Fall of the Confederate Government, vol. 2 (New York: D. Appleton & Co., 1881), 554–55.

Grant

Lieut. Gen. James Longstreet toast quoted in Helen D. Longstreet, Lee and Longstreet at High Tide (Gainesville, GA: published by the author, 1904), 108.

Lieut. Gen. Nathan Bedford Forrest quoted in Anonymous, "N. B. Forrest Interview," Cincinnati Commercial, August 28, 1868; New York Times, September 3, 1868.

Sheridan

Gen. Ulysses S. Grant quoted in George F. Hoar, "Some Political Reminiscences," Scribner's Magazine 25, no. 4 (April 1899): 462.

Conclusion

Box Quotation

Henry W. Elson in Francis Trevelyan Miller and Robert S. Lanier, eds., The Photographic History of the Civil War, vol. 2 (New York: The Review of Reviews Co., 1911), 96.

INDEX